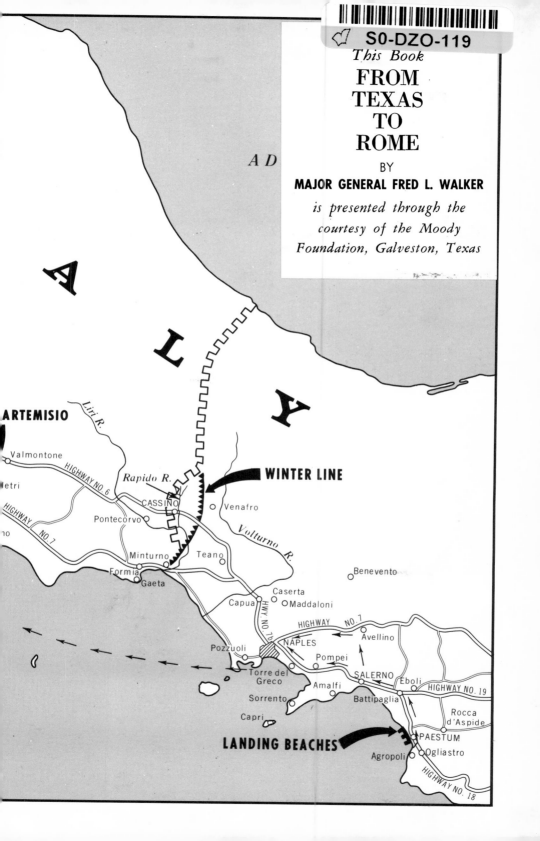

This Book

FROM
TEXAS
TO
ROME

BY

MAJOR GENERAL FRED L. WALKER

is presented through the
courtesy of the Moody
Foundation, Galveston, Texas

A D

A L Y

ARTEMISIO

Liri R.

Valmontone

HIGHWAY NO. 6

Rapido R.

WINTER LINE

etri

HIGHWAY NO. 7

CASSINO

Venafro

Pontecorvo

Volturno R.

no

Minturno

Teano

Benevento

Formia

Gaeta

Caserta

Capua

Maddaloni

HIGHWAY NO. 7

HWY NO. 7b

HIGHWAY NO. 7b

Pozzuoli

NAPLES

Avellino

Pompei

Torre del
Greco

Amalfi

SALERNO

Eboli

HIGHWAY NO. 19

Sorrento

Battipaglia

Capri

Rocca
d'Aspide

LANDING BEACHES

PAESTUM

Agropoli

Ogliastro

HIGHWAY NO. 18

D
756
I8
W3
c.2

Walker

From Texas to Rome

TO
THE MEN OF THE 36th

Whose patriotism, steadfastness
in time of trial and valour in
combat are an imperishable
memorial to the Texas Division

Major General Fred L. Walker

ABOUT THE AUTHOR

General Walker was born June 11, 1887, in Fairfield County, Ohio. He graduated from Ohio State University with the degree of Engineer of Mines as of the Class of 1911.

In 1907 he enlisted in the Ohio Cavalry in which unit he served four years from Private to 1st Sergeant. He entered the Regular Army from civilian life, as a result of a competitive examination, February 11, 1911. He was first stationed at San Antonio, Texas, where he reported for duty with the 13th US Infantry. He served in the Philippines with that Regiment from 1911 to 1914. Upon returning to the United States, he was assigned to duty with the 17th Infantry at Eagle Pass, Texas. He served with that unit in Mexico in 1916 and when the Punitive Expedition was withdrawn from Mexico he was stationed at El Paso, Texas for several weeks. In the fall of 1917, he was assigned to the 30th Infantry, 3rd Division, having been promoted to the grade of Captain. He served overseas with the 3rd Division, commanding the 1st Battalion of the 30th Infantry. For outstanding leadership as Battalion Commander during the second battle of the Marne, July 15-18, 1918, he was awarded the Distinguished Service Cross, and the Purple Heart for wounds. Later, he was assigned to Division Headquarters as the Division Inspector and promoted to the grade of Lieutenant Colonel.

Upon his return to the states, he was assigned to duty at the Infantry School, Fort Benning, Georgia, as an Instructor for three years. He is an honor graduate from the Command and General Staff School at Fort Leavenworth, class of 1927. From 1927 to 1932 he was Commandant of Shattuck School, Faribault, Minnesota. He graduated from the Army War College, 1933, and was an Instructor at that institution from January, 1934 to June, 1937; after which he was assigned to the 15th Infantry at Tientsin, China. After his return to the States, he was assigned as G-3, 2nd Army at Chicago. He was appointed a Brigadier General April 19, 1941, and assigned to the 2nd Division in San Antonio, Texas as Assistant Division Commander.

He commanded the 36th Division from September 1941 to July 1944. He was promoted to Major General on January 15, 1942. For the outstanding manner in which he met his responsibilities as Commander of the invasion forces which made the successful landing at Salerno, Italy, September, 1943, he received the Distinguished Service Medal. He commanded the 36th Division during the foolhardy and unsuccessful attempt to cross the Rapido River below Monte Cassino, January 1944. He received the Distinguished Service Cross with Oak Leaf Cluster for his leadership in originating and carrying out the plans which broke the defenses of the Germans at Mt. Artemisio and precipitated their retreat north, through and beyond Rome in May and June, 1944.

He was Commandant, Infantry School, Fort Benning, Georgia, from July 1944 to July 1945. In July 1945 he was made Director of Military Training, Headquarters, Army Services Forces, Washington, D. C.

He retired from the Regular Army April 30, 1946, and was immediately appointed Lieutenant General and Commander of the Texas National Guard by Governor Coke Stevenson to reorganize the National Guard of that State.

FOREWORD

My mentor and friend for more than thirty years, Major General Fred L. Walker, U.S. Army (Ret), has written an unusual book. Most retired military men writing about World War II have concentrated on the strategic or tactical situations they faced. While General Walker relates the part played by the 36th Infantry Division during certain battles in the Italian Campaign, the bulk of his narrative is devoted to a more fundamental purpose—the story of the creation of a fighting division.

I regret that my own involvement in that process was confined to the first year that General Walker commanded the division. As he records, I was his aide when he took over the division on 13 September 1941. When I was ordered elsewhere in late August 1942, I was commanding the 2nd Battalion, 141st Infantry. His notation on 26 August 1942, when he declined to intercede with the War Department to have my orders changed, that "I suspect he (Wheeler) thinks I am trying to get rid of him ..." is an erroneous conclusion. I knew very well that he was acting—as he always had—in what he believed to be my best interests.

Nevertheless, I was unhappy. During the preceding year, I had become deeply involved in the life and future of the division. I was closely associated with General Walker. I knew the problems of personnel, organization, training, standards of performance and discipline with which he had to cope. I did my best to help and, in so doing, my duties went considerably beyond those usually assigned to an aide. In the course of my work I came to know, like and respect a large number of officers and enlisted men. In short, I was at home in the division, and I hated to leave it ...

As mentioned earlier, this is not the usual military memoir. It is, in General Walker's words, "... a record of the transformation of civilians into disciplined soldiers ..."; but it is also more than that. General Walker's narrative reveals the meticulous attention he devoted to detail, his clear understanding of the objective, and his driving sense of obligation and duty.

Veterans of the 36th Division—whether they are old-timers who traveled from Camp Bowie, Texas, to Camp Blanding, Florida, to Camp Edwards, Massachusetts, or replacements who joined in Africa or Italy—will find in these pages the explanation of what were probably to them mysterious happenings at the time.

Above all, any reader will certainly be struck by what the author reveals of himself. There is no posing for posterity; indeed, I have the feeling that parts of it were deliberately underwritten. Nevertheless, it comes through clearly that this talented soldier was a sensitive man, a compassionate yet determined leader and commander, and a follower of the highest ideals. It comes through clearly also, I think, that General Walker understands what war is about and the human qualities required in the men who win battles.

EARLE G. WHEELER
General, U.S. Army
Chairman
Joint Chiefs of Staff

Fort Myer, Virginia
February 1969

PREFACE

This is a personal journal of my service with the 36th Infantry Division (Texas) from September, 1941, to July, 1944.

It is based on a journal in which I made entries—often terse, incomplete and sometimes caustic—at the time, or soon after the events described. However, there were periods, some extending over several days, when my duties and responsibilities allowed no time for entering comments in a journal. To substantiate my recollection of the events during these periods, and to verify the details in the entire record, I have referred to my Chief of Staff's Journal, the daily notes kept by my Aide, the official records of the 36th Division, and to letters written at the time. In doing so, I have been especially careful to insure that this expanded journal is factual.

This is not an account of strategy or tactics, or of the Italian Campaign. It is a record of the transformation of civilians into disciplined soldiers, the provision for their welfare, the development of their esprit, their training for teamwork in battle, and finally, how the strategy and tactics of the battles in Italy affected them, the Division, and me.

. I wish to acknowledge the encouragement given me by the men of the 36th to gather my records into a document that would round out their memories of the Italian Campaign; a view from the "top side" of which they could have had no knowledge at the time.

I acknowledge with gratitude the support of my wife and sons in preparing this journal for publication. I also wish to acknowledge the help received from former members of the 36th Division. Without the urging and encouragment of Oran C. Stovall, H. Miller Ainsworth, Carl L. Phinney, Clayton Price Kerr, Andrew F. Price, Wright Armstrong, and many others, this book would never have been published.

PROLOGUE

THE NATIONAL GUARD—HEIR TO THE MILITIA

In the thirteen original Colonies, all able-bodied males between specified ages were subject to call for military service. This great pool of manpower was divided into two groups: the companies and regiments into which men were enrolled for military service constituted the Organized Militia; those men who were not enrolled in any military organization, but who were subject to call, constituted the unorganized militia.

The Organized Militia Companies were on a permanent basis during peace and war, but the men were paid by the Colony only when on active duty. These companies were formed by patriotic volunteers who agreed to arm themselves and assemble for service in return for authorization from the Governor to organize. They enjoyed military prestige, took pride in military drill, competed in marksmanship and drill, organized hunting parties for sport, and made practice marches to neighboring towns when they were invited guests of another Militia Company. They gave their units such descriptive names as Greys, Blues, Rifles, Grenadiers, Hussars, combining these with the name of the commander, as in Riley's Rifles; or with the name of their city, as in Richmond Blues. The companies, which were part of the Massachusetts Volunteer Organized Militia, were called Minute Companies. Their members were Minute Men who have been memorialized in history.

But, each Organized Militia Company was a military club, some very exclusive, with each commander determining his own standards of training, and the company electing its officers and choosing its own uniforms. Consequently, when the Militia Companies and Colonial Volunteer Regiments were called for field service, they were generally lacking in discipline, physical fitness and uniform standards of military efficiency.

Also, when the Governors wished to increase their Organized Militia, they called for volunteers. Thousands of unorganized militiamen would enroll and be formed into companies or regiments.

Whenever the regiments had time to be trained for battle under capable leaders, they did well. They fought side by side with the British troops in King William's War, 1688-1697; Queen Anne's War, 1702-1713; King George's War, 1744-1748; and the French and Indian War, 1754-1763.

X

Massachusetts Organized Militiamen took Port Royal, Nova Scotia, in 1690, and helped recapture it in 1710. The most important event of King George's War was the capture of the strong Fortress of Louisburg on Cape Breton Island by the New England Organized Militia.

There was no effective Organized Militia on the fringes of the colonial frontier. Here and there a few forts were located miles back of the forward settlers, but these forts could not be relied upon to deal with surprise attacks by Indian marauders. These attacks had to be met by the settlers themselves, who constituted the unorganized militia of their area. When necessary, they turned out voluntarily, formed themselves into armed bands, repelled the raiders, and disbanded as soon as the danger passed. There were also occasions when the unorganized militia, composed of settlers who had suffered extreme losses, rushed into the territory of the raiders, burned their towns, destroyed their crops and stores, and then returned home.

But, the Organized Militia did a more effective job to reduce Indian raids on the settlers. Strong forces under experienced commanders marched far into the Indian territory, defeated the Indians who attempted to defend their domain, forced them to move to more distant lands or to agree by treaty to discontinue their wars upon the isolated settlers. The invasions by Colonel Henry Bouquet and by General Anthony Wayne, into what is now Ohio, are examples of invasions of this nature.

THE REVOLUTION

During the years when the Colonists were opposing the Acts of Parliament, but before they declared their independence, many militiamen were members of the revolutionary movement. Gradually their views grew to dominate the membership and upon the outbreak of hostilities, their companies joined the revolutionary forces.

The Minute Men who assembled to oppose the British on the Commons at Lexington in April, 1775, were members of the Lexington Company of Massachusetts Volunteer Militia. Other Organized Companies of Minute Men were called out that same day and hurried to Bunker (Breed's) Hill near Cambridge, across the channel from Boston.

In similar fashion the Militia Companies of other Colonies were aroused, assembled into regiments and marched to Cambridge. For nearly two months before they were attacked in June by the British troops from Boston, these various Organized Militia Regiments were throwing up breastworks and preparing for battle under the leadership of Israel Putnam and William Prescott.

However, there was no overall commander. Each Colony controlled its own Organized Militia. The forces in Cambridge were being depleted by expiration of enlistments; there was dissention among the officers over prerogatives; and the civil population was resentful of the military presence and damage done to property.

Meanwhile, George Washington was appointed Commander in Chief of the Continental Army by the Second Continental Congress which met on May 10th, 1775. His principal duty was to create a Continental Army, independent of the various Colonial Governors, which would owe its allegiance only to the Continental Congress. It would need men, who would have to be enlisted from the Organized and unorganized militia by the Colonies. It would need arms, equipment, a code of justice, a code of regulations, and most of all, an espirit de corps. The men in the Continental Army were to serve wherever needed, and were not to be limited to service within their own Colonies.

Washington took command of the 16,000 troops at Cambridge in July, 1775, and appealed to them to enlist in the Continental Army. He proceeded at once to create an effective fighting force by organizing his troops into six brigades of six regiments each, keeping in each regiment, as far as possible, the troops from a single Colony and placing over them a commander from that Colony. Officers were recommissioned in the Continental Army. Enlistments were for a longer period and of a set duration. Foreign officers with military experience made application for, and were accepted for, positions of high command.

Troops enlisted for the Continental Army from New Jersey were known as the "New Jersey Line." Those from New York were the "New York Line," and so on for each Colony. Troops from the Colony Lines constituted the "Continental Line" or the Continental Army; the forerunner of our Regular Army.

In addition to maintaining its part of the Continental Line, each Colony maintained other Organized Militia units which operated within its own boundary, independently of the Continental Army, but in cooperation with it. These Organized Militiamen harassed the British, followed their movements and attacked them as a surprise when they found them at a disadvantage.

AFTER THE REVOLUTION

After the Revolutionary War, the Continental Army dwindled to a few troops. The majority of veterans returned to the Militia Company near their homes, or became a part of the huge unorganized militia. The Congress of the United States, operating under the new Constitution, provided for raising troops for the common defense by passing the Militia Act of 1792.

Each State was to register all able-bodied men within its borders between the ages of 18 and 40. Districts large enough to contain the number of men needed to constitute a company were given specific boundaries and a volunteer captain was responsible for registration of each company.

On Muster Day, once or twice each year, the registrants assembled to answer the roll call. That having been done, the remainder of the day in most company districts was a holiday devoted to drinking, picnicking, horse racing, and competing in individual contests of strength and agility. These registered companies were not organized military units, but were merely lists of names of men who were subject to call for military service and who lived within the company district. The only requirements placed on these men were to arm themselves, which was no great burden for nearly every citizen owned a musket, and to appear on Muster Day.

Ten registered companies made a registered regiment for which a volunteer colonel was appointed by the State Governor. Enrolled regiments were grouped into enrolled brigades and enrolled brigades formed paper divisions under an appointed volunteer general. The duties of these commanders of enrolled units were anything but arduous. Each provided himself with a uniform, often of his own design, appeared on Muster Day, renewed acquaintances with his subordinates and noted and signed the muster roll.

This paper system of providing military forces, while practically cost free for the States and Federal government, was a worthless method of producing reliable soldiers, as was proved at Bladensburg in 1814. When the fleet of British Admiral, Sir John Cockburn, suddenly appeared in Chesapeake Bay, officials at the Capitol became panic stricken. Congress called upon Maryland, Virginia, and the District of Columbia to rush, overnight, enrolled companies and regiments to Washington to fight the British. These enrolled companies, some without weapons and all without any military experience or adequate training, constituted a mob rather than a military organization. They were still converging on Bladensburg when the British arrived there. The battle was a farce and of short duration. Although supported by a Regular regiment at part strength and by a small force of Regular Marines, the enrolled militia was a rabble in battle. It was confused by the conflicting orders of bewildered leaders who were officers in name only, and by the directives of the Federal officeholders who by virtue of their official positions presumed to take charge. Such a performance proved once again that men cannot fight unless they are organized, trained, equipped, and placed under competent leaders.

In contrast, the Organized Militia Volunteers performed well at the Battle of New Orleans where there was time to assemble and organize before battle. General Jackson's total force was about 5,700 men. Of these, the Organized Militia Volunteers from Tennessee, Kentucky and Louisiana numbered about 3,400. About 1,300 were hastily assembled recruits from the local unorganized militia. The Regular Army units had a strength of only about 1,000 men. The Organized Militia Volunteers constituted the main forces of Jackson's defense.

After the War of 1812, the practice of creating citizen military units by registration was discarded. The policy, used during the Revolution, of calling upon the State Governors for Organized Militia Volunteers to defend the nation was reinstated. As a result many more Militia Companies were voluntarily formed. They took their military duties seriously, met periodically for drill and practice marches, provided their own uniforms and accouterments, and offered their services to their States. These military units fought Indians, put down rebellions, controlled civil disturbances within their own States, and served beyond the boundaries of their States when their Governors made them available upon call to the Federal government as State Volunteers.

General Zachary Taylor's army was composed of large numbers of Organized Militiamen formed into State Volunteer Regiments and furnished by State Governors on call from the President, or on call from Army commanders in the field so far distant from Washington that an emergency could not wait for the slower procedures. Again, as in the Revolutionary War, the same discrepancies of military efficiency existed between regiments.

THE CIVIL WAR

This same method of raising troops was continued during the Civil War, by both the Federal and Confederate Governments. In April of 1861, President Lincoln called upon the states to provide 75,000 Volunteers who would serve three months under Federal control, but not as members of the Regular Army of the United States, which was stationed in the far West or in the South. The troops in the West continued to protect the frontier, while the Regulars in the South were either made prisoners, joined the Confederate ranks, or made their way North.

In the South, where the Regular Army of the United States ceased to exist, the Confederate Congress called for 400,000 Volunteers.

In cities, towns and villages, both North and South, volunteers were enlisted, formed into companies, and together with the long-standing Organized Militia Companies, were formed into regiments. In some cases, regiments were formed by individuals who hoped to command them and who offered them to the Governors of their respective States, and through these State officials to their Federal or Confederate governments. The Civil War was fought by citizen soldiers on both sides.

By July, both Washington and Bull Run were armed camps, occupied by uniformed State Volunteer Regiments hastily assembled, poorly trained, lacking in discipline and physical fitness, and some without qualified leaders. That same month, Congress authorized a Volunteer Federal army of 500,000 men.

The first important battle of the Civil War was fought at Bull Run on July 21st between a Federal Army of about 29,000 under General McDowell, and a Confederate Army of about 28,000 under Generals Beauregard and Johnston. Only about 18,000 on each side were actually engaged. On each side the troops were inexperienced and poorly trained. At first, the Federal forces fought well, but when surprised by an attack on their right flank, their formations were broken up and they were driven from the field. The defeat became a panic. The demoralized troops fled in disorder toward Washington. The Confederates, disorganized almost as much by victory as the Federals were by defeat, made no attempt to pursue.

This battle impressed the Federal and Confederate leaders, both military and civil, that soldiers, to do well in battle, must have self-discipline, an esprit de corps, and sound tactical training.

Although there were battles of minor importance during the remainder of 1861, responsible leaders in both the North and the South devoted the remainder of the year to a sensible program of preparing the Volunteer units for battle. This included physical conditioning, marksmanship, disciplinary drills, field sanitation, respect for authority, and development of a sense of belonging to and being responsible to a military team.

After the Battle of Bull Run, the State Volunteers, both North and South, were organized into well-trained regiments and divisions, even though some of the commanders were political appointees. These regiments and divisions fought honorably throughout the Civil War. At the close of the war, the strength of the Organized Militia in the North was 1,000,516 men. The strength of the Regular Army of the United States was only 22,310 men. Many veterans returned to their homes in the North and the South with a personal appreciation for the discipline and good order they had experienced in the military service.

THE NATIONAL GUARD

After the Civil War, the Organized Militia Companies were recreated as before, but there were certain veterans in these companies who saw the need for coordination and uniform training standards for these companies. Gradually, the officers of various units banded together and in 1879 the National Guard Association, made up of commissioned officers of units of all States, was formed. Slowly the term National Guard was substituted for the terms Organized Militia and State Volunteers.

Congress gave Federal assistance to the Guard and recognized it as a reserve for the Regular Army in time of war. Although not a part of the military system, the National Guard Association took over the policy-making for the National Guard. It exerted a powerful influence in Congress because many senators and representatives had been members of the National Guard in their home states, and were familiar with its ambitions and problems. They usually supported legislation favorable to the Guard, even when the legislation was opposed by the War Department. Active and former members of the National Guard in cities and towns throughout the States, their relatives and their friends, were a great influence on legislation favorable to the Guard.

On the other hand, the War Department had no lobbying agent. The officers of the Regular Army were in the military service as a fulltime profession. They devoted their lives to it and eventually retired with reduced pay. In the past, the War Department had presented legislation unacceptable to the National Guard.

As an example, in 1898, the War Department introduced a bill to greatly increase the Regular Army. Officers for the new units were to come from the Regular Officers Corps. The National Guard Association, acting on behalf of the Guard, opposed the bill because the Guard would have remained inactive and would lose the promotions that go with active duty. Its opposition to expanding the standing Army received the support of Congress and it amended the bill as desired by the Guard.

The war with Spain and the Philippine Insurrection were fought and won by both the National Guard and the Regular Army whose increase was limited. But the Spanish-American War again exposed the weakness of the National Guard called to serve as volunteers. Many regiments, under strength, had to take on raw recruits and were unprepared for field service. Their equipment was obsolete and had to be replaced. Their uniforms were left over from the Civil War.

THE NATIONAL GUARD OF 1903

Our modern National Guard came into being with the passage of the Militia Act of 1903. The law made the National Guard a reserve to the Regular Army and provided for it the same organization, armament, uniforms and equipment as the Regular Army. In return for Federal assistance, the law required 24 armory drills and one five-day encampment each year.

The Militia Act of 1908 prescribed that the President could call any Guard unit to defend the nation, without asking the Governor to volunteer its services. This placed an obligation on the officers of the Guard to devote more of their time for study, drill and camp. Officers who were in the Guard merely for prestige and pleasure began to disappear. Recruiting became more difficult and service in the National Guard less attractive. To improve this situation, the National Defense Act of 1916 authorized pay for armory drills and authorized a peacetime strength of 425,000 men and officers for the National Guard.

THE WORLD WARS

When World War I was declared, and the President called the National Guard to serve beside the Regular Army, it was again necessary to spend a great deal of time bringing the Guard up to combat efficiency. However, the Regular Army was in no better shape than most of the Guard. Because the Regular Army had to expand, many of its regiments had to be split to form three regiments, and these had to be filled to full strength by raw recruits. Consequently, the Rainbow Division was made up of the best National Guard units from many different states in order that a division could be made ready for combat in minimum time.

Prior to World War II, Congress improved the efficiency of the National Guard. It added more hours of armory instruction, increased the period of training camps and assigned Regular Army instructors on full-time duty with the National Guard. But, while the Guard units were greatly improved, they were not ready for field service, and had to undergo a long period of training to prepare them for combat duty.

This was the status of the Texas National Guard when its 36th Infantry Division was inducted into the Federal Service on November 25, 1940. Although not combat ready, this Division reflected the glorious heritage of its citizen soldiers of the Organized Militia of Texas who fought at Gonzales, The Alamo, San Jacinto, Gettysburg and the Argonne.

At this time it was made up of officers and men who had voluntarily enlisted in the Division, drilled and trained in their home town armories, attended several annual encampments of two weeks each, and received pay from the Federal Government for their military training. Many of the older officers and noncommissioned officers were veterans of World War I.

Prior to induction into the Federal Service, the training of the 36th Division was elementary, as was true of all National Guard Divisions. Its units were dispersed in cities and towns throughout the State, and occasionally local politics crept into the management of the unit. Being dispersed in this manner, and being assembled for only two weeks each year, opportunities for training had to be devoted principally to the individual soldier and smaller units. Although there was little or no time for practical training of the larger units, some of the commanders and staffs of these units had received some theoretical instruction by Army Correspondence Courses, map exercises, tactical walks, and by individual studies in their own homes.

Consequently, after induction into the Federal Service, the 36th Division, like any other National Guard Division, had to undergo an extended period of instruction on all phases of military excellence, and had to meet Regular Army standards and procedures before it could be qualified for combat duty.

During this extended period of instruction, it was the job of the Division Commander to attain and maintain high standards of performance. The degree to which he succeeded depended upon how well he applied his knowledge, his personality, integrity, and his physical energy as well as other qualities of character. Success depended not only on imparting knowledge, but also upon developing morale and esprit de corps, and such habits as respect for authority, cheerful obedience to command, and careful performance of duty.

During its combat service in World War II, the 36th Infantry Division was composed of the following Texas National Guard units:

    Division Headquarters and Headquarters Company
    Headquarters Special Troops
    Military Police Platoon
    736th Ordnance Company
    36th Signal Company
    36th Quartermaster Company
    36th Military Band
    36th Cavalry Reconnaissance Troop
    111th Medical Battalion
    111th Engineer Battalion
    141st Infantry Regiment
    142nd Infantry Regiment
    143rd Infantry Regiment
    36th Division Artillery:
        131st Field Artillery Battalion
        132nd Field Artillery Battalion
        133rd Field Artillery Battalion
        155th Field Artillery Battalion

Each infantry regiment had one antitank company, one cannon company, and three battalions; each battalion had four fighting companies. Each artillery battalion had three batteries and each battery had four howitzers.

Each Infantry regiment had about 3,600 men; the Division Artillery totaled about 2,400 men. The total strength of the 36th Division was about 16,000 men. Units attached to the Division in battle sometimes brought the strength to approximately 26,000 men. Although not a part of the official organization of the Division, the 636th Tank Destroyer Battalion was assumed by the men and officers of both to be a part of the 36th. It had three companies, each with eight tank destroyers.

THE GUARD TODAY

As always in time of peace, the Guard is available, upon call by the Governor, to suppress riots, control civil disorders, and aid in the relief of victims of disasters.

The important difference is that, today, the Guard is mobilization-ready for war. Its officers are Federally recognized as qualified for active duty. Its enlisted men have received 23 to 26 weeks basic training. They are familiar with the equipment they will use in combat. All members meet required physical standards, and all units are at 80 per cent of their required strength. Guardsmen receive the same rates of pay as their corresponding grade or rank in the Regular Army, and may retire on reduced pay.

When mobilized in time of war, the National Guard and Regular Army troops are required to undergo the same training and must attain the same degree of combat efficiency before being permitted to enter the combat zone. Guard units need a much shorter time than previously to develop physical stamina, review military subjects and improve their skills. Within months, the Guard is ready for combat. Its weapons, equipment and organization are identical in every respect to the Regular Army. Both receive replacements from the same source. Some commanders of National Guard units have had previous service with Regular troops. After the initial ordeal of battle, the combat efficiency of National Guard units is, in general, equal to that of Regular units alongside of which they fight.

The National Guard is a proud and patriotic organization. Its members are civilian volunteers loyal to their State and dedicated to the defense of the United States. It is the hard core of the ground forces, ready to defend the nation.

References:

The Minute Man in Peace and War, by Jim Dan Hill; The Stackpole Company, Harrisburg, Pennsylvania.

The National Guard in Politics, by Martha Derthick; Harvard University Press, Cambridge, Massachusetts.

Two volumes: Forth to the Wilderness, and A Company of Heroes, by Dale Van Every; The New American Library.

The International Encyclopaedia.

TABLE OF CONTENTS

The 36th Division in Training
September 1941—March 1943

The 36th Division in Combat
April 1943—July 1944

Part I

**The 36th Division in Training
September 1941-March 1943**

CHAPTER ONE
Joining The 36th

My service with the 36th-Texas National Guard-Division began prophetically in the middle of a hurricane alert during maneuvers in Louisiana in the Fall of 1941. I say "prophetically" because the Division had something of the quality of a hurricane. It was potentially the great fighting force which was to culminate in an overwhelming break-through of the German defenses at Velletri—thereby opening the road to Rome.

Merryville, Louisiana
Saturday, September 13, 1941

I was tired and went to bed early, but before 9:00 PM a messenger awakened me to deliver an order from Division Headquarters that all equipment should be made secure immediately. A hurricane was expected to strike during the night.

I got up, routed out my orderly and drivers, and with their help was staking down my tent when I spotted someone with a flashlight approaching from the direction of Headquarters. I thought, "Order, counterorder, disorder."

The orderly reported that General Greely wanted to see me at his tent. Major General John N. Greely, Commanding General, 2nd Infantry Division—the son of Adolphus Washington Greely, the Arctic explorer daringly rescued by Admiral Schley when a young officer—was my Chief.

"Why me? And at this hour of the night?" I wondered as I rapped at his tent.

"Come in," he said.

I entered and, without any comment, he handed me a telegram. It read:

"WASHINGTON, D. C., 3 PM, SEPTEMBER 13, 1941. BY DIRECTION OF THE PRESIDENT, BRIGADIER GENERAL FRED L. WALKER IS HEREBY PLACED IN COMMAND OF THE 36TH DIVISION, REPLACING GENERAL CLAUDE V. BIRKHEAD."

I was so surprised I read it twice, just to be sure.
When I looked up at last, Greely said, "I congratulate you."
"Thank you, sir, but I don't want it."
"Why not?" Greely shot at me.
"The 36th is a National Guard Division. The Guard won't

like having a Regular as a Commanding General."

"Oh, no! You are really very fortunate. All you have to do is treat them right. If you do, they will soon respect you."

"When shall I move to the 36th?"

John had anticipated my question and gave me some help. "Theoretically you have been in command since 3:00 PM and you are now six hours late. You should go at once. On your way, stop at VIII Corps Headquarters. General Strong may want to talk to you."

Another salute and I was on my way, but I was not happy about it. I felt I knew the Guard and recalled my service as an enlisted man in Troop B, Ohio National Guard, during my college days at Ohio State University. I remembered how rightly proud we were of our unit, which was a good one. After I had been commissioned in the Army, I heard some regular officers speak in a critical fashion of the Guard and imply a lack of cooperation. On the other hand, I remembered that when I was on duty in Washington, I had attended some sessions of the National Guard Association during its conventions and had heard speakers make equally critical remarks about the Regular Army.

When I told my Aide, Captain Earle G. Wheeler—I call him Bus—and my orderly and drivers, they were delighted, all smiles and apparently did not share my skepticism. They suffered no pain in pulling up stakes, cheerfully undoing what they had been doing for the past half hour. The hurricane was completely forgotten.

On my way to the 36th Division, bivouacked about 12 miles to the north between Merryville and DeRidder, I stopped to see Major General George V. Strong, commanding the VIII Corps.

General Strong is a cavalryman. He impresses me as a person who is quite unhappy. I have never seen him smile or laugh. In my opinion he does not have a sense of humor. He is pessimistic and is anything but physically strong. It may be that he has indigestion. He is known in his command as the "Little Scorpion."

He seated me on a campstool inside his trailer which serves as an improved substitute for a tent. Without congratulating me on the appointment, he explained that I had been placed in command of the 36th upon his recommendation; that Major General Walter Krueger, Third Army Commander, had concurred, and that he would help me in any way he could to get the Division into a proper state of training and discipline.

"Do you know the Division?" he asked.

I did not.

"Well, then, you've got a lot of cleaning up to do. The Division has been in the Federal Service and the active Army for only ten months."

Then he took up each general officer in turn, appraising his capabilities. He didn't consider any of them qualified for combat duty. He told me flatly that I would have to replace them.

I did not like this. It was contrary to the generally accepted rule that a Division Commander has a free hand in the selection and rejection of his subordinates, but is held responsible for the efficient performance of his command.

I thought to myself, "There goes my military career. I am being made a whipping boy for Strong. He is giving me an unpleasant job which he should have done himself."

If I am to be responsible to Strong for the proper functioning of the 36th Division, the means by which I accomplish this should not concern him—so long as I use good judgment, obtain desired results and maintain a high morale. But, in effect, he had said: "You are indebted to me for your command and I expect you to be my hatchet man, using my judgment and not yours with respect to the qualifications of your subordinates." That is not my idea of my duty as a commander.

When all the general officers had been raked over the coals, Strong gave the division staff officers and some regimental commanders individual attention. In his opinion some possessed no promise. Some could be utilized, if they had the capacity to learn. Others had ability but would have to have proper leadership. I did not know a single one of them. They were just names to me, and I decided to reserve my judgment until after I had lived and worked with them. It seemed to me there was some Regular Army prejudice in his remarks. I listened carefully, but made mental reservations.

Continuing on our way to the 36th, I discussed with Bus much of what Strong had said. Wheeler and I are close friends. We served together in Tientsin, China, and at Fort Lewis, Washington. He is blessed with a high IQ and has unusually good judgment. To me he is more than an Aide, and I do not hesitate to discuss my problems with him.

NOTE: My judgement has been completely justified, since he is now Chairman of the Joint Chiefs of Staff.   ·

When I finished my account of Strong's version of the 36th,

Bus said, "Well, General, it looks like we are going to have a hell of a time."

When we arrived at Headquarters, 36th Division, General Birkhead of the Texas National Guard was waiting for me. I introduced myself and Wheeler, and at the same time presented the telegram. Birkhead did not glance at it.

"I've been expecting you," he said, "and I want to tell you you are not welcome here."

I was shocked, and at a loss for an immediate reply. I fully appreciated the blow his removal from command must have been and his natural, if illogical, resentment at my appointment. But professional courtesy is obligatory with rank, rooted as it is in the determination to keep things running smoothly.

When I had recovered, I told him I hoped that he would not look upon my replacing him as a personal matter; that I had been surprised by my assignment. My remarks received little or no attention and, as I felt there was nothing to be gained by prolonging the unfriendly conversation, I asked if there were any place for visitors where we might spend the night.

"No, none," was the curt answer. "But you may put up your tents in the open space in the rear."

We had brought with us only pup tents. Not a soul showed up to help us get settled. Wheeler, with his usual ingenuity located a vacant tent for the two of us and my orderly and drivers slept in our vehicles.

Near Hunter, Louisiana
Sunday, September 14, 1941

Last night I did not do much sleeping; my thoughts were a jumble. "What kind of an outfit is this, anyway? Will the members of the Division Staff, having been appointed by Birkhead, find it difficult to transfer their loyalty to me, a Regular Army officer? Strong may be right. Maybe the Division does need changes.

"On the other hand, he could be wrong. I will find out for myself. I will treat them right, but I won't trifle. I will meet situations as they come. I will not let myself leap to conclusions. True, in some National Guard Divisions, personalities and politics play an important role. But this Division is in the Federal Service and I will not let personalities interfere with my official responsibilites. One thing I know. I will get the job done."

The hurricane never arrived.

Wheeler and I were up soon after daylight. When we stepped from our tent to get a look at our surroundings, I noticed that General Birkhead was up, so I went over to say good morning. He apparently had been up for some time, for he was neatly dressed and gave the impression of a man all set and ready to go. I saluted and meticulously paid every respect to his seniority of rank and age.

He returned my salute and it was every bit as smart as mine. His reply to my "Good Morning, Sir" was friendly. He stated that he was going to leave right after breakfast and take his Aide, sedan and driver with him. He did not ask my permission to take his sedan and driver which courtesy required.

I wanted to be generous and correct. "Of course, and take any other personnel or transportation you may desire. You may keep the sedan and driver as long as you like. Return them when you are through with them." I extended this courtesy to him. As for myself I shall send my vehicles and drivers back to the 2nd Division tomorrow.

The question of breakfast then arose. He pointed out the mess tent and mentioned the hour. Wheeler and I were there on time, as was Birkhead. As the three of us were entering the tent in order of rank, Wheeler said to me in a low voice, "I hope they don't put poison in our coffee."

The Division Staff officers had preceded us and were standing at attention. Birkhead told me to sit on his immediate right, where I belonged. Wheeler was ignored, but he found a place at another table.

During the meal, General Birkhead talked mostly about his dieting habits which were rather unusual. He ate only one item of food at a meal—and this morning it was chocolate cake.

At length he signaled that the meal was ended by rapping on his plate for attention. He arose and introduced me as the new Division Commander, adding that he knew the members of his staff would give me the same high quality of loyalty and service that they had given him. Then he sat down and indicated that it was my turn to speak.

He had not warned me that he was going to do this—and certainly his actions of the previous evening had given no intimation of his intention—but I made a few remarks. I simply said that the staff was to carry on as usual; changes would be made only if necessary and when changes would be an improvement, but that there would be no changes until I had become acquainted with personnel and procedures. Outside I asked Birkhead to give me his personal appraisal of the military qualifications of each of his General Staff officers. He rated them all superior.

> NOTE: The Staff of a Division Headquarters is divided into two groups. The General Staff is composed of five executives who form the principal study group and who supervise all of the activities of the Division. Their responsibilities are coordination, intelligence, personnel, supply, operations and training. The Special Staff is composed of chiefs of services such as ordnance, medical, signal, religion, quartermaster, finance, military justice, chemical, administration and military police. Also the commanders of artillery, engineer, reconnaissance, armor, tank destroyers and tank units were Special Staff Officers.

What I must do is to prevent speculation and political maneuverings by maintaining the personal dignity of men who are serving their country. When the axe has to fall it will, but not until I know when and where it is essential.

I arrived at the 36th just in time for a five-day maneuver under the direction of GHQ, so we buckled down to work at once. The Second Army under Lt. General Ben Lear, and the Third Army under General Walter Krueger, are going to butt into each other tomorrow. I checked the part the 36th will play and made no changes in Birkhead's plans.

Shortly after noon I assembled the regimental commanders and their staffs. They are a splendid-appearing group of officers. Their faces reflect intelligence, friendliness and curiosity. Perhaps General Greely was right. Anyway I am favorably impressed.

I spoke to them briefly, reiterating what I had said to the Division Staff at breakfast, adding that I considered it a serious responsibility as well as a high honor to be their Division Commander. Then, after commenting on the coming maneuver, I described a certain procedure I wanted them to follow on our first contact with the troops of the Second Army. They were intensely interested.

After they were dismissed, Colonel Nat S. Perrine, whom I had not spotted previously, came up to speak to me. I was delighted to see him again. As a part of his National Guard training he served four years on the War Department General Staff. During the years I was an instructor at the Army War College, he was on duty in the College Map Section there, and voluntarily attended the College lectures whenever he could find the time. I saw him almost every school day and we became good friends. I am pleased to learn that he is in command of the 142nd Regiment.

Saturday, September 20, 1941

Not all casualties in the military service are suffered on the battle field. There is one enemy I can see we will have to fight before we become a real combat Division. That enemy is carelessness, which can be deadly and which, if allowed to expand, will be responsible for deaths—even defeat—when it comes to combat.

During the five days we were on maneuvers, some men were killed and others severely injured because of carelessness.

The troops had to move in and out of bivouacs at night; no lights allowed. Of course the men were tired and some would lie down in the open spaces and fall asleep. Later trucks would roll into the area. In the dark a few men were run over. Also some trucks missed bridges and turned over into deep water or mud. Others mired down in ditches.

This is inexcusable carelessness and is due to laziness on the part of drivers and assistant drivers of the trucks, and to lack of foresight on the part of the junior officers and NCOs in charge.

I explained to my commanders, and published orders, that whenever trucks move off the main highway without lights at night onto poor roads or across country, they **must** be preceded by a guide on foot.

I am surprised that these subordinate commanders have not taken care of this long ago on their own initiative. It is just ordinary common sense.

In these maneuvers we opposed the 27th Division from New York, and there was very little left of it when we finished, for they lost 6,000 men. We captured or put out of action one brigade headquarters and nine battalions of infantry. We captured 170 trucks, twelve 155 mm, and five 75 mm howitzers. We advanced 42 miles by motor and 30 miles on foot. The Associated Press gave us a big write-up which was picked up by papers across the Nation. The members of the 36th are delighted. Their enthusiasm and energy convinces me that I am most fortunate to be their Commander.

I issued a Division citation commending them for their splendid performance. One of my staff officers told me that this was the first citation the Division had received since it was inducted into the Federal Service. It made a most favorable impression.

Perhaps I did not do just what the 27th expected, for I used some short-cuts. At my first conference I had instructed my infantry regimental commanders not to halt on making contact with the enemy, but to place a small blocking force to hold his attention while the remainder of the regiment continued to move forward off the road in a wide, concealed flanking movement. When sufficiently far into enemy territory, they were to turn and attack on the flank.

The 27th played it according to the book. They halted, reconnoitered, assembled for order and formed for attack. We had them defeated before they got to the formation stage.

A brigade commander of the 27th was captured. Near midnight two MPs brought him to my headquarters which had been set up hastily in a thicket with almost no conveniences. Our people referred to him as "Black Mike" because of his shock of jet black hair. He was as angry as a bull and refused to talk or accept any courtesies.

I tried to appease him. I was tired and had promised myself a few hours sleep, but I knew that "Black Mike" was tired, too, and that he could look forward to a chilly, sleepless night since he had no equipment. I thought a victor could afford to be generous, so, taking pride in my magnanimity and self-sacrifice, in the spirit of a welcoming host, I invited him to sleep in my bunk, telling him I did not intend to use it. He spurned my offer with contempt.

I withdrew, but not being disposed to run at the first rebuff, I told Wheeler what had happened with the hope that, with his usual tact, he would find a way to get the man to relax and enjoy his tour as a prisoner of war.

Wheeler tried his own type of diplomacy. After some minutes of conversation, which started with "Mike" still angry and disgusted, he loosened up and agreed to occupy my bunk.

Through the rest of the night the troops of the 36th were "blessed" with an unannounced inspection by their new Division Commander who found this a convenient way to while away the sleepless hours.

Colonel Nat Perrine did an outstanding job in carrying out the instructions I had given and was responsible for the greater part of our success. Brigadier General Preston A. Weatherred also had much to do with the defeat of the 27th Division. His 72nd Brigade captured "Black Mike" and his headquarters. Weatherred is one of the National Guard officers whom Strong criticized the night I took over the Division.

At the conclusion of this maneuver the concentration areas assigned to the 2nd Division and to the 36th were located so that their routes to them crossed each other. General Greely is senior to me so he had the right of way. This meant that most units of the 36th would be delayed until tomorrow. The infantry units were tired and some of them wanted to get back to Gillis and get settled in camp this afternoon, even though supper might well be long after dark.

Back when I was with the 2nd Division, I had successfully passed one moving column of trucks through another, although some of my contemporaries said it could not be done expeditiously. So, I tried my formula again. I gave the job to First Lieutenant Armin Puck, Military Police Company.

When a truckload of infantrymen approached the intersection, it would pause and then cross over in the space between the moving trucks of the 2nd Infantry Division, Puck signalling them through. This was done without slowing down the 2nd Division column.

I observed this procedure from a distance and it was pleasing to watch. Puck handled the job like a master, and when it was over, I told him so.

Gillis, Louisiana
Tuesday, September 23, 1941

I have heard it said that even the devil must receive his just dues. I received the following letter from Major General William H. Haskell, commanding the 27th Division:

"Prisoners who were captured from this Division by the 36th Infantry Division during the first phase of the GHQ maneuvers are unanimous in their praise of the considerate and extremely efficient manner in which they were handled. They were shown every consideration by the officers and enlisted men with whom they came in contact while in the custody of the Third Army. They were particularly impressed by the fine attitude of Captain Jack L. Rhodes and Second Lieutenant Fred L. May of the 36th Military Police Company.

"Please accept my thanks for the kindness shown to the officers and men of my command. It is heartening to know that the

systematic and humane handling of prisoners by the 36th Infantry
Division is quite commensurate with its splendid fighting qualities
on the firing line."

Near Hunter, Louisiana
Sunday, September 28, 1941

Our Louisiana maneuvers ended this afternoon.

This last exercise was not nearly as interesting as the preceding
one. The Division had to operate over poor roads and cross weak
bridges and was bedeviled by congested traffic. It was mostly
a problem in overcoming these handicaps as rapidly as possible,
both by day and by night, in order to maintain a constant advance
of the front lines and, at the same time, a proper supply of the
troops.

The Division CP (Command Post-Headquarters) moved four
times: from Gillis to Caney; to a sawmill at the road junction west
of Anacoco; to the vicinity of Negreet, and to Hunter—all in
Louisiana. The conditions were trying, but we did well and I am
pleased.

The maneuvers were very valuable for my troops and I am
sure they learned a great deal. It was fortunate for me that I
came into command of the Division during the last two exercises,
for they gave me a splendid opportunity to become acquainted
with all of the units. I am especially pleased that at no time have
I discerned any feeling of resentment toward me because I, a
Regular officer and not a Texan at that, am their commander.

Field maneuvers are a very important part of training for
combat. They provide practice in moving and deploying troops
in simulated war conditions in accordance with accepted combat
principles and tactics. Commanders are tested in making tactical
decisions and workable plans. Staffs are tested in standing operating procedures, in methods of procuring and distributing supplies,
in complying with health and sanitary regulations, in maintaining
an efficient communication system, and in many other staff responsibilities. Small units are tested in the execution of tactical
orders, methods of deploying for combat, effectiveness of camouflage and maintenance of discipline and morale. After maneuvers
everyone knows his job better.

In a training maneuver two forces, usually designated Red and
Blue, simulate fighting each other. The opposing commanders
must comply with the rules and administrative restrictions of the

game which are established by the Chief Umpire.

Sometimes, however, the unexpected occurs. A maverick runs wild. Just prior to my taking over the 36th, I met with such an occasion.

I had been designated to defend an area from a tank attack. The Army had not bought any anti-tank weapons except for experimental purposes since World War I, so we plastered "Tank Destroyer" signs—that could be seen 600 yards away—on a couple of 1 1/2 ton trucks; labeled little caliber 30 machine guns as big anti-tank guns; and propped up some logs to represent an artillery battery. We had to have some kind of physical evidence to show that we knew how to defend against tanks even though the equipment was a sham.

I checked the whole position and explained the defense plans to my subordinates and to my umpires. Then we waited for an armored onslaught, like six-year olds with pop guns playing "Cowboys and Indians."

Late in the day, Major General George S. Patton, whose Armored Division "Hell on Wheels," was a part of the opposing forces, sent his tanks into, over and through my sham defenses, ignoring the umpires who tried to stop him. I was furious, but I was not as angry as my men who had to take to the brush to keep from being run over. If any of them had had live ammunition, I am sure some would have felt like using it.

At the critique, which took place later, Georgie boasted of destroying our anti-tank defenses, but he did not mention that he willfully disobeyed the umpires. I did not want him to get away with this, but as an Assistant Division Commander, as I was then, and a mere Brigadier, I was not slated to speak, and the umpires were too timid to mention General Patton's disobedience of their orders.

Only Patton could get away with this, but everyone in the Third Army knows how he likes to brag and that tanks cannot be stopped by umpires waving red flags nor by make-believe weapons.

During maneuvers I told Generals Weatherred, Eugene V. Eversberg, Robert O. Whiteaker, and Colonel George D. Sears, Chief of Staff, that General Strong felt they should be replaced by Regular Army officers. I asked them to think the matter over and let me know how their replacement could be accomplished with the least embarrassment to them.

They are all men of excellent character. They are patriotic and, as far as I have observed them, possessed of good judgment and ability

General Weatherred is one of the leading lawyers in the city of Dallas. He is the granddaddy of the 36th Division. He served with it in combat in France in World War I as a Major in command of a machine gun battalion.

After the war he took a prominent part in reorganizing the Division, looking after its welfare and devoting much of his spare time throughout the years to its interests, having been promoted step by step to his present rank. All the men know him, respect him.

General Eversberg is a successful executive in the wholesale grocery business. He, too, has given years of his own time to keeping the Division intact and recruited up to prescribed strength. He may not be a tactician, but he is a fine gentleman.

General Whiteaker has been through all the ranks of the artillery and is proud of being an artilleryman. During the time he has been a commissioned officer in the Texas National Guard, he graduated from the Field Artillery School at Fort Sill in 1918, from the Army War College in 1925, and from the Advanced Course, Field Artillery School in 1929. In World War I he commanded a battery and served as Battalion Adjutant and Regimental Operations Officer. While he may lack the leadership qualities and technical knowledge necessary to successfully command an artillery brigade in combat, he has an excellent staff that would not let him fail. In private life he is a civil engineer, and a good one, according to all reports.

Colonel Sears is a prominent and successful attorney in Houston.

Today I received an admirable letter from Sears in which he expressed his views. I quote:

"As you requested, I am sending you herewith my executed request of relief from active duty on the expiration of my one-year tour of duty.

"Standing unexplained, this makes a record by which it might appear that I sought to avoid military duty on the eve of war, should one presently occur. My grandchildren might well wonder why, having been active as a civilian soldier all my life, I had suddenly quit of my own volition when the Nation was faced with an immediate danger of war. I am sure you do not wish me to be put in a false light now or hereafter. Hence this letter.

"If it is to be merely further peacetime training, then it is my desire to be relieved. A place in the Army simply as a job has no attraction to me. I have made a better place in civil life for myself than the Army can offer me, and if the government has no further need of me, I can gracefully take my place again as a civilian, being conscious only of having done my full duty, however inexpertly.

"If it is to be war, then I want to serve in any grade and in any assignment within my capabilities.

"In any case, the War Department action on the accompanying request will tell me what is wanted of me and set at rest any doubts I might have as to what should be my proper course.

"I write this to you privately. I have not discussed this question with anyone, and I do not intend to do so, nor do I intend to advise the brigadiers. In response to his question I did tell Weatherred that I was going to do as you asked, because I think he has worked faithfully at his job, and is entitled, for what it might be worth, to know what course I planned.

"Meanwhile it is my purpose to aid you faithfully and frankly in your work, not so much on the professional side, for you have little need of that, but on the question of personality, background and many similar facets, knowledge of which, it seems to me, may greatly facilitate the task in front of you, and prevent outside influences from causing any serious trouble or involving the Division"

I agree completely with the sentiments expressed by Colonel Sears. They prove him to be loyal, frank, patriotic, unselfish and gracious.

In the modern streamlining of all forces—including the Army—I wonder if those who plan for efficiency do not overlook—if, indeed, they ever knew—the potential power of personal loyalties. Many of the victories of war have come about through loyalty to men or traditions. Light Horse Harry Lee's men followed their leader against all odds, in our own Revolution. The men who served with Phil Kearny in the Civil War wore proudly the patch that signified they "rode with Kearny." Nor must we forget the extreme loyalty of Stonewall Jackson's troops to their commander in the Valley Campaign. In today's Army, the highest compliment a commander can have is to have the rank and file refer to him endearingly as "The Old Man."

I can see where I must move warily in handling this problem of personnel. The good of the Division must be my first consideration.

Just received a letter from Lt. Colonel Harold L. Reese, who was my battalion adjutant in World War I. He writes that he was seated next to General George C. Marshall at the annual dinner for distinguished guests given by the Commander of the American Legion in Milwaukee on the 15th. Marshall told Reese that he knew me; that he had placed me in command of the 36th on the previous Saturday morning, and that as he was leaving the airfield in Washington on Monday morning, he was waved back to find a message from Senator Tom Connally of Texas strenuously objecting to the relief of Birkhead and to my appointment. Marshall told Reese that he proceeded on his way, confident that I would remain where he had placed me. I am still on the job.

Monday, September 29, 1941

When I stepped out of the mess tent this evening I noted that my subordinate commanders and some members of a band were assembling about 100 yards away in the open.

I realized that this was a surprise reception, arranged by Colonel Sears, to make it possible for all of us to enjoy an informal get-together with music.

After I had received the guests, a bonfire was built, for it was a chilly evening. We gathered on one side of the fire, some of us sitting on logs and improvised seats, with the band formed on the opposite side. When Sears gave the signal, the band struck up a rousing song I had always known as "I've Been Working On The Railroad." I was surprised when everyone stood. So I did, too. The words they sang were new to me.

There was a twinkle in Sear's eyes, and I realized that I was being introduced to a Texas tradition. I asked Sears to "let me in" and he told me the song was "The Eyes Of Texas Are Upon You" and that while it was originally a University of Texas song, it has been adopted by all Texans and they always stand during its rendition.

I was very favorably impressed and shall encourage its being played and sung on all appropriate occasions hereafter. I shall also learn the words.

Tuesday, September 30, 1941

I attended the final critique at Camp Polk. After much fault finding and very few compliments, all the umpires enthusiastically claim that the maneuvers were a great success. Everyone is glad they are over and is happy to depart for home stations. We are going to Camp Bowie, Brownwood, Texas.

CHAPTER TWO
Back To Bowie

Camp Bowie, Texas
Thursday, October 2, 1941

The first echelon of the 36th began its return to Bowie yesterday. It stopped overnight at Mexia and arrived today. All troops will be in by tomorrow night.

Although I had some misgivings when I was assigned to the 36th, I have become devoted to its personnel during the past two weeks because of their whole-hearted cooperation and enthusiastic desire to comply with all of my directives. I now feel happy and content with my assignment. I am especially pleased to be associated with the people of Texas whose hospitality I have known from past tours of duty within their state.

In a way it is a little like coming home. My first station as a brand new 2nd Lieutenant was Fort Sam Houston. That was thirty years ago, at the time Julia and I became engaged by mail.

Saturday, October 4, 1941

My first task as I see it, is to concentrate on setting up an administrative system that will be fool-proof. Once the Division has such an operating system, the emphasis will go on training and coordination of forces. Training will not be neglected at any time, but it is essential that each officer and man know precisely what is expected of him. This is vital—for I cannot help but feel that I am getting this Division ready for combat.

I can see where I will have to prepare statements on various points as questions arise—even at the risk of seeming dogmatic.

Therefore, in order to impress upon all concerned that I am interested in the welfare and just treatment of enlisted men, I issued the following memorandum today:

"As a general policy, soldiers of this command will be granted permission to discuss their personal problems with the Commanding General. Such interviews must be at a time when the soldier is off duty. It is not intended that the men be allowed to bring forward trivial, routine matters, but where a man feels that he has a just grievance, or if he is faced with difficult home or family conditions, or if he feels that sufficient consideration or impetus is not being given to his case, he should be permitted to take the matter up with the Commanding General. These examples indicate only generally the application of the announced policy. This must be applied intelligently and liberally and, in case of doubt, the permission will be granted."

It is my intention to release this memorandum at intervals of six months in order that recruits coming to the Division will be aware of this privilege. I do not anticipate many callers because the unit commanders now know that they cannot be negligent or unfair in dealing with their men and that if they do not take care of these problems themselves, the men will come to me.

Tuesday, October 7, 1941

We are in camp, engaged in routine training, so I assembled all subordinate commanders and took up several administrative matters that needed immediate attention. Administration is only as good as its administrators.

I also laid down some new policies under which I expect these officers to operate:

1. When not on duty, members of the Division may wear civilian clothing off the reservation.

2. Organization commanders may issue passes good after taps.

3. Soldiers now in the guard house for minor offenses are to be returned to their units.

4. Organization commanders are to write a letter to each of their men who is absent without leave, encouraging him to return. Many men are absent without leave because the maximum punishment they will receive under the Articles of War is so light that they are willing to trade a good absence-without-leave for the punishment. Our records show 183 men now absent—the equivalent of more than one whole infantry company. This condition is not confined to this Division; all training camps and all new Divisions are cursed with it.

5. Promotions are to be given to qualified personnel only. Unqualified personnel, who do not know their jobs or do not show improvement from day to day, are to be sent before reclassification boards.

6. Athletics are to be encouraged.

7. Noncommissioned officers who are lax and careless are to be instructed in their duties and taught to be thorough in everything they do. If they do not respond to this help, they are to be "busted." A unit is no better than its noncommissioned officers.

8. If the families of Division personnel wish to live in the vicinity of Brownwood, they are welcome to do so.

In addition I told my subordinates that the commander of a military unit, be it a squad or division, is not only responsible to his superiors. He is also responsible to his subordinates. He serves the men who do the fighting. He feeds and clothes them, and provides for their welfare under all conditions of service. He is their teacher. By means of appropriate training exercises he improves their skills, develops a fighting spirit and molds them into a coordinated combat team. A good combat commander is able to estimate correctly the capabilities of his enemy as well as the capabilities of his own troops. He assigns practicable missions and brings his troops into battle under conditions which offer the greatest possible advantages over his enemy. In battle he constantly strives to bring order out of disorder.

Thursday, October 9, 1941

Sometime ago, with the thought of doing something to create a Division esprit de corps, and to obtain for the Division the goodwill of its veterans and the support of the relatives of the present personnel, I designated October 8—yesterday—as "36th Division Day" and invited them to attend.

Transportation was made available to and from Brownwood. The chaplains arranged special services for the occasion; the bands gave concerts, and the unit messes served meals. The camp was filled with visitors and everyone seemed to enjoy the day. I believe this event will do much to create a feeling of mutual interest and confidence.

General Strong sent for me today. He is after me again to relieve the three Brigadiers and the Chief of Staff. I told him that during the recent maneuvers I asked them what method would be the least embarrassing to them, and they all agreed to submit applications to revert to inactive status at the end of their first year of service, which will be on November 24th—a little over a month from now—and that Sears had already submitted his application.

Strong made no comment, but brought up other subjects.

In addition to these four officers, I am going to lose several others who will be discharged because they are overage in grade. The rumor is that Marshall thinks there should be no infantry division commander over 45 years of age. There must be exceptions.

I am 54.

The filling of vacancies, together with the promotions which are involved, is a matter of great importance to me. It is a constant, nagging problem, which is going to require my careful and personal attention. I want to be certain that only well-qualified officers are promoted. I do not want to do an injustice to anyone, yet I know from experience that some mistakes are unavoidable.

Tonight the nurses at the Post Hopsital gave a dance at Lake Brownwood and invited Bus and me. They sent a committee to do the inviting and made it appear that if we should not attend, their party would be a flop.

Being conscious of my duty to encourage any and all worthy efforts to provide recreation and entertainment, Wheeler and I dressed in our best "spit and polish" and took off for the dance. On the way we discussed our probable reception by the nurses' committee and agreed we would take no offense if they should violate some of the military protocol, since they are not supposed to be military-minded.

We arrived with great expectations, found the unlit entrance with difficulty, and went into the reception room where there were a number of medicos and their dates sitting around with drinks in hand. When they saw us they became alarmed and tried to hide their drinks. I am sure they thought I was conducting a raid. Some were so flabbergasted they did not even get on their feet.

There was no music and no dancing at the moment. No one came forward to greet us. They just sat or stood where they were, looking at us, and, I suppose, wondering when the paddy wagon would back up to the door. To relieve their embarrassment, I walked on through the ballroom and onto the patio.

Were we let down! We withdrew as best we could. As we drove back to camp, Bus remarked that we could have had a lot of fun out of the incident, if we had not been so taken by surprise.

Friday, October 10, 1941

Bus tells me the nurses did not realize they should have appointed a committee to receive their guests, so no one was primed or prepared to greet anyone last night.

Strong sent for me today.

I went, secure in the knowledge that I had made the relief of the key officers easy and satisfactory for all concerned by their

agreement to revert to inactive status. They had made it clear
to me that they were not going to vacate their position under
any cloud or stigma—and I agree with them. But Strong does
not like this. He is all for finding them unqualified. To me this
is not customary military procedure.

In my opinion he is unreasonable, unsympathetic, stubborn, and
plain looking for trouble. I told him that to date I could find no
fault with these officers and that I could not declare them inefficient unless I had some evidence to support such a charge. He saw,
I guess, that I have no enthusiasm for persecution, for he proposed
that a series of field tests be given the officers by the members of
his own staff.

This afternoon I spoke at the dedication of the eleven chapels at
Camp Bowie. When I arrived at the scene of the ceremonies, I was
surprised to see only one chair on the platform where the VIPs
were to congregate, a big upholstered one. Being suspicious, I inquired of the Division Chaplain, Father Marius Chataignon, "For
whom is that chair?"

He explained, with considerable respect, and a show of deference,
that it was for me. I probably disappointed the chaplain, as I did
not sit in that chair. I do not want to be mollycoddled nor do I want
anyone to get the idea that I sit while others stand.

Saturday, October 11, 1941

Julia, who has been in Brownwood for the past week, found a
furnished house on Austin Street which will serve our purpose
until we can do better. The rent is $65 a month, but that is better
than our one room at the Brownwood Hotel at $85. Before Camp
Bowie was established, rents were lower, but the influx of people
has naturally raised the rates.

Brownwood is not a typical West Texas town—though it is on
the edge of West Texas. There are many fine trees, a rarity in this
area. They make the riverside most attractive. I am sure we are
going to like it here.

The fact of its being a college town gives Brownwood a settled
air. I remember how, in my part of Ohio, we were told that as the
settlers came in after the Revolutionary War, they built first a
church and then an academy—the forerunner of the modern college—and the houses clustered around these two places to make a
town.

Maybe Brownwood hasn't all the conveniences of a large city, but

I think we are all very fortunate to be in the 36th's home town.

Sunday, October 12, 1941

The businessmen of Brownwood are pleased as Punch to have the 36th back at Bowie. After we arrived, I was promptly invited by Mayor Wendell Mayes; by the President of the Chamber of Commerce, F. S. Abney; and by the City Manager, Gene Mattox, to attend a planning meeting for a homecoming program of elaborate entertainment and speech-making with me as the honored guest.

This program was to continue throughout one whole day and well into the night. I noted that all of these leading businessmen were studying my expression for my reaction to their plan. They wanted to make a most favorable impression. But I could foresee possible future requests for special encouragement of business, such as collection of soldiers' debts, extension of call to quarters to a later hour, and some lenient pass privileges. I'm not suspicious of any ulterior motive—but I have been in such situations before.

Furthermore, the proposed program would have required considerable expense on their part and that was unnecessary.

I'm afraid they were disappointed, for when they asked my views, I replied, "Do you gentlemen think all of this is necessary? I do not have time for an all day affair, and neither do any of the other officers of the Division."

"Well, General, we are just trying to let everyone know that we are happy to have the 36th back home."

"We're all happy to be back home," I said. "Let's limit your reception to a dance in the evening at the hotel for the officers, and, for the thousands of enlisted men, since you haven't a hall big enough, sweep the streets clear and scatter cornmeal. I'll provide the music."

They were disappointed but they adopted my suggestions. Last evening the town was flooded with music from the eight bands of the Division. The well-lighted streets were crowded with soldiers and their girls. Dancing went on as long as there were dancers. The bright lights, the gay and carefree crowd, and the music of the bands gave Brownwood the appearance of a joyous Mardi Gras.

The Municipal and Military Police were instructed to interfere only in extreme cases. A few drunks had to be helped to their quarters, but there were no arrests. However, many are thankful that today is Sunday.

This morning a mother from Dallas called on me. Her son, a

lieutenant, is in a peck of trouble—forgery, false official statements, breaking arrest, absence without leave several times, drunk and disorderly, and fighting with enlisted men. She pleaded with me to let him go, unpunished. After talking with her, I found that she had always allowed her son to do as he pleased. Self-expression, she called it. I pointed out to her that if the youngster had had to practice some self-restraint during boyhood, he might not now be in so much trouble.

She asked me to spare him, his mother, his wife, and his brother, from the disgrace of his being court-martialed.

I told her I had to be fair and impartial. I pointed out that her son apparently had no regard for her feelings, nor for the feelings of his wife and brother, at the time he committed his many offenses. I explained that she was asking me to spare her feelings, which is the responsibility of her son. He, not I, had placed her in this unpleasant situation.

I assured her that I would see that her son was not imposed upon; that he should have a fair and impartial trial; that as little publicity as possible would be given the case; that the sentence, if he were found guilty, would not be greater than is customary for such offenses.

I believe she departed feeling that it was right and proper for her son to pay for his offenses. She said she now realizes that she has been too lenient with the boy.

I have started to read Sandburg's **The Prairie Years** and hope I can finish it without too much delay and interruption.

Monday, October 13, 1941

The greater part of the 72nd Brigade is on duty in Dallas at the Texas State Fair, where, each evening, it stages a demonstration of a night-attack. I consider this a good time to grant leave and furlough to the men who live far away. Many of them have not been home since they were brought into the Federal Service almost a year ago, while the men who live nearby get home nearly every weekend.

The few that are left in camp are struggling along in a haphazard manner awaiting their turn to go next week. By November 9th, all will be back and we will start to work in earnest.

I am not attempting to do anything in the way of training other than cleaning, preparing, and properly storing our equipment, putting our living quarters and areas in good condition, getting our transportation in good order, and improving our paper work.

I find my job most interesting. The esprit de corps of the Division is superior to that of any other with which I have come in contact. The officers, in the main, are quite capable and enthusiastic. Eventually we will be better prepared for combat than the Third Division was when it fought its initial battle on the Marne, July 15, 1918, when, as a Major, I commanded the 1st Battalion, 30th Infantry.

Once the administrative problems of the Division are solved to my satisfaction, I shall put my mind to the question of leadership. I know they say that leaders are born. But I have learned that they can also be trained—and a leader who has not had leadership training is too apt to make a mess of things.

A good leader shows the way. He knows where he is going and how he will get there. He determines the difficulties that lie in the way and makes intelligent plans to overcome them. He sees to it that his followers have the necessary equipment for the job. He sets a personal example of loyalty, energy and devotion to duty. By just treatment of his men, by rewarding them for attaining high standards of excellence, and by virtue of his own personality, he promotes a high morale and inspires respect for and confidence in his ability to lead.

Tuesday, October 14, 1941

Brigadier General Dallas Mathews, formerly the Adjutant General of Texas, is with the Division, not as a member but as a representative of Governor Coke Stevenson. He has given me a lot of help evaluating personnel qualifications. He told me that soon after the mobilization of the Division, Colonel Perrine transferred and shuffled all the officers in his 142nd regiment in order to break them away from their home-town units.

By doing so, he obtained a better distribution of his capable personnel, and also broke up the "home-town" cliques that are a natural result of the geographic limit placed on the Guard. This required going contrary to local wishes but demonstrated the excellent judgment and capabilities of Perrine.

Thursday, October 16, 1941

The life of an enlisted man in a training camp is none too good at best. I have looked into this phase of army life, and have found a number of unnecessary restrictions which I have removed. My action drew the following comment in a letter which I have just received from the Chairman of a Selective Service Board:

> "I am quite happy to state that since your taking charge, the boys have a happier spirit and say that changes are coming through fast and furious as to their treatment. I can appreciate your position, and know the task you face where many of your senior officers are political appointees, instead of professional soldiers."

Friday, October 17, 1941

Just received a letter from Colonel R. I. Burnell, Chief of the G-2 Section, Command and General Staff School, in which he referred to the recent maneuvers in Louisiana and stated:

> "In our critique of the maneuvers, there were few bouquets thrown. You might be interested in the following: 'Troops of the 36th Division were especially adept in close-country fighting. They advanced and created salients and then picked off opposing forces by flanking action with marked success. They even enfiladed an armored attack with artillery which had been advanced to positions within the salient.'"

Colonel Burnell surely knows that to do this we improved on some of the elementary routine procedures taught in our army schools. Skill and confidence in military tactics, as well as in the other professions, is improved by continued study and experience.

Sunday, October 19, 1941

On Thursday the 16th, the Director of the State Fair of Texas arranged a luncheon at the Esplanade, Dallas Fair Grounds, in my honor. At least 200 officers of the Division were invited guests, together with some 100 businessmen of Dallas, and the Fair officials.

A first class stage show was presented during the luncheon with Orrin Tucker's orchestra and Wee Bonnie Baker as the headliners.

I made a few remarks of appreciation and received applause when I referred to the present members of the Texas Division as having the same courage, spirit, morale, and fighting ability as those who proved their courage at the Alamo, at San Jacinto, and at Gettysburg.

In the Cotton Bowl after dark, I watched the demonstration of a night attack by Weatherred's brigade. The Fair officials asked us to put on this display as a feature, and Weatherred and his staff had worked it up. We knew it could not be a realistic demonstration because of the limited area of the stadium and the great number of troops employed.

I was surprised when General Strong showed up from Brownwood. I thought, "This is going to be a farce, nothing like the real thing. Maybe he is looking for an excuse to declare us all incompetent." He sat on my right throughout the show.

Needless to say, it was just a show. There was lots of firing of blank cartridges; many "killed and wounded" carried off the field; lots of talk over the loudspeakers designed to entertain and impress the civilian audience. I knew the show was unrealistic. I assumed that Strong felt the same way, so I tried to keep his mind off the show by bringing up other matters.

At the conclusion, the enemy having been duly destroyed or captured, Strong arose, turned to me and said, "General, I congratulate you on a fine demonstration."

I was surprised, not to say startled.

Weatherred **had** done a good job. He had put on an exciting and interesting show—for civilians.

I have arranged with the Commanding Officer of Camp Bowie for soldiers of the 36th to be confined in the camp stockade when they receive less than a 30-day sentence. Formerly the camp stockade would not receive them unless they had a sentence of over 30 days, which meant that my regimental and other unit commanders had to set up a guardhouse within their own units. This has been wasteful of personnel. I also arranged for prisoners to have coffee, sugar, and dessert, which the camp formerly withheld from them.

Once again I had a long talk with brigade and regimental commanders about promotions and reclassifications of officers and enlisted men. This business is very important to me, and I expect it to become a constant nagging problem along with countless nagging problems in other phases of our work. The capability of this Division in combat depends upon how well we treat these problems and I am demanding high standards of excellence in all activities.

Hereafter, I shall meet with brigade, regimental, and separate unit commanders each Friday at 10:00 AM to consider current problems.

Friday, October 24, 1941

Weatherred, Whiteaker and Eversburg have now submitted requests to return to inactive status a month from now, at the end of their year of active service. Sears is going to be detailed for duty at Third Army Headquarters, which shows that he has a lot more ability than Strong would have me believe. He did his job here as Chief of Staff in an excellent manner and he will always have my very best wishes.

To replace the infantry brigadiers, I have asked the War Department for Colonel Charles W Ryder, Lt Colonel Matthew B Ridgway, and Lt Colonel Charles Bolte. For replacement of Whiteaker, I have requested either Colonel Herbert Clarkson or Colonel Charles G Helmick. I am asking for Colonel Percy W Clarkson for Chief of Staff, and Colonel William Triplett for Division Inspector. I have served with these men and know them personally. They would give me a team of experienced Regular Army officers. I will retain Lt Colonel Carl L Phinney as Quartermaster. Even though he is not Regular Army, he is doing an excellent job.

Sunday, October 26, 1941

My enthusiasm for recreational activities gets me into some unusual experiences. On a recent evening I had my driver take me to the Service Club on the reservation in my spick-and-span sedan. The hostess was pleased at my visit and welcomed me most graciously. She wanted to show me the place, and I wanted to see it.

We had just started our tour when I saw an MP in duty uniform, playing checkers. Leaving the hostess rather abruptly, I walked over to the MP and asked if he were on duty. He said that he was.

I said, "There are many enlisted men present in mixed uniform." He confessed that one of his duties was to see that all enlisted men were in proper uniform.

I asked him why the checkers. He answered that the hostess had given permission for him to amuse himself, and for others to wear comfortable clothing while inside the Service Club. "Well," I wondered, "how long has this been going on?"

The hostess with some degree of self-satisfaction, supported the statement. When I explained, as tactfully as possible, that she had no authority to disregard official orders, she grew somewhat indignant, and completely lost her enthusiasm for my visit.

I gave the MP a lecture on obedience to orders and put him on the job at the Club entrance. I told another MP, on duty there, to inform all enlisted men who were not in proper uniform to go back to their quarters and change into the prescribed clothing.

The offending soldiers stared at me, and I could read on their lips certain uncomplimentary appellations. Reluctantly they sauntered off into the night. I noticed my driver was watching the proceedings from the side lines with a great deal of glee. The hostess gave me black looks and was glad to get me out of the building.

I was entering my sedan when my driver discovered that all four tires were mysteriously flat. I walked to my quarters through the Fall darkness, expecting to be struck at any moment by an egg or a brick.

The problem here is how to get across to the men that there are reasons for all regulations and that observing a regulation should become a habit.

Saturday, November 8, 1941

This week has been a hectic one.

Two officers have, through carelessness, "lost" part of their post exchange coupon book funds; one $1,940, the other $584. This indicates a laxity which may extend into other accounts. The two have gone to Ft. Worth and Dallas to borrow the money to balance their short accounts. Such carelessness is inexcusable.

I do not see how this can happen. When a soldier has no money, he may obtain one or more coupon books, valued at $5 or $10 from his company commander, receiving credit until pay day. These are good for purchases at the post exchange and theater. The company commander, in turn, receives his books on credit from the post exchange. On pay day the soldier pays for his books and the company commander settles his account with the post exchange. Either somebody has been negligent or the money has been stolen.

Yesterday was payday.

Last night about 300 Negro soldiers from Camp Bowie—

Strong's garrison troops, not the 36th—took possession of the colored section of the city of Brownwood. Many of them were drunk and disorderly. They threw bottles and stones at white people and at passing automobiles.

The few white MPs and local civil authorities were run out of the area, but later, after being reinforced, they returned, arrested about 100 of the Negro soldiers, and put them in jail. I was informed of the disturbance and immediately ordered one battalion of the 143rd Infantry to the scene, and went there myself.

By the time I arrived the disturbance had quieted down and order was restored. The battalion was not needed and returned to camp. No one was hurt except one Negro soldier who was accidentally shot through the foot, but the situation could have developed into a serious riot. I commended the MPs and the civilian authorities for their prompt and efficient action.

I found the local sheriff and Lt. Puck discussing the situation. In the area there were still a number of surly Negro soldiers who were insubordinate and inclined to cause more trouble. When Puck explained this to me, I said, "If they give you any more trouble, use whatever force is necessary." He replied that he would do so.

Monday, November 10, 1941

I was well pleased with the performance of the Division while on maneuvers, but upon returning to Bowie, I find that some of my people are ignorant or negligent in matters of administration, keeping records, accounting for money and property, execution and supervision of official orders, customs of the service, military courtesy, exactness in the technicalities of military exercises, relationship between officers and enlisted men, and troop organization.

I find that in some units privates, particularly if they were friends of their company commander in their home towns, have more authority than some sergeants. In some cases, motor transportation has been used for joy-riding. In other cases soldiers are not punished justly, but according to the whims of their superior, in violation of the Articles of War. Some company commanders are in the habit of reducing in rank, or disrating, enlisted men who are absent from their units on detached service or special duty.

In my efforts to correct these deficiencies, I have an uphill fight. I have held conferences, issued orders, given instructions, passed out commendations, punished delinquents, but, in general, there has been little improvement. They all seem so hurt when I point out errors, omissions, and negligence.

I have come to the conclusion that they just don't know what I am talking about, or that my orders and desires are not being made clear to the NCOs who are responsible for the execution of the details.

So I have given Wheeler the job of going to each regiment and separate battalion to inspect its paper work and property accounts and to instruct the responsible enlisted men in how to keep their records. I am taking over the inspection of all funds and instruction of the custodians until I have a Division Inspector.

A few custodians of funds have strange ideas. They deposit the unit's funds in their personal bank accounts and borrow back and forth as occasion demands. Some company commanders loan money from the funds to soldiers until pay-day.

Tuesday, November 11, 1941

The weakest spot in the administration of the Division is the care and preservation of, and accounting for, government property. It has been the habit of some investigating officers to relieve persons from responsibility and accountability for property when they should not be relieved. Very few get stuck for negligence, loss or damage. Many hearts are going to be broken when I disapprove of investigation reports, where negligence is indicated, and require the offenders to pay for their carelessness. This seems to be the only way in which to call a halt to carelessness.

Normally, when government property is damaged or lost the custodian reports the circumstances to his regimental commander, who appoints a disinterested officer to investigate the cause and determine whether there has been negligence, and if so, whether the custodian should pay for loss or damage.

Since I know that all is not well in the property business, I am ordering a complete check in all units by disinterested officers. The check of all units will be made on the same day to prevent property being loaned back and forth for display several times before the inspector. Surplus property is to be turned in, and shortages are to be placed on a Report of Survey at once. I have the impression that most units will be short some items, and when they finish paying for all missing property, the Treasury of the United States should be better off by quite a sum.

I hope that as a result of my orders the Division will become property conscious. Of course, General Walker will be a "stickler" among other things, but property and records must coincide, and I hope the personnel will never forget the lesson they are learning the hard way.

Wednesday, November 12, 1941

I have received a letter from Brigadier General J. Watt Page, Adjutant General of Texas, in which he welcomed me "most heartily as Commander of the 36th Division." He also wrote:

> "You will find, I feel confident, a most creditable organization. True, you have found therein some officers and men who, because of age, are rendered unfit for duty with combat troops. You have found some who are not professionally trained to a high degree in a military way. These will, of course, have to make way in the combat forces for other men.
>
> "While some of these men are not highly trained in a military way, and while some who have had a great deal of training are still not adaptable, it must be remembered that they have been the men who have been able to hold these organizations together during 'piping times of peace' and that is no small contribution to our country. In spite of all, you will find a most loyal and hard-working outfit, endeavoring to do its full part in preserving the democratic things for which we stand."

I have found conditions to be exactly as General Page states them. I am thanking him for his frank appraisal and hearty welcome. We see alike.

In all fairness, I must say that in loyalty and willingness to cooperate, the great mass of members of the Division need no standards set for them. In this respect they are all any commander could want.

Friday, November 14, 1941

A Negro delegation, representing themselves to be from the NAACP, came to my headquarters, and asked to be admitted to "interrogate the Commanding General of the Division."

Wheeler met them and then informed me.

"What do they want to see me about?" I asked.

"They want to know if you gave orders to the MPs during the recent unpleasantness to 'knock the heads off the niggers'?"

"Where did they get the idea they can conduct an investigation on a military reservation? Tell them I cannot give them permission to do so and to leave at once."

"General, don't you think they might make a rough time for you if you tell them that?"

"No matter what the group nor how rough a time they might give me, there are military regulations that must be adhered to."

Wheeler must have made it clear for they apparently departed without being offended.

Saturday, November 15, 1941

General Strong assembled military and civil authorities at his headquarters today to discuss the race problem. He started out by declaring:

That under no circumstances was he going to have his colored troops abused further;

That they had as much right to enjoy themselves as white troops;

That any prejudice the South might have against colored troops would not be permitted to interfere with their rights; and some other declarations along the same lines.

The Sheriff of Brown County, his deputies, the Mayor of Brownwood, and members of the municipal police, all listened intently. I was sitting some six or eight feet off General Strong's right, facing the assembly at an angle of 45 degrees. All of them would glance at me from time to time to see how I was taking the implication that the rioters had been abused and deprived of their rights.

When General Strong finished, I do not think he intended that there should be a discussion. He was just laying down the law. But the sheriff spoke up, with some feeling:

"Well, General, as long as I am Sheriff of Brown County I intend to protect the lives of our citizens."

"Yes, but you arrested a lot of soldiers who were not involved. You put them in jail and took away from them their personal possessions."

"General, every soldier there was involved. I saw them. I know. We did put some in jail, but we turned them loose as soon as they sobered up."

"I have reports from my soldiers that they did not receive back all their money and personal belongings."

"They are lying to you, General."

"I don't know that they are."

The faces of the Sheriff and the Mayor, and a number of others, showed anger at this remark, but no more was said and the meeting broke up. Outside, the Sheriff and Mayor Mays stopped me and asked, "What kind of a man is this General Strong?"

"Well, he probably has had a session with the NAACP and is not feeling well. He'll get over it."

Monday, November 17, 1941

There has been a deluge of applications from soldiers for hardship discharges. Many of them are not bona-fide cases, and I have disapproved all such requests. This is often done contrary to the wishes of Senators and Representatives in Congress from whom I receive letters almost every day urging me to discharge so-and-so because of dependents, when actually, there is no hardship. I presume that eventually I will know their wrath.

I quote from a letter I received today from Coke Stevenson, Governor of Texas:

"I have not had the opportunity to meet you, but I am looking forward to an occasion when I shall have this pleasure.

"I am deeply interested in the Texas Thirty-Sixth Division, and am pleased to have heard that you have commended the Division for its spirit and efficiency.

"I am deeply concerned because of the repeated reports that all of the higher officers have been requested to retire from their commands. I am interested, as are the Texas people, in the Division both during its period of active service and its being returned to the State intact after this emergency has passed, and I sincerely hope that at least one or more of the Division's higher officers can be retained. This would seem to me to be the only fair course, if the Division has been brought to the state of efficiency I understand it to have attained.

"I wish to express my pleasure at having heard members of the Division give praise to your leadership, and I am looking forward to an opportunity to meet you and talk over these and other matters with you."

I plan to visit him soon and discuss this with him.

I designated yesterday, Sunday the 16th as Visitors' Day. I did this for two reasons. I wanted the relatives of the members of the Division to become familiar with our living conditions and at the same time I wanted to keep as many of our soldiers in camp as possible.

On every weekend since our return to Bowie hundreds of soldiers who live within travelling distance leave camp at noon on Saturday and return in time for reveille on Monday morning.

But not one weekend has passed without a number of automobile accidents; cars wrecked and men killed. These accidents and deaths are the direct result of driving at high speed to and from home, especially by those who live at greater distances; getting little or no sleep while absent; and drinking parties staged at their homes or en route.

I have tried every means I can think of to stop this slaughter with no real results. I have spoken on the subject. I have put out bulletins encouraging careful driving. I have had commanders personally caution their men when they are about to depart on Saturday. Nothing seems to help.

So I tried Visitors' Day yesterday. It did not help either. We had just as many smash-ups as before. I look upon an approaching weekend as an impending calamity. These calamities may not cease until the Division leaves Texas.

We have had a most regrettable accident on the Ranger Training Course because a soldier charged with handling a dynamite charge was careless. Corporal Barrett will probably lose his right arm. I have not had the final word from the hospital where the surgeons are trying to save it. Private Bayles was also seriously injured. This is bad! There are enough hazards in a soldier's life without adding to them by carelessness.

Wednesday, November 19, 1941

I got angry on the rifle range. I had visited the range before, found many errors in instruction methods and pointed them out for correction. Today I found little change from former indifference, so I "laid down the law" and went back to my office. It never does any good to get angry, so I'll try to control my temper hereafter.

Thanksgiving, November 20, 1941

Today Julia and I ate dinner at the headquarters officers' mess at Camp Bowie. We had an excellent turkey dinner with all the traditional accompaniments.

Colonel Percy W Clarkson reported for duty last Monday as Chief of Staff. He will take a lot of administrative detail off my shoulders and make it possible or me to spend some time actively supervising the tactical training of the troops. Administration of a Division is a 24 hour a day job with a 7 day week. And no alibis or excuses are acceptable.

Colonel Clarkson, "Perque" as he is familiarly called, and I know each other well. We first served together as instructors at the Infantry School in the early twenties and later in the office of the Chief of Infantry, 1923 to 1925. There we sat side by side for months proof-reading the original training and combat regulations which were being issued to the Infantry at that time. I had a hand in writing some of those combat regulations while at the Infantry School before I went to Washington.

Perque is a native of San Antonio, a graduate of Texas A and M, and will be welcomed by the Division personnel.

.I am not going to get Ryder, Ridgway, Bolte, Herbert Clarkson, Helmick or Triplett. The War Department says they are not available. I consider myself lucky to get Perque. I will appoint Lt Colonel Clayton P Kerr to be Division Inspector. He has served in the Texas National Guard for over 20 years and has been a building contractor in private life. He is the author of **Pointers for Infantry Troop Leaders** and is well-qualified for his job.

Saturday, November 22, 1941

Last evening I attended a dinner given at the officers' mess of the 111th Quartermaster Regiment in honor of its former commander, Colonel Ernest O Thompson. Thompson now commands the 141st Infantry, but will leave the Division in a few days to return to civil life as Chairman of the Texas Railroad Commission which regulates the production of oil and gas, as well as railroad rates in Texas.

Colonel Thompson has an inspection procedure which he claims to have originated. When, as regimental commander, he inspects kitchens, mess halls, and barracks, he requires the NCO in charge of quarters to present to him, upon arrival, a spotlessly clean pair of gloves. These he puts on and as he goes about, wipes his gloved hands on tables, shelves, benches, window sills and similar objects. At the end of the inspection the gloves are displayed to the NCO as visible proof of perfection or neglect. Then follows commendation for perfection; other comments for neglect. Not a bad idea, if applied with intelligence.

Sunday, November 23, 1941

Some members of my staff have been inclined to act on their own initiative without consulting me or learning my wishes. This has caused some embarrassment. After all, military procedure was designed to make for smooth operations.

The Artillery Brigade is a little kingdom of its own. Its members are proud of being artillerymen, as they should be, but they also seem to feel superior to the rest of the Division. They hold themselves aloof and do not like to receive instructions or orders from Division Headquarters when and if the orders interfere with their own way of doing things.

In order to proclaim their esprit de corps to the world, a number of artillery officers have spread red paint liberally on equipment that does not have to be olive drab. General Whiteaker painted his field equipment and the inside of his cottage red. Being a doughboy I look upon all this as quite unnecessary, but have no real objection to it.

The Medical Regiment is not enthusiastic about the administrative details I have thrust upon it. Medical responsibilities having been performed, they think other matters may be slighted. Some time ago, when I spoke to the Regimental Commander, Colonel John J O'Riley, about the disorder of the equipment in his storage tents, he flared up: "General, do you want me to neglect the sick in order to move these supplies and this equipment around just so it will look nice? We know where everything is."

"Colonel," I said, "I'll be back one week from today and I want to find these storage tents in good order."

The organization that gives me the least concern and is the most cooperative and, I may say, the most efficient at this time is the

111th Engineer Regiment under Colonel Richard B Dunbar.

Slowly but surely the various organizations are coming to "join" the Division and feel themselves a part of it. Slowly but surely a Division esprit de corps is developing that will do justice to the great state of Texas.

Monday, November 24, 1941

Last evening the various units celebrated the end of their first year of Federal Service. My Headquarters' mess gave a special dinner and dance in the mess hall to which the members brought their wives and other guests. Those who wished brought their own liquor, but setups were furnished by the mess. Everyone seemed to enjoy the party.

It is November 24th but there is no word from General Strong on the requests of Weatherred, Whiteaker and Eversburg to return to inactive status.

Wednesday, November 26, 1941

Yesterday afternoon Julia, Perque, Bus and I drove to Austin and called on Governor Stevenson. I wanted to explain to him my policies with respect to the Texas Division.

The Governor made a special request that I retain the brigadiers. I told him no action had been taken by higher headquarters on their requests, but that I felt they should be replaced. I told him they were men of ability and gentlemen of importance, but that they were not sufficiently experienced to handle troops in combat, and that I wanted to fill their places with officers more experienced in tactical leadership.

I explained that it was my duty to give the enlisted men of Texas, their parents, wives, sisters, brothers, and children the best possible leadership, if and when war should come.

He seemed to appreciate that the personal interests of the enlisted men and their relatives, probably as many as 80,000 in all, are important.

I found the Governor to be courteous, frank, reasonable, understanding and personable. I formed a high regard for him as an individual and as the Governor of Texas. In my opinion, Texas is fortunate to have an able, sincere and devoted servant like Coke Stevenson.

Friday, November 28, 1941

Last night an automobile carrying soldiers of the 36th Division, while travelling at high speed, attempted to pass a truck on a hill and collided with a civilian automobile. Two soldiers and three civilians were killed instantly. One other soldier will probably die.

I published a memorandum to the Division pointing out the nature of the accident. I referred to the soldier driver as being criminally negligent and stated that I hoped every member of the Division would realize that laxness in obedience to law and good order must be paid for; not necessarily with material things but often with the lives of innocent people. The line of demarcation between carelessness and criminal negligence is slight. Carelessness is **never** an excuse when an accident occurs.

My Judge Advocate, Lt Colonel Jesse E Moseley, told me after he read the memorandum, that I had committed a libel in charging the driver with criminal negligence, and advised me to recall it. I explained to him that the soldier had committed a criminally negligent act, according to the laws of the State of Texas, and that I would take a chance on being sued for libel. I will not have much difficulty if I should have to prove my charge.

Sunday, November 30, 1941

When I went back to inspect the storage tents of the Medical Regiment, I found them in good order. Colonel O'Riley was as pleased as I.

Thursday, December 4, 1941

Although I do a great deal of observing, inspecting, and pointing out need for improvements, it seems that progress is at a snail's pace and in some cases, not at all. I have been trying to think of ways to speed things up.

Some days ago I decided to test the basic military knowledge of the senior officers. It seemed to me that they did not always understand my language.

I prepared a schedule of written tests. I could have conducted them orally, but that method might have been extremely embarrassing to the older officers if they should fail in the presence of their subordinates. Since the purpose of the tests is to improve everyone's basic military knowledge, I published the subjects of the tests a week in advance. The questions are to be elementary and the answers should be common knowledge to every unit commander.

When I announced the tests at our regular Friday morning meeting, there were expressions of righteous indignation on the faces of the senior officers especially.

They seemed to be thinking: "The very idea of subjecting me to a petty and tedious written test. We know our business. Why waste our time? We are being treated like children."

The tests came off as scheduled. There was a surprising amount of interest. I collected and marked the papers, returning them promptly. All grades were to be kept secret. Most did well, but a few were unable to answer all the questions. One colonel, who prided himself on his long service and splendid regiment, had a rude awakening. His face turned red with anger when I returned his paper with the notation, "Obviously you have not prepared for this test. Too many incorrect answers. Come to my office next Saturday for reexamination."

When the others had departed, he spoke to me, showing his hurt feelings, "Why the embarrassment of taking the test over?"

"Because I want to be sure you know the basic elements of the subject."

"Well, General, if I don't know my business now, I never will know it."

"You certainly do **not** know all you should know about military law. Look it up before you report Saturday."

When Saturday came, he reported full of confidence, passed the test easily and went away happy as if to say, "I told you so."

CHAPTER THREE
After Pearl Harbor

Camp Bowie, Texas
Friday, December 12, 1941

This is the first breathing spell I have had since last Sunday, December 7th. General and Mrs. Paul Paschal visited us over that weekend. After they departed around noon Sunday, I lay down for a nap, got up around 4 o'clock, turned on the radio and learned that the Japanese had bombed Pearl Harbor.

Since that moment, I have been on the jump with a flood of special instructions about troop movements, cancellation of peacetime policies, and emergency plans.

Monday we received orders to prepare one infantry regiment to move to the West Coast on short notice. The 144th Infantry was designated. Preparation for departure was of first importance and Lt Colonel Harry Steel, Division G-4, was instructed to assist in every way possible and to maintain close liaison between the 144th and post headquarters, which is responsible for supplying the railroad trains.

It is one thing for a unit to move out of camp when it is going to return. It is quite another when it is leaving permanently.

All the units in the regiment have property in their possession which belongs to the Texas National Guard, such as supplementary kitchen equipment, recreation supplies, and furniture. This property is to be properly packed and sent to Camp Mabry at Austin, since it must not be moved from the State. Packing lists are to be placed both inside and on the outside of the containers. Surplus Federal property, if any, is to be turned in to the post supply officers, and receipts procured.

The 144th had just started to carry out these instructions when word was received from VIII Corps that the regiment would move by rail to Fort Lewis, Washington, the next day. Then things started happening.

The regiment was to take full field equipment, woolen clothing, heavy tentage, five-day rations, initial allowance of ammunition, foot lockers, company property—everything. Persons on furlough and away at schools were to be returned to accompany the regiment, if time permitted. Otherwise, they were to remain with the Division at Bowie.

The officers and men had to look after their army duties and their families and personal affairs, all at the same time. The officers who were responsible for procuring and preparing property to go with the regiment were also charged with disposing of the surplus. In the midst of all this, the Regimental Commander, who is overage, had to be replaced.

I went to the 144th's area to see how they were getting along. They needed help! I designated the Supply Officer of the 142nd to take over any of the property the 144th couldn't dispose of promptly. He is to turn it in to the post and send the receipts on to them later.

Three or four hours later I visited the area again. As I came around the corner of a mess hall, I saw a pile of property almost as big as a house in front of the 142nd's storeroom. I could hardly believe my eyes, and was quite irritated. Weeks ago I ordered all units to dispose of their surplus property. I had been told they had done so.

As I approached the pile and saw trucks pulling along side and men throwing property onto it, helter-skelter—most of it was obsolete—I began to see something ludicrous about all the running about and running to and fro to get things done. The property was being dumped faster than the supply personnel could check, count, and write out receipts.

There were too few men to handle the job, and since I was determined the regiment would get off on time, I directed the Commander of the 111th Engineers to use all the personnel and resources of his regiment, day and night, to assist the 144th to get on the trains and away for Fort Lewis on schedule.

I went to see the first train-load pull out. Colonel Erle D Sandlin, whom I had never met, and who had been Regimental Commander only about 24 hours, was leaving on that train. He told me he had been pulled off another job suddenly and unexpectedly by the VIII Corps, and that he did not know a soul in his own regiment or the 36th Division.

When he first visited his new command he could not distinguish between his own personnel, those of the 142nd, and those of the 111th Engineers, all of whom were quite busy within his area. As affairs became more and more confusing to him, he had sought his own brand of escape from his predicament and was now sufficiently "relaxed" to accept the whole situation with resigned amusement.

The train, with Sandlin aboard, departed at 8:57 PM and the other detachments pulled out at 10:40 PM, 12:45 AM, 4:19 AM, and 5:20 AM—all on time.

But that wasn't all. The next day, Wednesday, Company K. 143rd Infantry, departed to protect Hensley Field, between Fort Worth and Dallas. Thursday morning Company L, 143rd Infantry, less two platoons, went to Raton Pass to protect a railroad tunnel. One platoon of Company L went to Phoenix to protect an airfield and another went to Tucson to protect the airfield there. The remainder of the 143rd is alerted to move on short notice.

Saturday, December 13, 1941

This morning the Military Police Company and Company A, 111th Quartermaster Regiment departed for Fort Mason, California, for duty at that port of embarkation.

All units are ready to move anywhere at any time. I have had a number of officers reconnoiter the border from Brownsville to the Big Bend in order that they may be familiar with housing conditions and tactical dispositions in case we have to send troops there. It is reported that General Whiteaker, contrary to my orders, crossed the border on a personal tour, and I will see him about this.

Yesterday we received orders to strengthen the loading platforms at Bowie so that we may load heavy equipment on two trains at one time. This we did immediately.

The expenditure of all types of ammunition has been discontinued by the War Department.

No more officers or enlisted men are to be discharged except for physical defects or incompetence.

The Nation appears to be united now in this war against Germany, Italy and Japan. The damage to Pearl Harbor and the island of Oahu is greater, I believe, than has been reported. We received a cable today from Fred Jr, at Schofield Barracks, Hawaii, where he is stationed. He, Florian and our two grandchildren are safe. This is a relief to Julia and me.

In the Philippines the Japanese have had some little success, but have met with some reverses. I studied the plans for the defense of Luzon while I was a student at the Army War College, and I note that the Japanese are acting exactly as we anticipated they would. I fear that the garrison in the Philippines is going to have a severe test before it can be reinforced by troops from the United States. It is quite probable that it may never be reinforced.

Sunday, December 14, 1941

I inspected the 71st Brigade yesterday. I found many minor defects and corrected them, I hope, in so far as material things are concerned. But I was disappointed with the apparent indifference to exactness and completeness in performance by some officers and enlisted men. They do not seem to understand how discipline is developed, nor why. So I am scheduling a number of conferences and shall take pains to explain my concept of discipline to my staff and to all my subordinates, in order that it may prevail in this Division.

The word "discipline" has a different meaning to different people. In a military sense the word does not mean punishment. Discipline is a habit of obedience. It includes an immediate willingness to obey directives and wishes of those legally appointed to command.

It is developed, like every other habit, by repetition. That is, by repeated obedience to all forms of military activity such as routine drills, details of administration, standards and procedures of maintenance.

Obedience is encouraged by rewards for good work and by appropriate penalties for negligence. A well-disciplined command is not a well-punished command. A good disciplinarian is not noted for dealing out excessive punishment. But he is firm.

I have served at many levels in many organizations, but I was happiest in those commands where a high state of discipline (the habit of obedience) was maintained. This is true also of others because in that kind of command there is a greater pride of service, a greater contentment, less bickering, less absence without leave and less punishment.

A soldier should not be penalized because of failure at some duty. If he is ignorant he should be instructed. If he is incapable, he should be given another job, one he can do. He should be punished only when he is qualified but negligent. He should never be permitted to do his duty in an indifferent and slipshod manner.

Careless commanders permit careless ways of doing things. This leads to a habit of negligence, a poor state of discipline, and an unhappy organization where duty is apt to become drudgery.

That is why I want everything we do done well, in accordance with prescribed methods and procedures. I want a well-disciplined and contented command, one with esprit de corps; a Division better than any other in the United States Army.

Many men are coming into the army at this time who have no pride of service, no desire to do their work well, no spirit of self-sacrifice and no sense of duty. They do not know how to work to advantage and they are satisfied with anything that gets by. We must get down to basic training and begin the development of discipline. The fact that we are at war should give us all a common goal, but transfers of personnel and the breaking-up of units do not help.

God give us the ability to produce disciplined soldiers before it is too late.

I am surely glad I bought the farm in Ohio last April. Now, with the war, I feel that I have an anchor out, if the Navy will forgive the phrase, a place for Julia, Florian and our grandchildren to go and a place to absorb their attention and interest while Fred Jr and I are in the service. Charles will be out of college in June and will undoubtedly go in the service, also.

General Eversburg has been reduced to the grade of colonel, to which he agreed, and has been assigned to the San Antonio General Depot. This will help. His request for inactive status, submitted while we were yet at peace, was disapproved. Eversburg is a fine gentleman, but he is not a combat soldier. Since he has a great deal of experience in the grocery business, this is a splendid assignment where his knowledge can be used to advantage.

I have packed all my civilian clothes and extra books in order to move quickly, if I have to. There is no telling when or where I may go. War Department orders and instructions are being issued on short notice these days.

Monday, December 15, 1941

I had a long conversation with General Strong regarding General Whiteaker. Strong wants to recommend him for reclassification, but I told him he does not have sufficient evidence to prove that Whiteaker lacks the professional knowledge to command an artillery brigade. Strong is going to try a field test on him to prove his ability one way or the other.

Tuesday, December 16, 1941

Received instructions at 3:14 PM from Headquarters VIII Corps to alert Whiteaker's 61st Field Artillery Brigade and Weatherred's 72nd Infantry Brigade, each for a separate field exercise.

At 3:35 PM the situations for the exercises to be conducted by the Corps Staff were received, and the two brigades moved out of camp without delay. I watched them go. Their departure was orderly and on time, although some of their equipment was not well packed. They had only 21 minutes to get ready; a very short warning period, indeed.

Thursday, December 18, 1941

The field tests, which Corps suddenly ordered held on the 16th and 17th for the 61st and 72nd Brigades, turned out to be quite elementary.

I observed much of each of the exercises, and failed to find anything wrong that was of real importance. One can find minor errors in any exercise by troops when they are suddenly rushed out out into the field on short notice.

Anyway, more than six weeks ago Weatherred and Whiteaker submitted their requests to be returned to inactive duty on last November 24th. Why all this harassment? In my opinion, the field tests revealed nothing that could be classed as inefficiency on the part of the two brigadiers. However, I am not informed of the official findings.

Last month we shipped off the 2nd Battalion of the 131st Field Artillery to the Philippines. Persons who have received letters from friends in that battalion tell me that it sailed from Hawaii on about November 28th. If this is correct, their transport may have been in the vicinity of Guam or west thereof on December 7th. It is my belief, however, that they have evaded the Japanese sea attacks and are now either at their destination or at some other port in the Pacific. We are all quite concerned about them.

In line with my continuous efforts to develop high standards of performance in this Division, I decided to introduce some competition between units. Some time ago I had my staff prepare tests on every military skill except tactics and paper work.

The first of the three-day competitive tests began today. They are conducted in the nature of an athletic field-day with many events going on at the same time at different locations. Each unit is represented by a select team which has been given an opportunity to prepare for its test.

Saturday, December 20, 1941

The band concert held last night at the Officers' Club closed the three-day competitive tests.

All eight bands participated and each played three numbers. The first was a warm-up number which was not considered by the judges. The second was a number required of all bands. The last number was chosen by the band leader. The concert lasted almost four hours. I invited most of the leading citizens of Brownwood, and everybody enjoyed the music and an opportunity to relax from the tension of the times.

First place went to the 142nd Infantry Band, second to the 143rd Infantry Band, and the 111th Medical Regiment Band was third. All eight bands were excellent, so the judges must have had a difficult time arriving at their decisions.

This morning, the Division was turned out for a dismounted review as a finale to the period of tests. I distributed awards to the winners or their representatives. More than 300 winning contestants were assembled before me on the reviewing field as a part of the ceremony.

After making the awards, I directed the winners to take their places in line on my left to witness the Division pass in review. This was the first time a group of enlisted men of the 36th Division had ever witnessed a review at their Commander's side.

The three-day competitive tests were very interesting. Unit commanders wanted to win and they made considerable effort to prepare their teams or groups for the competition. Officers and men, who had the time, observed their teams and did some loud cheering. Now, since high standards have been demonstrated by the competition, it is the job of all unit commanders to bring their personnel up to these levels.

Sunday, December 21, 1941

Charles arrived home this morning from Knox College for Christmas vacation. He said, as a joke, that he would like to have a ride in my official automobile before he goes back to school, with flags flying and MPs on motorcycles with sirens screaming out in front; alluding, of course, to similar childish displays by some generals we have known.

Monday, December 22, 1941

There is a feeling on the part of those who administer justice in some of our penal institutions, and on the part of some judges of our courts, that men found guilty of misbehavior should have their sentences remitted provided they will enlist in the military service.

Those who feel this way should know that a troublemaker is a troublemaker wherever he may be—in the army, in jail, or on the loose. The army is not a reform school nor will it put up with the criminally inclined. We need reliable men who will carry out orders when the going gets tough. It is an honor to serve.

A soldier of this Division was discharged some time ago for the good of the service and now he is in trouble again and I am being asked to take him back. This I will not do.

I had to tell the civil authorities, "The long record of offenses committed by this soldier bears out his bad military record. He is an habitual offender and is a liability rather than an asset to the military service.

"It is not felt that any good purpose could be served by returning him to military control, and we would only be handicapped in the performance of our mission, during these critical times, by having to take care of this individual.

"I therefore feel it incumbent upon me to inform you that no steps will be taken by the military to secure his return, nor do I feel justified in assuming any responsibility to the civil authorities, should he be released.

"Your offer to cooperate with the military authorities is appreciated deeply and in case where a man is of any value to us, I shall be glad to take him off your hands and assume responsibility for his future conduct."

Tuesday, December 23, 1941

My Christmas greetings to the officers and enlisted men:
"To each and everyone of you I extend my sincere wishes for a joyful Christmas season. We should be grateful that a divine

Providence has decreed that most of us will have the opportunity of spending a portion of the holiday season with our loved ones. May the happy events of Christmas, 1941, linger long in your memories."

Friday, December 26, 1941

I have just learned that our enlisted MPs are under the impression that they are not to arrest an officer under any circumstances.

I have informed them that any officer whose conduct is unbecoming, and such as to bring discredit on the service, especially if he is drunk and disorderly, is subject to arrest. He is to be taken into custody and delivered to his unit Officer of the Day, following the same procedure as for enlisted men. If the officer's condition requires restraint, he is to be confined in a cell in town, or in the guardhouse, just the same as anyone else.

Saturday, December 27, 1941

An automobile carrying seven soldiers enroute to Bowie from their homes ran into a truck outside Brownwood yesterday. The soldiers' car was on the wrong side of the road and struck the truck head-on, killing four soldiers instantly. Two died later, and the seventh is in serious condition. The truck driver was not badly hurt. He said he saw the soldiers' car coming toward him at a considerable distance, tried to signal them with his horn, and failed. The crash followed. He believes that the driver was asleep. This is a terrible way to end our holiday.

The Japanese ruthlessly bombed the city of Manila after it had been declared an open city by the American forces.

I first saw Manila in October, 1911, having arrived with the 13th United States Infantry as a married 2nd Lieutenant of only six months service. The Bridge of Spain over the Pasig River, the Escolta, the old walled city, the Luneta, the General Hospital where our first child was born, all these and many other interesting places became familiar to us during my three year tour of service in the Philippines. I greatly regret the destruction of Manila.

Monday, December 29, 1941

Today I received a directive from the War Department to institute a series of lectures explaining to our officers and men why we are in this war and how it all came about; some 18 lectures, each 50 minutes long. To my mind this is a lot of foolishness. It may be based on an assumption that soldiers do not read papers, attend picture shows where newsreels cover the world events, listen to radio commentators, and do not discuss the causes of the war among themselves.

The directive is the brainchild of some enthusiast, a "do-gooder," occupying a desk in the War Department, who does not know that our soldiers fully realize that we are at war and why we got into it.

Although the lectures will be a great waste of time, I will detail two officers and two NCO assistants from each regiment to give them. We will do them 100 per cent, but I cannot for the life of me understand why the War Department fell for this program, but turned a deaf ear to our pleas for some time for athletics on the training schedule. The esprit and morale of the army can be greatly improved by reducing training from 44 to 40 hours per week and devoting the four hours to athletics. Anway, there will be some benefit from the lectures—the men will have a chance to catch up on their sleep.

Carelessness again creates problems. General Krueger is very displeased, and so am I, because of the unusually high number of pistols, rifles, and field glasses that were lost by this Division during the Louisiana maneuvers. He was kind enough to warn me that I am going to get a very stiff "skinning" for the lack of care of government property. Really, this loss of equipment indicates poor discipline and just plain disregard of regulations, and most of the loss occured before I came to the Division. Nevertheless, I am responsible; i.e., I must explain the loss and accept the consequences.

Sunday, January 11, 1942

A lot has happened since I entered the hospital on the evening of December 29th for a minor operation. After several days of discomfort, I was able to leave and resume work on January 9th.

Since the war began we have been transferring personnel hither and yon, within and without the Division. We have sent officers away to the Field Artillery School, Infantry School, Engineer School, Command and General Staff School, Cooks and Bakers School, Army Junior Officers School, and others.

In addition, we have our own schools within the Division for cooks, promising NCO's, motor mechanics, truck drivers, radio operators, medical technicians, etc. We have organized and trained 19 gun crews and sent them off to New Orleans to serve aboard transports. It seems that everybody is either going to school, at school, returning from school, or being transferred away permanently. This keeps us in a state of confusion and uncertainty, and makes it impossible to carry on unit tactical training. However, this is all necessary and must be done.

I have let it be known that in this program of education and transferring of personnel, there are going to be opportunities for promotion and transfer to more favorable positions, and that no one is to be denied the right to better himself on the grounds that he is indispensable and his services cannot be spared.

At noon on the 30th we, and the 64th Medical Regiment, received a directive from the War Department to transfer 250 men to a General Hospital at El Paso, over 500 miles away, and have them there within 24 hours. I don't know why.

All were to be physically fit and qualified for tropical service. Inoculations were to be started as soon as possible, but were not to delay the movement. The following skills were required:

4 barbers	2 stenographers
1 butcher	2 technicians, dental
8 chauffeurs	6 technicians, laboratory
4 clerks, mail	12 technicians, medical
20 cooks	6 technicians, x-ray
2 mechanics, general	4 pharmacists
1 operator, electrical	9 typists
8 clerks, general	148 non-specialists.

This was some job! We could not furnish all the specialists fully trained, but we sent men who will be able to perform the skills after they have had an opportunity to improve by doing. At dawn on the 31st, they departed on a special train for Fort Bliss. The Division staff, the unit commanders and the men complied with this directive by working all night. This is a sample of the problems we are facing daily. Praises especially to Lt Colonel Marvin D Steen, the Adjutant General.

On New Year's Day, Senator "Pappy" O'Daniel and General Weatherred, who was the senior officer on duty, visited me in the hospital. A photographer wanted a group picture of us, so we stepped outside. When the photographer was about to snap the shutter, Senator O'Daniel said, "Wait a minute. I don't want any of our friends up North to think we have to wear overcoats in Texas. Texas is a summer resort."

So saying, he removed his overcoat and the picture was taken.

Brigadier General Terry de la Mesa Allen telephoned on January 2nd to say that he has been assigned to the 36th Division. He was enthusiastic about his new assignment, and said he would be here on the 8th. He arrived yesterday, the 10th, the day he was due.

Although he is senior to me, I am to continue in command of the Division, according to the War Department. This is a very unusual situation. I am the junior Brigadier in the Division—there are three others—yet I command it. My guess is that either Terry or I will be promoted soon, and one of us will leave the Division. I have known Terry since we were second lieutenants serving together at Eagle Pass, Texas, in 1915. Terry has served most of his Army duty in Texas, and his wife is from El Paso. I am pleased to renew our friendship.

I have received the report on the field tests of the 61st Field Artillery Brigade and the 72nd Infantry Brigade from the VIII Corps. It indicates many deficiencies in the 61st Brigade, and I sent it to General Whiteaker for an explanation. Then Krueger and Strong informed me that they expect me to do something about the unsatisfactory condition, so on the 9th I notified Whiteaker that I intend to recommend him for reclassification. This means that he will have to appear before a board of officers appointed by either Strong or Krueger to determine what duty he is qualified to perform.

The test on Weatherred's brigade was reported satisfactory. I have the feeling that he was ordered out in an attempt to make it appear that Strong was not concentrating on Whiteaker. For the life of me, I do not understand why General Strong did not permit Whiteaker to return to civilian life on his own request.

I had Moseley, the Division Judge Advocate, send a letter to the president of a general court martial which had prescribed a sentence of six-month's restriction to camp for a soldier, informing the court that I am displeased with the sentence for the reason that it is illegal. Three-month's restriction is the limit, and a sentence of extended restriction to camp is impractical.

There are times when a man has the right to lose his patience. Due to cold weather and just plain indifference (this is becoming a frequent word with me), we have five frozen and cracked engine blocks, maybe more. An inspection has been ordered to determine the total number in the Division, the officers responsible, the cost of the blocks, and the shop where they can be repaired.

I wonder how many of those responsible would have gone to bed in freezing weather without draining the radiators, if the vehicles had been their own? Carelessness in care of government property is indicative of poor discipline.

Wednesday, January 13, 1942

Today I received notice that I have been nominated by the President for the rank of Major General. Of course, this is good news. In order to do this, the War Department had to jump me over brigadiers who are senior to me in length of service. While this is a compliment to me, I know that those I jumped will not like it.

Perque and Lucy Kent Clarkson and their son Bill presented me with a set of stars for my new rank, along with their congratulations. They are pleased at my being nominated for promotion, and I appreciate their kindness.

Thursday, January 15, 1942

During the past ten days the Division has been required to organize a tank destroyer battalion, submit names of qualified personnel to form part of the cadres for a new Army corps staff, an engineer regiment, the headquarters of a reception center at Fort Dix, an ordnance company, and a quartermaster company.

The Division is now really a replacement depot, and I am glad we are doing as well as we are in meeting the demands of the War Department for personnel. This means promotion for practically everyone who leaves and everyone who stays, and is an incentive to all in their new jobs.

Sunday, January 18, 1942

It has developed that the Division has overdrawn its allowance of rations by 1200 already this month, due to erroneous accounting by regiments. The Morning Report shows the number of men for duty each day, and all that is necessary is to add up the total for the number of days in the month. The problem may be that the responsible persons are arriving at their ration strengths by pure guesswork. Captain Burton Miles is going to conduct a school on this subject next week.

Wednesday, January 21, 1942

The VIII Corps Inspector has finished inspecting the Division. He found only a few minor errors (not nearly as many as I can find). He said he was impressed by the professional knowledge and efficiency of the general and special staff officers whom he interviewed, and that he noted particularly the orderly and efficient procedure in the office of the Division Adjutant General, Lt Colonel Steen. He is quite right. I have found that General Birkhead was correct when he told me that his general and special staff officers were superior.

Friday, January 23, 1942

At our conference today I read to my subordinates the law regarding the unauthorized use of government vehicles for private, personal purposes, and explained the necessity of complying with the spirit of the law. The use of government vehicles to transport officers to and from Brownwood to attend to personal matters is not within the meaning of the law. Also, a number of army vehicles have been seen parked, during working hours, at the Service Club, various places in town, and at roadside eating spots. Drivers who are sent on official errands must not stop and hang around such places.

I told them also that the time has come for officers and NCOs to get out of the pre-war attitude of talking about what is to be done; to start doing, instead. Commanders must punish men who fail to do their duty, and must have the courage to do so whenever necessary. Careless and casual performance of duty will surely result in our men being unnecessarily killed or wounded. We are responsible to the parents and relatives of these men, as well as to ourselves, to see to it that everyone does his full duty.

Saturday, January 24, 1942

I have a letter from Bus Wheeler, whom I sent to take the short course at the Command and General Staff School at Fort Leavenworth. He has heard rumors that are disturbing to him and is concerned about being separated from the 36th. He writes, "If such is the case, perhaps you'd better ask for me by name to return to the 36th Division to fill my own vacancy as Aide de Camp. This is based on hearsay, of which this institution has a God's plenty."

In answer, I wrote, "I have just received a telegram in which the War Department has asked whether or not you are available for assignment to duty in the G-3 division of the War Department General Staff. To this I replied that you are my Aide; that you are now in school in Leavenworth; that I intend to use you in a key position on my own staff; and that I request that your present assignment be not changed. What the outcome will be, I do not know.

"Colonel Nat Perrine has been transferred to the 141st from the 142nd. He wants you in his regiment, and promises to promote you. He says that his property records are in a deplorable state and he needs you to untangle them. I told him I would talk to you first."

I have a problem with officers who go to service schools and fail. Any person with average intelligence can pass these courses, if he applies himself. The officers who fail either do not have the intelligence, in which case we cannot use them, or, having the intelligence, do not apply themselves, thus being derelict in their duty, in which case we cannot use them, either.

Officers who lack intelligence or application are unworthy of wearing the uniform and cannot possibly command the respect of their men and fellow officers. Yet indications are that the Third Army Commander is going to require me to keep them in the Division. If he does, it will be bad for discipline and efficiency. It will put me in an embarrassing position and will place a premium on indifference on the part of service school students. Of course, each case has to be investigated on its own merit.

On Wednesday, the 21st, I received official notice of my promotion. Unfortunately, due to the pressure of work, I could stop only long enough to take the oath of office, pin on the second star, call Julia and tell her, and pose for the news photographers.

If I had received this promotion in peace time, we would have given a real party. With this new rank I feel more secure in my assignment, and I hope to remain with the Division, for I have come to feel really a part of it.

I want to retain as souvenirs the brigadier flags I used. I have received many letters and telegrams of congratulations which I will also save. They may be of some interest to my posterity.

This promotion increases my pay $183 a month, which will be a little more than enough to pay the increased taxes. So, my pay in the future will be only slightly more than in the past, in so far as any amount I can use to meet personal needs. This reminds me of that ancient, but persistent, old-soldier doggerel, "You'll never get rich, you son-of-a-bitch, you're in the Army now."

Wednesday, January 28, 1942

I talked to Major General John N. Williams, Chief of the National Guard Bureau in the War Department, today by phone; Brownwood to Washington. I had previously received a letter from him containing a plan for reducing the 36th to a triangular division, and called him at his request to clear up some errors and omissions in his plan. According to him, the War Department will issue orders for the change next week.

By triangular division I mean that we will have three infantry regiments instead of four, four artillery battalions instead of six, one engineer battalion instead of an engineer regiment, one medical battalion instead of a medical regiment, and the service units will be reduced. After the reorganization, our strength will be reduced from 22,000 men to approximately 16,000 men, and we will have more than 2,000 vehicles. The infantry regiments will have about 3,600 men each. Weatherred's 72nd will be absorbed, and will not exist as a brigade.

This so-called triangular division is of the type that has been adopted by most European armies. It is expected to be more maneuverable and more economical in manpower and material than the square or four regimental divisions without sacrificing fire power.

Thursday, January 29, 1942

I inspected the 636th Tank Destroyer Battalion today. It is in a deplorable condition. The men are dirty, and the NCOs indifferent. The officers do not do their duty or assume responsibility. I am going to assign Major Van W Pyland to the battalion to get it organized, equipped, and disciplined.

It must have proper leadership, and there is no time to lose. When we organized the battalion recently, certain units, principally field artillery, were required to transfer personnel and equipment to it. What they did was to transfer their least desirables, which was contrary to the spirit of my instructions.

I should have kept an eye on this business. Now I have to select qualified personnel from throughout the Division, transfer them to the 636th, and send the undesirables back to their original units. Also, I have to return the unserviceable equipment.

In a way, they can't be blamed for trying to shove off their undesirables onto somebody else. This is an old army trick, but they made the mistake of doing it in a wholesale rather than a retail manner. My viewpoint is a little broader than theirs. If the undesirables were leaving the Division, I would not complain, but the 636th will go overseas with us.

The day may come when that battalion will save us in battle. Right now, it would ruin us.

Friday, January 30, 1942

Many of my officers are disturbed by the change to the triangular division for they think they will lose promotion if the Division is reduced.

Their anxiety is unwarranted because there is going to be a flood of promotions in any case. There are some who are eager for advancement in rank, but not so eager to qualify professionally. If they will but determine what their duty is and will then qualify to perform that duty and consistently perform it under all circumstances, promotion will take care of itself.

Now that I am a Major General, I need two Aides, especially since Bus is still at school in Leavenworth. I asked Colonel Phelps of the 133rd Field Artillery Regiment to recommend an officer because I want an artilleryman for my junior Aide—thus combining the knowledge of the Infantry and the Artillery. He recommended Lieutenant Frank L Reese, an excellent officer whom I have just promoted to Captain. It just happens that his birthday is the same as mine, June 11.

Sunday, February 1, 1942

Troubles never cease.

Several officers and NCOs failed to pass our own school course in methods of preparing ration returns.

I have six officers on my hands whom I cannot use in any capacity. They are lazy, have no pride of service, no ambition, and no sense of duty. It will take a month or more to get them reclassified, but in the meantime I suppose I could keep them busy by organizing a school, detailing one of them as instructor, and sending the others as students.

Actually it is only a small group I have to keep prodding. The others are really marvelous. They are enthusiastic and want to do good work, and they have accomplished wonders. I am fortunate in having outstandingly able general and special staffs, and there is no Division, Regular Army or National Guard, that has any better.

Julia and I attended the dance given by the doctors and nurses at the Post Hospital at the Officers' Club. It was a very pleasant party; quite a contrast to the one Wheeler and I "attended" at Lake Brownwood when we were invited by the same people.

                                    Tuesday, February 3, 1942

Brigadier General Weatherred has been informed that he will be reassigned.

Last night Terry Allen invited a number of persons, including myself, to a reception he arranged at his cottage in camp for the General. I was pleased to go, and at Terry's request, proposed a toast complimentary to the honor guest. This was followed by many other toasts. General Weatherred tried to enter into the pleasant conversation and joviality, but I could sense his sadness at leaving. I do not know where he is going.

I am not satisfied with the progress we are making in preparing the Division for field service. GHQ, Army and Corps now prescribe 44 training hours per week. They then prescribe what will be done and how we are to do it so that little is left to the Division Commander's discretion. He is the only man who really knows the status of his Division in training and combat efficiency, and he should have some time on the schedule to devote to his own needs.

We are required to practice loading and unloading trains. We must take our men to the camp theatre for lectures on how the war came about. Then, we must follow an inefficient method of teaching known-distance range markmanship and combat firing. The ammunition available for this is below requirements. One and one-half hours must be spent each day in motor maintenance. We are continuously sending officers and enlisted men away to service schools and as cadremen to new units.

Now the Division is to be reorganized on the triangular plan. This means new types of units. Much of the personnel will be assigned to positions different from those they are used to.

All personnel, including Division Headquarters, must turn out and march with packs two days each week while instruction, courts, boards, current business, preparation for the next day's work, all go begging. Just imagine engineers, artillerymen, medical troops, quartermaster troops, and signal troops devoting two days each week to marching up and down roads when they have so much to do! If it is physical fitness that is wanted, they get plenty of that going about camp in their ordinary work.

A well-meaning professor from the University of Texas came to my office today from higher headquarters and wanted me to assemble the troops in conveniently-sized groups so he may teach them to sing. He is authorized to teach singing, if I wish him to do so, but it is not required by higher headquarters.

There is a time and place for soldiers to sing, but not on a training schedule. Besides, as I have already discovered, Texans will sing without urging. I will not be surprised, however, to get a positive order from above directing us to develop disciplined soldiers by giving singing lessons.

Thursday, February 5, 1942

Some time ago I invited Governor Stevenson and General Page to visit the Division as my guests. Today I received a letter from Page in which he enclosed the following note from the Governor: "I have thought several times recently of slipping away and paying the 36th Division a visit. I don't want any notice given about it, but if I could just go up there some day and range around and meet the officers and men and tell them how much interest we have in the 36th Division, I would like it."

I told Page that the Division would be pleased to have the Governor as its guest at any time convenient to him. Personally, I think this is a splendid idea, and I will be delighted for him to come and see how the Division works and lives. Furthermore, the Governor's visit will greatly encourage the Division personnel.

Monday, February 9, 1942

This is going to be a busy week. Effective at midnight the 36th square Division becomes a triangular one. This is a real job in itself with all of the personnel and property transfers that are necessary. But, to top it off, I received orders today to move the Division on the 15th to Camp Blanding at Starke, Florida. Now we will do both jobs at once.

In spite of my orders, many units still have property that belongs to the State of Texas and this must be delivered to Camp Mabry at Austin. All this will be a real test of the Division's ability to do a lot of detailed paper work.

I have directed that the persons concerned must work from reveille to 10:00 PM, if necessary, to get it done. We are to receive recruits to fill out units to war strength after we arrive at Blanding.

This movement to Florida is to be secret; the War Department insists. How come? Since all the families living in Brownwood have to cancel their leases, it will take only a few hours for the word to get all over town: "The 36th is moving to Camp Blanding."

However, I assembled the leading people of Brownwood today and told them what is taking place so they will not be victims of rumors. The newspaper men and radio station owners promised not to give publicity to the move. I am trusting them.

The mother from Dallas called at my office again today. She has discussed with me a number of times the status of her son who is in the stockade awaiting review of his case by the President. He was sentenced by a General Court Martial to be dismissed from the service, to forfeit all pay and allowances due or to become due, and to be confined at hard labor for one year. I think the court was very lenient in view of his offenses—drunk and disorderly, fighting with enlisted men, direct disobedience of orders, forgery, breaking arrest, and absence without leave. She wanted to know if the President had taken any final action in his case. He has not.

"Perque" Clarkson is worth his weight in gold to me. He handles his job as Chief of Staff in a superior manner, and he ought to be promoted to brigadier general.

Friday, February 13, 1942

I received a note of appreciation from the Brownwood Chamber of Commerce which says, "This letter is a most sincere expression of the esteem and high regard in which the people of Brownwood hold you, your fellow officers, and the men of the 36th Division. We regret very much to see you and your associates leave Brownwood.

"It was our thought for the city of Brownwood, the Brownwood Chamber of Commerce, and our leading citizens to give you a departing banquet as concrete evidence of our regret in seeing you leave. Due to the press of official duties and respecting your wishes in the matter, we are instead trying to express in writing our feeling toward one of the finest Divisions in the United States of America.

"All our dealings with you and your fellow officers, including Municipal and Chamber of Commerce business, have been most satisfactory. Many mutual problems have been worked out to the entire satisfaction of the army and the people of Brownwood.

"We wish you all the success in the world in your new location, and hope that sometime you can return to Brownwood. Please remember us kindly as your friends."

The letter was signed by Wendell Mayes, Mayor; F S Abney, President of the Chamber; and Gene Mattox, City Manager.

On behalf of the personnel of the Division and myself, I have prepared and mailed letters of appreciation and farewell to the leading citizens of Brownwood. All the people of Brownwood have been most cooperative, especially the business men. It will be a long time before we will enjoy a similar hospitality, if ever.

A sergeant has asked me to discharge him so he can go home and look after a grocery store now being operated by his aged uncle, mother and sister. I told him to advise his mother to hire some reliable person to help her. I have had many other applications of a similar nature. Everyone is going to have to work. Women may have to take over the jobs of clerks, chauffeurs, bellboys, elevator boys, and other workers in order to provide the manpower necessary to win this war.

As soon as we received orders to leave Brownwood, many soldiers, whose homes are in this general area, ran to the hospital claiming they were sick. Today I decided to take all hospital patients along to Camp Blanding on a special train with doctors in charge. I expect the majority of them to recover rapidly.

Last night I attended a basketball game at the Field House between the 111th Engineers and the 111th Medical Regiment. I presented the trophy to the captain of the medical team and congratulated the losers on their fine sportsmanship. This was a good game, and there was enthusiastic cheering on both sides. Insofar as I am concerned, any team may win, but I do require good sportsmanship and an orderly performance in all athletic contests.

Saturday, February 14, 1942

On the eve of departure, I received the following telegram from J Watt Page, and published it to the Division: "Without going into detail you will know the reasons prompting this telegram. My very good wishes go with you. You have the confidence and respect of officers and men of your command. You can depend on them because they are Texans and are being led and not driven. You and those under you will be much in my thoughts during the months to come, and each day I shall offer up my humble prayer for the outstanding success of any mission to which you and your Division are assigned."

This message was much appreciated by the Division personnel, coming as it does from the Adjutant General of the State, who has over the past years had much to do with the creation and maintenance of the Division. The Texans consider, rightly, that the 36th is their own Division, and the sentiments General Page expresses undoubtedly reflect the feelings of all Texans.

As far as I can determine, we are going to get away to Camp Blanding in good order. The property officers are on the job, and all the supply officers have their plans completed.

Advance parties have gone ahead to notify the police of each state of this motor movement and to request their cooperation. These parties will also select and rent the five overnight camp sites. They have been provided with funds to procure fire wood, gasoline and other necessities at each camp.

The motor elements of the Division consist of some 2,000 vehicles: trucks, trailers, jeeps, command cars, guns. They will be grouped into six columns each of approximately 325 vehicles commanded by a colonel or a lieutenant colonel.

The columns will depart from Camp Bowie at intervals of one day because their rate of speed, their length (approximately

8 miles), the distance between successive camps, plus a half-hour refueling and lunch stop, and time to make and break camp will require a full day. Each column will travel six days to reach Camp Blanding, and all will travel the same route. It will take 11 days to complete the movement of the motor elements.

Each column is divided into serials of approximately 70 vehicles commanded by a transportation officer. In order not to disrupt normal civil traffic, a half-mile interval will be maintained between serials. The drivers will obey traffic signals at intersections not controlled by the State Police or our MP's.

The motor elements will be fully loaded with rations, gasoline, baggage, equipment and personnel. Personnel and baggage which cannot be moved by motor will go by trains which are being loaded and will be on their way before the last column leaves Bowie. The train trip will take two-and-a-half or three days. Because I want to relieve the men from having to wash their mess kits on the train where there are no proper facilities, I told Carl Phinney, Division Quartermaster, to buy paper plates and cups for the troops to use enroute. I have washed enough mess kits on troop trains to know that it is messy and unsanitary.

Generally the camps are in fields near towns where there is an adequate supply of water, preferably from hydrants, within easy traveling distance for the water trucks. The vehicles must have easy ingress and egress to the main highway and to the fields.

However, it has begun to rain, and if it should continue, the men who have to sleep on the ground will be miserable. Although we have provided the wood for open fires, the cold, at night, will be bad enough without rain.

I have let it be known that families of Division personnel who wish to move to Starke, Florida, will be welcome there.

I had to talk to a major about paying his house rent. His landlady came to see me and complained that he owes her $10 back rent, which he refuses to pay. When I spoke to him about it, he put on an air of hurt feelings and of being unjustly accused. But he did admit owing her $5 and implied that the landlady was misrepresenting his obligation. I told him to pay the landlady the $5.00 now and argue about the other $5.00 later. My guess is that the landlady is right, judging from past events.

I have received orders from General Strong to transfer General Whiteaker to VIII Headquarters where he will remain until he appears before a reclassification board, which will be appointed by General Strong. Now all four officers whom Strong set out to get rid of are gone. The 61st Field Artillery Brigade becomes the Division Artillery, 36th Division, and I will need a new commander for it. In the meantime, Colonel Tom Bay will command.

CHAPTER FOUR
Plans Change In Florida

Camp Blanding, Florida
Saturday, February 21, 1942

Here I am at Camp Blanding. I departed from Camp Bowie at noon on the 16th accompanied by Perque Clarkson and Frank Reese. We traveled by official sedan and arrived at Blanding on the 19th. We spent a cold Monday night with Colonel Tom Bay's motor column, east of Terrell but near the camp site originally picked. The previous night it had rained and the trucks in Colonel Perrine's column had mired down to their hubs in the field, and he had had the devil's own time getting them back on the highway. When Bay came along the next night, one of the advance party had arranged with the State Police to park the vehicles off the main highway on secondary macadam roads. The men slept in and under the vehicles, or along the roadside. A farmer allowed us to use his yard for our pup tents.

Tuesday night we bivouacked with the column commanded by Perrine even though we had to travel 400 miles to overtake it. This time Perrine also camped along secondary roads where his vehicles could be parked on pavement. Because of the rain and mud, the camp sites we had rented were never used after the first night out.

Wednesday night we stopped at the Ralston Hotel in Columbus, Georgia. That evening I paid a visit to Brigadier General Leven C Allen, Commandant, The Infantry School, and to Colonel W A Burress, Assistant Commandant. The Infantry School is a familiar place for I was an instructor there for three years after World War I, specializing in the combat principles of the infantry battalion.

On Thursday we drove on to Blanding. Along our route I visited each bivouac site and made myself familiar with the conditions under which the troops were living. The whole movement from Bowie to Blanding was conducted in an excellent manner in spite of the disagreeable weather. I have heard no criticism from any source, and I am most favorably impressed with the fine spirit displayed by everyone. Harry Steel, Carl Phinney and Bob Ives worked unceasingly to make this movement a success, and the several States' Police were most cooperative and helpful.

We found the buildings we were to occupy at Blanding very dirty. Although the Post Commander is cordial, this camp is far from being as comfortable or suitable for training as Bowie. We burned natural gas there, but here we burn soft coal, and the place is sooty. The tents are black from coal smoke and burned by sparks. Everyone speaks of the contrasts, but the spirit of the officers and the men is excellent.

Colonel Louis E Hibbs has arrived from West Point to command the Artillery Brigade. I am delighted to have him. He, Terry Allen and I were together at Eagle Pass, Texas, when we were 2nd lieutenants—Hibbs in the artillery, Allen in the cavalry, and I in the infantry. He was a student at the Army War College when I was an instructor there.

Louis tells me that Clarkson will soon be transferred to one of the new divisions and promoted to Brigadier. I will be sorry to lose him. But, of course, I am pleased to see him promoted, and Perque will make an outstanding general officer.

Wednesday, February 25, 1942

We have been working hard since arrival to get settled in this camp, wash our vehicles, clean their motors and other equipment. Everyone seems quite cheerful but anxious to get this cleaning business finished.

I had a conference at Jacksonville with Major General Lloyd R. Fredendall, who greeted me with, "Hello Freddie." After a brief conversation about our individual wanderings in the past few years, he said, "I suppose you know why you are here."

I did not have the slightest idea.

"I asked the War Department for you. I'm going to take you overseas with me. I don't know what kind of a Division the 36th is, but I know you and I know you will have a good one."

Then he explained what we are to do as a field force overseas, but naturally that must be kept secret. The operation is going to be most interesting, but we will not leave here for three or more months.

This sounds wonderful. He could not have paid me and the Division a greater compliment, and I thanked him.

I would like nothing better than to command a Division in Fredendall's Corps and go with him overseas. We served together as instructors in the tactical division of the Infantry School at Fort Benning from 1920 to 1923. I also participated in writing, from scratch, the initial series of training manuals on the combat principles of infantry which were issued by the War Department to include the lessons learned in World War I. Having specialized in the combat principles of the infantry battalion, Major Jess Ladd and I wrote the first correspondence courses for teaching the combat principles of the infantry battalion. All this under the direct supervision of Major Lloyd Fredendall.

Bus Wheeler has just returned from the Command and General Staff School and has gone to Perrine's 141st Infantry to straighten out an unsatisfactory property condition in that regiment. He will do it. I'll continue to get along with one Aide for a while.

We had a false alarm today. This afternoon we were suddenly told that unidentified planes were over Jacksonville flying toward Blanding. We immediately turned out our machine gun squads to take positions about the camp, but the planes never showed up. Of course, they could have been here and gone before we could have been in position to fire on them, but this incident will put us on guard, and we will devise a plan of defense against aircraft so that we can get ready for quick action in case of a real attack. Such an attack is not probable, but it is good practice to be prepared anyway.

Wednesday, March 4, 1942

Julia arrived from Bowie today and has rented a place at Keystone Heights. It is a very cheerful house on the edge of a small lake.

We have just received 4,000 recruits from the northern states who are from all walks of life and older than those we have received in the past. They are serious-minded, especially attentive during instruction periods, and are making good progress. I will not be surprised if some of them are better soldiers, after they complete basic training, than some of our men who were with the Division before induction and have formed careless habits that still dominate them.

I have been trying to get a recreation program started for the enlisted men. They have so little time off and so little in the way of recreational facilities that this is a difficult problem. There are no baseball fields, and only a few basketball and tennis courts. We need many more.

The War Department is still taking away my best officers for instructors at schools, for cadremen for new units and for special assignments. Our best NCOs are being sent to officer candidate schools and to the Air Force. This cannot be helped because good officers are urgently needed for expanding the army, but it is tough on the 36th Division and me. However, we are developing many good officers in company grades who will be of great value to us later. Last Sunday I sent in a long list of officers whom I recommended for promotion because they have been doing good work.

Sunday, March 8, 1942

I want to establish friendly relations with the 1st Division which is stationed here at Blanding with us, so I arranged for the senior officers of the 36th to invite their counterparts in the 1st, as our guests at our regular Saturday night hop, last night. We went all out to make our guests welcome. Unfortunately, my counterpart, Major General Donald C. Cubbison, was ill and unable to attend, but I went.

Everyone had a good time. During an intermission between dances, Terry Allen and his guest, Brigadier General Teddy Roosevelt, strode to the center of the dance floor, and holding their glasses high, toasted each other's Division.

Terry was first. The gist of his toast was:
"To the 1st Division.
First in War, First in Peace, First in the Army.
May it always be First."

Teddy tried to out do Terry, so his toast went something like this:
"To the gallant 36th Division.
Born in blood at the Alamo
Nurtured in glory as Hood's Texicans,
Famous in 1898, renowned in 1918,
Destined for greater glory in 1942."

Well, after all that it seemed to me that as the senior officer present, I should say something that would apply to both Divisions. So I stepped out toward the two enthusiasts and gave my toast:

"To the 1st and 36th Divisions:
May their luck be as great as their glory."
The audience was pleased. The band broke into a medley of the "Sidewalks of New York" and the "Eyes of Texas," and dancing was resumed.

Tuesday, March 10, 1942

General Cubbison sent for me and told me that over the weekend there had been some fights in Jacksonville between the enlisted men of the 1st and 36th Divisions. I probably know more about this than he does.

He said he was not going to have this fighting, and wanted it stopped. He told me to order my men to stop. I told him I would, if he would order his men to stop speaking insultingly of the Texans as "the damned national guard."

I did not tell Cubbison, of course, but I had told my men not to take any insults from the 1st, and they have taken me at my word.

I guess we should have arranged a "get together" to promote friendliness between the enlisted men of the two Divisions last weekend also.

Friday, March 13, 1942

I gave all of the new recruits a pep talk today.

"I have assembled you here today in order that I may welcome you to the 36th Division. We are pleased to have you with us.

"As you know, the 36th Division is from the State of Texas. Almost all of the officers and most of the enlisted men are from Texas. They are descendants, either in fact or in spirit, from such Texas patriots as Bowie, Travis, Crockett, Houston and Austin. These Texas patriots, at the Alamo and at San Jacinto, built a superior fighting spirit and a tradition of devotion to duty and self-sacrifice that has been adopted and carried on by all Texas troops that have ever fought in any war.

"You are expected not only to absorb the Texas fighting spirit of this Division but also to improve upon it. You should strive to show our Texans that you are even better fighters than they. You, too, must develop a high sense of devotion to duty and self-sacrifice. We want you to be proud to serve in the Texas Division just as the Texas Division wants to be proud of you.

"Sooner or later you are going to be fighting for your very life against well-trained troops of your enemy. And this may be sooner than you think. I want to warn you that you have a tough job laid out for you and that it will require the best that is in you. You must begin now, in deadly earnest, to learn your jobs as soldiers.

"I want you to know what to expect when you meet your enemy. He will show you no consideration. In the front areas he will take every possible advantage of you to shoot you down. And you, likewise, are going to take every possible advantage of him and his mistakes to shoot him down. In the rear areas he will bomb your camps, your bivouacs, your supply bases, your motor and troop columns, wherever you present to him a profitable target.

"Your various commanders will become casualties, and you will find yourself without your accustomed leaders. At times there will be no one to tell you what to do. You will have to take charge of those about you and direct their actions without orders. You will witness scenes of destruction and death that will nauseate you. Your buddies will fall all about you. They will call to you for water and for help. But you cannot and must not leave your place of duty to respond to them. This is the job of our medical personnel.

"Through all of this you will sleep in the mud and the rain and the cold. Much-needed food and ammunition will often fail to arrive on schedule. When you are hungry and thirsty and exhausted by fatigue, you will have to carry on, nevertheless, without adequate rest.

"These conditions are the usual, not the unusual, to be expected in battle. Your enemy intentionally makes it that way. Your job and mine is to bring order out of disorder, to accept these trying conditions cheerfully, to laugh them off, and to send them right back with compound interest. The ability to do this has characterized all victorious troops since the creation of man.

"When the going gets tough, when the future looks black, keep up the fight all the more. Remember that many a campaign has been won because the victorious troops, at a critical hour, at a critical location, in the face of difficult and discouraging conditions, carried the fight to their enemy.

"When we meet our enemy you are going to carry a heavy responsibility. Now is the time for you to acquire the knowledge, skill and speed which you must have. Take pride in doing your work well. Everything that you are called upon to do should receive your very best thought and effort and you should not be satisfied with any result short of perfection. The loss of your life, or that of your buddy, may result from some little failure on your part.

"If you are assigned to drive a truck, treat that truck as if it were your own. Do all that you can to keep that truck in the best possible condition.

"If you are assigned a weapon, you must know how to shoot straight, how to make your first shot a hit rather than a miss. If you miss your first shot, you may never fire another.

"If you are assigned to operate an instrument, train yourself to be accurate. Carelessness in reading scales and angles may be fatal to some of your buddies.

"If you are assigned to the communication system, strive to acquire accuracy and speed. Delay in encoding or decoding a message, delay in transmission, slowness in repairing broken wire lines, may have grave results.

"Any of these may mean delays in troop movements, or in the delivery of ammunition, or in the protection of a flank, or in the warning of a command against surprise. Any such delay may be the direct cause of failure which we can ill afford. It is only by doing our work well that we can hope to gain an advantage over our enemy.

"You are expected to conduct yourself in a respectful and orderly manner at all times and in all places. Any soldier who disobeys the laws, either civil or military, is heading for trouble. There is no standard of ethics, no code of morals, no religion that has a greater regard for good conduct or a greater disgust for bad conduct than the military code. A good soldier will always do his duty. We want you all to be good soldiers."

Monday, March 23, 1942

Terry Allen is enthusiastic about his training program and asked me to accompany him on his rounds. When we arrived in the training area, we saw three soldiers standing together about 100 yards off the road. Terry told the driver to stop, and called to the men in a spirit of friendliness, "Hey, you sons-of-bitches, come over here."

"Terry," I said quietly, "we don't call men sons-of-bitches in this Division."

He replied, "Oh, they like it."

The men arrived promptly with no indication that they resented their hailing, but after the men were dismissed, I made it clear that such terms, even though jocularly applied, were not to be used in addressing personnel of any grade in this Division.

Wednesday, March 25, 1942

Florian and our two grandchildren arrived Sunday evening from Hawaii, and Julia and I met them at Jacksonville. They were tired out and were in bed and asleep soon after we were back home. They were glad to be at the end of their long journey and away from the strenuous times at Oahu where the Army, Navy and Air Force are busy building a strong base for carrying the war to the Western Pacific. The Japanese attack was still fresh in their minds. At first they though it was a planned maneuver by our own Air until they saw bullets kicking up dust and striking houses. Then they huddled inside and waited. They said the attack was so sudden and so unexpected on Sunday morning that nobody had time to get excited or alarmed.

Lt. Colonel Troy Middleton joined the Division yesterday. I first met Troy at the Infantry School in 1920 when we were instructors there. He had had an outstanding World War I record and was an excellent tactical instructor. He was also an instructor at the Command and General Staff School when I was a student there in 1926-27. I have been associated with him for short periods at other times. He is known throughout the army as an outstanding officer. I am delighted to have him, but I know that he will be with me only a short while. I have assigned him to the 142nd Infantry as its commanding officer. Lt. Colonel Karl Wallace has been in command of the 142nd since Colonel Perrine was transferred to the 141st, but I know that General Marshall wants Middleton given command of a regiment so he can be promoted.

I am having a difficult time getting officer replacements and officers promoted. We are short 202 officers, and I can't get any anywhere. I have also tried every way I know to get the major items of equipment for the Reconnaisance Troop, but had no success.

Friday, March 27, 1942

I am going to stop hoping for the War Department to send me officer replacements, so I am going to create acting officers by selecting qualified NCOs and placing them permanently in command of platoons. We will give them all the privileges of lieutenants, and will think of them as lieutenants. Thus, we will attempt to create officer substitutes, and eventually they will be sent to officers candidate school. My purpose here is to establish some permanency of command over the platoons that are now without officers. The NCO "lieutenants" will study the same lessons, attend the same schools, assemblies, critiques, as other lieutenants and will carry the same responsibilities. This will overcome the handicaps of these platoons and will be good for all concerned. Besides, it will encourage some competition in training performances. No lieutenant will want to be excelled by a noncommissioned officer of his company.

I directed the organization of five baseball teams by next week, even though it is necessary, in order to have a suitable field, to cover the Florida sand with four inches of clay. The teams should pay big dividends. I hope the games may be the means of encouraging a lot of our men to spend more time in camp over weekends.

Thursday, April 9, 1942

Bad news from the war fronts. Bataan has fallen; the British Navy has been defeated in the Indian Ocean; and India is being invaded by the Japanese. General Marshall is in London, probably to arrange for operations in Europe or Africa by U. S. troops.

Twelve hundred of our men are home on furlough. Now is the time to let them go. I do not believe they will have a chance after the middle of May, if we go with Fredendall.

Saturday, April 11, 1942

Terry Allen is quite interested in physical culture. He has been running two miles cross-country before breakfast each morning. He told me some time ago how beneficial all this was, and I encouraged him to continue. But today he told me that I would be greatly benefitted physically, and that it would be a fine example for everyone in the Division, if both he and I would turn out together each morning for a two-mile run. "Terry, I admire your energy," I said, "but if the welfare and physical stamina of this Division depends on my running two miles before breakfast each day, there just won't be any welfare and physical stamina."

Saturday, April 18, 1942

Brigadier General Otto F Lange has arrived to succeed Allen as Assistant Division Commander. I knew him as an instructor at the Infantry School, but I did not know him well.

Terry will remain with the 36th until he is assigned to command a division. There he can set a top example for physical stamina, and I presume that everyone in his division will bubble over with enthusiasm.

Brigadier General Mark Wayne Clark visited the 36th yesterday. Now he is Chief of Staff of the Army Ground Forces. Wayne has come up fast within a year from Major to Brigadier. I first met him when I was an instructor at the Army War College and he was a student there in the 30's. I served with him at Fort Lewis, Washington, after the 15th Infantry, of which I was the Executive Officer, returned from Tientsin, China, in March of 1938. We were together there for some 18 months and became very good friends, although he is much younger than I.

Clark was here on an observation tour, looking over some of our training activities, and he seemed well-pleased. He asked me when I thought the 36th would be ready for battle, and I told him it would be ready June 1st. He replied that he had reported to the War Department that it would be ready July 1st.

Wayne also told me that we are going on maneuvers in Carolina this coming summer. I'll be damned! What kind of monkey business is this? Fredendall said we were going overseas with him. Now Wayne says we are going on maneuvers which will continue until late August. There is some shenanigan going on behind the scenes, and it looks like the 36th is being shoved around.

Wayne said that I am on General McNair's list to be a Corps Commander. I told him I was pleased, but knowing his predilection for such "carrots," I do not take it too seriously.

I suppose if they ever offered me a corps, I'd take it, but I would hate to leave the 36th. I have become very fond of this Division, and feel a very personal attachment to the men. I have watched it build, from week to week, from a bunch of raw recruits to a fine fighting force. I am really quite proud of these confident and able soldiers, and take special pride in having a hand in molding them. This is a great personal satisfaction. A corps commander has more authority, but a division commander has a more interesting job. He lives with his men. A corps commander deals with three or more division commanders and a few corps troops. To me, a corps commander's job is a bore, except in combat. But it is a stepping stone to something higher.

This past week I have had Master Sergeant Bronkhorst here, from Fort Sam Houston, to teach some of our officers and NCOs how to fight with the bayonet. He is an excellent bayonet instructor, and we needed his help.

Frank Reese, my Aide, being an artillery officer, has never had any real infantry training. It seemed to me that he might get some first-hand knowledge of how infantrymen are trained by taking Bronkhorst's bayonet course. So, after some discussion, he said he would like to take the course.

Each day, at the appointed time, he got himself properly dressed for the occasion and took off. When he returned each day, I noted that he was exhausted, giving me the impression that he was not enthusiastic about the bayonet course.

When he came in after the last class he looked quite worn out, and I asked if he were glad the course was finished. He gave me a rather determined and serious look, and said, "General, that man Bronkhorst tried to kill us today. He gave us a terrible workout. He made us all mad. I felt like using my bayonet on him. Yes, sir, I am glad it is over."

"Well! If he did all that, he is an excellent bayonet instructor," I said.

Frank looked at me askance, and walked away to his bath, feeling, I believe, that I was unsympathetic. But I was not.

I suspect that Sergeant Bronkhorst, with 25 or more years of service, picked on Reese a little more than the other young officers because he is my Aide and an artilleryman. You can't blame him for that. Old NCOs feel that that is their privilege. I, too, had my period of "instruction" by old NCOs who wanted to test my patience, and they can be quite clever at this. They helped me a great deal, but I did not know it then. A unit is no better than its NCO's, as I have said before.

My orderly went crazy last week—literally. I guess I must be hard on orderlies for he was the fifth one I have had since I joined this Division.

When troops are in the field it is very necessary for a senior commissioned officer to have an orderly to look after his personal needs, such as run errands, put up and take down tents, clean and repair equipment, look after baggage, serve meals, drive vehicles, prepare baths and a dozen other needs. Junior officers need orderlies, also, but not to the same extent. Officers do not have the time to do these things for themselves. If they do, they are neglecting their professional jobs.

It is a real pleasure to see so many of the men of the Division enjoying a swim in the lake near camp. At first a few of them deliberately got themselves sunburned, hoping to be excused from duty. But when they went to the hospital at sick call, the doctor marked them "not in line of duty" and their pay stopped until they recovered. "The best laid schemes o' mice an' men gang aft agley."

Sunday, April 19, 1942

Brigadier General Preston Weatherred, accompanied by his Aide, Major Sam Elliott, arrived today to visit the Division and meet old friends. He had to travel close by Blanding on an inspection trip and took advantage of the opportunity to visit us. In the course of our conversation he told me that he had heard that Terry Allen might be leaving soon and had thought there still might be an opportunity for him to return to the 36th. But, after he arrived, he learned that General Lange was already here and realized that he would not have a chance.

I was pleased to have him visit the Division, and his old friends were delighted to see him. He commands the Eastern Security Section (Florida to Virginia) with headquarters at Fort Bragg, North Carolina.

Tuesday, April 21, 1942

Today is San Jacinto Day. It is the 106th anniversary of the battle which won for Texas its independence and raised the fourth flag of the six to which its citizens have sworn allegiance. To commemorate this event, a patriotic ceremony was held on the drill field of the 142nd Infantry which included the playing of "The Eyes of Texas Are Upon You" and an inspiring address by Jesse Moseley, the Division Judge Advocate.

Sunday, April 26, 1942

"Perque" Clarkson and I attended the firing test of the 132nd Field Artillery Battalion which was conducted by the II Corps Staff.

The gun positions were well dug in and camouflaged; the transportation was well dispersed; and the signal communications worked well. I was proud of them.

General Marshall will pay us a visit and will require one infantry and one artillery battalion to do a tactical exercise for him. He is just back from England where he may have promised this Army Corps for operations in Europe. I can see no real reason why he would single us out for a personal visit except to see first-hand whether or not we are ready for battle. If he is favorably impressed, we may be on our way soon, and not go to maneuvers as Clark indicated.

A woman from Chicago came to see me to make a mother's plea that her son be transferred to some locality near home, where she would be able to see him more often. She claims that her son is not physically fit for field service. This mother is typical of the many who petition me for special preference for their sons. They all say that they are patriotic and want to do their part to win the war, but their part is to let some other mother's son endure the hardships, face the dangers, and do the fighting.

If I were to weaken in the presence of their tears and grant their requests, I would be unworthy of my position. The mother and son who do their duty without complaining must be protected. Mothers, as well as sons, must adjust to conditions of war, reduce their standard of living, and make the best of the curse that Hitler, Mussolini, and the Japanese have forced upon us.

A month ago a live round was unintentionally fired from a 37mm gun during drill. One man was killed instantly, another permanently injured. Investigation of this accident indicates that it was the result of gross carelessness on the part of the company commander and the platoon commander. They are being charged with negligence.

Automobile tires are denied to army families by the local ration board on the grounds that we are not government employees and are not engaged in work that requires us to have transportation between our homes and work. But any civilian employee, no matter what his job, can have tires because he is working. Those of us who are going to do the fighting are not considered worthy of having tires on our privately owned automobiles in order to get back and forth from our homes.

What was it Kipling said:

"For it's Tommy this, an' Tommy that, an'
'Chuck 'im out, the brute!'
But it's 'Saviour of 'is country' when
the guns begin to shoot."

I encourage all the officers to participate in our regular Saturday night dances. One of the regimental bands provides the music. It always plays three or four typically Texas numbers, each of which has its special step, such as "Put Your Little Foot" and "Ten Pretty Girls." Of course, all the Texans know these dance steps, but some of the "foreigners" do not. The men have no time for dance instruction, so their wives are meeting with some of the Texas ladies at the Woman's Club in Keystone Heights to learn the dances. Then they will teach their husbands at home.

Saturday, May 1, 1942

Lt. Colonel Kerr, Division Inspector General, reports that the motor transportation in the Reconnaissance Troop and in the Division Headquarters Company is in poor condition because of indifferent and careless maintenance. Paper work regarding personnel in these units is also poor.

He recommends that both units be placed under the authority and control of the Quartermaster Battalion for instruction. I think the suggestion is a good one for the delinquent units, but it would be hard on the Quartermaster Battalion. In my opinion, it is better, initially anyway, to require them to make their own corrections. Let them learn that their own carelessness means more work for them.

Sunday, May 2, 1942

Yesterday, General Marshall, Lt. General Lesley J. McNair, Brig. General "Pinkie" Bull, and British Field Marshall Sir John Dill visited Camp Blanding. We turned out for a dismounted review and set up some demonstrations in firing on the ranges for them. Lt. Colonel Burke Brewster, Division Surgeon, demonstrated a method he has developed for carrying wounded men on litters on a jeep. They seemed impressed with what they saw.

The 1st and 36th Divisions gave a luncheon for the guests. I sat on Marshall's right and discussed old times. I first met George Marshall in the Philippines in 1912 when he was a 1st lieutenant and I was a 2nd lieutenant in the 13th Infantry at Fort McKinley. General Henry "Hap" Arnold, now Chief of the Army Air Force, was a 1st lieutenant in the 13th at the same time.

Marshall had come to the regiment from duty as an instructor at the Army School of the Line, now the Command and General Staff School, at Fort Leavenworth, Kansas.

We all looked upon Marshall, who possesed greater tactical knowledge than we, as headed for an outstanding future. He was with us a year or so, during which time he was the instructor in garrison school subjects for all the other lieutenants. As a result he and I know each other quite well. I have served with him on a number of occasions since.

Therefore, at one point in the conversation when Marshall turned to me and said, very seriously, "Walker, you know I still think of you as a lieutenant," I was speechless. It has since occurred to me that I should have replied, "Lieutenant General, I hope."

I turned my cottage over to Sir John Dill who slept in my bed. He said he had a good night's rest. He is the type of man who inspires respect and confidence. I noted that Marshall always addressed him as "Sir John."

Tuesday, May 5, 1942

Yesterday and last night I was with the Division Artillery during a test given by an inspection party from II Corps. This problem was a simple one, involving an extensive survey, moving into position at night, night firing, and firing concentrations after daylight in support of an attack; all by map-corrected data. In general, the artillery did well, but there are many weak spots still to be corrected. Lack of discipline is responsible for 90 per cent of the weaknesses.

Wednesday, May 6, 1942

I have made it known that when we get into the Theater of

Operations the Division Artillery observers are to be well up front. They are to display personal energy and initiative in selecting and firing on targets without waiting for requests or orders from the infantry commanders. We may have to provide more observers than the Tables of Organization authorize in order to do this. General Hibbs shares this view.

I received sugar ration books today for Julia and myself, good until next June 30th. Before this war is over, everyone will have to reduce his standards of living and eliminate all unnecessary waste. Some families will have to double up in houses, and everybody will have to reduce expenses and save food and materials.

One gets the impression that the civilian workers at home are expected to win the war by their sacrifices and hardships. This view is being broadcast over the radio, shown in the movies, and printed in the newspapers. Of course there is not going to be any real down-right sacrifice or hardship except by the men in combat who will die or be wounded in battle, and by members of their families.

Thursday, May 7, 1942

A. P. Long, Senior Military Products Engineer of the Goodyear Rubber Company, has been inspecting the maintenance of tires of all units at Camp Blanding. He has obviously visited most of the camps in the United States, but he told "Perque" Clarkson that the conditions in the 36th are excellent and much above the average. Furthermore, he said that he had told the 1st Division that they could learn much about the care of tires from us. Well, what do you know? The old Regular Army 1st Division can learn much from a National Guard Division! They won't like that. Thanks, Mr. Long. They can learn much on other subjects, too, if they will cast aside their prejudices and visit some of our other activities, especially our Adjutant General's Office, our Quartermaster Battalion, and our kitchens.

Friday, May 8, 1942

A very sad accident occurred early this morning. A privately owned automobile carrying seven soldiers of the 1st Division plowed into the rear of Company C of our 111th Engineer Battalion. The Company was returning to camp from a night exercise. It was on the left side of the road, facing oncoming traffic where it belonged. The automobile which was also traveling toward camp, crossed the center line and struck the Company. Twenty-seven soldiers were hurt and had to be sent to the hospital. Two of them are critically injured and not expected to live. Terrible! The driver of the automobile was guilty of gross carelessness. This is another example of the great damage and sorrow that just a little inattention can cause.

I received the following telegram from Colonel Ernest O. Thompson, Chairman of the Texas Railroad Commission, and formerly the Commanding Officer of the 141st Infantry: "Governor Stevenson and I will arrive on the train, Jacksonville, 6:15 Wednesday morning, May 13th."

This was followed almost immediately by another message stating that General Page, Adjutant General of Texas, and Colonel Paul Wakefield, a staff member of the Texas Selective Service, would accompany the Governor and Colonel Thompson and that all would leave Jacksonville at 9:20 Wednesday night to return to Texas.

I replied: "We are pleased to have you, Governor Stevenson, General Page, and Colonel Wakefield visit us. Will meet you with transportation at railroad station 6:15 AM, May 13th."

I directed Perque Clarkson to arrange a suitable reception and review for the Governor. I presume this is the result of my invitation of April 23rd.

Sunday, May 10, 1942

As I expected, I am going to lose Troy Middleton. He has received orders to report to the War Department in Washington next Wednesday for special instructions. It would be wonderful if I could keep him in the Division for he is a good friend and a capable officer. But, of course, I know that he is slated for greater responsibility.

Wednesday, May 13, 1942

While I was at Fort Jackson, S. C., for two days, serving on a board to reclassify a brigadier general who had, until recently commanded an artillery brigade there, there was a great security hullabaloo originated by somebody in the War Department over Governor Stevenson's visit.

At 6:00 PM on May 11, Brigadier General Albert M. Gruenther,

Chief of Staff, Third Army, called Colonel Clarkson from San Antonio and said that the War Department had contacted him about the Governor visiting Blanding. He said the War Department was very much upset about the visit and wanted steps taken to stop him.

Gruenther asked if the Governor had been issued a specific invitation, and stated that neither the Third Army nor VIII Corps Area at Fort Sam Houston knew anything about it. Perque told him that I had issued no specific invitation, but had written the Governor sometime ago that if at anytime he should be in the vicinity of Blanding, we would be pleased to have him visit us; that while we were at Camp Bowie, General Page had proposed that his office present a Texas flag to the Division, but had not got around to doing so before our departure. On May 8th, he said, word was received from Colonel Thompson, of Austin, that the Governor would visit the 36th Division on the 13th to present 'the flag. No word had been received by us to date from any higher headquarters about the visit.

General Gruenther called a half hour later to say that he had received information from the Headquarters of the Fourth Corps Area*, in Atlanta, Ga., to the effect that our own G-2 had told them that we would stop the Governor at New Orleans. Gruenther was informed that this report was incorrect. We had taken no steps to stop the Governor's visit, and did not intend to do so unless so ordered by higher authority.

*NOTE: An Army Corps, or just Corps for short, is a battle unit composed of 2 or more divisions. It moves about. A Corps Area is a territorial region composed of several states. It does the housekeeping for the combat troops.

Next day, May 12, at 8:20 AM, Colonel Clarkson informed Colonel Watkins, II Corps G-2 in Jacksonville, of the proposed visit of the Governor. Thirty minutes later Camp Blanding's Public Relations Officer called and stated he had received a call from the War Department pointing out that there had been a news release to the effect that the Governor was departing for an unannounced destination to visit the 36th Division; that there was to be absolutely no publicity in connection with the Governor's visit; and that no press photographers would be admitted to the camp. Lt. Colonel A. B. Crowther, the Division G-2, went to call on the Camp Publicity Officer and explained the situation to him. At 9:00 AM, Colonel Shue, Acting Chief of Staff, II Corps, telephoned that he had talked to Colonel Watkins, the Corps G-2; that he knew about the Governor's visit and would let us know if he received any instructions.

At 12:45 PM, Colonel Shue called and stated that General Fredendall, CG of II Corps, directed that the presentation of the Texas flag would be made at II Corps Headquarters to a small group of the Division staff, that all schedules for ceremonies and social activities in honor of the Governor would be called off; that the Governor might visit Blanding as a private citizen, but that there must be no publicity, no newspaper men and no photographers.

At 12:50 PM, I called Colonel Clarkson from Fort Jackson, for I had also received, by phone, some very specific orders from the War Department. I told him that in accordance with those instructions the Governor's party was not to be allowed to go to Camp Blanding; that he, Colonel Clarkson, should arrange with Colonel Shue to receive the Texas flag at II Corps Headquarters in Jacksonville; and that he and Shue should take care of the Governor's party during the day. I suggested a sightseeing trip to St. Augustine and Silver Springs or some other place of interest. When Perque told me that Fredendall had said that the Governor might visit the Camp as a private citizen, I told him to follow the instructions from Fredendall.

Colonel Shue called again at 1:30 PM, to say that the Governor might go to Camp Blanding as a private citizen, but that there would be no ceremonies, no social or semi-social gatherings, no newspapermen and no photographers. Shue also stated that the Mayor of Jacksonville wanted to meet the Governor of Texas at the railroad station and to have some ceremony for him, but that he, Colonel Shue, intended to send his Publicity Officer to explain the situation to the Mayor. Colonel Watkins, II Corps G-2, called Crowther, our G-2, that afternoon to arrange procedures to prevent any publicity, ceremonies, social gatherings, or photographers in connection with the visit.

The Governor and his party were met this morning at 7:00 AM at the railroad station by Terry Allen, Perque Clarkson, Carl L. Phinney and Lt. Colonel James Taylor. Phinney and Taylor are close personal friends of the Governor, both having served recently in the Texas legislature; Phinney as Clerk of the House. They took them to the Roosevelt Hotel where reservations were made for them in the names of Colonel Ernest Thompson and Colonel Miller Ainsworth, but the hotel was well aware that they were for the Governor's party.

I arrived in Jacksonville from South Carolina this morning, and Perque briefed me as we drove to II Corps Headquarters. I got there just in time to receive from the Governor a Lone Star flag, a gift to the officers and enlisted men of the 36th Division from the people of Texas.

The ceremony was simple. I accepted the beautiful flag as a symbol of the soldierly qualities of courage, energy, and self-sacrifice which have characterized all Texas troops who have fought in any war since the Alamo. Travis' famous message, ending in "Victory or Death," is contained in a metal capsule inserted in the flag staff. After the presentation, both parties drove to Blanding where I arranged for the Governor to speak to and shake hands with most of the officers and NCOs. I invited him to view the troops at work, which gave him an opportunity to see various types of troop activities.

On his departure, the Governor expressed to me his very sincere appreciation for the hospitality he had enjoyed while with the Division and said again that his visit had been a real pleasure. I do not think that he knew about all of the events that took place behind the scenes which were a lot of fuss and much ado about nothing.

Security is important, of course, but security measures can be overdone. When some 16,000 men of the 36th Division are mailing thousands of uncensored letters each day, all postmarked Florida, to relatives and friends throughout the United States, and hundreds of civilians are visiting the camp every week, it seems a bit ridiculous to be concerned that a few hours' visit from the Governor of Texas would reveal any more information to the enemy than is already known. Of course, there should have been no publicity, and there would have been none in any case because military forces should never allow themselves to be used for publicity purposes.

Saturday, May 16, 1942

I had to speak very frankly to a company commander. He works hard, tries hard, means well, but does not know how to organize his responsibilities, delegate them to his subordinates and then check to see that the work is properly done. He wants to do everything himself. As a result, he wears himself out while those who are there to help him stand about idly.

Sunday, May 17, 1942

Orders were received on May 15th relieving "Perque" Clarkson as my Chief of Staff and assigning him to the new 91st Division as Assistant Division Commander. I regret very much losing him because he is a close personal friend, a superior officer, and has taken a big load off my shoulders. My best wishes go with him. He left a personal note when he departed today:

"Freddie: Goodbye and thanks again for a most enjoyable and instructive tour with your Division.

"I feel that this promotion is due to the boost you gave me with Clark and General McNair. If I am successful in my new job, it will be due to the training I have had under you.

"Cannot tell you how much I hate to leave you. This English and such things are difficult for me.

"Good luck and I know you will leave soon. What will happen to the poor old 36th when you go, I hate to think about.

"Hope you send for me again."

Monday, May 18, 1942

Terry Allen is now assigned to command the 1st Division and Otto Lange officially succeeds him as my Assistant Division Commander. Allen told me that he felt "very humble" upon being given the high honor of commanding an Infantry Division. All Terry had to do was move across the road to the Headquarters of the 1st Division.

Today we began a series of tactical exercises in which the 141st and the 143rd Combat Teams were opposed. They did very well, but many minor corrections must still be made, such as coordination of movement, teamplay, concealment, communication, and sanitation. In this exercise I deliberately intermingled the tactical units, attaching and detaching companies and battalions so that at the end of the exercise regiments and battalions were composed of some units of their own and some units from other battalions, and even from the other regiment.

I did not warn them ahead of time because I wanted to observe how they would operate when surprised and in command of "foreign" units. They were surprised and somewhat confused at first, but by the time the exercise was over they were doing a very good job.

I explained at the critique that I had given them this experience in scrambling and unscrambling units because such procedures are sometimes necessary in emergencies in combat because of tactical surprise, lack of time, or when action is demanded on-the-spot by the nearest troops available. I also explained that such scrambling of units does not cause confusion when they are placed under the command of an appropriate higher headquarters.

The 141st Combat Team marched 15 miles, half of the distance on roads the rest across-country, in very hot weather, and only six men fell out. The soldiers of the 36th are becoming hardened physically.

Tuesday, May 19, 1942

Lt. Colonel Russell Skinner arrived today and is assigned to command the 142nd Infantry in the vacancy left by Troy Middleton. I do not know Colonel Skinner. He is here by direction of General Fredendall. I took some pains to point out to him that he has a big job that will require all of his intelligence and energy. I explained fully what I expect from him because he has had no experience in command of a regiment.

Wednesday, May 20, 1942

Dallas Mathews, former Adjutant General of Texas, has been with the Division since its induction into the Federal Service. He is a liaison agent for the Governor and for the present Adjutant General of Texas, General Page, in matters concerning the State of Texas only. He has never attempted in the least to influence any of my policies or directives, and has been unbiased and most helpful in giving me information about the qualifications and service-history of the Division personnel. He and I served together in the 3rd Division at Andernach on the Rhine during the occupation of Germany after World War I. He was a battalion commander in the 7th Infantry, and I was the Division Inspector. So, I am pleased to have him with the 36th Division.

But, General Fredendall has a different view. He told me to "get rid of old man Mathews." I said that I had no objection to Mathews being with the Division and that he had helped me in many ways. He replied impatiently, "I don't want him around. Get rid of him somehow."

When I told General Mathews, his feelings were hurt, and he showed it, but being the good soldier that he is, he made arrangements to return to Texas without malice toward anyone. I shall miss him.

Troy Middleton writes that he is assigned as Assistant Division Commander, 45th Division. He was a real help to me as commander of the 142nd Infantry, although he was here only a little more than a month.

I have received gasoline ration cards. These various ration cards serve two very useful purposes. They make people realize we are at war, and they ensure equitable distribution of a scarce product.

A mother and her daughter came to see me today. Both were quite upset and hostile. The furious mother told me that her daughter had been raped by one of our soldiers in a hotel room in Jacksonville. She handed me a piece of paper on which was written his name and organization.

"I want this man punished for what he has done to my daughter. This is a terrible thing."

I directed a few questions to the daughter, but her mother answered them all. Of course my sympathies were with her and her daughter, but her behavior and manner of speaking indicated that she felt I was not showing as much enthusiasm for punishing the soldier as she wished. This is not the first case of this nature I have had to deal with, but it is the first one in which the mother took over so completely.

She took from her purse a newspaper clipping, handed it to me and said, "I don't want this man let off and whitewashed as they did there."

I read the item which reported, in effect, that a soldier had been tried for rape by a general court martial in a military command, and had been acquitted. When I finished reading she said, "How can they do such a thing?"

I explained to her that the Articles of War govern the legal procedures of the Army and that the one applying to the offense of rape states that any soldier found guilty in time of war shall suffer death or life imprisonment; that the sentence is mandatory and that the court cannot give the soldier any lesser punishment; that in the case out West either the evidence did not support the charge or the court did not consider that the circumstances required the soldier to be hanged or spend the rest of his life in a penitentiary. I also explained that in all previous cases that had come to my attention, when the girl involved was asked if she wanted the man hanged or sent to prison for life, she withdrew her charges.

I then asked them the same question. Reluctantly, they calmed down and then the mother said, "This is terrible. Can't something be done? Does this mean that a soldier can go on doing such things and not be punished?"

I told her that a soldier could be tried by a military court for attempted rape and be given an appropriate sentence or he could be tried in the civil courts. But, I pointed out, even attempted rape is very hard to prove in a case where a girl goes willingly with a soldier to a hotel room and remains there.

Finally the mother said, "We don't want to go to the civil court. There will be too much publicity. There is no use to talk about a charge of attempted rape in a military court. They won't do anything anyway. What I want is for you to punish the man yourself."

"That I cannot do."

Some people think that just because a man has been given the title of "General," and happens to be in command of a military organization, he is some kind of a superman with complete freedom to do as he pleases. This may have been true in the days of Caesar, but it is not true today. Generals, like everybody else, have to obey the law.

Anyway, when they departed I had the feeling that the mother was quite frustrated—but that the daughter was pleased.

Saturday, May 23, 1942

Yesterday and the day before I had the Division, less certain detachments, out in the field for combat team practice.

The 141st did especially well in organizing a defensive position and in conducting a withdrawal at night. The 142nd did well also, but because its reserve battalion did not do its job the command post of the 142nd was captured by the 141st. This will serve as a good lesson to all.

We have begun instruction and tests in swimming. About 10 per cent of our men cannot swim, and we must teach them so they may meet minimum swimming standards before July 1st, the date Clark says we will be ready to go.

We received 1100 recruits this week.

They have a lot to learn, and we are going to be rushed to get our program finished by July 1st. We must complete the GHQ tests for all infantry and artillery battalions, require everybody to swim 100 yards, put the entire Division across an unfordable river without the aid of engineer equipment, conduct a series of air-ground exercises in cooperation with the Air Force, complete training in landing on hostile shores, and do all this while maintaining a large post guard.

In addition, we must make two marches per week of at least 10 miles each to build up marching stamina. Before July 1st, each unit must complete a march of 25-miles in 12 hours with full packs. This is going to be tough on the personnel of Division Headquarters who, because of their many administrative and training duties, have little opportunity for a gradual buildup of marching stamina. I jokingly told Otto Lange that we should keep our Aides near us on the march in case we need someone to lean on during the last mile.

Tuesday, May 26, 1942

A private, who is suspected of being a Communist, has been speaking disrespectfully of the President and our war effort. He has been praising Hitler and the Russians and has been holding meetings in his tent in an attempt to convert other soldiers to his views.

After an investigation, I had him tried by a General Court Martial for his slanderous accusations against the President which border on treason. Today the Court found him guilty and sentenced him to be dishonorably discharged and confined at hard labor for 20 years. I will approve the sentence and send it on to the War Department for confirmation.

After the conclusion of the trial, Jesse Moseley reported to me that for the first time since the Division was inducted into the Federal Service there are no soldiers in confinement awaiting trial, no cases pending before a general or special court, no cases referred for investigation and report under Article of War 70. This shows that the discipline of this Division is far superior to the average. In fact, it is tops, and I am pleased.

Thursday, June 4, 1942

Colonel Carnes Lee, General Staff Corps, has been assigned
to the 36th Division as Chief of Staff by Headquarters II Corps.
He reported for duty today and will take the vacancy left by
"Perque" Clarkson. I have served with him before at the Army
War College, when he was Aide to General Craig, Commandant
of the Army War College and later Army Chief of Staff. Everybody liked him.

Frank Reese has returned from the anti-tank school at Gaines-
ville. Texas. I am glad to have him back for everything operates
better when he is around. I will not keep him as my Aide but
will assign him to the G-2 Section of Division Headquarters, to
take effect as soon as Major Ives becomes G-1. This new assignment will mean a promotion for Reese.

Charles received his commission as a second lieutenant in the
infantry reserve upon graduation from Knox College. He is now
home (here) on leave and will report to Camp Blanding for
active duty on June 12. He then goes to the Infantry School at
Fort Benning for a three months course of instruction after which
he is to be assigned to the 36th. He is enthusiastic about his new
rank and his forthcoming tour of active duty, and has been observing the training activities of the Division in order to learn
about them.

Wednesday the staff officers of Division Headquarters received
instruction in firing the Tommygun on the target range. They did
remarkably well although most of them had never fired the gun
before. Charles had an opportunity to fire the gun also. Although
he, too, had never fired it, he made a score of 84; the same as
mine.

After the firing, we all walked back to camp in the rain, four
and one half miles.

Again, before we go overseas I am letting several thousand
men go home on furlough prior to June 14th. Yesterday I went
to see them off. There were so many that two special trains
had to be provided.

We have been having lots of rain since last Saturday. Each
night this week a battalion of infantry and a battalion of field
artillery have been going out into the field to participate in prescribed GHQ tests under the supervision of General Lange, who

has a very strenuous program. They are out from 4:00 PM to 11:00 AM and most of the troops have been soaked.

The nights have been wet, cold and miserable, and I doubt if the men really learn anything under such conditions, or are able to put forth their best efforts. Nevertheless, it is good training because battles don't wait for fair weather these days. I am going to spend tonight with these troops.

I presented a test case for tires needed by Louis Hibbs to the local ration board last week and received a flat refusal. The ration board takes the stand that army personnel are not entitled to tires to go back and forth to home, although every janitor working in camp is given tires for the same purpose because he is furthering the war effort. Soldiers are not furthering the war effort, according to the members of the board.

The soldiers who are going to do the fighting and dying cannot be blamed if they lose patience with discrimination in favor of civilians.

Friday, June 5, 1942

Some months ago General Cubbison and I agreed that there should be no fighting between the men of the 1st and 36th Divisions, but it did not mean a thing.

There were insults and fist fights although the Texans have the odds in their favor for they are bigger and stronger. The enlisted men of both divisions have been roaming the streets in groups for self-protection. If one group occupied a bar or restaurant, the opposing group gave it a wide berth. It was quite the thing for the Texans to require a 1st Division group to sing, loud and clear, "The Eyes of Texas Are Upon You" or "Deep in the Heart of Texas" and to repeat it until they did it perfectly. The 1st Division men under similar circumstances would demand that the Texans sing "The Sidewalks of New York." The 1st Division has no song of its own.

This eventually got to be funny with the result that the fighting has now stopped and a spirit of comaraderie has grown up between the men of the two divisions. But, until they made peace, there were some heads broken.

Monday, June 8, 1942

I was with the 3rd Battalion of the 143rd Infantry on an exercise last Friday night and the next forenoon and was pleased with the excellent way the men did their jobs. They were absolutely silent; no lights whatever. They were well dug-in; well protected from attacks by ground troops, tanks, artillery fire and aerial bombing. They conducted their attack from the line of departure in an excellent manner. The supporting artillery fired over their heads, but it was too foggy to see the bursts of the shells about 700 yards in front of them.

Wednesday, June 17, 1942

Higher Headquarters are still taking away our trained men. Just received a call from II Corps for 127 specialists of 13 different categories to be in Jacksonville by 5 this afternoon. They don't mind asking for specialists on short notice. They have no idea how much time it takes to locate the men, get them relieved from their present duty, get them ready to depart, make out all the papers, and actually transport them. Nor do they seem to realize how much trouble they cause by asking that things be done in a hurry. This is "lousy" staff work on the part of the II Corps Headquarters, and I am tired of it. We will do it, of course, but we would like a little consideration, especially since there is no need whatever for these 127 men to be in Jacksonville this evening.

Back some months ago when we were about to leave Camp Bowie for Camp Blanding, the custodians of our company funds were told by the Camp Post Exchange Officer that he could not redeem their stock in the Exchange because he did not have enough cash on hand to do so. He advised them to go on to Blanding and said that the money would be sent to them later, wherever they might be.

I did not like this. I thought of the old army saying: "Never separate yourself from your baggage." Here was some very valuable baggage, indeed. The Camp Post Exchange owed the 36th Division some $68,000 which the Division had invested in the Post Exchange to set it up in business when the Division arrived there after mobilization. Lt. Colonel Kerr, Division Inspector, insisted that the Camp Post Exchange Officer give me a note over his signature for the amount owed to the 36th Division. After some argument he did so. This insured that our units would get back their capital investment as well as accrued dividends.

Now Camp Bowie Post Exchange has sent us the money and the

note has been cancelled. Once again we have our "baggage" with us.

Sunday, June 21, 1942

On June 11, 12, and 13, I attended a demonstration at Fort Benning of air-ground liaison and cooperation. All the division commanders from all divisions within the States were present, together with their operations and intelligence officers, 300 in all.

The purpose was to impress all general officers with the importance of air-ground cooperation and to demonstrate an approved method of cooperation between air and ground forces.

I saw five former members of the 15th Infantry whom I served with in China: Lt. Colonels Coates, Elmore, Starr, Thomas, and Triplett. I also saw Colonel George Howell who is now with the paratroops. I was pleased to see them all again. They look a lot older than when I saw them last. They probably think the same of me.

I had to get after one of my lieutenant colonels yesterday. He has been talking too much and stirring up animosity between the National Guard and the Regular Army, charging that the Regular Army is going to steal all promotions away from the National Guard. I told him to cease such talk, that anyone who engaged in it was unworthy of the uniform of an American soldier. I do not expect to have any more trouble with him.

Wayne Clark has been promoted to Major General and assigned to command the II Corps. Fredendall has departed, but I do not know when or where he went. What happened to his promise that he was taking the 36th with him? Why did Clark report that we would not be ready for combat before July 1st? Why are we being sent on maneuvers instead of going with Fredendall? Somebody is giving other divisions priority over the 36th. I swear, I do not know whom to believe.

Clark, who is many years my junior, is now in command over me. This is in line with the policy of General Marshall and the War Department of putting youth in command in the Theater of Operations. I think this policy is a mistake. To replace experience with inexperience means a slowing down in battle efficiency until the youngsters acquire the knowledge they lack. Many of us, who served with combat units in World War I, have a lot of practical experience that should be used now.

The II Corps has robbed the 36th Division of many of our best stenographers, typists, cooks and other technicians. They have been ruthless in fixing themselves up at our expense. Rank surely has its privileges. The ranked submit and hope for better days.

Last week I qualified as a swimmer by swimming 100 yards twice, a rest between each effort. This means that I can swim across a small river, if I must.

Thursday, June 25, 1942

Last night Division Headquarters, including myself and General Lange, made a foot march of 25 miles, beginning at 7:00 PM and ending at 5:45 this morning. We had a two-hour rest from 12 to 2 AM. The conditions for the march were excellent. Nevertheless, a few of the staff officers were unable to complete it and fell out at the midnight halt. Many of those who finished were in no condition to go another mile. Many had very bad blisters on their feet, but General Lange and I came through without any. I did develop a troublesome pain in the tendons back of my knees. The last two halts found several exhausted, but they continued to the end determined not to let two old men outdo them. We made the whole march in a little less than nine periods of fifty minutes each, 2 2/3rds miles per each fifty minutes.

This is a foolish and inhumane way to treat soldiers who have no opportunity to build up the stamina and endurance needed to make long marches. In my opinion, the person in the War Department, and I do not care who he is, who ordered these long marches is impractical and ignorant of the effect of his orders.

When will a Division Headquarters, or any other group of soldiers, have to march 25 miles on foot in 12 hours? Maybe he contemplates a "Bull Run" somewhere in Europe or in the Pacific and is getting us ready. It all seems silly and childish to me. Physical endurance training is desirable and necessary, of course, but it is being overdone in some respects.

I found out afterward that some individual troubles were caused by wearing new shoes. The Division received 100 pairs of experimental shoes four days before the march. The untried composition soles were to be tested. Some of the staff officers, inexperienced in marching and not knowing that new shoes never should be worn on a hike, decided that the 25 mile march would be a good time to test them. The sharp shell surface of Florida roads cut and wore the composition soles to such an extent that those who wore them had terrible blisters and severe damage to their feet. Needless to say, the shoes were reported as unsuitable for infantry.

Saturday, June 27, 1942

Last Friday Carnes Lee, my Chief of Staff, recommended that I send 1350 recruits to camp at the rifle range until their rifle practice is completed. Ordinarily this is a good idea. But, under present circumstances, I do not agree because the level ground is frequently flooded by heavy rains at this season of the year. This would make a temporary camp very miserable for the men, especially when the preparation and serving of meals must be done without adequate shelter or facilities.

He made his recommendation in the presence of Lt. Colonel Richard Werner, G-3, and Major Albert Hoffman, both of whom wanted to do what I had decided previously; that is, to transport the men back and forth by truck. Colonel Lee became irritated and made a number of sarcastic criticisms of my decision, which embarrassed my officers. I endured this in my office, intending to correct him later when no one else was present, but before I had an opportunity to speak to him, we all went to lunch.

At the table, Lee again let loose his sarcastic remarks and criticisms. The other staff officers kept their eyes on their plates and gave full attention to the business of eating, obviously embarrassed. I had to tell him then and there in unmistakable language to cease any further discussion of the subject. I told him that he had a perfect right to disagree with my views, but that there was a proper way to express his disagreement. After a decision is made, it is up to him to comply, the same as anyone else.

After thinking over his insubordination and disrespect for more than 24 hours, I decided to relieve him as Chief of Staff and report him for reclassification. This I did. He seemed very sorry for his conduct and said that he meant no disloyalty or disrespect.

Monday, June 29, 1942

Recently I have had several persons come to my office trying to convince me that I should transfer their friends, sons or husbands to some duty which will permit them to remain in the

United States. They all say they do not want their relatives or friends to avoid doing their full duty as soldiers, even fighting on the battlefield, but feel that they can best serve their country by staying in the United States and supporting their families while on duty nearby.

I also get a lot of letters on the same subject. A typical one:

"Dear General Walker:

"You most certainly have received several requests of this kind, but won't you please listen to one more. My husband JHP of your division is crippled. One leg is just about an inch shorter than the other one, also the bone is cracked. He isn't allowed to walk very much, and has to stay in camp when the other boys go out for hikes. He is being left at Camp Blanding when the 36th goes on maneuvers. I need him at home very badly now. I am going to have a child in October and I am in no condition to obtain a position to support myself and it will be quite a while after the baby comes that I will not be able to work. My family has been kind enough to let me live at home, but they are in no position to support me or my child and it certainly takes more than kindness to raise a child.

"If my husband was at home, he could secure work here in Akron in one of the defense factories and contribute more to the war effort than he is now doing, and support his family too.

"My husband wanted to see and talk to you himself but he hasn't been able to get permission from his company commander to see you, so won't you at least talk to him and if possible help him to come home. Thank you very much."

My reply:

"Dear Mrs. P:

"I have had an investigation made of your husband's physical handicap, and I find that proceedings are already under way to have him transferred to the Corps Area Service Command, an organization that does not require field service of its members.

"The provisions of the new pay bill make it possible for him to provide adequately for you while he remains in the service. If he establishes that you are his dependent wife, the government will provide $28 monthly which will be augmented by $22 mandatory contribution by him. Should you have any children, you will receive $12 for the first child and $10 for each additional child. Your husband may, from the balance due him, of course, provide directly to you such additional funds as he may desire.

"I can well understand your anxiety under your present condition, and I regret that I cannot do more for you."

There are many deserving cases and Congress has at last taken steps to ameliorate hardship, but the greater number, by far, of requests for special consideration and personal preference that come to my attention are from people who do not have the spirit of self-sacrifice. The will to fight and the will to undergo privation are attributes of character which maintain the freedom of a people. The absence of these characteristics in a citizenry will eventually result in national decay and finally in subservience of one kind or other.

Tuesday, June 30, 1942

I had to tell Major Dallas J. Mathews, Jr., today that he could not go overseas with the Division on account of his physical condition, overweight and flat feet. I advised him to take immediate steps to transfer to one of the air-fields in the United States. He was disappointed but saw the necessity for my action.

I had to tell a lieutenant colonel that I had lost confidence in him; that I did not intend to recommend him for promotion and command of an infantry regiment; that he could either stay on in the Division in the hope that he would do excellent work from now on, or arrange for a transfer to another organization. He said that he would like to stay in the Division and convince me that he can qualify for command of a regiment. I agreed to this and assured him that I was in no way prejudiced against him. I really want him to do well.

I called Major General Ernest J. (Mike) Dawley, Director of the coming maneuvers, and requested permission to assign umpires to their own units since we are so short of company officers. This would permit them to command their own units, be with their government property and also do the umpiring. This arrangement would provide better instruction during maneuvers. He did not appreciate my views, so we will go to maneuvers with only one officer per company. Dawley did permit me to detail a few NCOs instead of officers as umpires.

A soldier came to see me today. He has a wife and three children who are destitute at his home in Texas. He has been released from military service on two occasions before because of dependency after the Red Cross investigated his home conditions. Here he is, back in the army again. I ordered him discharged for the third time. Do you suppose he will be back here again? I presume he was called back into the service because of a clerical mistake or oversight on the part of the Induction Board.

Saturday, July 4, 1942

I had a telephone call today from my old boss Ben Lear, Commanding General, Second Army. He is not going to let my recommendation to reclassify Colonel Carnes Lee go through. He asked if I knew that Lee is a friend of Generals Marshall and Craig. I replied I did, but that I could not use Lee. He then told me to send a telegram recommending that Lee be assigned to another division, but to do so only if I so desired.

Of course, I desire to do anything my superiors tell me to do. I sent the telegram, and I suppose Lee's reclassification papers will be thrown into the waste paper basket. That will be all right with me. I know Ben Lear well enough not to start an argument. I was Operations Officer of the Second Army for two years, the last six months of which he was the Army Commander. In fact, I was promoted to a brigadier and assigned to the 2nd Division while I was on his staff. I like Ben Lear, and I enjoyed serving under him, but he can sure raise hell when he wants to.

Yesterday I received a telegram from III Army Corps to which we are now assigned, directing that I submit data upon which a citation for merit for myself could be based. I am not interested. It appears that we are going to beat the Germans and Japanese with mutual admiration citations for merit.

We had to send 14 automobile mechanics and 12 expert radio operators to the 1st Division yesterday. I suppose they are going to cross the Atlantic soon, probably where we originally were to go.

I received a telegram day before yesterday requesting that a man in the Division, whose father is secretary to a Congressman and a friend of Senator Barkley, be reported and available for transfer from the 36th to the Corps Area Service Command at Fort Knox, a "stay-at-home outfit." I talked to the man and he admits that he does not want to fight or belong to a fighting unit. He wants to be transferred so he can stay home while others do his fighting for him. I am surprised that a Congressman or Senator would take such unpatriotic steps as to have favoritism shown to himself and his constituents. I replied: "Not favorably considered because of need for men with clerical ability in this Division." However, I know that sooner or later I will be required to transfer him.

When our politicians are willing to insist on safe jobs at home for their friends and send substitutes off to war, God help us.

And when our able-bodied proudly state that they do not want to fight for their country, deterioration has set in. The disease will spread, and it can be only a matter of time, perhaps a hundred years, until our people, being no longer willing to make sacrifices for their own welfare, will be governed by those who can and will fight for a place in the world. I am not a politician, and maybe we are not as badly off as it appears. I know that one General George Washington had a hell of a time with politicians in his day but the United States of America is still here.

Sunday, July 5, 1942

There was not much rest for the command today. Almost all units are turning in their excess property so they will have everything taken care of in an excellent manner when they leave for maneuvers. I am insisting on this because we may not return.

CHAPTER FIVE

More Maneuvers, Then Massachusetts

Wadesboro, North Carolina
Sunday, July 19, 1942

The Division has moved from Blanding to the vicinity of Wadesboro, N. C., for maneuvers. Two field exercises have been completed already. In one I was in command of the II Armored Corps for two days while General Alvan C. Gillem was in Washington. I tried no "funny stuff," just straight coordination of effort on one main objective. It worked, and the tactical mission assigned to the Corps was successfully accomplished.

I find the same old attitude in those in charge of these maneuvers as I have found before. They refuse to acknowledge conditions as they really are and expect the same standards of maintenance, appearance, and discipline as prevail in permanent camps. Neither they nor anybody else can attain these same standards in the dirt and sweat and long hours of maneuvers, where adequate facilities and routine procedures do not exist. Therefore, they are unhappy and frustrated most of the time and complain to subordinate commanders, implying that they are inefficient. One of the most important attributes of a good troop commander is the ability to correctly estimate the capabilities of his troops and those of his subordinate commanders under various conditions of service.

On July 11, I had the pleasure of listening to Major Henry Cabot Lodge, 2nd Armored Division, speak on his experiences in the Lybian campaign. His talk was instructive and interesting.

Tuesday, July 21, 1942

Today I received the following letter from Clark, thanking us for the splendid cooperation and assistance rendered him and his staff in preparing the II Corps Headquarters for its movement overseas:

"During the last week of its stay in Jacksonville, Florida, quick action was called for in expanding this headquarters to full strength and it became necessary to call upon you to furnish trained personnel on short notice. Your Adjutant General met these calls in a prompt and efficient manner, giving them his personal attention.

"I wish to extend my personal thanks for this splendid cooperation given my staff during my absence.

"P.S.: Hope to see you before very long."

I am pleased to receive the thanks and appreciation of my friend Wayne and I am glad that we were able to meet the needs of his II Corps, but we did a lot of faultfinding at the time, which is an old soldier's privilege.

Maybe the 36th will go overseas after maneuvers, now that II Corps Headquarters has gone.

Recently I ordered that the NCOs and rated privates who have venereal disease be reduced to the grade of private for allowing themselves to become incapacitated not in line of duty. Brewster, the Division Surgeon, has gone to great pains to provide prophylactic stations in every convenient place. Failure to promptly use the prophylaxis constitutes negligence.

Near Pageland, South Carolina
Thursday, July 23, 1942

I am in a woods about eight miles southwest of Pageland. S. C. Poison ivy and poison oak are all about us. Many of the officers and men have gone to the hospital already. Fortunately, neither poison ivy nor poison oak bother me. Gnats, spiders, chiggers, flies, and mosquitoes abound.

Yesterday my stenographer asked me to approve a request for him to join a group of men who are being made ready, within the Division, to go to the Air Force. When I asked why, he replied, "I can't stand the bugs." He is a new man from Brooklyn, has never been out in the woods before, and finds it difficult to adjust to camp life. Of course, I disapproved his request. He will get used to bugs.

Friday, July 24, 1942

The sky is cloudy and it is raining. To be in the midst of a dense woods during a long rainy day is anything but a delightful experience: dismal, cheerless, damp and chilly.

About all that we can do is to wait until it stops. We are in reserve awaiting orders and are better off than the troops that are deployed and on the move.

My tent consists of four ordinary shelter halves sewed together.

By tying a rope between two trees and suspending the tent from this rope, I avoid the use of poles and thus make more room inside.

Night before last it rained nearly all night but I did not get wet. I cannot stand up inside the tent, but I can sit in a chair, if I sit under the highest part.

I have a quilted sleeping bag with a canvas outer covering which can be closed with a zipper all around. This rests on a rubber air mattress. My cot, which is only about six inches off the ground, together with the air mattress and sleeping bag, makes a very comfortable bed in either cold or warm weather.

The other night, during blackout, I had to go to the latrine, so I started out into the inky black woods to find it. I had an awful time: ran into brush, trees, stumps, vines, spiderwebs and fell down a couple of times. The latrine was marked by a green lantern, burning low, which I finally discovered and made for, arriving just in time. I had almost as much trouble getting back to my tent where there was no light. Hereafter, when there is to be a blackout, I intend to get my bearings before going to bed. All a part of learning-by-doing.

For breakfast this morning we had hot cakes and syrup, bacon, butter, coffee, and fruit juice; all very good.

I sent our assistant mess officer out to buy some fresh fruit. He returned with a bushel of green peaches and a bushel of green plums which no one can eat. The poor devil thought he had better bring back fruit, or else. Maybe they will ripen in time.

In general, young officers, and some older ones, too, follow the literal meaning, rather than the spirit, of an order. They do not feel safe in assuming personal responsibility and exercising their own judgment, although it is an old army axiom that when an order does not fit the situation at hand, the person responsible must do what he believes the commander would do, if he were present.

Those who get ahead have good judgment and do not hesitate to use it.

The 142nd Infantry has not been doing well on these maneuvers. I talked to the commander yesterday and explained to him some of his shortcomings. I told him that I wanted him to make good and that I intend to give him every opportunity to do so, but that I will have to put someone else in command of the regiment unless there is an immediate change for the better. He received my talk in the proper spirit.

Tuesday, July 28, 1942

Conferences, critiques, inspections, and official visits go on apace. These, together with the solving and execution of the various exercises which go on day and night, give a division commander little spare time. He has to catch his sleep when he can.

Thursday, July 30, 1942

I have received a letter from Brigadier General Preston A. Weatherred, the granddaddy of this Division. He is overage as far as field service is concerned, but he had hoped to accompany the Division overseas. Since he left the Division last January, he has maintained a cheerful and patient attitude, free from rancor or personal enmity "with malice toward none." In his letter he stated:

> "Orders have just been received transferring me to inactive status effective August 1st. This comes as not much of a surprise. General officers of my age are being relieved around these parts pretty freely, and I sensed that my turn would come sometime in the near future.
>
> "As my heart's desire was to remain with the Thirty-Sixth, I accept with greater resignation my return to civil life. Of course, the adjustment is going to be hard, but I have the consolation of having gone as far as I could for the service and for the country, and of having given them the best that I have in me.
>
> "You and my many friends among the members of your Division know of the warm place all of you have in my heart. I will follow with deep concern the career of the Division, and it goes without saying that I wish for you and your fine command the best of a Soldier's Luck.
>
> "Those of us who feel as I do toward the Thirty-Sixth will always believe that our lucky star was up when you were assigned to command. You have the affection and respect and the sincere best wishes of all of us.
>
> "When a convenience offers, I would like to have you pass this bit of news on to the officers of the Division. In doing so, please express to them my deep interest and my best wishes. I had hoped that I could make a visit to the Division during the maneuver period, but the turn affairs have taken now makes that impossible.
>
> "Again, wishing you the best of luck, I am, Sincerely."

Watermelons, watermelons everywhere, and not a slice to eat. We are in the midst of the watermelon country, and I have received orders from higher authority that nobody in the military service will enter any watermelon field without the owner's permission. I have transmitted these orders to the personnel of the 36th Division. One may as well issue orders for the rains to cease.

Knowing that its orders are impracticable, Army Headquarters has directed also that any claims for damages to watermelon fields or fruit orchards are to be investigated and settled by the troops themselves, and the offending persons are to pay the claim out of their own pockets. When offending individuals are not identified, the unit involved pays the bill by assessing each member a pro rata share, all in accordance with the Articles of War.

Several farmers came to see me today. They said that soldiers have stolen their melons and destroyed the vines. One farmer reported that ingenious soldiers crept into his field last night, cut melons in half, ate the insides and put the tops back on. They deceived the farmer but a short time for a close look revealed quite a mess of damaged vines. I sent the farmer to Kerr, the Division Inspector, whom I have charged with investigating such claims. Members of the Division Inspectors Section have become quite expert in estimating claims. They count the number of hills, vines per hill, and average melons per vine. When confronted with such accurate data, the farmer usually accepts the amount offered without argument.

Lt. Colonel John Garner was quite embarrassed when the men of his Artillery Battalion, charged with stealing watermelons, were lined up and each was required to put a dime on a camp table as he walked past. He claims the melons were stolen by infantrymen, not by his men. But he was not the only unit commander to be disillusioned and embarrassed.

Camp Edwards, Massachusetts
Wednesday, August 26, 1942

I am in Camp Edwards, Massachusetts.

The maneuvers were terminated on August 14th and the 36th Division began moving by rail to Edwards on the 15th. By August 21st all units had arrived. Forty trains were required for the movement.

Julia has rented a room in a private home at 140 Locust Street in Falmouth, Massachusetts, until she can find something more suitable.

When Major Earle G. Wheeler finished the course at The General Staff School last February, I received the report of his work. He stood number one in the G-4 course, and either number one or two in the other courses. I knew the moment I saw the report that the War Department would mark him for General Staff duty. Sure enough, I received a telegram assigning him to General "Tommy" Lawrence's new 99th Division.

Bus came to see me. He does not want to leave the 36th nor do I want to lose him, but if I know the War Department—and I think I do—they will not rest until they have him on the General Staff.

He asked me to make a personal request to have his orders cancelled, but nothing would be gained by my doing so. He is marked for better and higher assignments and he should comply with orders. I am sorry to lose him, but he paved the way to the General Staff by standing high at Leavenworth. He was disappointed at my action, said I did not understand his problem, and was not happy. I suspect he thinks I am trying to get rid of him, and does not realize that I am doing what I believe to be in his best interest.

Nat Perrine of the 141st has been promoted to a brigadier. I do not like to lose him, but he deserves the promotion. I am assigning Lt. Colonel Werner to command the regiment.

As a result of my request for a regular army Officer for Chief of Staff, Colonel John D. Forsythe was assigned to the Division during the later phases of the Carolina maneuvers. I have not known Forsythe before.

> NOTE: Brigadier General Nat S. Perrine was the only National Guard officer inducted with the 36th Division who became a general officer during the war. He was assigned to duty in Puerto Rico where he did an excellent job. He would have done as well with combat troops. I would have been satisfied to have had him as my Assistant Division Commander.

Thursday, August 27, 1942

Last evening my staff, subordinate commanders, and I were guests of honor at the Hyannis Service Club. Mrs. Gerard C. Besse, Chairman, Hyannis Chapter, Red Cross canteen, served a turkey pie dinner. Dr. Charles E. Harris, Chairman of the USO committee on management, presided during the evening. After the meal I introduced my division guests, one at a time, and as each stood up

I tried to say something humorous but pertinent:

"BRIGADIER GENERAL OTTO LANGE is my assistant and does his best to keep me from doing the wrong thing. He looks after his doughboys like a mother hen looks after her chicks.

"COLONEL JOHN D. FORSYTHE is my Chief of Staff. His job is to see that all the other members of the staff are kept busy and working efficiently. He keeps them from getting in each other's way.

"LT. COLONEL JOSEPH B. McSHANE is my Operations Officer. He thinks up work to keep everybody busy at what he describes as training programs. When we get overseas he will be telling us how to beat our enemy.

"LT. COLONEL ALBERT B. CROWTHER is our Intelligence Officer. He knows all about our enemy, Japanese or German; at least he is expected to know all about them. He has ways and means of spying on them, and when we are overseas he can tell us where our enemy is, how many there are, and what they are up to.

"LT. COLONEL HARRY V. STEEL is our G-4. His job is to see that those who are charged with our supply and transportation obtain everything we need and are authorized to have. Sometimes he may have to get a little rough with some of his people to get the desired results.

"LT. COLONEL JESSE E. MOSELEY is our Judge Advocate, our attorney at law. He sees to it that we do nothing illegal. He supervises our court martial procedures and does not permit anyone to be punished unjustly. When he pulls the law book on us, we all take cover.

"LT. COLONEL CLAYTON PRICE KERR is our Inspector General. He is not really a general. But he inspects everything in general. He goes about looking for anything that anybody may be doing improperly. He keeps us all on the qui vive. If we do our work well, we like for him to pay us a visit; otherwise, no.

"LT. COLONEL WALTER G. JENNINGS is our Ordnance Officer. His job is to keep us supplied with arms and ammunition. That includes everything from big tanks to 22 caliber target rifles. He also keeps our tanks, guns and other arms in a good state of repair.

"LT. COLONEL HERBERT E. MacCOMBIE is our Division Chaplain. He comes to us from your state of Massachusetts and is affectionately spoken of as "Our Damnyankee Chaplain." He looks after the spiritual welfare of the Division, and sees that church services are provided. We have some fifteen other chaplains with the battalions and regiments who are of various religious faiths. He keeps them tolerant and tolerable.

LT. COLONEL CLARENCE B. BREWSTER is our Division Surgeon. He does his best to keep us well. He sees that our food is wholesome, our shelter adequate, our clothing proper. He takes care of our sick, but woe unto him who pretends to be sick for he will be sent back to duty in a hurry.

"LT. COLONEL CARL L. PHINNEY is our Quartermaster. He supplies our food and clothing and provides our shelter and transportation. We all like to be on good terms with him for he can do much to make our lives comfortable and happy. He is always busy.

"LT. COLONEL ROBERT L. COX is our Signal Officer. He is our telephone and telegraph company. He installs wire lines, switchboards, telephones, radio sets and operates a messenger service. He has to have the patience of Job. Everybody wants a telephone and wants it **now**. When we move he tears down a splendid system of communications, and then sets it up again. It is like marching up the hill, then marching down again. He does not talk much himself, but he makes it possible for the rest of us to talk all day long.

"MAJOR ROBERT L. PHINNEY is our Finance Officer. He is our banker. He is very popular because he pays each of us on the first of each month. He has a way of showing up with money when it is needed. We don't care where nor how he gets it.

"MAJOR EDWARD N. HARRIS is our Chemical Warfare Officer. He teaches our people how to use gas and other chemicals to subdue our enemy and how to carry on without interruption if the enemy gasses us. If neither we nor our enemy use gas in this war, Harris will be envied because he will have the only soft job in the Division. But we have to be ready anyway.

"MAJOR FRANCIS R. REESE is my Aide. He looks after my personal needs so I can give my full attention to the Division. He and I were born on June 11th, but not the same year. I am a little older than he.

"LT. COLONEL MARVEN STEEN is our Division Adjutant General. He does our paper work, writes letters, publishes orders, keeps our records, knows how to short cut red tape. He runs his office with firmness and efficiency. He has received several commendations from inspectors of higher headquarters who snoop about trying to find fault with his records, but never do.

"COLONEL FLOYD E. MARTIN is our Division Engineer. He makes roads, constructs shelter, provides us with water, not pure water, but germ-proof, if it must come from creeks and rivers. He can do almost anything in the way of construction. If and when our infantry becomes hard pressed, he is prepared to come to its aid and fight by its side.

"MAJOR VAN W. PYLAND is commander of our Tank Destroyer Battalion. He is our insurance against defeat. If the time ever comes when we are being attacked by overwhelming numbers of tanks, it will be up to him and his tankers to knock them out before they can harm our infantry. For this purpose he has 24 armor-piercing guns.

"CAPTAIN RUSH S. WELLS is our Reconnaissance Officer. He is a cavalryman who does not ride a horse. It is his job to keep us informed of the movements of our enemy. For this he has many lightly armored motor vehicles. These reconnaissance vehicles have replaced the horses of other days, but we still call them cavalry.

"BRIGADIER GENERAL LOUIS A. HIBBS is commander of our Artillery Brigade, which is a very important part of the Division. The brigade has four firing battalions, the 131st, 132nd, 133rd, and 155th. These battalions have the job of saving the lives of our doughboys by destroying the enemy's forces and equipment. The infantrymen and artillerymen may contend with one another when all is peace and quiet, but in battle they work together like brothers. We are proud of our artillery.

"COLONELS WILLIAM H. MARTIN, RUSSEL SKINNER, and RICHARD WERNER are commanders of three infantry regiments. They are fighting men. The rest of us are their keepers; their servants, if you please. It is our business to keep the ten thousand men in these three regiments provided with everything they need in the way of care, equipment, and assistance so they can give their full time and attention to their job of defeating our enemy. These three men are very fortunate, for they have the jobs that all good soldiers would like to have."

Monday, August 31, 1942

I have been quite busy during the past week. General Dawley, VI Corps, (to which we now belong), was here on Friday to observe the activities of the Division. Just after noon I received word that Major General George Patton would arrive at Falmouth Field at

4:30 PM on important business, and a request to have someone meet him. During his visit utmost security and secrecy is to be maintained. General Dawley said he would remain to meet General Patton with me. Patton had said nothing about his visit to Dawley, the Army Corps Commander. This was a real military discourtesy and Dawley did not like it although he did not show his feelings to Patton. As soon as Georgie arrived, he requested that the three of us go to some private place to talk.

We went to my office at Camp Edwards where, after some mysteriousness, he told us that he had been assigned to command a task force; that the 36th Division was a part of the force; and that some day we would be going overseas to somewhere. This was very valuable information, indeed! At least I suppose he meant it to be. After his talk, during which there was much beating around the bush but no flushing of game, he borrowed my automobile and driver, Sergeant Clay, and departed for Hyannis in civilian clothes. Object, a deep secret.

Next morning at Camp Edwards, having informed me again that the 36th was to become a part of his task force, and that he was here for the purpose of orienting the troops to his way of thinking, he directed that I arrange for him to speak to the officers of the Division assembled in one group. I told him that our troops were located in two areas miles apart and that it would ruin a day's amphibious training for the group now in camp on the beaches, if they were required to travel to and from one assembly. I recommended two assemblies. He did not like this because he would have to make two speeches instead of one, but finally agreed to two assemblies. I provided a loudspeaker and a truck for a platform. He required that a strong guard, consisting of many officers and NCOs, be posted around the assembly area in order to prevent unauthorized personnel from hearing what he had to say. I provided the guard from the 636th Tank Destroyer Battalion. We expected to hear something important, but there was nothing in it of value nor of a classified nature. I watched the faces of my officers during his "oratory." They showed surprise, bewilderment, and disgust. They were not favorably impressed by his profanity and vulgarity.

After his talks I accompanied him on a visit to our units in camp and to those undergoing amphibious training on the beach. He seemed pleased with what he saw except on one occasion when he gave my driver hell for not saluting him although Clay was not at fault. I do not require him to salute when I am getting in and out of the car frequently. Patton said when he departed, "Walker, you have a good outfit here." He was not telling me a thing. Nevertheless, he did show good judgment in this one instance.

When my Aide, Frank Reese, and I returned to my cottage, he opened the door to let me in and closed it behind him. He stood there with his hand on the knob for several seconds in deep thought. He then said:

"Sir, I think General Patton is crazy."

"He does give some people that impression when they first meet him. They will get used to him."

Almost immediately after arriving at my cottage I was summoned to the telephone. General George C. Marshall was on the other end, in an unhappy mood. He said, "Walker, when I want to talk to the Division Commander I do not wish to be delayed." I was at a loss to understand his unfriendliness. He said that if General Patton should arrive at Camp Edwards he is not to be allowed to speak to the assembled officers and is to be told that the Chief of Staff directs that he return to Washington at once. When I got a chance to get in a word I told him that Patton had already arrived, had already spoken to the assembled officers, and had already taken off by plane for Washington. In a frustrated state of mind, General Marshall made an appropriate and well-chosen remark and hung up the receiver with some irritation. It is only natural that he would.

Then I learned that General Marshall had called while I was accompanying Patton to the airfield. The NCO in charge at Division Headquarters who took the call, having been greatly impressed with the necessity for utmost secrecy in connection with Patton's visit, could not mention Patton's name and could merely report that I was not available. This went on for some minutes until General Marshall got on the phone himself and was using some rather plain language when I took up the receiver.

I would like to be present when Marshall and Patton meet.

Now that I have had some time to reflect on the day's events, I catch myself laughing.

We are being filled to war strength, and the equipment we need is being sent to us. We expect to be prepared for overseas movement by October 5th.

I have had several talks with my Chief of Staff, Colonel Forsythe. He is new at the job and has much to learn. He is inclined to proceed along theoretical lines as laid down in the books and to overlook practical requirements. He thinks I am difficult to work for because I want to know the what, where, when, why and how of activities within the Division. I have explained to him that I must have complete knowledge of things if I am to make proper decisions. Otherwise, I will do poor work and degenerate into a "rubber stamp," having to depend on recommendations of others, without mature ideas and suggestions of my own.

Three Red Cross representatives have joined the Division. They are intelligent and robust men. Another representative will join later. Their principal duty will be to arrange for investigation of home conditions of needy soldiers' families and to procure loans for the soldier's return when home conditions require it.

I disapproved an application by a soldier from Brownwood for discharge because of dependents. His father is paralyzed, his mother is not well, his wife, 23, lives with them. This soldier can contribute as much as $115 per month, including the government allowances. I do not believe they can be suffering extreme want with an income of $115 per month.

For humanitarian reasons the soldier ought to be with his parents and wife, but I am not authorized to discharge soldiers for humanitarian reasons. Our people should realize that we are engaged in a destructive and critical war in which all must do their bit—and that includes disappointment, sorrow and hardship.

Some people in the States feel that, somehow, the suffering, hardship and sorrow of this war should be borne by the other fellow. Maybe I feel the way I do because I get so many requests to send men home or to duty away from combat units. Sometimes I wonder if I am too tough and inhuman. I am sure there are many people who think I am.

I am sending Frank Reese to the Command and General Staff School for a three months' course in staff operation. He wants to go and he will be back before we go overseas, I hope. If he does as well as Bus Wheeler, I'll lose him, too.

Thursday, September 3, 1942

Some time ago I organized a commando platoon in each infantry battalion. These platoons have received special training in stalking tanks at night, patrolling inside enemy territory, capturing enemy patrols and outguards, blowing up bridges and the like. The members are very much interested in their assignment, and I am going to give them some exercises that will test their special knowledge.

Friday, September 4, 1942

On about the 10th of August a general court martial was convened at Camp Blanding and tried a lieutenant charged with the theft of two automobile tires. It found him guilty. He was sentenced to be dishonorably discharged from the service, to forfeit all pay and allowances, and to be confined at hard labor for six months. Today I received a letter from a friend of his family in Texas. The friend made a very earnest plea for me to disapprove the sentence in order to save his parents and sisters from the sorrow that they will undergo when his sentence is made effective. Of course, I cannot grant this request. I feel very, very sorry for him, his parents and his relatives. He should have thought of their feelings before he stole the tires. An officer who is a thief cannot command the respect of his superiors nor his subordinates. He is untrustworthy and unreliable and is of no value as an officer in the army.

The Commanding General, Fourth Corps Area, sent me a bill for more watermelons. This claim for $500 was submitted after we left the area. This means that each member of the three combat teams will contribute 4 cents with which I will pay the bill.

From 3:30 AM to 6:30 PM I watched the 3rd Battalion, 143rd Infantry, in a movement over water in small boats between K and L beaches. The movement was well-handled throughout, and I was pleased. The officers and men are very enthusiastic about the type of training they are getting. They are acquiring confidence in themselves and in each other. This Division is going to give a good account of itself when it meets the enemy for it is in an excellent state of training.

Monday, September 7, 1942

Spent all day today on the beach witnessing demonstrations of loading and unloading assault boats, moving vehicles over deep sand, and distributing personnel and equipment in the landing craft of the various boat-waves. It was cool; a breeze was coming from the sea; the sun was shining, but it was not sensibly warm. Nevertheless, everyone who was on the beach today has a very red, sunburned face tonight. All of us were surprised.

Monday, September 14, 1942

Some time ago, in June, I sent Captain Frank Coker, 142nd Infantry, from Camp Blanding to England to attend the British school for commandos. He returned on the **Queen Mary** and last Thursday called at my cottage. He said that he had gone to England in a convoy of twenty-odd vessels, all carrying personnel. It required sixteen days to cross the Atlantic because they took the long northern route and zigzagged all the way.

He spoke in complimentary terms of the course of instruction he received. He brought back one of the automatic weapons which is being manufactured in Britain by the thousands at a cost of $4.37 each. It fires the type of pistol ammunition used by the German, Italian, and Japanese armies—7mm. It is rather crude in appearance and finish, but thoroughly practical, with a cyclic rate of 600 rounds per minute.

Tuesday, September 15, 1942

Mr. Williams, who is the head of the Field Service of the American Red Cross, called on me today regarding the assignment and duties of the four members of the Red Cross who are to accompany the 36th Division to the Theater of Operations. We had a very friendly visit, and I am sure he went away with the feeling that we appreciate the help we are getting—as we really do—and that harmony is going to reign within the Division as far as the American Red Cross is concerned.

Together with the members of my staff, I have been attending the lecture course given by the Amphibious Command which is responsible for our amphibious training here. Today the school gave us a tactical map exercise to solve, requiring the movement of the entire Division from a friendly beach to a hostile one, as a landing expedition. We are now engaged in solving the problem.

I visited the camp ordnance shops and saw our new 75mm antitank guns mounted on half-track scout cars. These guns are to be issued to our three antitank companies; one in each regiment. They are highly mobile and should be able to cause a lot of destruction.

I also saw the new 105mm howitzers mounted on lightly armored carriers for our Infantry Cannon Companies. We have six of these 105mm howitzers for each regiment. They are to be used for close support of our infantry.

Colonel Werner told me this evening that Charles had conducted a class for NCOs, his first military duty, in an excellent manner and that he led his platoon at night ten miles across country by use of a compass through brush and woods without getting lost. They did it in a little over seven hours, which is three hours better than the expected time under such conditions. I am pleased that Charles is doing good wook.

Thursday, September 17, 1942

This afternoon I inspected the new 3-inch, self-propelled anti-tank guns that have just arrived for our Tank Destroyer Battalion. They are of the latest model and we have 24 of them. When the battalion learns how to use them, we will be able to give the Germans hell.

This was a very busy day as far as military justice was concerned. I fined one officer $25 for negligence, wrote letters of a disciplinary nature to two others, laid the ground work for reclassifying a fourth, and signed 16 court-martial cases of enlisted men who were sentenced to confinement and forfeiture of pay for from one to six months each. I have caused a lot of men a lot of grief today as a result of their own misconduct.

Friday, September 18, 1942

I witnessed a demonstration by our engineers of a flame thrower. It is a very effective fire gun, throws a flame 75 feet, and if the wind is favorable, 100 feet. It has a huge hot flame that will burn a human being to a crisp in a second, but it can be used only in special and unusual situations.

Colonel Conrad, VIII Corps Area, has especially requested me to give him the names of twelve good field officers for transfer to the Eighth Corps Area Service Command. I do not want to lose twelve good officers, but we gave him the names of those we can spare with the least inconvenience to ourselves, and I presume it will be only a few days until they leave for San Antonio.

I witnessed a parade by the 143rd Infantry today. It was only fair. Too many men were out of step, and the guides did not know how to get onto the line. Salutes were ragged. The adjutant did not know his business and made one mistake after another. But their spirit was excellent. They wanted to do well but did not know how. After all, a lot can be done with people who have the right spirit.

A Texas flag flies over the entrance to my headquarters. Last night some members of a nearby unit, not a part of this Division, climbed up and tore it down. When our men discovered what had happened, they were very angry, and, if they could have gotten their hands on the guilty parties, they would have given them a real beating. Luckily, it was not the flag Governor Stevenson gave me. It never pays to stir up ill feelings between units in the army; they are expected to cooperate in battle.

Thursday, September 24,1942

Today I learned that we will be here two more months, until the first of December. Either Patton did not know what he was talking about when he told me we were a part of his task force and were going overseas in October or Marshall was irked because of Patton's visit and took us off the task force list.

The Chief of Staff, VI Corps, called and discussed a number of reports that Negro soldiers at Camp Edwards have been mistreated. These complaints are based on incidents of colored soldiers being called "niggers." Some cases of actual mistreatment have occurred. But on the other hand, the tendency of some Negro soldiers is to make a great deal out of a little and cry out like children when they feel offended. When two white soldiers call each other names, or beat each other up, they go on about their business and nothing is made of it. But if a white soldier and a Negro soldier call each other names or beat each other up, the Negro runs to the nearest authority and cries mistreatment because of race. We have no Negro soldiers in this Division.

Today the Division Chaplain, Herbert MacCombie, brought Francis J. Spellman, Archbishop of New York, to call on me. He just wanted to pay his respects and invited me to call on him at St. Patrick's Cathedral in New York, if I should ever be in that city. We had a very delightful visit.

In the presence of Chaplain MacCombie, who is a Baptist, I made a very inappropriate remark. I told the Archbishop that in my opinion the best chaplains in the army, as a whole, are the Catholics. As soon as it was out I realized that, even though this is my opinion, I should not have said it for it must have offended Chaplain MacCombie and I do not want to offend anyone, unintentionally.

A Mr Pearson, Passenger Manager for the New Haven Railroad, called this afternoon. He came to discuss the case of a major of the 143rd Infantry, who was removed from the train while returning to Camp Edwards from a weekend in New York.

He had an argument with the conductor, used some strong language, and the conductor appealed to the MPs, who put him off the train. Pearson came armed with statements from the conductor accusing the Major of hitting him in the chest, fracturing two ribs and bruising him. I could well believe it for the Major is a solid chunk of muscle. The Major said that the conductor had mistaken him for another, who was creating a disturbance, and that he had resisted being put off the train because he had done nothing wrong. Mr. Pearson and I agreed that we would drop the case and cooperate to prevent ill feeling between the railroads and the army.

A Task Force Headquarters has asked for a captain qualified for duty as Assistant G-3 at that headquarters. I feel that I should send them a good officer, one who is sure to succeed, so I will send Captain Paul Dresser.

Wednesday, September 25, 1942

Colonel Bell, Air Corps, and myself had an interesting conversation today about methods to be employed by the Air Support Control personnel when in support of an infantry division.

The Air Corps has adopted a method that is purely theoretical; no practical experience to support it. I told Bell that the method would not get results. I gave him my views on the subject, which were, in short, that the Air Support Command must find its own targets when a battle is in progress, which should be just beyond the accurate range of our artillery; and that it should attack those targets at once without orders from corps or division. In order to avoid bombing our own people, we should designate a bombing line well in front of our own troops, the bombing to take place on the enemy side of that line. A bombing line is necessary because the pilots have difficulty determining the exact location of our own front line troops.

Bell was delighted with my views. He said that he had learned something new and important. I thought to myself, "amen."

I have directed that charges be preferred against a lieutenant in the 143rd Infantry. He was absent without leave from September 7 to September 22, and he failed to obey an order sent to him by his regimental commander, Colonel William Martin, to return to duty.

Monday, September 28, 1942

Members of my staff and I have been attending classes to refresh our knowledge of the strength, composition, type of equipment and capabilities of the German ground forces, and the design and appearance of the German airplanes. We have to know our enemy's army as well as our own. After a few preliminaries, a good bridge or poker player knows how his opponent will play his hand. So it is with good soldiers.

Monday, October 5, 1942

On Friday and Saturday of last week the Division participated in a landing exercise. We departed from a point several miles east of Falmouth and were transported across Vineyard Sound to Martha's Vineyard. We landed on the west portion of the island, beginning at dawn.

This required the infantry to arrive at the embarking shore, organized into boat teams with all their equipment, after a night march. They silently boarded the boats assigned to them in the blackout in good order, each man in his proper place. The boat crews—engineers from the Amphibious Command—moved them to the debarkation shore in formation so that the troops would be let out at the proper time, at the proper place, and in the proper order for combat. The troops were required to advance in combat formation over strange territory to successive phase lines as directed by the umpires. The exercise extended over two days and two nights. It was principally a test in maintaining control, coordination and good order under different conditions, and was a means of familiarizing our personnel with the technique of a landing operation. The Division and three regimental combat teams were given three days to prepare the detailed plans.

It is interesting to recall how old is this training. In the Revolutionary War Glover's Marblehead fisherman practiced it on the beaches north of here. Glover used the technique when he ferried Washington's Army across the Delaware.

We all traveled with light baggage. I carried a small inflatable rubber mattress, a blanket, and a pup tent and slept on the ground —when I had an opportunity to sleep.

The Division did especially well, and I received many compliments on the excellent work of both officers and men.

General Dawley was here again yesterday. He told me that he had no information about our future. He gave me permission to schedule schools for officers and NCOs between 3:30 PM and 5:00 PM instead of between 6:00 PM and 7:00 PM, after supper. This was granted because we have no proper place with adequate light for classes after dark.

He also told me to go ahead with my plans to check all the property in the Division, and granted my request to give furloughs to the men who have gone through thirteen weeks basic training, the Carolina maneuvers, the amphibious training, and who have not had a furlough since joining the Division. After the property check I will announce a policy regarding furloughs, and I am going to make it as liberal as possible. The men will be pleased to get back home for a visit; maybe their last.

Tuesday, October 6, 1942

I discovered today that a prisoner in the artillery guard house has been kept in confinement a full month after he had served his sentence. This is disgraceful! The officer who failed to do his duty in this case is guilty of the worst kind of negligence. I have directed an investigation to determine who is at fault.

I have received a questionnaire regarding the reclassification of Major General John Greely, my former boss. My answer was favorable to him. He had been relieved from command of the 2nd Division on the ground that he lacked the aggressiveness and forcefulness for a division commander. I served under his command from April 20 to September 13, 1941 as his Assistant Division Commander, and I saw no evidence of a lack of agressiveness or forcefulness on his part. He was well-qualified to command a division in my opinion.

I think Greely's trouble was that he was outspoken in his criticism of the VIII Army Corps Staff whenever they bungled their plans and orders in a way that harassed the 2nd Division.

They were amateur staff officers, and on several occasions issued orders that were not based on mature thought and study. As a result, the troops were made to suffer, and Greely resented this. On occasion he requested changes to which the amateurs gave no heed. His adverse comments followed.

The staff undoubtedly ran to General Strong and charged Greely with indifference and failure to carry out the orders issued to him. It could be that Strong became prejudiced in favor of his staff and started the reclassification.

Much injustice will be done to commanders during this war because their higher commanders will be misled by staff officers of limited ability, narrow vision, or with personal axes to grind.

Friday, October 9, 1942

Yesterday a lieutenant came to my office and requested permission to resign for the good of the service. He is charged with conduct unbecoming an officer. He lived with a woman to whom he was not married and received government allowances and railroad transportation for her, certifying over his signature that she was his wife. I am going to let him resign, and I will withdraw the charges. If he should be tried and found guilty, I doubt if the court would give him any more than "to be dismissed from the service." Since he will get out without the trouble and expense of a trial, I am willing to grant his request.

Sunday, October 11, 1942

Yesterday I was informed by the VI Corps and Army Ground Forces in Washington that the 36th Division will go to Indiantown Gap soon. That relieves me of worrying over procuring proper housing here for my Division this winter. Our men will be glad to get out of here for almost anywhere.

Monday, October 12, 1942

Today I went to Boston to see General Sherman Miles, who commands the First Service Command (formerly First Corps Area), to receive instructions regarding some special mountain training for members of the 36th Division. The plan is to rent a hotel at Lincoln, New Hampshire, and conduct mountain training there for approximately 100 officers and enlisted men who will return to the Division later and, in turn, instruct the other men in their units. Schools for teaching the Norwegian language are also to be conducted at Lincoln, and also here at Camp Edwards. All of this is to be kept very secret. How? Please tell me.

> NOTE: Although we were supposed to keep this a "secret," it was a deception, a part of an intelligence plan to make the German agents think we were about to invade Norway. Even I was not informed of the real purpose until later.

I also received an order to move the 36th Division to Indiantown Gap, Pennsylvania, as soon as accommodations are ready for us there. Probably this will be the first part of next week.

Friday, October 16, 1942

Lt. Colonel Napoleon Rainbolt, Executive Officer of the 143rd, called to see me this evening. He has been ordered to duty in the Eighth Service Command at Fort Sam Houston. He wanted to know whether or not he was being transfered because his services were unsatisfactory. I assured him that his services were entirely satisfactory, and that I will give him a letter of appreciation. He does not want to leave the division.

Our move to Indiantown Gap was suspended on October 14th, and everyone in the Division is disgusted. Since then, we have been having a squabble over barracks here at Camp Edwards. The Engineer Amphibious Command is trying to crowd us into too few barracks so that they may not be crowded in their area. I have opposed this, but I have lost out because the Service of Supply controls the housing here, and the Engineer Amphibious Command is a part of the Service of Supply while the 36th Division belongs to the Army Ground Forces. Since we are not getting proper housing here, I am recommending to Army Ground Forces that at least part of the Division be sent to Indiantown Gap for the winter.

I have been giving some thought and study to the problem of reducing the paper work in this Division. I am also considering a method of punishing delinquents without putting them in the guard house. We have too many men in the guard house. Most of them are men who have been absent without leave.

Sunday, October 18, 1942

I have had the Adjutant General investigate whether or not company commanders are appointing noncommissioned officers in accordance with their IQ ratings and other qualifications. It was found that inexperienced officers are appointing some men with low IQs to positions of responsibility while men with higher IQs and otherwise qualified remain in the ranks, their ability not being utilized. I realize that a man's IQ is not his only qualification, but wide differences between IQs do mean something. This appointment business is a condition that I am taking steps to correct. Unfortunately, too many officers of company grade want to favor men for whom they have formed a liking or because they are fellow Texans. They do not take pains to know all their men and appoint those most able.

Colonel Falk, from the Inspector General's Office in Washington, has been here making an informal inspection of the records of the Division. He told me upon departure that this Division is in better condition from an administrative point of view than any other division he has inspected to date. Thanks go to Colonel Marven Steen and Major John Deane who are the supervisors of administration. Although we have placed a lot of emphasis on administrative work, we have placed a greater emphasis on tactical training.

Sergeant Fay, my stenographer, the boy who does not like bugs, has been transferred to the Air Force. He asked me some time ago if he could have my permission to apply for appointment as an aviation cadet. He was the only good stenographer at Division Headquarters, and I could ill afford to lose him. For a while I will have to do most of my work in longhand. This will take some of the time that I should devote to thinking and planning. I have to be preparing for possible future events and have a solution ready if prompt action is required. However, the Air Force needs pilots and I cannot oppose his going merely because of convenience. I will find another secretary.

The transfer of our key enlisted men to officer candidate schools, to the Air Force, and to new units as cadremen has materially reduced the combat efficiency of this Division but we are carrying on, making the best of the unfavorable situation and will be back up to my standards in a short time. Some of my officers are not playing the game whole-heartedly. They cannot quite bring themselves to the point of undergoing a little inconvenience in order to help somebody else in greater need. They have to be pushed.

Tuesday, October 20, 1942

Last night the four bands participated in a competition for best band in the Division. The judges were three civilians, experienced musicians, who did a good job—at least I agreed with them. They selected the 142 Infantry Band as the winner, the same band that won a similar contest last year at Camp Bowie.

I presented the trophy, a loving cup, to the band's director, Mr Irwin Young, Warrant Officer, Junior Grade. The winning band then played an encore. After that it played "The Star Spangled Banner" while 4500 people stood at attention, many of whom were local civilians. This was a most delightful event.

I am proud of all four bands. They have been living in tents in the woods since last July 6th and have had to practice in the open air during some unpleasant weather in September and October. One band is still living in tents because there are no barracks available for the 141st Regiment.

I received a telegram yesterday from Fred Jr., from San Francisco where he landed on Saturday. It has taken him a month, after receiving his orders, to procure transportation and make the journey to the States. Colonel Martin told me today that he expects to assign Fred to the job of S-3, regimental operations officer of the 143rd.

I visited the school for the cannon company personnel yesterday, made a few remarks to start the school off, and remained to witness the first instructor in action. He lectured on organization and the duties of individuals in key positions, but he was obviously rattled by my presence for he violated many principles of pedagogy. He walked back and forth continuously; played with the pointer; turned his back on his audience; spoke in a conversational tone; asked students to answer questions before he had explained the subject; and did not emphasize his points so they would stick in the minds of the students. During the intermission I assembled the instructors and explained to them what not to do when giving a lecture. I probably hurt the first speaker's feelings, but I hope he has a sense of humor.

When I announce the furlough program there will be cheers from the enlisted men. The Red Cross is prepared to lend them expense money.

Wednesday, October 21, 1942

I learned today that an enlisted man was illegally confined in the guard house of the 141st Infantry because the inexperienced officer who was responsible did not know his job.

The investigation into the cause for a man remaining in the
Artillery Brigade guard house one month after his sentence ex-
pired reveals that guard duty in the Brigade has been performed
in a perfunctory manner. An NCO of the Guard made an error
in transcribing the length of confinement of the unfortunate
prisoner onto a new Guard Book, and the Officer of the Day
signed the record without checking it. Result: the error was
carried forward from guard to guard. I have directed the Brigade
Commander to reprimand the negligent persons, and to take steps
to insure that members of the Guard are meticulous in performing
their duties.

The President signed the big tax bill today. This bill will take
about one-fourth of my income, perhaps more. But this is quite
all right. I am willing to give it all, after living expenses are
deducted, if others do the same.

Thursday, October 22, 1942

Today I had occasion to talk to a young officer who has been
in the habit of writing personal checks without funds credited to
his account. He is a big man, pillar of strength, who looks like a
splendid soldier. But I am amazed at his ignorance. He has little
imagination, talks incoherently, writes incoherently, has no desire
to learn his job tactically, and lacks personal initiative. How this
man ever became an officer is a mystery. He will never be any
help to the men in his platoon; they will have to look after him
instead of his looking after them. I wonder if there are others
like him in this Division.

I have made it a point in recent months to place a letter convey-
ing birthday greetings on the desks of my staff officers. Included
in the letter is an authorization for the officer to be absent for
the remainder of the day. I now find that each of them, when his
birthday is approaching, looks forward to receiving this letter of
greeting and the leave that goes with it. They appreciate this far
more than I thought they would when I instituted the practice. I
will keep it up as long as I remain in command.

The 141st Infantry is living in tents in primitive surroundings.
Last night and today have been rainy. The men have no mess
tents, so after they fill their mess kits at the kitchens, they must
hurry over duckboards to their own tents to eat. They have only

candles for light. To have a bath, they must go to the barracks of our more fortunate units, or take a soldier's bath in the open, standing on a newspaper, a board or a flat rock, while dousing themselves from a bucket of warm water with a tin cup. I hope to overcome these inconveniences by getting all of the Division into barracks at Camp Edwards as soon as possible, since I was not permitted to send any units to Indiantown Gap. So far I have had no success.

Sunday, October 25, 1942

Yesterday I had 25 members of the Army and Navy Munitions Board as visitors. Mr. F. Eberstadt, Chairman of the Board, brought the members here to see just exactly what shortages in equipment exist in a division destined for early embarkation for overseas. I arranged for them to be shown one of each of the items we were short in each class of equipment, and to the item was attached a placard showing the number authorized, the number on hand, and the number short. In cases where substitute articles were furnished the fact was shown on the card. In cases where we had no item on hand we tacked a placard on a stake with appropriate information thereon.

Our important shortages are radios and up-to-date weapons and improved vehicles. For these shortages we have substitutes which are less effective than the authorized items. As a result, we may have greater casualties and accomplish less tactically than we would if we had the improved equipment. It is important also from our point of view that we have the improved equipment sufficiently in advance of battle to become familiar with it, and that a reserve supply be built up at the point of debarkation to insure replacement of equipment which may be wrecked in battle.

Upon departure, Mr. Eberstadt told me that our program was exactly what he wanted, and he expressed his appreciation of all that we had done to give them a true picture of our shortages.

I drove to Providence today to confer with Mike Dawley, my Corps Commander, about the future training and furlough status of the 36th Division. The more I come in contact with Dawley, the more confidence I have in him. He told me that he considered the 36th Division "topnotch." Maybe that's why. He agrees with me. No! I don't think I am that naive.

I received a donation package (soldier's) from Mrs. Ray Reelhorn, of Kirkersville, Ohio, today. It was packed by Mrs. Bigony.

The package contained cookies, chewing gum, candy, writing paper and envelopes, a pencil, a package of raisins, needle and thread, smoking tobacco and cigarette papers. These packages are being prepared and distributed to soldiers from Kirkersville by the ladies of the Baptist and Methodist Churches. Many communities are doing the same.

Friday, November 6, 1942

A medical officer in the 141st Infantry is a Seventh Day Adventist. He says that he is not a conscientious objector. However, he refuses to do any duty on Saturday that he himself decides is contrary to his religious scruples.

Two weeks ago he refused to do any duty on Saturday. His commanding officer was deemed by him to be incapable of deciding what duty he should perform. He refused to make a physical examination of a patient. Charges for refusing to obey orders were preferred by his commanding officer.

The medical· officer says that the War Department accepted his oath of office with the provision that his duty would not interfere with his religious practices. I am writing to the War Department to verify his statements. If his statement that his oath of office was accepted by the War Department with a personal limitation is correct, I shall take steps to have him transferred out of the Division. Our loyalty to the United States of America comes first.

Tuesday, November 10, 1942

Fred Jr. arrived from Metuchen on the 8th, and we had the first family assembly we·have had in years. Julia had been saving a bottle of champagne for this occasion, but when we opened it, it had turned to vinegar; too sour to drink.

The three Walkers have come into the Service from three different sources. I came directly into the Army from civil life after a mental and physical examination during my senior year at Ohio State University, from which I graduated as of the class of 1911, with the degree of Engineer of Mines. I must have transmitted my enthusiasm for army life to my two sons because both have sought a military career. As soon as he was old enough Fred Jr. entered the United States Military Academy, graduating at the age of 21, class of 1936. Charles graduated from Knox College in June, 1942, with the degree of Bachelor of Arts, and came into the Army as a Reserve Officer, directly from the Reserve Officers Training Corps.

Fred is now in the Division as a Major in the 143rd Infantry and Charles is a Lieutenant in the 141st Infantry. They know that they are going to have to work harder than someone else to get the same credit, since they are my sons. This probably should not be so, but it is. They want to be here, and I want them here. There will be some who will cry "nepotism." I would be a poor father, indeed, if I denied them assignment to this Division merely because they are my sons. Both will do well.

The Allies have been successful in their invasion of Africa. Eisenhower, Clark and Doolittle have done a grand job. The only thing I do not like about the whole affair is that the 36th Division was dropped out of the show.

I have been informed that the 45th Division is moving from Camp Devens to the port of embarkation, and I presume that we will be on our way to the port in due time.

I have resumed the 5 mile hikes for members of the Division Staff to improve their physical condition. I march with them and set the pace.

We have just completed the specially organized school for personnel of the cannon companies. They now have the basic information to enable them to do their work. From here on they need plenty of practice to develop skill and speed.

Saturday, November 14, 1942

Last night was a very cold night; 18 degrees above zero. This is the coldest spell we have had to date. We are not going to get much effective training done during such cold and windy weather. We can go through the motions, but the men will not learn much. However, we are required by higher headquarters to carry out the training schedule, and it is well to avoid idleness.

We received many anti-tank rocket launchers this week; bazookas. The grenades which are launched by them have a range of 400 yards and are very effective against tanks. This improves our anti-tank defenses. Enemy tanks that come in contact with us are going to get hurt.

We have a 1st Sergeant Bull in the 141st Infantry who has been refused a commission as a 2nd lieutenant because he has calcium deposits on his lung. Otherwise he is well-qualified to be a lieutenant. I am taking his case up with the War Department to obtain special consideration for him, if possible. If he is physically able to serve as a 1st sergeant, it would seem that he is physically able to serve as a lieutenant.

The Seventh Day Adventist doctor, who chose to do such duty as he wished on Saturdays, cannot be used in this Division, and the War Department is transferring him elsewhere to non-combatant troops. This is exactly what he wants. Our other medical officers could just as logically choose to do such duty as they wish on Sundays, but they are made of sterner stuff.

Sunday, November 15, 1942

Wanted: A lieutenant colonel, who is intelligent and possessed of good judgement, who knows the details of operation of an infantry division, has a pleasing personality, and who views his duty impersonally. This officer must be one who will be firm in his demand for efficient performance of duty, and for high standards of discipline and honor. He must be loyal to me and to my way of doing things. He must be capable of proceeding toward objectives, guided by general policies only. He must have imagination, curiosity, mental initiative, a spirit of self-sacrifice, a proper sense of justice. I am looking for an officer to fill a possible vacancy of Chief of Staff.

Wednesday, November 18, 1942

Julia has rented a small house near the Coonamessett Club, 3 miles from Camp. It has a living room, one bedroom, a kitchen and a bathroom. It is quite modern, convenient and heated by oil. Because it is necessary to save fuel during the war, the thermostat is set at 65 degrees during the day and at 60 degrees at night.

I have been trying to find a way to get the officers of the Reconnaissance Troop promoted. They are cavalrymen and do not want to serve in Infantry units, but I have no positions for cavalrymen in the Division except in the Reconnaissance Troop. They may change their minds later and be willing to transfer to an infantry regiment where vacancies exist and where I can promote them.

Yesterday, during ranger training in the use of explosives, a corporal who was handling some dynamite was injured by a premature explosion. His hand had to be amputated. Two officers were hurt also but will recover. Men get careless, and when they do, accidents occur. This accident was due undoubtedly to careless handling of the explosive. I always feel especially sorry for the men who are killed or injured in these training accidents. Training for war, as well as war, is dangerous.

Thursday, November 19, 1942

Today I sent a request to the Commanding General, Army Ground Forces, for Lt Colonel Clayton P Kerr to be released from assignment as Inspector General of the Division in order that I may assign him as Chief of Staff. I also requested that Lt Colonel Harold L Reese, whom I know very well, be assigned to this Division as Inspector General. I will assign Colonel Forsythe to the 142nd Infantry to succeed the present commander, whom I am forced to recommend for reclassification because he does not have the knowledge nor ability to command an infantry regiment satisfactorily. He means well, works hard, but does not know how to get results. Personally, I like and respect him.

Friday, November 20, 1942

A soldier came to see me today and requested that he be transferred to a service command unit near his home so he can be near his aged father. Of course I sympathize with him. Thousands would like to do the same, but somebody has to do the fighting, and I will not approve his request.

I notice a great difference in the attitude of our people toward their obligation to defend their nation and toward the military service from what it was at the beginning of World War I. Men then considered it an honor to serve in the Army or Navy and to do their part as patriotic citizens. They did not (except for religious or political agitators) avoid hazardous duty.

Monday, November 23, 1942

Today I sent the following to each of the noncommissioned officers in the Division because I want them to know what I expect of them:

"It is not going to be long before this Division will be fighting with a clever and cold-blooded enemy. The success of this Division will be no greater than the efficiency of its noncommissioned officers. To them is entrusted the direct care and control of the men who do the fighting. If our noncommissioned officers do their full duty, this Division will be invincible.

"The following responsibilities and duties of noncommissioned officers are stated in general terms, but they are the foundation of battle efficiency. Study them, reflect upon them, and adopt them as your own:

"1. Set a proper example of soldierly conduct, attention to duty, military courtesy, bearing and appearance for those who serve under you and for those with whom you come in contact. Instruct those under you in these subjects and maintain a high standard by constantly checking and periodically inspecting your men. See to it that your men wear their uniforms and equipment correctly.

"2. See that all government property used by your personnel is, at all times, in perfect repair, properly safeguarded and ready for immediate use. Report lost or unserviceable equipment, and report the individual or individuals who are responsible for the loss or breakage if because of carelessness or neglect.

"3. Carry out, and see that those under you carry out, all orders and regulations, and promptly report violations of orders and regulations, which you cannot correct, to your immediate commander. This is not tale bearing; it is your obligation. Do not evade it.

"4. Use your initiative to cause personnel in your charge to maintain their health, in order that they may, at all times, be able to do their full duty as soldiers. See to it that areas occupied by you and your men are well policed and sanitary.

"5. Train your personnel to obey orders cheerfully under all circumstances. Cheerfulness during hardship and battle will insure teamwork and confidence in each other and will help get the job done well. Never fail to do everything you can to reduce the hardship of your men within the requirements of duty.

"6. Develop in your men a fighting spirit and teach them to realize that they are out to kill any enemy that gets in their way. Teach them to be clever, resourceful, fast and accurate in order to kill their enemy and avoid being killed themselves.

"7. Do not wait for someone to tell you to do these things; do them on your own initiative."

Tuesday, November 24, 1942

It has been raining for the past 48 hours and I have cancelled the Division track and field meet, and also the Division Review scheduled for today, the second anniversary of the induction of the

36th into Federal Service. The parade ground is a sea of mud and water.

The following is an address I intended to make to the officers and men of the Division at the review but will publish it to the Command instead:

"Two years ago on the 25th of November this Division was inducted into the service of the United States. These past two years have been a period of preparation for hardship and battle. Much has transpired. There have been many changes in personnel, many changes in equipment, and many changes in organization. You all realize, I am sure, that there has been much improvement in the battle efficiency of all units and all individuals. There is still much to be learned, much to be done.

"The next year of active service will test your ability as soldiers and will bring a crisis in our lives. Hardships and battle, for which we have been preparing, will be the rule. By November 25th, 1943 we will have fought a number of battles. Hundreds of us will have met with a soldier's death on the field of honor and will have passed on to join the immortal heroes of the armies of the past. A year from this anniversary, in some distant theater of operations, the men of this Division will again commemorate their induction into the federal service and will stand in silent reverence to honor their departed comrades.

"In view of the difficult job which lies ahead, it is important that you make of yourselves skilled soldiers, whose purpose is to kill your enemy wherever found. Some of you still think of yourselves as skilled only in your trade or vocation prior to entering the service. Forget your civilian trade or vocation. That is of secondary importance now.

"Develop within yourselves a strong heart and a strong soul. You will need these to withstand the strain and confusion of your first battle, where you will undergo great hardship; where you will find yourself in the midst of deafening, destructive shell fire; where you will pass over the dead bodies of your comrades. In spite of these incidents, you must go on killing every enemy soldier that gets in your way.

"By doing all that I have mentioned you will make your Division invincible; you will preserve the American way of life, and you will attain the objective for which you were inducted into the Federal Service."

General Dawley stopped in to see me yesterday. He said that we are now in A-2-A priority for supply of equipment. That means "at the top" so we should be able to get all our needed supplies soon.

Had a letter from Perque, now Major General Percy Clarkson. He has been selected to command the new 87th Division, soon to be filled to full strength. He says he is having trouble trying to get things done "with a bunch of slovenly, indifferent officers who sit on their fannies in the midst of dirty and disorderly conditions." I know how he feels. The fact is they do not know how to assume responsibility, have never had to, and it will take time for Perque to teach them how.

Friday, November 27, 1942

Julia, Charles and I had an excellent Thanksgiving dinner yesterday at the Division Headquarters mess. I attended the Thanksgiving services at the Chapel presided over by Chaplain MacCombie. In his prayer he asked God to give the President of the United States and the Division Commander the power and strength to do their full duty to those who serve under them. I hope that I may have that power and strength.

I visited several officers' schools today. In some classes the instruction was not well done. Some students had no texts. They can learn very little under such conditions. The younger instructors do not know how to use the English language. They hesitate for words, express their thoughts clumsily, repeat unnecessarily, place no emphasis, lack enthusiasm, and do not know even their subjects.

I don't understand why our public schools systems cannot turn out graduates who know how to analyze, how to think, how to manage, and how to talk intelligently. If there is one thing our nation needs, it is a renovated school system in which emphasis is put on application and practice of the theory that is taught from books. Generally speaking, our schools stop with theory; the application or practical phase is often slighted.

The President has issued a proclamation removing all limitations of punishment for soldiers who go absent without leave. Now they can be punished as a court martial may direct. This is an excellent step forward. Heretofore, the punishment for being absent without leave was fixed by regulation and was inadequate.

Men went AWOL because they were willing to pay the price of punishment. I look for a reduction in the number of these offenses, and soon.

I admire the officers and men of the French fleet who sank their ships and went down with them at Toulon today, to keep the Germans from getting the ships. The French people are in a terrible situation; their liberties are gone for they are under military government headed by a German Governor General.

CHAPTER SIX

Order, Counterorder, Disorder

Camp Edwards, Massachusetts
Sunday, November 29, 1942

We hear a great deal about the difficulty of preserving our democratic form of government. Many people feel that our government should not be revamped during wartime to give the President dictatorial powers, although this action establishes a more efficient and practical administration. Under the present conditions, where various pressure groups and self-seeking blocks are striving to procure every possible advantage for themselves, regardless of the effect upon others, there has to be somebody in authority who can override them and look after the welfare of the United States.

Just received a telephone call from General Dawley. He said the XIII Corps is being activated at Providence to replace the VI Corps after it departs for overseas. Major General Emil F Reinhardt, my junior, is being placed over me to command the new corps. Major General Charles Hall was recently passed over me to command the XI Corps at Chicago. I must not be doing so well in the eyes of those who choose corps commanders.

I wonder if we are ever going overseas.

Last night a great disaster, caused by fire and panic, occurred at the Cocoanut Grove night club in Boston. Four hundred and seventy-two are reported dead, and many others who were injured are expected to die. Two of my lieutenants were seriously burned and may die. Many of our people were in the place but kept their heads and were able to escape. I am told the fire was caused by a careless bus boy who allowed a lighted match to come in contact with the flimsy interior decorations. Again carelessness was a killer.

Tuesday, December 1, 1942

I visited the troops on the firing range today. It was quite cold, several degrees below freezing. The men and officers were out all day, firing. They were uncomfortably cold but they were doing passable work and were in a cheerful mood, which is evidence of a fine spirit.

I received a complimentary letter from Governor Coke Stevenson which contained Christmas Greetings to the Texans in the Division. I will publish it to the Command.

Dimout regulations for civilians as well as soldiers went into effect last night. All outside lights must be extinguished. Windows are to be covered by curtains, blinds or canvas. Automobiles must not travel more than 30 miles per hour. The upper half of all headlights must be painted over, and only low beams may be used.

Friday, December 4, 1942

I discovered that the various companies and batteries do not have the equipment which they are supposed to have, and which I thought they had. I find it necessary to institute a check by teams of officers detailed from Division Headquarters. Some company commanders do not have the necessary experience and knowledge to do the work that is expected of them. They have many responsibilities but do not manage well. They do not delegate them to their subordinates. But they will learn rapidly after we arrive in the theater of operations.

Sunday, December 6, 1942

I had the unpleasant duty of informing Colonel Tom Bay, Executive Officer, Division Artillery, why he is being transferred from the Division. While Hibbs and I were perfectly satisfied with Bay's work, Dawley was not. He felt that Bay was incapable of handling the Division Artillery should Hibbs become a casualty. Colonel Bay is an excellent officer and a fine gentleman. His heart and soul are wrapped up in the Division Artillery, and he is greatly disappointed. I don't think that Tom has been treated properly in this matter, and I regret that he is leaving the Division. He is going back to Eighth Corps Area in Texas. Dawley has assigned Lt Colonel Thomas J Shryock, a National Guard artilleryman on his staff, to fill Bay's vacancy.

Wednesday, December 9, 1942

Last Monday I sent John Forsythe to command the 142nd Infantry. I had a long talk with him and pointed out the necessity for getting the regiment on its feet, cheering up the officers and men, putting good officers in key positions, encouraging athletics and other forms of recreation, checking up on his supply arrangements, administration, discipline and training procedures.

Kerr has been released as the Division Inspector, and I have appointed him Chief of Staff. I intend to unload all administrative matters on to him and give my time to training activities.

Since he and I will work together, it is important that in addition to the official duties of his office as laid down in regulations, he know some of my own personal views. So, I have prepared a memorandum for his guidance which includes, but is not limited to, the following:

"Follow the regulations but vary prescribed procedure whenever better results may be obtained by so doing. Strive to reduce paper work, ritual, time consuming processes.

"Disciplinary action may be taken only by the Division Commander insofar as the Division staff is concerned.

"Recommendations of staff sections should be brought to the attention of the Division Commander in order that he may know what is going on in his command. This does not include trivia.

"Division Heaquarters exists solely for the purpose of serving the subordinate units, especially the enlisted men.

"Guard the rights and privileges of all personnel.

"Always grant requests of subordinate commanders. If you think they should be denied, bring them to the Division Commander, who alone should deny them.

"Be courteous and considerate of all regardless of rank, grade or position. Promote cheerfulness. No gossip. Express appreciation of work well performed. Do not 'bawl out' or reprimand anyone. Instruct and advise in a sympathetic manner.

"Do not deny nor discourage anyone who wishes to discuss his problems or troubles with the Division Commander.

"When a major decision has to be made and the Division Commander is not present, you make it. Consult the Assistant Division Commander in appropriate cases. Have good reasons for what you do.

"Make daily notations in 'Chief of Staff's Journal'."

Soon we are to undergo a number of tactical tests by the VI Corps which will require us to stay out overnight. Snow is on the ground and the temperature goes down to 16°. The tests should be written so that we will not have to stay out all night, since our troops are not equipped for winter campaigning. I discussed this matter with Dawley, but he is opposed to bringing the troops into their barracks at night. So we will have to be miserable for no real purpose.

Last night I attended the school for the officers and NCOs of the 636th Tank Destroyer Battalion. Afterwards I made a few remarks explaining why, in battle, the Tank Destroyer Battalion must be kept concealed, fast in getting started, skillful in getting into position and accurate in marksmanship. They were very attentive and applauded when I had finished. Applause under such circumstances is irregular, but it was spontaneous and they meant well.

We received eighteen new M-10 tank destroyer mounts today. Six more will come later. These are of the latest design. They carry a 3-inch gun with greater penetration than any previous anti-tank gun, and I am pleased to receive this new equipment.

Friday, December 11, 1942

Yesterday I conducted a command post exercise for the Division. About twelve staff officers arrived as observers from VI Corps Headquarters. They expected something spectacular, and were disappointed because I was emphasizing radio communications and use of the combat code. They ran all over the area looking for errors and they found some, of course. Most of their comments dealt with minor points of no real importance. Observers from higher headquarters are of no real help. They learn of unsatisfactory conditions for the first time whereas they have been known to me for weeks, but because of restrictions of one kind or another placed upon us by high headquarters or transfer of personnel, weather, equipment, shelter, terrain, or lack of qualified instructors, it is difficult to get desired results in all respects at one time. I know that, while we must strive for perfection constantly, we will never be perfect. My test developed weaknesses in proficiency of our communications personnel which I shall correct at once.

Saturday, December 12, 1942

The Special Services Officer requested that one of his assistants be let out of the guardhouse because he is an artist who is needed to help publish **The T-Patch**, the Division publication. He said he thought the man should receive special consideration. The man was tried for being drunk and disorderly in the streets of Falmouth and was sentenced to three months in the guardhouse. My reply was that artists, like everyone else, must obey the laws and regulations. He will remain in the guardhouse.

Sunday, December 20, 1942

Last Tuesday evening, Lt. Colonel Harold L. Reese, Inspector General's Department, reported for duty as Division Inspector. Hal was my battalion adjutant when I was in command of the 1st Battalion, 30th Infantry, during WWI, and was my assistant when I was Division Inspector, 3rd Division, after the war, with headquarters at Andernach on the Rhine. I am greatly pleased that he has joined the Division and that we will serve together again. He is going to have to adjust to his new surroundings and responsibilities. In the intervening years he has been a business executive and has been able to hand out work to others. Here he is on the receiving end and will have to get down to details and work hard to do his job well.

All last week staff officers from the VI Corps have been conducting tests of various units of the Division, tactical and physical. Last Wednesday the temperature dropped to 10° below zero. This sudden change in temperature, together with a 6 inch snowfall threw the Texas men completely off balance. Most of them had never seen so much snow or felt really cold weather before. To be confronted with a testing board, below zero weather, and 6 inches of snow was more than some could adjust to; hence they did not do so well on the tests.

Two companies of the 636th Tank Destroyer Battalion had 109 men disabled—frostbitten feet, fingers, faces, severe colds and fever.

Although Dawley intended to keep the men out overnight, after the first night I finally persuaded him to let them come into barracks at midnight. Keeping men out in subzero weather until they are disabled is a lot of foolishness and mismanagement, in my opinion.

I have exceeded my authority and directed that all men in the Division be supplied with high overshoes. It is perfectly silly to require our men to wade about in the snow and cold without overshoes. In the name of promoting the health of the command, I have ordered the overshoes supplied. Eight thousand additional pairs are needed for the infantrymen. We already have eight thousand pairs for the men in motorized units, artillery, engineers, and supply services. Some of my staff feel that I should conform to the tables of basic allowances which, after all, is somebody's guess at what is needed in the normal situation. This is not a normal situation.

Chaplain MacCombie is arranging a special Christmas entertainment for the children of the Division and Julia is helping him with some of the details. The officers donated funds for the presents. Last Christmas I would have bet money that this Division would not celebrate this Christmas in the United States.

Last Friday a sergeant of Company F, 141st Infantry, was very seriously injured by a shell fragment which pierced his skull. Another fragment broke his leg. I do not see how it is possible for him to get well. His company was on a combat firing problem and the 81mm mortar crew supporting his platoon fired a shell over the heads of the troops. It fell short of the target, however, and exploded near the sergeant.

I am told that the accident was caused by faulty ammunition. It is possible that the gun crew was careless and let the propelling charge get wet from the snow while waiting to fire. An investigation is being made.

I know of no situation in which the expression "a little learning is a dangerous thing" is more applicable than in the handling of explosives. I feel very sorry for the injured soldier, his relatives and friends.

Yesterday I saw two trains off for Boston and New York City, carrying men on weekend passes. Each train was made up of twelve crowded coaches. The men like to get away from camp whenever they have time off. Camp conditions here are far from comfortable.

Last Friday I heard a lecture by a Marine officer who had participated in the fight for Tulagi Island. His lecture was very interesting and I got a lot out of it. I wish every officer and man in the Division could have heard it.

He said that the Japanese do not surrender; hence almost no prisoners are taken by the Americans. He stated also that accurate rifle fire is absolutely necessary in fighting with the Japanese. Accurate rifle fire is absolutely necessary in fighting anybody.

Tuesday, December 29, 1942

Private First Class Pablo F. Bernal, Co. E, 141st Infantry, of Waco, Texas, presented to me an artistic Christmas greeting he had done in crowded barracks under very difficult conditions. It is a framed nativity scene painted on a piece of 12" x 14" light gray satin. He gave a lot of his time to making this Christmas gift and I greatly appreciate it.

Headquarters, VI Corps, relinquished command of the 36th Division at midnight, and we then come under command of the XIII Corps, Major General Emil F. Reinhardt, Commanding. I do not know Reinhardt well for I have never had the good fortune to serve in the same command with him. There are several things I want to talk to him about, especially some changes I want to make in our training program. I regret that Dawley is leaving. We understood each other.

We have several quiet officers in the Division who do their work well; so well that they do not attract attention. They don't boast about how good they are, so they are not in the limelight and are overlooked when promotions are in order. They must not be overlooked hereafter. It is difficult for me to acquire all the information I need when considering recommendations for promotion. As a result, I have made some mistakes which I have learned of later.

Wednesday, December 30, 1942

We have received notice to prepare an infantry regiment for movement overseas at an early date. Everything is in good shape so this will be an easy job. We checked the property last week and will check the individual clothing Monday. I selected Forsythe's regiment because he, being an experienced regular army officer, will know how to get things done after he is out of contact with the Division Staff and on his own.

If only all officers could be depended on to do their duty, it would be much easier for everybody. I have been trying to get the property accountability of the units corrected for more than a year. I have had their property checked at least five times and have prescribed in detail just how it should be done.

I have relied upon the regimental and battalion commanders to see that a proper check is made. But some of them don't do it. They will not do the tedious work of checking personally, but leave the details to junior officers or untrained noncommissioned officers. The result is that the work had to be done over and over. I am having another check made this week, using my own staff officers to do the inspecting and counting. I hope that at last we are going to get a proper accounting.

One officer is asking for relief from responsibility for the loss of one camouflage net and three pairs of shoulder pads! The investigating officer found that the articles were never really lost, but are still in the company storeroom. This officer will be penalized under the provisions of the 104th Article of War, as has been done in the case of others who have been careless and indifferent.

Some battalion commanders do not realize that they must actually be present and supervise the work of their company commanders.

A battalion commander illegally confined one of his men in the stockade for seven days during the Christmas Holidays. This is just plain damn indifference to the rights of enlisted men. I'll speak to the battalion commander, and I don't think he will imprison an enlisted man illegally again. He was just too damn lazy to check the sentence with the table of maximum authorized punishments or use his common sense. I hope that officers who are careless in administrative matters will be good fighters when we get into combat.

All these troubles are the result of our lax methods in training the National Guard in times of peace.

Friday, January 1, 1943

I was in an ill humor when I made the previous entry. The National Guard is composed of patriotic people who give up a great deal of their spare time and personal convenience to serve in it. If some of my officers are not perfect, it is not because they have served in the National Guard. Really, no combat division, be it regular army, national guard, or reserve, has any better personnel than the 36th. I doubt if any division has as good. I have served in six regular army divisions and I should know.

This morning at 11 o'clock Julia and I received the officers and wives of the Division Staff and subordinate units at the Officers' Club at Camp Edwards. About 130 persons attended. We served eggnog, small cakes and nuts. An orchestra from the Artillery Band played during the reception. The nog must have been very good for out of 17 gallons Julia made only one third of a gallon was left. The sale of whipping cream being prohibited by law because of rationing, Julia used ordinary cream and added a few drops of glycerine to make it whip easily.

At the reception Julia wore the beautiful orchid Clayton and

Clara Kerr sent her.

Saturday, January 2, 1943

I sent Chaplain MacCombie to Providence today to confer with the Chaplain, XIII Corps, in order to resolve some of our chaplains' problems.

Again the War Department robs me of my best men! This morning I had to send to an overseas destination 2 officers and 33 enlisted men from our Ranger personnel. I trained them for use within the Division. Yet I am glad to have qualified officers and enlisted men for this assignment. I still have many Rangers left and shall develop more. However, I don't like to have them taken away. Now, 40% of the Division personnel are replacements from all the States.

There was a good attendance at the Division hop this evening and I was pleased to note the happiness and enthusiasm that prevailed. The morale of this Division is excellent—none better.

The check of the property is completed. There are still some property accounts that do not balance. Kerr has explained to me that the property methods prescribed for National Guard troops while under State control are quite different from those prescribed for the Regular Army. When the 36th Division was inducted, it had to switch from one accounting system to another overnight. Personnel were untrained for this change. Training manuals were not available. The War Department had not foreseen nor provided for the great quantities of manuals and blank forms that would be needed. Company commanders were transferred willy-nilly without regard to their property responsibility. Successors were careless and negligent. Vouchers for unserviceable, lost, damaged, and stolen property which were credits to the company commanders' accounts were processed at a snail's pace. Some were lost or forgotten. Others that should have been processed were never prepared and submitted. Accounting officers of the Regular Army Supply Services were transferred, too, their places taken by inexperienced personnel who became swamped by floods of vouchers. Without adequate help the mass of papers increased from day to day. To the young, inexperienced company commander and supply sergeant of the National Guard, this sudden switch to the Regular Army way of doing things, without having received any previous instruction, was confusing, complicated, impracticable and more than they could handle along with their other demanding duties. It was one great big mess, and we are still suffering from its backlash.

One of my chaplains has been doing as he pleases. He has failed to obey instructions regarding his duties, has been absent without leave and has deliberately disobeyed orders that he be present at certain scheduled classes of instruction. When brought before the Chief of Staff to explain his deficiencies, he broke down, cried, and declared he was being persecuted. His only trouble is that he wants to do as he pleases. This cannot be permitted. He was told to stop disregarding orders, quit being a cry baby, and start being an army chaplain. I will observe his conduct and hope for improvement.

Tuesday, January 12, 1943

I learned that two soldiers of the 36th from Sweetwater, Texas, had a big time in a Boston hotel recently. The hotel manager tells me that they registered for a room and then proceeded to have a little war of their own. They burned a good woolen blanket and defaced a door with a piece of glass or other instrument. From the condition of the room he believed they both must have black eyes. He wants $15.00. He'll get it.

Saturday, January 16, 1943

Last week a businessman from New York, accompanied by a lawyer, called on me to get his son transferred out of the Division. His son is a graduate of the University of New York and is now an assistant gunner in one of the companies of the Tank Destroyer Battalion.

They want him transferred to Fort Jay so he will be close to his home. There he is to render a great service as a soldier and help win the war by practicing rodent extermination, his civilian occupation. I told his Dad we needed men to exterminate Germans and Japanese. The father has no patriotism. He is just a plain selfish man trying to put his son's obligation off onto someone else.

I sent for the son and after talking to him decided he would make a good soldier, if his father would leave him alone. The boy told me that a few years ago he killed a child while backing an automobile out of a garage and that he did not like being a member of a gun crew which would deal out more death. I had him transferred to the office of the Division Sanitation Inspector where he can practice extermination of bedbugs, roaches, flies, mosquitoes, and even mice and rats within the area and installation of the Division.

The next day a mother from Philadelphia called on me. She wants her son home near her so she can take proper care of his health, which, she says, the Army is neglecting. Think of it! His company commander makes him go on long marches and makes him carry 50 or 60 pounds on his back while his feet are all broken down; he is lame and suffers pain. The Army is so cruel to him. She can't understand why we are so cruel.

I wanted to tell her to leave my office, but I made a mistake and remained calm. She said she would buy me a dinner if I would come to Hyannis where she is staying.

She asked me three times to promise I would let her son transfer to Schuylkill Arsenal near her home. Each time I told her very postively, but politely, that I would not transfer him, if he is physically fit.

Later I had the boy examined by a medical officer who reported him physically sound. Then I sent for the boy. After talking to him, I decided he is a quitter, weakling and coward, and will be of no help to the Division. As much as I hate to see such people get out of fighting, I, nevertheless, need good soldiers who have courage and are men. So I transferred the boy to the 1114th Service Unit at Camp Edwards.

I learned today that he is going to Alaska to work on the Alcan Highway. Good riddance. They may make something out of him. At least he is not going home to mother.

Last Tuesday General Reinhardt came down from Providence to witness the artillery fire over the heads of the infantry. I had the artillery fire so the shells would burst about 400 yards in front of the advancing men, in order to get them used to the sound of the shells and the explosions near them. I feel they were greatly reassured by the exercise.

Both the artillery and infantry are undergoing battle practice exercises. The men are required to crawl from one trench to another, about 75 yards apart, while blocks of TNT are exploded near them, and two machine guns shoot over them constantly. The trajectory of the bullets is only 4 feet above ground.

This gives the men a fair idea of battle conditions and puts them under real strain. After the exercise they have the feeling of having accomplished something valuable and different from the usual training routine.

I am going to arrange an exercise in which a whole battalion will attack over unfamiliar ground and fire all its weapons to support the advance.

Yesterday I arranged and conducted a Division exercise to stress radio communication and our standing operating procedure for establishing command posts. There was some improvement since the last exercise, but not enough. Many vehicles were poorly concealed and often were parked too close together. Some of the radio operators need more practice. They must acquire much greater skill and speed in encoding, decoding and transmitting messages, and especially improve their traffic discipline to keep the enemy from picking up information.

Last night Julia and I attended a basketball game at the Arena between the 142nd and 143rd Infantry Regiments. The personnel of both regiments turned out in force. The regimental commanders were there with their bands to cheer their men. It was a very inspiring crowd for the players. The 142nd team won and I presented a trophy to the team captain.

Sunday, January 17, 1943

Our departure for a theater of operations has been postponed again for the fifth time. This is disappointing and will lower morale. I wish the War Department would make up its mind.

I understand that this postponement is because there are many thousands of French troops in Africa which can be used instead of American troops, providing they are equipped with suitable weapons and supplies. Ship space is, therefore, being taken up with supplies for the French and our own infantry divisions are being placed farther down on the priority list.

This is the situation today. It may be different tomorrow.

Monday, January 18, 1943

It rained all day. I went out to the target range this afternoon and found two infantry companies and a battery of artillery trying to conduct range practice in the cold rain. The men had been out since morning, were wet and cold, and had no interest in their work. I sent them back to barracks.

I picked up one soldier who was especially wet and cold and took him back to camp in my auto. He did not want me to show him special preference in front of his buddies, and apologized for getting my automobile dirty with his muddy boots. This is a fine spirit from a man who was obviously suffering from exposure. There are many thousands in the Division who have a similar spirit, thank God!

I sent letters to the War Department recommending Louis Hibbs for promotion to major general. Recently a number of officers have been promoted over him for no good reason.

I broke the news to John Forsythe that the 142nd Infantry probably will not leave for overseas very soon. He was greatly disappointed and said that the morale of his men will go down, but only temporarily. That's normal.

Last Tuesday during dinner at the officers' mess Lt. Colonel Miller Ainsworth presented a certificate from Governor Stevenson, declaring me a "citizen of Texas." All drank a toast in wine to my good health and bright future as a Texan. The Lone Star Flag of Texas hung on the wall behind us. Miller had arranged for all the staff and unit commanders as well as Julia and Clara Kerr to be present. The orchestra played "The Eyes of Texas Are Upon You" and "Deep in the Heart of Texas."

Miller also gave me a typical Texas Stetson hat as an additional emblem of citizenship and then had several photos taken of me wearing it.

We all felt that I was properly initiated into the brotherhood of Texas citizenship, but I will have to learn to wear the Stetson.

I can now brag on the size of Texas, the grace and beauty of its women, the magnificence of its scenery, the virility of its men, the superiority of its soldiers, and the best Division in the Army. I greatly appreciate and shall keep the Governor's certificate and the Stetson hat as most cherished souvenirs of my service as commander of the 36th Division.

I received six copies of a resolution, passed by the Senate of Texas, congratulating me on being named a citizen of Texas. This week's issue of **The T-Patch** carried a pen and ink sketch of me wearing the Stetson. The artist, Private Jack Burnett, did an excellent job.

Julia has been trying to find a house for Fred Jr., Florian and the children, when they return from Leavenworth next week.

There are very few available. Those that are, either will not allow children, are heated with oil which is rationed, or are not on a bus line. With restrictions on the use of gasoline and rubber it is important that one live on or near a bus line.

All careless officers are not in the 36th Division. Some staff officers in the War Department must be crazy. Last month we received orders to turn in our khaki clothing to the Post Quartermaster. We completed the job yesterday. Today we received orders from the same source to provide every man in the Division with khaki clothing. This little deal will cost the taxpayers some money. Maybe we can win the war anyway.

I have issued a number of certificates to lieutenants who have completed certain courses of study: motor maintenance, military law, mess management, supply, and company administration. We are working constantly to improve the proficiency of our personnel.

Wednesday, January 27, 1943

I have awarded the Soldier's Medal together with an appropriate citation to Sergeants Howard I. Fore and George W. Coston, both of the 142nd Infantry. They threw themselves in front of a truck in order to push a child from the path of the vehicle. The truck stopped just before it would have crushed the two men. Fore is now attending Officers Candidate School and will receive his medal at Fort Benning.

I granted these awards, the first that I have issued, not only because Fore and Coston deserve them, but also because I want the men in the Division to know that outstanding deeds will be recognized and rewarded.

One of the men of the 141st Infantry, who was crawling under machine gun fire on the battle practice course, got a tracer bullet through his pack. The pack caught fire but the man threw it off and finished the course. I've had the trajectory raised 6 inches.

The court martial proceedings of a soldier tried for desertion have come to me for review. The court sentenced him to confinement for life. There were no extenuating circumstances. Since we are not in a combat zone, I reduced the sentence to ten years. Ten years is a long time to spend in a penitentiary. After the war Congress will probably release all prisoners confined for purely military offenses, so he will serve only a part of the ten years. The war will not last that long and he should still be alive when it is over. Some of his comrades will not be.

I sent nine prisoners to Fort Devens today. All of them have more than three months confinement to serve and are of the type that will not conform to good order and military discipline. They are being transferred out of the Division.

General Lange likes to talk. He came to my office today, did almost all of the talking and never hesitated for words or thought. Anyone who can do this is bright and intelligent. We had a good visit for an hour and a half.

Tuesday, February 2, 1943

Recently I reduced the sentence of a private from life imprisonment to ten years. Yesterday his wife, accompained by Chaplain MacCombie, called at my office to plead for leniency. She seemed to be a very intelligent woman and insisted that it was her fault he deserted and that she had not tried to persuade him to return. I felt sorry for her and for him. I told her that there would be no change in the sentence now, but if her husband is a good prisoner and convinces me that he means to make a good soldier of himself, I shall be glad to review his case after he has served six months with a view of restoring him to duty. I explained that he would not have it easy as a prisoner and that it would be hard for him to prove his worth.

I have the impression that the Chaplain thinks I am rather heartless. I know she does.

This afternoon half of the staff went out to the range for practice in firing the pistol and Thompson sub-machinegun. One can shoot a Tommy gun without aiming. You hold the stock at your belly, point the gun, pull the trigger and correct your hold by watching the strike of the bullets. A crouching position is more stable than standing. The gun is accurate.

Friday, February 5, 1943

Our military police arrested four soldiers who were stealing food from company kitchens where they were on duty. This is too bad because all of them are married and some have children. They may be reduced to the grade of private and their families may suffer from loss of pay.

Another soldier was arrested while trying to sneak ten quarts of liquor into camp. He was from a company quarantined in barracks for a few days and where, according to reports, the NCOs permitted drinking. I suspect that the soldier intended to sell the liquor to other soldiers at a profit, but he said he was taking it home for a party he was giving for his friends. Some party! He will be tried by special court martial.

During the past week the Division Artillery was tested on going into position and firing at a target, both by day and by night. They did not do very well. One section chief did not look through the tube before firing: result, the muzzle of the howitzer burst because a large wad of waste was left in the tube.

In another battery a section chief was too lazy to get off his truck and lead it into position: result, one of the 155mm howitzers turned over when it struck a large boulder.

Another truck, towing a gun, ran into a large boulder and broke the front axle because the lazy section chief would not get off his seat and lead the way.

When noncommissioned officers will not do their work, defeat of the enemy is doubtful. Commissioned officers cannot do it for them. To arouse their determination to do their best I made a talk to the artillery officers and section chiefs. I doubt if I was successful for they sat and stared at me with disinterested faces, indicating that my talk was just another inconvenience to be endured and forgotten. It is no easy chore to have to make soldiers out of careless and disinterested young men.

Wednesday, February 10, 1943

I have received a **confidential** letter from the War Department stating that absenteeism has become a serious problem. The letter points out that punishment for deserters and absentees, as presently prescribed, only plays into their hands, since most of them want a long term of imprisonment so they will be removed from combat duty. The new War Department policy is that deserters and absentees are to be sent to their units in the combat zone when apprehended and not be allowed to escape combat duty.

This sounds good on the surface, but I wonder if the General Staff really thinks that these shirkers, physical cowards, men with no sense of duty, are going to stick with their units in battle. If they do think so, they have no proper concept of battlefield conditions.

Shirkers have no intention of fighting, no intention of entering the area of small weapons fire and hand-to-hand combat. They will sneak away from their unit at night, or lie concealed in woods or brush until their unit passes beyond them.

Then they will "beat it" for the rear, looking for a kitchen with kindly cooks who will feed them after hearing their imaginary tales of heroism and achievements at the front. They will always say, if asked, that they got lost from their unit and have been doing their best to find it. In this they are always safe because nobody in the rear area knows exactly where a certain company or battalion is located during battle.

When and if directed to a locality where his company may be found, the straggler appears thankful and moves off in the indicated direction until out of sight. Then he moves in a wide circle back to another part of the rear area and to another benevolent cook and kitchen.

These are facts that I know from personal experience, having had to deal with stragglers in WWI. I'm not disturbed by the fact that the War Department General Staff doesn't understand battle conditions. But what depths of decadence have we reached when the War Department is afraid to discuss the serious problem of desertion openly? Why must this condition be concealed from the public? Why must an impractical solution to a problem be circulated among commanders, who know better, under cover of "CONFIDENTIAL."

The War Department letter even implies that commanders are at fault if their men desert; as if commanders can remove danger, hardship, dirt, and filth from war. The Articles of War state that deserters, in time of war, will suffer death or such other punishment as a court martial shall direct. Leave it at that.

Hannibal, Napoleon, Wellington, Washington, Scott, Grant, Lee, and Jackson, all took deserters out and shot them, except that Hannibal used no gun powder. A scimitar or rope did the job as well. By doing so, commanders removed those who spread the disease of desertion throughout their armies and provided a deterrent for any who toyed with the idea of running away.

We temporized with deserters in the last war. As a result, absenteeism in this war is rampant. The apprehension and sending of deserters to the combat zone will not solve the problem. When the authorities were lenient on desertion in the last war, hardboiled officers and noncoms took matters in their own hands and used their own methods. There were even ugly rumors that men were shot when trying to run away from battle.

A soldier who crawls through mud, shellfire, and hail of bullets for many hours, does not have a normal outlook. He may feel no hesitation in shooting one who runs away, when that one is physically able to do his job and assist his comrades.

This may seem cruel and inhuman to persons who do not know what it is to be a soldier in combat, constantly exposed to danger and resigned to death. To be deserted by a despicable member of the fighting team, who refuses to help when he is needed most, sometimes arouses a hatred that knows not reason.

A soldier of the artillery was badly injured while placing a charge of dynamite on a battle practice course. He lost one hand and both eyes and is expected to die. The charge was to have been exploded electrically. I feel that someone was careless, closed the circuit prematurely and caused the tragedy. Careless men can cause untold damage and destruction.

Thursday, February 11, 1943

I observed the 111th Medical Battalion in a terrain exercise and was well-pleased with their work and spirit.

General Hibbs, back from detached service at the Port of Embarkation of New York, has given me some detailed information regarding the disposition of our troops in Tunisia. From his statements I have formed the opinion that Rommel is regassing, refitting, and getting ready to take the offensive. Fredendall's front opposite Rommel is very thin. If Rommel drives at him, there will be little resistance.

Wednesday, February 17, 1943

Last week the War Department notified me that the 36th Division will not be needed in Africa before May. Today I was notified that the Division will move to Camp A. P. Hill, in Virginia, as soon as practicable, for special training and will not return to Camp Edwards.

I understand that there is nothing at Camp Hill in the way of shelter, warehouses, running water, electricity, bathing facilities, or toilets. To put troops there in the middle of winter without adequate shelter and sanitary arrangements can be expected from an inexperienced staff that does not realize the hardship they inflict on the troops. We can live there, of course, but while we are in the United States we would like to have the same conveniences as other troops.

However, this is about the sixth warning order we have received, so nobody is especially disturbed. We may never move from here.

Camp A. P. Hill, Virginia
Friday, February 26, 1943

On the 19th I received orders to move the entire Division, with the 636th Tank Destroyer Battalion attached, to Camp A. P. Hill, Virginia, by rail, without delay. To make the problem even more difficult, the 142nd Combat Team was ordered to Lowesville, Virginia, for mountain training. At Lowesville there are no Army facilities, so tents, stoves, gasoline, oil, coal, straw for beds, rations for 6,000 men had to be sent there from the Richmond Depot. Also, medical, telephone, mail and censorship arrangements had to be made for the arrival of the troops.

Naturally I was quite busy with the coordination of movements and supplies. I decided that I would set up advance Headquarters at Camp Hill, taking part of the staff and leaving Lange in command at Camp Edwards until all the troops departed—about 30 train loads. I sent Major Nichols and Captain Bob Travis to Lowesville to get things ready to receive the 142nd Combat Team.

On Sunday morning, the 21st, Julia, Carl Phinney, Sergeant Clay, Corporals Bell and Jeter, Privates Bay and Smith, and I left for Camp Hill. We had three government and three privately owned automobiles.

We stopped Sunday night at a hotel in Trenton and arrived in Fredericksburg Monday afternoon. There we stopped at a motel which had such comfortable, clean rooms and such reasonable prices that I engaged a room for Julia for the duration of our stay at Camp Hill. I also arranged with the management to hold vacant rooms for the families of the officers who will shortly follow. We practically took over the place, and those who were fortunate enough to get rooms were well-pleased.

Tuesday I drove to Hill and conferred with the commanding officer about setting up facilities for the troops, while my staff looked about for a good place to set up Advance Headquarters.

On Wednesday I set up an office at Hill in the corner of a small and chilly storeroom, and took charge of the reception arrangements for the troops that will arrive here and at Lowesville. I went to Lynchburg to meet General O. S. Rolfe, his instructors, and Travis. Rolfe will be the director of the special mountain training we are to receive. He explained his plan for the training at Lowesville, which caused me to change my training plans for the troops at Hill. In fact, several units, when they arrive at Hill, will have to start for Lowesville by motor as soon as they get off the trains. This is poor staff work on the part of the higher echelons. The last ten trains should have been sent to Lowesville instead of Hill, which would have saved a lot of gasoline and rubber.

Apparently the War Department expects to use this Division in mountainous terrain—maybe Sicily, Sardinia, Corsica, or even Norway. Since we are to receive khaki clothing, I don't think it's Norway.

Thursday I drove over to Lowesville and found Forsythe's troops going into camp in an orderly manner. Nichols and Travis had handled their jobs in an excellent manner with only three enlisted men to help them, except that I had authorized them to hire civilian labor to unload the supplies. When the first train of the 142nd Combat Team arrived, all needed supplies were on hand for them.

Today I received word from the Richmond Depot that General Marshall has informed them that all shoes for the 36th must have composition soles. This sounds like we are being prepared for operations in a mountainous area, sure enough. Leather-soled shoes have a greater tendency to slip on rocks.

Twenty-four self-propelled mounts for 105mm guns have been shipped here, Camp Hill. These are to be used at Lowesville and should have been shipped there.

This movement and training job for the 36th was poorly co-ordinated by the inexperienced staff of the XIII Corps. By attending to our business instead of their own, they made things difficult. They meant well and tried to help, but they would have been of greater assistance if they had given us a mission and told us where to obtain supplies and send the sick. As it was, they gave some orders which were in opposition to mine, and, of course, confusion resulted.

As an example, G-4, XIII Corps, ordered the K-rations intended for the 142nd CT shipped from Piney River—the railhead for Lowesville—to Camp Hill after the rations had already arrived at Piney River, where they belonged. Luckily I received a copy of this order in time to cancel it.

The Corps staff officers lack knowledge, experience and training, all of which indicates that they have been selected for their present assignments from sources other than combat troops. This is an unsatisfactory way to recruit staff officers who are expected to visualize the capacity, equipment, and needs of combat troops.

But they have to learn their business and they may as well experiment on us as any other outfit.

I note that the Boeing plant in Seattle has been closed down. The workers have quit until their demands for higher wages are granted. This is disgusting to any soldier. He goes out and does the dirty work of fighting and dying to perpetuate such unpatriotic procedures. He is tempted to ask why the government tolerates delay in delivery of equipment needed on the battlefield.

Sunday, February 28, 1943

Last night at about 10 o'clock I received a telephone message from an officer in the War Department that the movement of the remaining elements of the 36th Division from Camp Edwards to Camp Hill is suspended until further orders; these to be issued in a few days! At first I thought someone was playing a joke on me and I refused to accept the order, but I was convinced after further conversation. At almost the same time my Chief of Staff called me from Edwards and conveyed the same information in double talk in an effort to maintain security.

Lange, at Edwards, was ordered to unload the troop trains that were ready to depart for Camp Hill. It is fortunate that these troops were not enroute. At least we will have troops at only two places—Edwards and Lowesville. It would have been worse if we had had troops at Edwards, Hill, and Lowesville, all at one time.

This change in orders by the War Department makes things difficult. Officers and men, returning from leave and furlough, from hospitals and schools, are now enroute to Hill. The same is true of weapons, vehicles and supplies, which are on their way from various depots to fulfill our requirements.

Many families have already arrived at Fredericksburg and Bowling Green. They have leased houses, and paid the rent for the first month. The cost of this needless journey will be hard to bear for lieutenants and enlisted men. Almost all families have given up their houses in the vicinity of Camp Edwards. Undoubtedly these have been rented by this time by families of other units there, because living space is in great demand. If we are to return to Edwards, the families may not be able to find a place to live. Everyone is disturbed.

I want to get back to my permanent headquarters at Edwards and find out what's going to happen to us. But I will have to leave a small staff at Hill for a few days to arrange for Camp Headquarters to take over and unsnarl the mail, equipment, weapons and supply mess.

My own view is the War Department has stopped this movement because it intends to put us on a convoy out of New York earlier than contemplated.

We don't expect efficient staff work nor thorough long range planning from the echelons above us. They are inexperienced and do not seem to have a clear concept of what they are trying to accomplish.

This is bad for discipline and morale. But it can't be helped. When an army is expanding as rapidly as ours is, inexperienced officers have to be employed in jobs quite new to them. They learn by making mistakes. But they don't deceive the troops.

Since I can only assume that the training program for the 142nd CT is to go on as planned, I discussed with Forsythe the necessity for providing suitable clothing for his men when they remain out overnight on top of the mountains. He will try various methods of carrying clothing which they need to keep them dry and warm: overcoat, raincoat, shelterhalf. I arranged for 24,000 pellets for sterilizing water in canteens to be issued to them. These will make it safe for men to fill their canteens from mountain streams and simplify the water supply problem. Since the troops will have to carry the K-ration, I suggested that he arrange for each company to carry along a few No. 10 empty tin cans for heating water for coffee and soup. I am concerned about their comfort while operating in the mountains at this season of the year, when we may expect snow and freezing temperature, and where supply is difficult because of poor roads—or none at all.

Monday, March 1, 1943

I visited the 142nd Combat Team at Lowesville accompanied by Chaplain MacCombie. While there I talked to General Rolfe at some length. He went over his program for special training which I approved. He also explained what the new field uniform is like. It is loose fitting with many big pockets, green to blend with the landscape and made of cotton cloth somewhat similar to denim. It is a work uniform, not dress. From his description, I believe it will be more practical than our present one.

Today I learned from the railroad employees at Piney River that the War Department is sending 60 flat cars there for loading vehicles of troops. This is the first indication I have received that we are going to load out for yet another destination.

Since we must be going to move, I obtained authority from the Army Ground Forces to leave the vehicles on the five trains which will arrive at Lowesville today, regardless of demurrage charges. They would not have granted my request if we were going to be here more than a few days. This will greatly expedite loading out, and receiving and disposing of all camp property now being used by the troops.

We should not have to do this, but the inexperienced officers at Camp Hill and at the Third Service Command Headquarters are so unfamiliar with their duties and so lacking in initiative that we will have to do their work for them for our own protection.

Phinney tells me that the Army Ground Forces want our quarters at Edwards released because they say our units will not return there. I called Lange and told him to sit tight until I can get there.

Several families of enlisted men are in Fredericksburg, stranded and confused as to what to do. I wish I could give them some help, but the War Department keeps me in complete ignorance of our next move. It is difficult to plan when one does not know what to plan for.

Camp Edwards, Massachusetts
Tuesday, March 2, 1943

Julia and I drove from Camp Hill to Washington this morning, and I stopped at the War Department to inquire about the status of the 36th Division.

All of the officers I talked to seemed very ignorant of what was going to happen next to the 36th. But General Tom Handy told me that they had stopped the movement to Virginia because they thought they might have some additional troop ships available, and if so, they intend to send us overseas.

What I saw in Washington did not make a favorable impression. Some officers of high rank occupy large private offices with thick carpets on the floor and with only a single desk. If I had that space, I'd put at least ten staff officers in it. And they're building additional office space!

Many of the officers who are making decisions in spacious offices in the new Pentagon are inexperienced in their jobs and lack the viewpoint of the troops. If I had my way, no officer would serve on the War Department General Staff until he had served on the staff of a division or lower tactical unit. I suppose this is impractical at the moment when the Army is expanding so fast, but if it were adopted as a policy, the troops would be better cared for.

We have been harassed by turning in and later re-drawing similar property, receiving and then having to get rid of unqualified replacement recruits, conforming to vexatious training programs, and by having to adjust our methods and procedures to meet change after change in regulations—many of which seem to serve no real purpose, from the viewpoint of the troops.

I found one officer in the Pentagon who was disgusted. He is a personal friend, a Major General in a very responsible position. He said he expects to be kicked out of Washington any day because of his outspoken, adverse comments about the continual changes being made in supply needs by Eisenhower's staff. He said he cannot plan supply arrangements for the troops in Africa because Eisenhower can't make up his mind what he wants and when he wants it.

Maybe, after all, our troubles really originate within the staffs overseas, composed of officers who can't create a workable plan and stick to it.

A good commander can estimate the capabilities of his own troops and those of his enemy and schedule his needs accordingly. A theatre commander should be thinking at least six months in the future.

I went from the Pentagon to Headquarters Army Ground Forces seeking information and help but without success. My conferences there were discouraging and unsuccessful so I boarded a government plane for Edwards, arriving at Otis Field at 3:30 this afternoon. Brigadier General Miles Cowles, my new Commander of the Artillery Brigade, accompanied me.

Things are not much clearer here. We have, however, been told that we are to prepare for embarkation on short notice; when and where, I don't know. My guess is we will leave from New York and go to Africa, since khaki clothing is on the way for issue to us.

Wednesday, March 3, 1943

I have had an amusing and informative talk with Lange and Kerr about our recent run-around. They tell me that two-thirds of the Division was still at Edwards when the movement was cancelled, much of it loaded on trains, all set to depart. Because it had taken several days to assemble the required railroad rolling stock (greatly needed elsewhere) the first troop train could not depart before 11:00 PM on February 27th. Trains were to leave at frequent intervals thereafter. In preparation for the movement, the troops turned in their station property to the camp authorities, packed and loaded their own equipment on their trains, vacated their barracks, marched to the loading area and went aboard.

Lange was at his home, just off the post, prepared to depart next morning by automobile for Hill. Kerr and Sergeant Neutts, my stenographer, were sitting in the bare office at Division Headquarters with one small folding desk, two folding chairs and two telephones, one to the camp switchboard and the other a scrambler phone to Corps Headquarters at Providence. Kerr's job was to collect the camp clearances reports from all units and then board the first train to depart. A call came in on the commercial phone at about 10:00 PM. The caller stated that he was the duty officer at Army Ground Forces Headquarters and wanted to know the location of the 36th Division. This statement was a gross violation of security regulations. Kerr told him that if he were the person he said he was, he already knew the answer to his question, and furthermore, he would not discuss such matters over the commercial telephone. The caller hung up after a sputter and many threats of punishment that would be forthcoming from General McNair.

Kerr then traced the call and found that it really had come from Army Ground Forces. A few minutes later the same person called again and insisted that he be told the location of the 36th Division. Kerr told him he would not give out any such information on the commercial line and that he could get it from Corps Headquarters. The caller continued to insist, lecturing and threatening as he went. Kerr stood his ground and finally hung up the phone and left him talking to himself. About ten minutes later the Corps Commander called Kerr over the scrambled phone, properly identified himself, and directed that the movement from Edwards be cancelled at once, that the troops return to their former barracks, that the trains be unloaded forthwith and the rolling stock be released.

Kerr then called Lange and told him to come to Division Headquarters at once. When Lange asked why, Kerr, quite properly, would not tell him on the commercial phone. Lange insisted but got nowhere. He then said to Kerr, in so many words, "I have always thought you were crazy and this confirms it."

Kerr then got in touch with me in Virginia, then sent for and informed the Camp Commander, who was quite upset because other troops were already on their way to Edwards to take over our barracks and facilities. However, he cooperated fully, returned our former barracks and reissued the property that we had turned in the day before. The troops pitched in, unloaded their equipment and the vehicles from flat cars. Within a couple of days, by the time I arrived, the place was back to normal.

Thus ended a run-around that cost the tax payers hundreds of thousands of dollars. I can imagine the choice comments the enlisted men have made about all this. They probably think that their Division Commander has gone crazy and is guilty of all sorts of damn fool things, and you can't blame them. Eventually, however, they may know how it all came about.

Thursday, March 4, 1943

Today I flew to New York with General Reinhardt to see Major General Homer Groninger, Commander of the Port of Embarkation, for the purpose of making ourselves familiar with the procedure for passing the 36th Division through the port. We obtained no new information and it was a needless trip, but Reinhardt said it would be helpful, so I went. I was pleased to meet my very good personal friend Groninger, whom I had not seen for years. We served together with Pershing in Mexico in 1916.

I selected an area for a battalion of infantry to conduct a combat firing problem. Its purpose was to develop initiative on the part of all personnel to carry out an attack and advance even when commanders and leaders become casualties. Unless an infantry battalion can do this, it is not fully trained for battle.

Friday, March 5, 1943

The War Department suspended mountain training for the 142nd Combat Team at Lowesville and directed that it remain there while awaiting shipment overseas.

Since there were no facilities or suitable terrain for tactical training at Lowesville and all that the troops could do was to climb mountains, sit in their tents, play cards, or do "bunk fatigue," I wanted them at Camp Hill where they could do some training and stay out of trouble. General Reinhardt has obtained permission for us to move the CT to Camp Hill by motor.

> NOTE: A combat team is a tactical unit usually composed of an infantry regiment, a battalion of artillery, and a company of engineers, all under the command of the senior officer, the commander of the infantry regiment. When the tactical situation requires it, other organizations may be added, such as tanks, anti-tanks, anti-aircraft, chemical, reconnaissance, and medical. When a combat team is off on a mission by itself, it is usually referred to as a "task force."

Another enlisted man was wounded today on the battle training course by a machine gun bullet that struck his helmet and caused a scalp wound. He is in the hospital but will be back on duty in a few days.

A letter to me from Captain Jack B. Street, former commander of our Rangers who departed some time ago, follows:

> "Dear General Walker:
>
> "I trust that my presuming to write this informal note to the commander of my old division does not exceed any bounds of propriety. My only desire in so doing is to keep you informed, insofar as the censorship regulations will permit, of the progress of your men.
>
> "Your preparatory measures for this group of men permitted them to be staged more quickly and efficiently than the other group that was assigned to my command. However, the entire group was staged in the allotted time. The only difficulty encountered was caused by lack of information from staging area headquarters as to what was required of us. This difficulty was enhanced by the fact that no standard operating procedure or check list was furnished any organization, thus causing them to learn solely by trial and error. This one fact alone caused most of the delay in drawing the necessary equipment and turning in other items for salvage or exchange.
>
> "Nevertheless, we are now on the sea and nearing the day of debarkation. The men are all well, in splendid spirits, and with several weeks of physical hardening will be fit for any mission. All are closely knit in our clannish little organization and eager for combat.
>
> "We aspire to combat glory for both our present and past organizations and, God willing, will bring honorable credit to

each.

"I trust that this finds you and yours in health, sir, and that we may soon be joined in our new stations together."

Saturday, March 6, 1943

I received warning orders today that the troops at Camp Hill are to have their property ready for shipment on March 14, their personnel ready by March 17. The troops here at Edwards are to be ready to ship their baggage on March 14 and personnel by March 28. In addition, an advance detachment, to precede us overseas, is to be ready to depart on March 19.

So it is beginning to look as though the Division is going to move again. Judging from past events, I would not be surprised if we would stop and unpack before we get to the port.

At a meeting, I issued warning orders to the Division Staff and subordinate commanders. They showed no emotion. They have been fooled many times.

After most of the officers and men had gone for a weekend leave to Boston or New York, I received orders to have a showdown inspection, prepare a list of shortages of equipment, and have the lists in Providence by 5:00 PM Monday. This is impossible. So we will prepare a list of shortages based on our previous inventories and records and will send that in. It is as accurate as any other list we can compile.

I am going to order all the men to have their hair cut short, no longer than two inches. This will bring grief to many men who are proud of their long, flowing locks.

Sunday, March 7, 1943

Fred, Jr. has been detailed as a member of the Advance Overseas Detachment and will leave about the 19th.

Propaganda, supporting President Roosevelt for a fourth term, is already being broadcast over the radio. Seems a little early to me since the nomination is more than a year away. Nobody will admit it and no one wants to hear it, but President Roosevelt is a dictator—benevolent, if you please—as a result of the extraordinary powers granted to him by Congress and by the votes of the people who repeatedly return him to office.

We had a high wind and heavy rain yesterday and last night. My cottage trembled and water was blown through the wall around the window frames. During the night I had to get up and pull my bed away from the wall in order to keep from getting wet.

A special court martial found a soldier guilty of being drunk and disorderly in a cafe in Falmouth, and sentenced him to be reduced to the grade of private and forfeit $10 of his pay per month for three months. I find, after reading the evidence, that all the soldier did was call an MP some inoffensive names and strike another soldier who tauntingly referred to his bald head as a "peeled onion." I reduced the sentence to forfeiture of $10 only.

On the other hand a general court martial tried a soldier last week for bringing 8 pints and 10 quarts of liquor into camp. The court found him not guilty. It is difficult to understand why men with mature minds will arrive at a finding which is directly opposite to the facts, for he was arrested in camp with the goods on him. They forget that their duty is to determine the facts no matter what their sympathies may be. Maybe he convinced the court that he was just going to throw a little party before crossing the ocean.

Thursday, March 11, 1943

We have had some very busy days this week. Packing and crating began in earnest last Monday and has been going on night and day. The Division is working three reliefs of eight hours each. All packing and marking must be finished by midnight tomorrow night. I think we will make it, but we will have to keep moving.

Last Monday I appointed 2nd Lieutenant Frank E. Burgher my Aide and have recommended him for promotion to 1st Lieutenant. I assigned Frank Reese to G-1 so I can make him a major.

A lieutenant, transferred to the XIII Corps troops today, came to me to ask that he be retained with the Division. The XIII Corps asked for him and his colonel concurred. He was arrested about two weeks ago for driving a vehicle while drunk and was fined in the civil court. He did his military work well, however, I told him that I was quite certain that his colonel would not have let him go if his personal conduct had been good.

Friday, March 12, 1943

We have sent many vehicles to Boston for shipment overseas

and will complete packing and crating today.

This morning Kerr and Lt. Col. Andy Price, 1st Battalion Commander of the 141st Infantry, came to my office and reported that last night two Camp Edwards MPs had slapped and beaten two men of the 141st in the camp stockade. I immediately called Colonel Smith, the Post Commander, and told him that I was going to call the War Department in Washington and ask for a special inspector to investigate the matter; that I intended to report him to the War Department as the officer in command of the camp who permits such things to happen, unless he took steps immediately to correct such procedure and punish the guilty MPs. He agreed to take action at once.

Later I sent Kerr and Price to see Smith and assist in the investigation, knowing that if I left it up to the camp headquarters they would gloss it over and let the guilty parties off. In the afternoon Kerr returned and told me that Smith had located the guilty MPs and would try them if I would be satisfied. This was a clever maneuver. By the time the MPs come to trial, we will be gone and there will be no witnesses to appear against them.

I asked Colonel Smith to transfer the guilty men to the 36th Division where I can look after their care and discipline. He agreed and is asking the First Service Command for authority to transfer them.

One man they beat up is a sergeant. If the MPs are transferred, I will put them in the platoon under that sergeant. He will not impose upon them nor mistreat them, but he will teach them to respect army regulations and their fellow comrades in arms.

Saturday, March 13, 1943

Louis Hibbs is to be assigned to command the new 63rd Division. I asked him if he had decided upon a Chief of Staff. He said he had not. I recommended Bus Wheeler, who is now with the 99th Division. He said he had not previously thought of him, but Bus was just the person he would like to have. He sat down at my desk and wrote a telegram to the War Department asking for him.

I'm glad for Louis to get a Division, but I do not like losing him. He's been a great help.

Tuesday, March 16, 1943

Last week I sent a 2nd Lieutenant, Chemical Warfare Service, with a convoy of several men and trucks to Camp Hill to deliver some chemical supplies to the 142nd Combat Team. Today I sent a similar convoy to Camp Dix to deliver the same supplies to the 142nd Combat Team, which is moving to Dix today. From there it will join me at the port.

This unnecessary trip came about because the lieutenant, who took the first convoy to Camp Hill, returned to Camp Edwards without delivering his cargo. His excuse was that he could not find anyone to whom he could deliver his supplies, so he brought them back without even finding the 142nd Combat Team or phoning Division Headquarters for instructions.

Such a fool cannot be trusted with any responsibility, and I have given orders for him to be transferred out of the Division.

The two MPs I requested transferred to the Division in order to teach them the viewpoint of a combat soldier have departed for parts unknown. Orders transferring them were issued all right, but they never joined, having gone "over the hill."

I don't like for them to put this over on me, so I am doing everything I can to apprehend them. The Division Provost Marshal has no other job but to find them before we depart, and civil and military officials have been notified to be on the lookout for them.

Last Sunday Julia and I attended communion services at the headquarters chapel. Afterward, Charles joined us for a visit with Fred Jr. at Falmouth Heights. This is the last family assembly for a long time, if ever.

Fred and Charles left for the New York Port of Embarkation yesterday, with the Advance Detachment. Its job is to make arrangements in Africa for receiving the remainder of the Division which will soon follow.

Had a telephone call from General Lange today from the Port of Embarkation where he is in command of the Advance Detachment. He said all the men arrived in good order; that they have nothing to do but eat, sleep and wait; but that Charles has plenty of work to do since he is the personnel officer. All have received typhus immunization and are feeling a little under the weather. Lange said the men and equipment, travelling together in a railway passenger car, had arrived all right. Harry Steel, the Division G-4, had told him it could not be done and that a baggage car for the equipment would be required.

I was informed today by the War Department that I will not get the 100 American Indians I requested some time ago. I regret this because with them I could have transmitted oral messages over the radio in the clear in a language the Germans could never translate, and thus could have saved time.

Colonel Werner has just returned from Africa where I sent him to observe operations. He has written his report and I have read it, but there is nothing new. The same old combat deficiencies that were present in Hannibal's day are found in our army today, and will exist in any army of the future. With more experience our soldiers will do better, but there will always be deficiencies. The conduct of war is a constant effort to bring order out of disorder.

Werner told me that General Moore, in the War Department, told him that Fredendall is being sent back to the United States. I wonder why?

A medical officer is trying, by every political means, to get out of the Division, now that he realizes he is about to go overseas. I have replied courteously but firmly to his petitioners that his services cannot be spared. But they are becoming a nuisance. I sent word to him to stop acting like a child and to start acting like a man; to make up his mind that he is a soldier; that if it should be his fate to be put into a hole and covered with the sands of Africa, then to meet that fate with his head up and chest out like a soldier. I doubt if Lt. Colonel Ben Primer delivered the message to him quite like I gave it, but his offensive efforts have subsided and he is now reconciled to going overseas.

The officers and men have done an excellent job of packing, crating, loading trains, and preparing reports and records, and I am very proud of them. Their spirit and morale are high, and they go about their work in a cheerful manner.

I am having the field laundry here make a special effort to wash the men's clothes so we can go aboard ship as clean as possible. I want our men to wear their fatigues while on the ship, and thus keep their other uniforms clean for going ashore.

I have given orders that no one shall go aboard who has not fired a prescribed course with the weapon with which he is armed.

Some officers and men are out today firing the carbine. We received 750 of them yesterday, the first we have received of this type of weapon.

I have issued one "cricket" to each officer and man in the Division. This is a clicking toy but it is to be used to give signals at night, in fog, and in smoke.

Inspectors are descending on us from Washington and the Port of Embarkation. They all say they are coming to help us. I hope so. I have been an inspector, too. It is always possible to find deficiencies, but there is no point in making mountains appear where only molehills exist.

I bought a hunting knife and sheath yesterday. Nearly everyone in the Division has a hunting knife stowed away in his legging, belt or hip pocket. This is becoming a custom in the 36th Division, so I carry one. At least I can use it to cut grass, brush and weeds.

Friday, March 19, 1943

Yesterday I flew to the Port of Embarkation at Brooklyn to check on our advance detachment, my Division party at Staten Island Terminal, and to visit General Groninger again. A number of minor matters were adjusted, after which I had lunch with him.

He took me for a tour of the harbor in his yacht and delivered me to the dock at Stapleton, Staten Island, where I was met by Bob Ives and Carl Phinney. I went with them to the temporary office the Division Advance Party is occupying while working with the various staff officers of the port, preparing the details for embarkation of personnel and equipment. I went over their plans, discussed some of the details to be certain they are fully understood, and approved them. I want to avoid disturbing or tiring the troops because of poorly prepared plans.

After visiting the advance party at Stapleton I went to Fort Hamilton where the Division Advance Detachment of 100 members is waiting to embark for Africa. Everyone was quite happy and in excellent spirits. I had a talk with General Lange and a chat with Fred, Jr., and Charles. They were quite cheerful and accompanied me out to Floyd Bennett Field where my C-45 plane was waiting for me. They all expect to sail soon on the fast ship **Andes.** It will go alone without escort. Its speed is about 22 knots which is too fast for submarines to catch it.

I notice a great letup in aimless telephoning, orders, counter-orders, and required reports since we came under the command of the Port of Embarkation yesterday. There is no more uncertainty. There are no more demands by the staffs of higher echelons to harass us. Everything is peaceful and calm. It is a relief to be under the command of people who know their business.

I still have the Division MPs looking for the two Camp Edwards MPs who mistreated my two men. I hope we catch them, but I am beginning to have my doubts.

Over 60 of our men have "gone over the hill" within a month. More will disappear before we go aboard ship. This is no compliment to the patriotism and will to fight of the American people.

Last Monday we received 750 carbines for issue to officers and key enlisted men. On Tuesday night, one of the inspectors from Army Ground Forces ordered me to turn them in to the Post Ordnance Officer. When I asked why, he said that the list of equipment we were to have does not include carbines. The Table of Basic Allowance, however, authorizes us to have them. We got those carbines because, some time ago, on my way back to Camp Edwards from Camp Hill, I stopped at the Pentagon and arranged with General Lutes and Colonel Bob Case, two of my good personal friends, to send us carbines before we left the States. They were kind enough to do this.

At the time I explained to them that Army Ground Forces and the XIII Corps had not shown any real interest in getting them for us.

So, when the inspector told me to turn our carbines back into the supply service it seemed like utter nonsense. I said, "I will not do it. The T/A authorizes me to have them."

The inspector said, "I hope you do not mean that. You had better think it over."

I did, and changed my mind.

We had had on hand 750 cumbersome, outdated Springfield rifles, model 1903, issued for the use of officers and key enlisted men, quite unsuitable for our purposes, as substitutes for carbines until those weapons were available. These undesirable, old-model rifles were turned in to the Post upon receipt of the carbines. Everyone who got a new weapon was delighted. Some men worked late into the night cleaning off the thick grease (cosmoline) in which they were shipped. Everyone felt that we had made a good trade.

I called General Reinhardt about the situation, but he was stubborn and instead of helping me keep the carbines, did just the opposite. Army Ground Forces were stubborn also, so I turned the carbines in on Wednesday.

When we asked for our old Springfield rifles back, the Camp Ordnance Officer had already shipped them elsewhere, so now we have 750 soldiers without arms.

But Colonel Bob Case, who had heard about the mess from Army Ground Forces, called me from Washington to say that he was shipping another 750 carbines to the Port to accompany us on the convoy. He also said that in the meantime, since the XIII Corps and Army Ground Forces had seen fit to require the carbines returned to the supply service, they could "rustle" for the 750 old rifles we needed, and get them wherever they could. I thanked him for looking out for us.

This is a typical example of the inefficiency of the staff of Headquarters, Army Ground Forces. Nobody minds the unnecessary work caused by all this foolishness because we have to work all the time anyway. The danger is that we lose confidence in our superiors, and that is bad.

Last fall I received orders to turn in all our cotton clothing. It was fitted to the wearer. All caps had piping on them. I succeeded in delaying this until December 17th. Then I was required, by the XIII Corps, to turn it all in. We finished the job on January 6th. On January 9th we received orders from the XIII Corps to equip ourselves with cotton clothing. We put in the requisitions. We have just finished issuing that clothing. We are exactly where we were last December, except that the clothing is not fitted to the wearer and there is no piping on the caps. Unnecessary harassment.

CHAPTER SEVEN
At Last, Embarkation

Camp Edwards, Massachusetts
Monday, March 20, 1943

This morning at a meeting of unit commanders and members of the Division staff, I discussed many details involved in our embarkation and preparation therefor. A number of staff officers from the Port of New York were here. I feel that everybody now is well-informed, knows what is expected, and how he is going to do it.

I note in the papers that the German submarine offensive in the North Atlantic is now under way. The allied nations have worked out a plan for combating the German submarines, and I hope it will be effective. I shall watch the submarine news very carefully during the next ten days, while the **Andes** sails to Casablanca.

Another medical officer came to my office today and requested transfer out of the Division to a base hospital where he would be able to do work in keeping with his specialty, eye surgery. I told him we needed his services with the Division and that he would have plenty of work to do fixing up wounded eyes after we get into battle. He said he did not want to avoid combat duty, so I told him he should be quite happy because he would have an opportunity for working at his specialty and for combat duty at the same time.

Some of our people cannot keep their mouths shut regarding our future movements. I saw a letter from Texas today which indicates too much talk, so I am making more rigid the enforcement of the recently imposed censorship.

At this time I am not putting men who return from being absent without leave in the guardhouse. They are not coming back now unless they really want to fight.

Monday, March 22, 1943

Saturday night Julia and I attended the Division dance at the Officers' Club. It was a very pleasant party and everyone had a good time. Some of the ladies of the staff placed a beautiful bouquet of flowers, including gardenias, on our table. We intended to leave at 10:30 but were enjoying ourselves so much we didn't leave until after midnight.

There were programs on each table, and I autographed a number for officers and their ladies. I kept my program, autographed by many of them, as a souvenir.

After we arrived home, Julia and I talked for an hour about the sterling character of the officers and ladies of the 36th Division. Many times during the party various ladies spoke to me of their love and admiration for Julia. This, of course, pleased me very much.

Willis Bell is washing my laundry since I do not have time to send it out and get it back before I leave. I told him that since he will have to do it from now on, this is a good time to begin. He is rather slow, but does a good job.

Julia left Camp Edwards for home this morning. She was very depressed, broken up, and had done a lot of crying in anticipation of her leaving. The fact that we are all going overseas at one time makes it all the more difficult for her. Yet she was very happy to have had us all together here for several months. She is going to stop at Florian's home in Metuchen for several days before she sets out for Ohio.

Staten Island, New York
Tuesday, March 23, 1943

I drove from Camp Edwards to Staten Island today and set up an office at the Stapleton Branch of New York Port of Embarkation, where an advance party of the Division has been working for two weeks. I hope to smooth out some misunderstandings and save some time and labor by being where the loading arrangements are being made.

I found that the ordnance people have placed some oversized tires on our 105mm howitzers and that they rub against the handbrake. The ordnance people here at the Port are working tonight to make the necessary modifications. These must be completed by next Saturday so the howitzers can be loaded not later than next Sunday.

I learned today that the **Andes,** on which Lange and the advance detachment sailed, departed last Saturday night and should be in Casablanca next Sunday.

Wednesday, March 24, 1943

Had breakfast with Carl Phinney, Bob Ives and Hal Reese. Reese looked at the sheath of my hunting knife and declared it was not good enough for a major general. He says, jokingly, that he is going to find a better one—one that will compete, in a newspaper reporter's mind, with the two pearl-handled revolvers Patton carries.

I told him to do his best, but that I was not looking for publicity. I just want to do a good job.

Sometime ago the Port authorities prescribed just how we were to substitute, at the gang plank, replacements for men absent without leave. Now they want to change their previous instructions. These will cause a great deal of confusion and require a lot of extra paper work. Same old story.

If I were king, I would teach all officers that they are the servants of the troops; that the troops are not the servants of staff officers or the echelon of commanders. And that includes the commander and staff of the 36th Division.

When the personnel of the higher headquarters begin to look upon themselves as the servants of the troops of lower units, we will begin to have a higher morale and a greater fighting spirit. I have preached this philosophy in this Division.

At 11:00 AM I visited the **USAT Brazil** which is to carry me, half of my staff, and nearly 5,000 men of the Division to Africa. I am surprised at the size and comfortable arrangements. The bunks for the men are arranged in tiers, four high. There is plenty of space between tiers and elsewhere for the men to store their baggage.

Although Colonel James L. Garza, Commanding Officer of troops aboard the **Brazil,** thinks that the men will be crowded, I don't think so at all. I think they will be comfortable, more so than on other transports on which I have traveled. There are adequate toilet facilities, and ventilation is good. None of the men will be below the water line.

Garza tells me that the ship moves through the water "steady as a house," and that very few persons will get seasick. I reserve my opinion in this matter. I have yet to travel on a transport that did not roll and make me seasick.

I was invited to have luncheon on board with Garza; the Captain, Harry N. Sadler; and Chief Officer Lloyd H. Thompson. The food was excellent—celery soup, steak, french fried potatoes, asparagus, mince pie, and coffee. If this is a sample of what we are going to eat during the voyage, we may expect the best. The Captain is a very pleasing person. Although he is quiet of manner, he impressed me as knowing his business. He spoke only occasionally, but when he did he had something interesting to say. There is no doubt but that he is the boss of the ship.

After luncheon, Carl Phinney and I went to Camp Dix in my official Packard to see how the 142nd Combat Team is getting along. We stopped at Metuchen on the way and saw Julia and Florian for a moment.

At Dix, I visited Colonel Forsythe and discussed various features of his personnel, supply and training problems. I also saw and talked to Captain Rush S. Wells, Jr., Commanding the Reconnaissance Troop, and Lt. Colonel Van W. Pyland, of the 636th Tank Destroyer Battalion. All were in excellent spirits and having only minor difficulties. I had supper with Pyland and returned to the Port via Metuchen for another short visit with Julia, Florian and the children.

Thursday, March 25, 1943

I visited the **Argentina** which is to carry the 142nd Combat Team. It is very much like the **Brazil,** carries almost as many troops and the facilities and accomodations are practically the same. We are lucky to have such good ships.

Colonel Steen called me from Camp Edwards to report that Jesse Moseley, Division Judge Advocate, has been sent to the camp hospital with a diabetic condition, which he had been concealing for the past two years. However, the condition showed up in the more thorough overseas exam. Moseley has been telling me right along how much he wanted to go overseas with the Division, never saying a word about not being physically able and hoping, I suppose, to get by the doctors. I am taking steps to have him transferred out of the Division and am asking for a replacement without delay. I will miss him. He did a good job.

Garza was right; we are going to be crowded. Major Wallock, of the Port Headquarters, tells me he is putting detachments of prisoner of war guards aboard each of our five ships, and that this may require some of our men to double up in using bunks and take turns sleeping. This is not as desirable as the men would like, but it can be done without a great deal of inconvenience. The War Department intends to bring back 1200 German prisoners on the return trip.

It looks as if we may sail on the 1st, 2nd or 3rd of April. I sailed out of New York harbor on the **Aquatania** with the 30th Infantry on April 1st, 1918, almost exactly a quarter of a century ago. Our mission then, as now, was the defeat of the German army and nation. I wonder if we will make another mess of the peace and send another army to Europe to destroy Germany in 1968.

Colonel Garza told me that two men who are employed in renovating the **Brazil** came to work at 7:30 AM, checked in and then locked themselves into a cabin and went to sleep, where they were found at 11:00 AM. He said there was no way they could be punished. If he should discharge them, the whole gang would quit and go on strike. He said that the union officials admitted that the two men were worthless bums and ought not to act that way, but that they could not be discharged, nor have their pay withheld for the time they were asleep.

I do not like to think that I am going away to risk my neck in order to maintain such conditions. Captain John Smith's Jamestown remedy was a good one.

Friday, March 26, 1943

In order to keep our strength in harmony with the Tables of Organization, I am appointing Major Stephen Brady as Division Judge Advocate to replace Moseley. The Judge Advocate General of the Army will not like this appointment because Brady is not commissioned in the Judge Advocate General's Corps, but he is an attorney, has been Moseley's assistant, and I am looking out for the best interests of the Division.

The officer here at the Port who is charged with preparing and checking the safe arrival cards and the passenger lists, found two mistakes in our papers for 16,000 men. This, he said, is marvelous and added that our lists and papers were the best prepared of any unit that has passed through the Port to date.

I told him that ours would probably be the best passenger lists and papers **ever** to pass through this Port. I have that much confidence in the ability of Colonel Steen and Major Deane, who have supervised the work, and I am pleased to know that our personnel people have done their work well.

I received a very encouraging letter from Mr. Miller, National Headquarters, American Red Cross, Washington, D. C., in which he stated that John Cattus, my friend and WWI comrade, would be called to Washington for consultation. This was done by Mr. Miller at my request, in an effort to get Cattus into the Red Cross and assigned to the 36th Division.

The number of men absent without leave from the Division has dropped from 80 to 43. This is a good sign. Frankly, I had expected the number of AWOLs to increase rather than decrease.

Monday, March 29, 1943

I learned today that some time ago a lieutenant of the 132nd Field Artillery Battalion went out for bazooka practice at Camp Hill and fired an anti-tank rocket into a building full of tents, burning up some $12,000 worth of government property. Four officers are being held back to appear as witnesses in the lieutenant's trial.

This is unfortunate but emphasizes the fact that just one careless officer or noncommissioned officer can do a lot of damage and disrupt plans. Hence the necessity of learning who are the careless and the incompetent, and getting them out of the Division before they can cause trouble.

No matter how much we try, we are going to have plans disrupted from time to time by careless persons. This was true in the days of Hannibal, in the days of George Washington, is true today, and will be true as long as imperfect human beings fight each other.

Major Burton Miles, Assistant G-4, has just arrived from Walter Reed Hospital. He returned recently from an observation tour of Africa where he visited the troops in Tunisia and at Casablanca. He had an infected leg and was admitted to Walter Reed while enroute to rejoin the Division. I was told by the hospital authorities that Miles would not be able to do duty prior to our departure, so I transferred him to the Quartermaster Replacement Pool, Fort Washington, Maryland. However, Miles succeeded in talking his doctors into letting him out of the hospital ahead of time so that he can accompany me overseas. This shows a fine spirit on his part, and I have told him that he will have no duty prior to our arrival on the other side. By that time he will be completely recovered.

This spirit is in marked contrast to that of a few officers who have tried to get out of the Division. One has deserted. He has been gone ten days. When a man is absent without leave after his unit is alerted for overseas duty it is prima facia evidence he is seeking to avoid hazardous duty and is therefore guilty of desertion in time of war. The officer in question had been tried last October for being absent without leave for more than 20 days. The court martial found him guilty and sentenced him to be dismissed from the service and to be confined at hard labor for six months. The President, however, restored him to duty and suspended the sentence. Now he has gone again.

Last Saturday I wrote a letter to the Judge Advocate General of the Army requesting that the sentence be put in effect. I presume the President will remove the suspension for I do not see how he can let officers of this type, who have no sense of duty, go on without punishment. No enlisted man can have any respect for such an officer.

I invited several junior officers to have luncheon at my table today. One, a captain, remarked that the attention he received from the waiter at my table was quite different from his normal service. He also commented that a major general receives more attention than a captain, and added that he would like to eat at my table regularly. I told him, jokingly, that if he would do his work well he might get to be a major general some day. However, I have little hope of his being one because he is too concerned with receiving service and attention, and not concerned with rendering service and attention to others. But then, he is rather young ... and combat service has a way of changing personal values.

This evening Bob Ives invited Carl Phinney and me to have dinner with him and his father. Doctor Ives is 73 years old, proud of his son, proud of the Ives family and proud of his professional accomplishment. What greater contentment can one have? I hope I have the same pride when I am 73. It was a real pleasure to meet him.

Tuesday, March 30, 1943

In spite of the order I issued two weeks ago that all persons in the Division should have their hair cut not longer than two inches by the 24th of the month, I still see some officers and men without proper haircuts. Same old story.

There are always some who feel that orders are intended for the other fellow. I can do nothing about those who evade the order until we arrive on the other side. Some people attach great importance to their wavy locks and cannot bear parting with them. Being bald, I do not share their view.

I received a reply to my letter to the Adjutant General in which I asked him to check on the MPs who mistreated my two enlisted men and insure that they are sent to the 36th Division as soon as they are apprehended. General Ulio states that he will comply with my request.

It remains to be seen whether they do finally join the Division in Africa. I will have to arrange for their assignment after we are on the other side because they will be shipped overseas as replacements for general assignment. Unless I pave the way, they may succeed in being assigned to some other Division.

Lieutenant Uzzio, assistant to the ordnance officer, tells me that my field glasses and pistol are not good enough for me. He says that the field glasses, though new, are not the latest model; same for the pistol. So I am letting him exchange them for the latest models, although I know there will be little, if any, practical difference. I have found it wise to permit subordinates, who mean well, to do as they like as long as their ways do not interfere with other plans. When they come around on their own volition to improve my equipment or my living conditions, it speaks well for their morale and confidence in me. I do not permit "bootlicking," and as far as I know, there are no bootlickers around my headquarters. But, one does not always know.

This afternoon I observed the advance parties of all Division units go aboard ship. They must board two days ahead of their units in order to organize and take charge of the embarkation and messing of the men, and to guard and police the ship.

They were carrying full field equipment and their overcoats, and each carried a barracks bag filled to the top—an awkward and burdensome load.

Three men stood beside a table at the foot of the gangplank, each with a copy of the passenger list. One man called out the names, the other two kept a check on the first man, in order to be certain that no mistakes were made. The man who calls the names announces the last name only, as "Smith." The man boarding calls out his first name and middle initial: "John T." After being checked off he struggles up the gangplank, lugging his heavy load.

Prior to arrival at the gangplank, the men are arranged in single file in the order in which their names appear on the passenger list, and each is given a card which indicates the deck, the compartment, and the number of his bunk. In spite of these precautions, some of the men have difficulty finding where they belong.

One man had the mumps. I had him fall out and sent him to the hospital. He was disappointed because he couldn't go with us. His spirit is quite different from that of some 35 men who disappeared yesterday. I now have 75 men absent without leave. All these deserters came to us as replacements from states other than Texas. Thank God, patriotism, a sense of loyalty, and devotion to duty are still considered virtues in that State.

When men are absent at the gangplank, their names are lined off of the passenger list; their service record is withdrawn and sent to the camp commander; and a replacement is furnished by the Port Commander. The replacements are immediately available.

We have five transports: the **Brazil**, the **Argentina**, the **Gibbons**, the **Barry**, and the **Hawaiian Shipper**. I have placed a regimental band on four of them and an orchestra on the fifth. The **Brazil** and **Argentina** are at pier 13; the **Barry** and **Gibbons** are at pier 16; and the **Hawaiian Shipper** is at pier 17.

These ships will carry the whole Division except one company of the 636th Tank Destroyer Battalion. Also, they will carry most of our equipment. One steel vehicle-carrying ship, especially built for the job, will carry the 24 new M-10 anti-tank, self-propelled vehicles. The one company of the 636th will act as guard on that ship.

I talked to Colonels Werner on the **Brazil**, Forsythe on the **Argentina**, and Martin on the **Gibbons**. Each was very much pleased with the comfort and arrangements for the enlisted men and officers on his ship.

On the ship I inspected, the galley was preparing supper and the men were already in line with their tin cups, waiting for mess call. The dining rooms are well arranged, with cafeteria-style service. The men file by a table where they pick up a partitioned tray, knives and forks. Then they move past tables of food in large pans kept hot by steam. There is no limit to the number of times a man can refill his tray. The tables are extra high so one must stand to eat.

After the meal, the men file by tanks of boiling water and dip their utensils into the water, returning them to the table for the next meal.

Passengers will have two meals a day. This is sufficient as the troops will have little or no physical exercise. If three meals were served, the kitchen crew would not have sufficient time to prepare and serve them and clean up properly. It requires two hours to serve each meal after it is prepared.

I have been told there will be about 70 ships in our convoy, of which ten will be transports. The others are freighters that travel fast enough to keep up. Our escort will consist of an aircraft carrier, a battleship, four light cruisers, and seven torpedo-armed destroyers.

This convoy could be a rich prize for the German submarines, and they may try to break through our escort vessels to get at the troop transports. I don't expect them to succeed, however, for this convoy means more to our allies than to the Axis, and our Navy is not going to leave any stone unturned to protect us. All ships carry guns, and any subs that appear within range will be in deep trouble, for many guns will open fire as soon as a target is visible.

Today, when the trains carrying the advance parties passed through New Haven, coffee was supposed to be put aboard each car for the men who were carrying sack lunches. When the attendant boarded the train, he announced that the coffee would cost $30.50.

Dick Werner, in command of the train, explained that he wanted the coffee, knew he was supposed to have it, and would sign a public voucher for it. But the attendant said he had to have cash. Werner rightly refused to pay, and the attendant left with the coffee.

Werner then sent a telegram to the Port Commander here explaining the situation. The attendant had planned to collect twice —once in cash and again from the government by presenting a voucher for coffee "delivered and payment therefor not received."

It is marvelous how clever some crooks are. The concessionaire knew the troops would be out of the USA in a few days and that there would be nobody to dispute his statement on the voucher.

Wednesday, March 31, 1943

I have just gone over the train schedule of troops coming from

Camps Edwards and Dix. A train will arrive each hour and stop within 100 yards of the pier to which the troops are assigned. The men will go directly aboard. Quite a little planning is necessary in order to insure that there will be no confusion or loss of time.

I watched the stevedores loading our equipment on the ships today. All are members of a union, and each does a minimum of labor. The port supplies every device known to handle freight mechanically so the stevedores wait for machines and cranes to carry and lift. As nearly as I could make out, there are as many, if not more, bosses than workers. Three workers have a straw boss over them. He stands by and sees to it that the other three do not risk getting hurt. For every three groups of four workers, which includes the straw bosses, there is another overseer who, after they have finished one job, tells the three straw bosses what to do next. There are other bosses of higher echelons who stand about as traffic directors or observers. Then there are the union delegates who see to it that union rules are enforced.

I saw a group working on a pile of our crates and boxes, moving them to the ship. Two men were on top of the 10 foot pile, rolling the boxes and crates off the top and letting them crash on the pier. Many of the boxes and crates broke open. I spoke to the overseer and asked him to put a stop to this. He looked at me and said calmly and unconcernedly that I would have to take the request up with the superintendent of the longshoremen's union, who would be back on the pier in about an hour, he thought.

I spoke to the army officer who was supervising the loading. He said he was powerless to do anything. If he gave any orders about the method of handling the cargo, the longshoremen would just quit work for a couple of hours until the union delegates could go into a huddle and decide the matter. He assured me that rough handling and breaking of boxes and crates was normal, and that the Port Authorities had a crew of repair men who would be along eventually to repair them. Thus, one group of longshoremen makes work for another group of carpenters. The officer also told me that both stevedores and carpenters dilly-dally while working on straight time so they can obtain double pay for overtime.

Our convoy will probably leave its piers and assemble outside the harbor some time Thursday night or early Friday morning.

The voyage will take 14 days, if all is well; otherwise the trip may require 16 or 17 days. A lot depends upon the route taken, and this will depend on the activities and location of German submarines.

Recreation for the men, where there is so little unused space, is quite a problem but is going to get a lot of attention. A long trip, without adequate lounging space and without any lights at night, is boring to everyone. Seasickness will make it worse. However, this discomfort is much better than the men will experience on the battlefield, where they will live in a 2' x 5' foxhole in mud, rain, heat and dust.

A few men break down under battle conditions and not only do not fear death, but actually welcome it. A few others become nervous wrecks and have to be sent back to base hospitals for special care and treatment ... what we used to call "shellshock" in WWI. The life of an infantry soldier in war is the most difficult and trying of all, and the nation should pay its greatest tributes to the infantry soldier. Air Force soldiers rarely miss a meal, never miss a bath, wear clean clothes, sleep in clean, comfortable beds, have normal recreation facilities, and in battle are only under fire for a few minutes at a time. Not so with the Infantry. Of all the combat forces, the Infantry suffers the greatest losses and deserves the greatest honor.

I complied with embarkation regulations and had a physical examination today to determine whether or not I am free from vermin and communicable diseases. I passed it. I don't know why the doctor took my blood pressure.

Our personnel now at the Port is restricted and confined to Stapleton Base, beginning at midnight. We will all go aboard Thursday and cannot leave the ship thereafter.

I took my baggage into my stateroom, No. 19, on the **Brazil.** The suite consists of two rooms, a private bath, and a private deck. The bedroom is about 12 by 20 feet with one corner out for a bath. There are two very comfortable single beds in the room which is painted light green. The bath has a combination shower and tub, and the fixtures are light and dark green. The other, or living room, is about 16' by 16' and is furnished with a table, comfortable chairs, reading lamps, and has a closet. I will have no one in the suite with me except when I invite them. There are many who would like to use my living room for poker or pitch, but their dreams will not be realized. I would not mind letting them play there, but they never know when to quit and go to bed.

The private deck is about 12' x 16', looks out over the sea and has a comfortable steamer chair. The Transport Commander told me that a peacetime cruise from New York to Buenos Aires and back to New York in this suite costs $2,700. Dick Werner and Clayton Kerr will have the stateroom next to mine, and we will share the bathroom.

Colonel Garza has the band aboard practicing so it can play to-morrow. He said this is the first time a band will play for troops going aboard a transport at New York Port, and he seemed very much pleased that it is available.

My Packard, which I have had since September, 1941, will be turned in to the motor pool at the Port. A new one—tagged with my name—has been put aboard for my use in Africa. But, I will have to have somebody on the job every minute after arrival at Oran to keep some officer at Eisenhower's headquarters from stealing it.

I will spend tonight at the Hostess House and go aboard ship to stay tomorrow morning. This afternoon I went over to Metuchen to say good-bye to Julia, Florian, Freddie, III, and Carolyn. I don't expect to get back home as quickly as I returned from the last war, 18 months.

Thursday, April 1, 1943

The Division has been embarking all day. The first train arrived at the pier at 6:30 AM, and one train arrived each hour thereafter. They were met by Port personnel and taken to the ship designated for each unit.

The officers and men carried a great deal of baggage, all re-quired by regulations. The men wore their field jackets and overcoats and carried all their field equipment which was very bulky and included gas masks and chemical equipment. In addi-tion, each man carried a very heavy clumsy barrack bag. The last train arrived with Lt. Colonel Charles Jones' battalion, 143rd Infantry, at 10:00 PM which was aboard by midnight.

I sent General Groninger a letter expressing my appreciation for the way his staff had cooperated with my staff in getting the Division through the Port in an orderly manner, fully manned and fully equipped. He visited me on board at about 10:00 PM and told me that the 36th Division had given him no difficulty in going through the Port. Several of his staff officers, Colonel

Ami, Lt. Colonel Beckworth, Major Wallock, and others, stated that the 36th Division was the best prepared unit that had gone through the Port to date.

Harry Steel remarked that the New Haven Railroad officials told him that the 36th was the only Division they had moved that had trains loaded and ready to go on time, without exception. This speaks well for the zeal, knowledge, initiative and esprit of the Division personnel. It's my job to tell them what to do; they do it.

Part II

The 36th Division in Combat
April 1943-July 1944

CHAPTER EIGHT
Prelude to Combat

At sea
Friday, April 2, 1943

The main body of the 36th departed from the pier at 7:00 AM and joined our convoy outside New York Harbor. Many ships are about us on all sides, and a battleship and a destroyer are steaming along not far away. Each ship carries several gun crews. This morning we held our first "stand to" and "abandon ship" drill. It was well done since everybody was familiar with the procedure. The police, guard, blackout and messing arrangements have been completed and all activities are being conducted in an orderly and soldierly manner.

I have begun rereading the first volume of Freeman's **Lee's Lieutenants.** I am not going to hurry through it, but rather I am going to go slowly enough to fully grasp Dr. Freeman's thoughts and descriptions, which he expresses so well. Dr. Freeman refers to himself as a layman in the military profession. Through his long, exhaustive study of the leaders of the Civil War and their campaigns, he has become a learned strategist and tactitian. It is interesting to reflect that the Virginia campaigns are still carefully studied in the tactical schools of the British Army.

Saturday, April 3, 1943

Yesterday was cloudy, foggy, rainy. Vision was limited. Today it is cloudy but one can see the whole of our convoy. I can count 20 ships. A battleship is leading at the center front. The transports are spaced in checkerboard formation following the battleship, and the whole convoy is surrounded by a number of destroyers. At about 9:30 AM a big Navy sea plane flew over the convoy and circled the battleship several times. All ships held gun crew and fire practice this morning. All guns on all the ships other than war vessels were fired to make sure they were in working order. The firing could be heard distinctly from various directions as different ships opened up as a part of their drill.

Tuesday, April 6, 1943

All ships carry anti-aircraft as well as surface guns. Each day the gun crews try them out by firing bursts in the air. Yesterday, I saw one of our destroyers drop a depth charge and saw the eruption of water. It was a drill, not an enemy submarine.

I had to punish two medical officers and a chief warrant officer today. One medical officer, while we were still at Camp Edwards, had made a false official report in that he, knowingly, had signed a captain's name on the regimental register as having departed at 5:00 PM on Sunday on leave, when, as a matter of fact, the captain had departed at noon the previous day. The collusion was undertaken in order to save a day of leave. I fined the medical officer $100 and administered a reprimand to the captain.

The chief warrant officer was placed on guard on one of the compartments of the ship. He tired of his assigned duty and at 10:30 PM, when he thought nobody would discover his absence, rounded up some of his friends and went to the dining room to play poker. Since he thinks more of poker playing than of doing his duty, I reduced him to warrant officer, junior grade.

I regret that I must punish officers and men at this time, prior to going into combat where a number of them are going to be killed and wounded. But, in justice to those who do their duty conscientiously, it is necessary that I do something effective to change the mental attitude of those who fail or neglect it.

Wednesday, April 7, 1943

I read over the manifests of all the ships in our convoy. From these I discovered there are other troops in the convoy besides the 36th. I note that our property is loaded on all of the ships and that the property of some units is distributed on several ships. This means that we will have to be especially careful not to let our property become mixed with baggage of other units after debarkation. It will be necessary to provide Division personnel at each unloading point to safeguard our interests.

This is a bright, calm, pleasant day. For the first time, one of the two small planes carried on the battleship took off for a two-hour reconnaissance of the sea.

I examined one of the life boats. Each contains a great deal of equipment for the "drifters" for a long period of time: food in the form of crackers, chocolate, pemmican, and fresh water, and canvas for catching rain water, sail, fishing tackle, canvas for protection from the sun, first-aid kit, signal flares and paddles. Although the life boats will be overcrowded in case of abandoning ship, their occupants can exist for thirty days without much hardship. I tasted some of the pemmican and found it good. It is a mixture of rice, raisins, kidney fat and cooked potatoes. A small amount is sufficient for a meal since it expands when moistened.

Everyone on the ship seems to be cheerful and happy. Several classes in German, French and Spanish have been organized voluntarily and are being conducted by members of the Division who have been trained for interrogation of prisoners of war.

We have a fuel ship in the convoy for supplying the seven destroyers. Refueling was done this afternoon while the convoy reduced speed and zigzagged in various directions. The destroyers are refueled, two at a time, one on each side of the fuel ship. Lines and hose are attached and the three ships continue moving forward at reduced speed. I do not think the destroyers are low on fuel but that the convoy commander decided to fill them today while the sea is calm and refueling is relatively easy.

I mathematically determined the distance of one of the destroyers from our ship by using the mil scale in my field glasses. I measured the width of the destroyer to be 15 mils. The known length of the destroyer is 341 feet. By using the formula $1000 : 15 :: x : 341$ and dividing by 5280 I find that the destroyer is 4.3 miles from us. If the destroyer can move at 30 knots at full speed, it will take it $22733 \div 6080 \text{x} 60 \div 30 = 7:47$ minutes to arrive here should a U-boat appear. By that time we could be one-third sunk. However, the destroyer will be more prompt than that because all destroyers can detect a submarine at a distance of three miles, and since the seven destroyers are disposed on the circumference of the convoy, they can usually discover a submarine and concentrate on it promptly before it can get into action. In dealing with a pack of enemy submarines the problem is not quite so simple.

Friday, April 9, 1943

Captain Sadler, Master of the **Brazil,** invited General Cowles and myself up onto the bridge where he explained the purpose and use of various instruments and other interesting features of the ship and the convoy.

The ships of the convoy are kept in formation at night and in fog by a radio control on the battleship **Arkansas.** Radar permits the Admiral to see, by glancing at a screen on his bridge, the relative location of all ships in the convoy. If one gets out of position, he can direct it how and when to get into place by blinker since we are observing radio silence. Each ship has a similar screen which shows its position with respect to the other ships. Thus, collisions at night or in fog, even with all lights out, are avoided.

The Captain explained that on his ship there are three ship's clocks, each with Greenwich time, which check on each other. They are used to determine the longitude of the ship. The sextant measures the angle to the sun and by calculation permits determination of latitude. In case of bad weather, when the sun or other suitable heavenly body cannot be seen, position is determined by dead reckoning; that is by plotting directions of the course and distances as revealed by the number of revolutions of the propeller. When near land, the ship is aided by radio beams and depth soundings.

From the bridge, the Captain can promptly locate a fire in any part of the ship. In case of fire, damage or collision, he can electrically close all bulkheads at one time.

The bridge of the **Brazil** is protected by a six-inch wall of concrete and by a concrete top about four inches thick. In addition, parts of the bridge are protected by half-inch steel plates. These will stop small-arms fire, but will not stop shell fire.

We are now passing to the south of the Azores and will be about 40 miles south of the southernmost island tomorrow morning. Captain Sadler said this is the most dangerous part of our course and that all crews will be especially alert for the next 36 hours. He says that German submarines are known to be in these Azores waters and will be looking for allied convoys both to the north and south of the island group. He is hoping for cloudy and foggy weather for the next two days.

A copy of the President's message has just been given to each man on the transport.

THE WHITE HOUSE
WASHINGTON

TO MEMBERS OF THE UNITED STATES ARMY EXPEDITIONARY FORCES:

You are a soldier of the United States Army.

You have embarked for distant places where the war is being fought.

Upon the outcome depends the freedom of your lives: the freedom of the lives of those you love—your fellow-citizens—your people.

Never were the enemies of freedom more tyrannical, more arrogant, more brutal.

Yours is a God-fearing, proud, courageous people, which,

throughout its history, has put its freedom under God before all other purposes.

We who stay at home have our duties to perform—duties owed in many parts to you. You will be supported by the whole force and power of this nation. The victory you win will be a victory of all the people—common to them all.

You bear with you the hope, the confidence, the gratitude and the prayers of your family, your fellow-citizens and your President.

Franklin D. Roosevelt

Saturday, April 10, 1943

The sea is as smooth as glass. The sun is shining brightly. There is very little breeze. The ships of the convoy are plowing through the water at full speed in perfect formation. There is a very inspiring and magnificent view from the top deck of our ship where one can look out over the convoy and the sea and observe its perfect uniformity and movement.

At about 8:30 AM what I presumed to be a passenger plane passed about 8 miles north of us, flying east. Our own patrol planes were out this morning to cover the environs of the eastern islands of the Azores group.

Abandon ship drill, which requires all personnel to take their station on deck, was completed in six minutes. This is the best time to date. If it were actually abandon ship, we would climb down rope ladders into the water, then swim to and hold onto floating rafts which have been thrown overboard. Meanwhile, life boats would be lowered which would pick up their allowed capacity from among the men holding onto the rafts.

The boats will take care of only a small portion of the total. However, all other ships will assist in rescuing the men on the rafts. The destroyers will assist also when threat of U-boat attack is passed.

I learned today that all ships of the convoy are equipped with an electrical device which will repel the magnetic mines used by the Germans during the opening months of the war. Nobody knows for sure whether the Germans are still using that type.

Sunday, April 11, 1943

Several airplanes came from out of nowhere and circled over our convoy this forenoon and again this afternoon. They were friendly British and American patrol planes.

Monday, April 12, 1943

During the night the battleship **Arkansas,** one sea-train vessel, and a couple of destroyers departed for Casablanca. Two British destroyers have joined us. We are now on a course a little north of east, moving straight for Gibraltar. The sea is calm and there is a mist that helps to conceal the convoy. We are making good time.

Toward 6:00 PM we passed a large convoy going west, a few miles to the north. I counted twenty-nine ships which were escorted by destroyers in the same manner as we are. One of our destroyers fired four depth charges at what it thought was an enemy submarine. I don't think there was any enemy submarine. If there were, the U-boat commander must have been inexperienced because he was between the two convoys all alone, a risky position in broad daylight.

This evening at about 9 o'clock we could see the lights of Tangiers and also the navigation lights along the shore. An hour later we could see signal lights and lighted towns on the coast of Spain to the north of us. In the darkness and haze we were unable to see the Rock of Gibraltar.

Our British escort of seven destroyers took us through the Strait without slowing down.

Harry Steel has completed, as far as possible, his plans for unloading, collecting, guarding and delivering our baggage and equipment.

Monday, April 13, 1943

The Mediterranean is much smoother than the Atlantic and the ships are moving along in perfect formation. The sun is shining brightly; there are a few clouds; and the temperature is ideal; we are about half way between Gibraltar and Oran.

Everyone is in the best of spirits. All are packing to be ready to leave the ship promptly so we will not be exposed to bombing at the pier any longer than absolutely necessary.

Lt. Colonel Robert A. Phinney, our Finance Officer, just called to pick up all my United States currency which he will exchange for francs. The same thing is being done for the troops.

Oran, Algeria
Later the same day

Arrived at Oran and debarked at about 6:00 PM. Prior to

entering the harbor, the convoy formed a single column of ships. Our ship was seventh in the column. It was a slow process to get into the inner harbor and up to the dock.

We were all surprised to find Oran quite modern. From the harbor there appeared to be many skyscrapers.

I was the first person ashore. After a half-hour or so General Lange met me and insisted on my going to the Grand Hotel where he was staying. There I met many old friends: Colonels Miller, Signal Corps; Humphries, QMC; Tom Brandt, IG; General Kingman and others.

Friday, April 16, 1943

Went to Ain Temouchent to see General Dawley, to whose VI Corps we are assigned. We had a very friendly visit, but he told me nothing about our combat assignment. He seemed very secretive.

I think he is going to take one of our bands away from us because he mentioned how nice it would be to have a band at his headquarters.

In this city I was shocked at the poverty, rags and filth of the Arabs. Terrible! One can scarcely believe that human beings can exist in such a state. But outside the city limits I was surprised to find highly cultivated fields on both sides of the road: oranges, olives, grapes, wheat, peas, and artichokes. All farm labor was being done by Arabs. Although for generations the French have been owners and overseers of these fields their habits and customs remain typically French. The countryside is very much like California.

Magenta, Algeria
Monday, April 19, 1943

We are beginning to get settled in our camp near Magenta, about eighty miles south of Oran. The troops came here on the dinky French railroad which is slow, unreliable and crowded. By shuttling back and forth we managed to move the personnel of the Division here in five days. The impedimenta was brought here in trucks supplied to us at the port. By running the trucks night and day we were able to move our baggage and equipment here in six days.

Much of our baggage disappeared at the port. Some was stolen and carried off by various army services; some was dropped into the sea by careless handling of the hoisting cranes and by care-less loading on lighters; and the Arabs have stolen some. The 750 carbines that Bob Case put aboard the convoy at New York for us have disappeared. Our fifteen artillery and command observation planes have also vanished. I gave General Cowles the job of finding them and he has his scouts out, but no results so far. Harry Steel is trying to find the carbines.

The first night in camp here the Arabs stole six barracks bags. The men hung the bags on a tree and moved off ten or twelve yards where they put up their shelter tents and went to sleep. The Arabs crawled up during the night, cut the rope, and ran off with the bags. We have to keep men on guard at all times to prevent theft.

Even though much has been stolen or lost, we find ourselves with a lot of things we don't need. We have overcoats and gas masks which we do not need at all, and far too much ammunition. I will turn the things we do not need into the Port at Oran and hope to get back the things we do need.

We are short on water here, only enough for cooking and drink-ing. There are bathing but no laundry facilities. Stovall has installed 128 shower heads on a nearby creek.

On our way here from Oran, accompanied by several of my staff, I stopped at Sidi Bel Abbes for lunch at the American Hos-pital.

Monday, April 26, 1943

Yesterday was Easter. Chaplain MacCombie held services in the mess tent today. I attended with General Lange. It is cold, damp, and cloudy, and I have not been warm all day. We have no heat of any kind except in the kitchens where loafers are not allowed.

Last Thursday Carl Phinney, Edward Harris, Frank Reese, and I went to Oran by auto and from Oran by plane to Rabat, a two and one half hour trip. We went directly to General Patton's headquarters and reported to him. I am not under Patton's command, but was there to receive instructions in case I later come under this command. Generals Maxwell D. Taylor, Geoffrey Keyes, Leonard T. Gerow, Arthur S. Nevins, Lucian K. Truscott, Russell P. Hartle, Kingman, Middleton, and Dawley were also there for the meeting. All of them are my personal friends.

After the meeting, which had to do with cooperation with the

French troops in case of an invasion of Morocco via Gibraltar by the Germans, we had lunch at the officers' club hotel. Later three staff officers and I obtained a government automobile to take us to Casablanca. There we visited the harbor and saw many ships damaged or sunk by the French on last November 8th. Salvage crews were working on the ships in an effort to get them back into service. I was especially interested in the battleship **Jean Bart** which was being repaired sufficiently to send her to the United States for refitting. Jean Bart was a very famous corsair in Louis XIV's time.

We drove through the main part of the city. I was surprised to see so much merchandise in the store windows. Our driver said that all this had come into Casablanca since November 8th. I have the impression that the French people are quite prosperous since the United States government and soldiers are spending huge sums here each month.

We went to visit the scene of the famous "no surrender except unconditionally" conference of President Roosevelt and Winston Churchill.

I called on General Arthur Wilson, the base commander. Although I have never served with Art, I know him quite well and we are very good friends. I have met him on many occasions in Washington, Fort Lewis, and Chicago. He has a pleasing personality and a host of friends.

On the road back to Rabat I saw many storks' nests on house tops and on old fortification walls. In every nest there was a stork.

On Friday I attended a conference at Rabat at which was revealed the plan for the next tactical operation, after Tunisia, and in which the 36th Division is to take part. After the conference I, with others, returned to Oran by plane, passing over the same route as before: Meknes, Fez, Taza, Oujda.

A new Packard sedan was put on the ship for me at New York, but some smart officer of the Base Port has succeeded in stealing it before it could be turned over to me. I have done everything I can to locate it but cannot find it. So I suppose he will ride around in it with great satisfaction. However, Harry Steel says that new Packard passenger cars are being unloaded at Casablanca on the west coast and he is going to send one of his officers there to get one for me. He didn't say how.

Cowles has located our fifteen observation planes hidden away in a hangar on an airfield near Oran. We are going to be allowed to have six of them. General Clark is appropriating the other nine. Harry Steel found our 750 carbines neatly stored in the ordnance storehouse at the port. I told him to steal them back.

Thursday, April 29, 1943

Last Tuesday I drove to Oujda to visit Wayne Clark, via Magenta, Tabia, and Tlemcen. The scenery along the route was most beautiful, especially in the valleys and over the mountains. Clark turned out a guard of honor for me, but when he explained that he just wanted to give the guard troops some practice, I did not feel particularly complimented. Clark told me that he classed the 36th Division as one of the very best and that he was going to keep it under his own control until he himself needed it, which pleased me.

The French farmers here preserve the straw, after threshing the wheat and oats, by making large, steep-sided stacks and then plastering them with a three-inch layer of mud mixed with straw. The rainfall is rather gentle and does not wash off the mud plaster. This keeps the straw bright, clean, and dry, and keeps it from blowing away. We have bought a lot of this straw for our men to sleep on. It comes to us baled and is quite suitable for stuffing bed sacks.

I have authorized our companies to buy wine for resale to their men because our soldiers are being exploited by owners of local wine shops. A quart bottle of wine costs our men $1.90. The standard price here for an empty wine bottle is 85 francs, which is equal to $1.70. The wine without the bottle is worth only 20 cents. It pays for soldiers to have their own bottles. The chaplains will not like my action in this matter and I expect a protest from them, but it won't change things.

Friday, April 30, 1943

Today we received orders to send one regimental combat team to the Infantry Training Center at Porte-aux-Poules. It is to be there not later than May 4. I am sending the 141st CT.

Sunday, May 2, 1943

Yesterday I attended a critique of a landing exercise made recently by the 3rd Division at Arzew. The Navy was there in force. The following Generals were there: Patton, Dawley, Huebner, Cushman, Taylor, O'Daniel, and Truscott. There was much talk about cooperation between the Navy and the Army, but I did not get anything of value out of the two and one-half hours of talks and discussion, beyond what I already knew.

The Navy made many errors in directing the landing craft to the beaches, but promised great improvement in the future. I do not have as much confidence as I should have in its ability to clear away mines or to land us on the correct beaches.

Higher authority requires that we take one tablet of atabrine on Monday and another one on Friday of each week to prevent malaria. Some of our people are having quite a time and say the treatment is worse than the disease. I was not affected by the last dose, and I hope I get by without too much discomfort in the future.

Now, nearly all of the personnel at Division Headquarters is sick except Kerr and myself. We took the atabrine along with them, but I am told that many suspect us of not taking the atabrine. One is called a lot of unusual names and accused of all kinds of silly performances in this business, but not to one's face. If you take a position of authority in the military, you must expect to be called uncomplimentary names and accused unjustly.

A cloudburst occurred last Wednesday in the nearby village of Bedeau, and the water in the creeks rose very suddenly to an additional height of twelve feet. We were warned by the French Commandant at Bedeau, but not soon enough, and one of our bath units was damaged before we could get it moved away from the creek.

I have sent our band to play in the nearby villages of Magenta, Bedeau, and Ain Tindamine. This will help promote friendly feeling between the natives and our soldiers, I hope. Besides, there is no musicians' union here to prevent them playing.

For dinner at our mess today we had the regular B-ration which consisted of stewed chicken, dumplings, creamed potatoes, peanut butter, and Jello. This was the first B-ration meal we have had to date, and it was well prepared.

I had to talk very frankly and firmly to my staff and commanders. They are letting the men grow lax in saluting, wearing of the uniform, details of training, and general conduct. This is a positive indication of a let-down in discipline, and I am going to correct these evils beginning now.

Soon after we assembled at Magenta, Lt. Colonel Van Pyland proposed that he be allowed to move his 636th Tank Destroyer battalion south a few miles to the desert where he can train it in the use of indirect fire. This involves, among other things, the training of forward observers and personnel to operate a fire direction center. He has the necessary equipment so I approved. The battalion went to Sebdue and began battlefield training, using live ammunition. The French Commandant at Bedeau moved out all Arabs from a large area so the TDs would have ample space for maneuvering and firing their weapons.

Monday, May 3, 1943

I noted improvement in the saluting today as a result of my peroration yesterday on errors to be corrected.

Steel's commandos have stolen back 749 of our carbines. One had been removed from its shipping case. They are issued to those who should have them, and 749 persons are delighted. I presume there is one delighted thief at the Port of Oran.

Arzew, Algeria
Wednesday, May 5, 1943

I moved my headquarters section to join the 141st Combat Team which is undergoing training at Arzew. General Dawley called and gave me some secret information regarding future operations.

Saturday, May 8, 1943

I had dinner with Patton and Keyes at Patton's quarters at Mostagenem. The menu: roast chicken, fresh creamed potatoes and chicken gravy. This was not the Army ration. Patton has commandeered one of the best furnished residences in the city, and also a boys' school for his headquarters. He has no less than six servants at his residence, all soldiers, and all expert in their respective jobs. I live in a tent and eat the government ration served in the division headquarters mess where only a tent fly is authorized for shelter from the weather. I could, of course, live like Patton, but I prefer to live with my troops.

Patton expressed pleasure concerning the various training exercises he witnessed yesterday in which the 36th Division was engaged.

I had to fine one officer ten dollars for violating the censorship regulations. Another lieutenant who does not have the courage to make his men do as they are told was recommended for reclassification and to be returned to the United States and discharged from the service. A lieutenant colonel is not doing well with his battalion, and I may have him reduced to the grade of major, if he cannot make good in the position to which I promoted him. He is not maintaining a proper discipline of his men, does not have the ability or desire to require them to do their full duty in the face of hardship. He temporizes with them. I can never be sure that he will carry out my orders, and so he is unreliable.

I had to reprimand one of my staff officers. He had deceived me into granting him permission to visit Oran, giving me the impression that he had official business there. I learned later that he had no official business there at all but wanted to go for his own pleasure and convenience. I gave him a lecture on his behavior, and I hope he will not attempt to deceive me again.

Monday, May 10, 1943

I went to Magenta yesterday and brought Crowther, Steel, McShane, and my secretary, Warrant Officer Hampton, to Arzew to assist me in working out plans for future operations.

A corporal from Co. C, 143rd Infantry, shot and killed a sergeant of our military police platoon and wounded another military policeman. A third MP shot and killed the corporal. The incident occurred when our MPs attempted to disarm the corporal who was carrying a pistol while off duty, contrary to orders. Too bad. Since the killing of the sergeant, I have issued orders that any military policeman in the division will shoot to kill any person who points a gun at him.

Three men from Co. C, 141st Infantry, drowned last Friday. They were rowing rubber boats for practice during a strong off-shore wind. The wind blew most of the rubber boats out to sea, and the high waves upset some of them. All men had life preservers but some must have been poorly adjusted. Rescue boats went out to pick them up. The bodies of the three missing men were later found on the beach. They were buried in Oran last Saturday with appropriate military honors. As I have said before, training for war is dangerous.

Magenta, Algeria
Friday, May 14, 1943

Since last Monday the mission for the 36th Division has been changed, and we are not going to be under the command of Patton but will remain under the command of Clark. We have been warned to be ready for a motor movement of over 500 miles—I presume to a training area somewhere near Rabat. The amphibious training of the remaining troops of the Division has been suspended.

When I inquired why we are not to serve under him in the next operation, Patton told me that he was very much impressed with the enthusiasm and excellent work of the 36th Division and that he had not asked for the 1st Division to be substituted for the 36th Division.

Clark told me yesterday that he considered the 36th Division better than the 1st Division, and for that reason, had made a special request to Eisenhower for the 36th to remain assigned to his command. Everyone seems to be pleased that we are going to serve under Clark instead of Patton. Because of this change I have moved back to Magenta to prepare plans for the movement to our new area.

The 3rd Battalion, 142nd Infantry, plus two rifle companies of the 141st Infantry will remain at Arzew to serve as school troops for training the 1st Division in amphibious and invasion work. The 1st Division will not be delighted to be instructed by men of the 36th. When these two divisions were stationed together at Camp Blanding, Florida, a year ago, there was considerable rivalry between them.

Within the past few weeks I have been at several higher headquarters, and I am amazed at the levity that some staff officers display toward their friends and contemporaries who are suffering hardships and making sacrifices in combat. I have heard some staff officers imply that only wise ones are on the staff and that those with the combat troops are dullards and naive. Battle is a very serious matter, and those who laugh and joke about their friends and belittle those who are engaged in it should be sent to the front to serve there, if they have the ability, which I doubt.

We have been advised by VI Corps that a number of German and Italian prisoners of war have escaped in Tunis after their

Capt. Henry T. Waskow, Company B, 143rd Infantry.

Rifle Company, 141st Infantry, on combat firing range. Camp Bowie, Texas, March 12, 1941—U.S. Army Photo

Company A, 142nd Infantry, on Third Army Maneuvers. Leesville, Louisiana, September, 1941—U.S. Army Photo

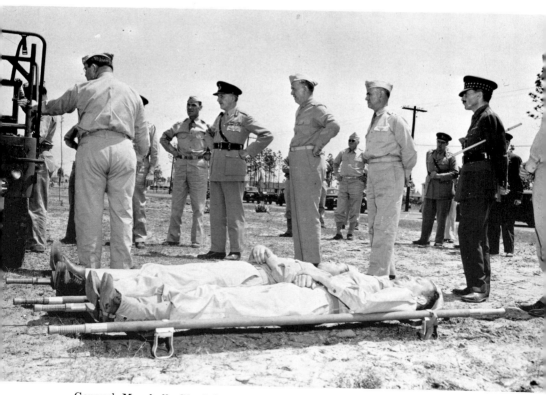

General Marshall, Sir John Dill and party stop to look at an arrangement that Lt. Col. Clarence B. Brewster, the Division Surgeon, 36th Division, made to carry two litter patients on a quarter-ton jeep. Camp Blanding, Florida, April 30, 1942

Generals Clark, Alexander and Dawley. Port-Aux-Poules, Algeria, August, 1943

General Alexander inspects the 143rd Infantry. Port-Aux-Poules, Algeria, August, 1943

The 143rd Infantry Regiment Combat Team on invasion boats landing on the beach at Salerno on D-Day. Setember 9, 1943—U.S. Army Photo

—U.S. Army Photo

Soldiers of the 151st Field Artillery lifting a 105mm howitzer out of a DUKW. Salerno, Italy, September 9, 1943—U.S. Army Photo

surrender and are probably trying to get to Spanish Morocco. We are directed to establish a line of straggler posts from the sea south to the desert to collect these escaped prisoners. Since we are going to move elsewhere, Lt. Colonel Van Pyland asked to have that job and I gave it to him. He will set up a line from Oran, through Sidi-Bel-Abbes and Magenta to Bedeau, the farthest French Legion outpost on the edge of the desert.

Rabat, Morocco
Thursday, May 20, 1943

Beginning last Sunday, the 16th, the Division started moving by rail and motor to the cork forest six miles east of Rabat.

I departed from the Magenta area last Monday morning with my staff section plus Majors Burton Miles and Robert Travis. We traveled by motor via Tabia, Tlemcen, Oujda, Guercif, Fez, Meknes, Klemisset, and Rabat; a most beautiful and interesting trip. We saw wheat being cut by sickle, as in the days of Christ. The Arabs grasp a handful of stalks and cut them off with the sickle, then bind the bunch into a small sheaf of about forty or fifty stalks. Men, women and children were cutting wheat by this method in many fields. We also saw wheat being cut by American binders drawn either by tractors, horses, oxen, or by a combination of horses and oxen. It was usual for eight oxen to pull a binder. Six to eight horses did the same job. Many of the wheat fields are on the sides of hills and mountains too steep for binders. I saw only one combine in use.

The fan belt on my command car broke soon after leaving Oujda, and we limped along with it to Taourit. At Taourit, a native Arab town, there is a French garrison composed of native Moroccan troops. I stopped at the French garrison in the hope that they might have a fan belt of the proper size. I arrived at about 1:00 PM. A French general, Beauclerc, was visiting the garrison, and he sent his aide to invite me to join him at his mess. Although I was in a hurry, I preferred not to be discourteous to him and followed the aide. He and all his officers of the garrison were there. They had finished the meal but were drinking coffee. I had a cup of coffee and one small drink of very strong and very distasteful liquor.

I recognized General Beauclerc as one of the French generals I had met at a demonstration at Arzew last week. He could not speak English and I had forgotten the little French I once knew, but through a lieutenant who spoke both, we carried on a fairly intelligent conversation. Beauclerc expressed admiration for the excellent demonstrations my troops put on for the French visitors at Arzew. After mess the general and his officers sat and drank wine until 3:00 PM when I excused myself, thanked them for their hospitality, and withdrew.

The lieutenant who acted as interpreter accompanied me and helped me procure a fan belt. He searched the town and found two which he borrowed from some of his French friends, but neither of them would fit. He then started off and was gone about 20 minutes. He returned with a borrowed belt which was just right in size, but the owner would not sell it; said he would lend it only. So we put it on the engine and drove on to Fez. I will send it back in a day or so.

Monday night we stopped at the Palais Jamai, a hotel in Fez. This was a most attractive place but obviously set up and organized for the tourist trade. The interior was decorated in true Arabian style. The floors and walls were inlaid tiles of bright colors; green, blue, red, yellow, white, and black. Each tile on the floor was about two inches square, smaller on the walls. These various colored tiles were set to form many attractive designs, all typically Arabian. The patio of the hotel was a beautiful, attractive and comfortable garden with terraces on which tables were set for guests. The hotel was requisitioned by the Air Force for quarters for officers who are stationed at the American airfield some nine miles to the west of Fez.

There were nine of us in my party, five officers and four chauffeurs. At first the lieutenant in charge would not agree to feeding and giving rooms to the four enlisted men. However, after I discussed the matter with him he changed his mind.

Our supper was a foreign dish, couscous, which did not appeal to me. The room I occupied was quite comfortable. A private bath was included, and there was plenty of hot water which I made the most of. The windows overlooked the patio and terraces. The entrance to the hotel was through the old fortification wall, probably more than a thousand years old. One would never suspect that such a beautiful and attractive spot existed behind that neglected and unattractive entrance. For breakfast we had fried eggs and ham. The coffee was made from parched grain.

Fez was a very interesting place, as was Meknes. I would like to visit these two cities after the war.

We arrived at our bivouac area at about 11:00 AM Tuesday. After setting up camp I went to Rabat and reported to General Dawley, Headquarters, VI Corps. I had a very pleasant visit with him. Afterward I drove throughout the area assigned to the Division and prepared my own plan for disposing the troops, which General Dawley approved, although it was quite different from the one prepared by his staff.

I had the detraining point for the foot troops moved from Sidi Ben Knabel to Rabat, thus saving them a 12-mile march—180,000 man-miles. I had the artillery detrain at Port Lyautey, a point better and nearer to their camp than Sidi Ben Knabel. They will go into camp in a neck of the cork forest about 6 kilometers south of Port Lyautey.

This whole change in disposition puts all units near a hard-surfaced road and will save much in motor maintenance.

I had a grand dinner today with Company B, 111th Engineer Battalion. Menu: pork chops, creamed potatoes, gravy, fresh boiled cabbage, fresh bread, fruit cocktail, and salad. This is government issue, much better than in the days of Julius Caesar whose soldiers carried their rations of wheat in a sack on their backs. We have been living on the C ration since leaving Magenta. It is very good but monotonous and consists of two cans. One is a mixture (stew) of meat or beans or vegetables. The other contains crackers, candy, sugar, and a beverage—either lemonade, cocoa, or coffee.

Near Rabat
Wednesday, May 26, 1943

We are now located in our new bivouac in the great Marmora Forest of cork trees about seven miles east of Rabat. Division Headquarters is located in a grove on a hill overlooking the city of Rabat and the Atlantic Ocean visible to the west. We have had a cool breeze each day so far. The temperature at noon today was 87 degrees.

In front of my tent, which is shaded by a big spreading cork tree, are four flags floating in the breeze, each on its staff thrust into the ground: the colors of the United States, the 36th Division flag, the Lone Star flag of Texas and the two star flag of a major general. On the next rise of ground about 75 yards north of my tent is a tall flag pole, which the engineers put in place. At its top a new, clean post flag waves lazily. A pretty scene.

Memorial Day. I accompanied General Dawley, General Les Cruex and others to a memorial service at the cemetery at Rabat. Dawley placed a wreath of flowers on the grave of each French and American soldier who fell in the fighting during the American landings last November.

An American battalion of infantry and a French battalion of marines composed the escort. They looked quite businesslike.

After the service I had lunch with Dawley. Major General Ernest Harmon, 1st Amored Division, was there also.

I was amazed to see radishes, green peppers and fresh spring onions on Dewley's mess table. These raw vegetables are strictly prohibited by orders from Eisenhower's headquarters because of cholera or other intestinal diseases which prevail. I have taken pains to exclude them from the messes of the 36th Division.

As so often happens, higher headquarters will prescribe rules and restrictions for their command which they expect the combat troops to obey, but pay no attention to those same regulations if they prove to be inconvenient to themselves. Naturally the combat troops don't like this. I wonder if my subordinates have similar thoughts about my headquarters. Many things take place that I know nothing about.

Last Friday General Lange and I called on General Desre, commander of the French Casablanca Division. He had a guard of honor for me and was most hospitable. I invited him to visit my headquarters next Wednesday at 11:00 AM.

While I was absent, a group of men from our engineers on a tactical exercise discovered a booby trap set to protect an enclosure containing beehives. A small gun about six inches long, loaded with a 16 gauge shot gun shell, was attached to a trip wire in such a way as to fire down the wire which ran along the side of the enclosure. Four such guns, one at each corner, were installed. I am told that one of the men tripped the wire and fired the gun, but for some reason he was not hit by any of the buck shot. He was fortunate indeed. I put out a notice at once to protect other men.

Yesterday at retreat, I decorated two lieutenants and two enlisted men of the 141st Infantry for saving the lives of their comrades at Arzew during landing exercises.

Monday, May 31, 1943

Temperature at 7:00 AM is 67 degrees seven miles east of Rabat.

Last evening at retreat I took charge of the drill of the staff officers prior to the sounding of retreat. They have been indifferent, inattentive, and sloppy in their dress. I put them through a course of command and movements that I hope will wake them up and get them looking like soldiers. Because of failure to respond to my instructions, I gave Captain Vincent Lockhart the job of committing to memory certain pertinent paragraphs of the drill book and reciting them to me each evening, beginning next Thursday.

Colonel John Paul Ratay, the Base Section Commander at Casablanca, has taken it upon himself to punish members of the 36th Division for not complying with the uniform regulations which he has prescribed for his own soldiers on duty at the Base. Of course, our men have no way of knowing what these regulations are before they visit Casablanca. Nevertheless, they are being arrested by Base Section Military Police, hauled before a drumhead summary court, and fined. Ratay directed Lt. Colonel Bob Phinney, the 36th Division Finance Officer, to deduct the amount of the fine from the soldier's pay on the next payroll and to report to him that this has been done. This is illegal and high-handed. I directed Bob Phinney to disregard Ratay's silly instructions.

This is just another incident in our long feud with base section people. They are there to serve the combat troops, but their attitude and behavior indicate that they consider combat troops a nuisance and an interference with their routine comforts.

Tuesday, June 1, 1943

Had a long talk with General Dawley last evening in his office in Rabat. He has some very perplexing problems of his own. I asked him to take Lt. Colonel Harry Steel to his headquarters and assign him to a position where he can be promoted. He gave me the impression that he would do so.

Yesterday an Arab woman complained to the Military Police Officer that she had been raped, and she identified a soldier in the 141st Infantry as the guilty party. I turned the case over to Colonel Werner, the regimental commander, to investigate.

He obtained a settlement and quit claim for four hundred francs, $8. Everybody satisfied.

Wednesday, June 2, 1943

General Desre and Admiral Renocre (French Army and Navy) visited my headquarters today and had lunch at the headquarters as my guests. Both are very charming and intelligent, even though they kept the guard of honor standing two hours. They liked our food, especially the hot biscuits and marmalade. A band from the 143rd Infantry played during the luncheon. I took them on a tour of the area to show them our various weapons, vehicles, radio sets and other equipment. I also showed them the organization of various types of tactical units.

They were pleased and are looking forward to the day when they will be similarly organized and equipped. The Admiral wore a white uniform and the trousers became quite streaked with oil deposited on the grass and brush by our supply vehicles. But he did not seem to mind. I enjoyed having them, and I have the impression that, if we ever fight together with them, they will be reliable and cooperative.

Saturday, June 5, 1943

Played a game of chess with Chaplain MacCombie. He won. When I told General Lange, he said, "Of course. The Chaplain has plenty of time to play chess. You and I are always busy with things military. He'll beat you every time." Of course, Lange did not mean what he said. Chaplain MacCombie is a dedicated and hard-working chaplain, and also an excellent chess player.

Sunday, June 6, 1943

General Dawley called me last evening and requested that I send a band to play a concert Monday afternoon for General Augusti Nogues, Governor and Commander of French Military Forces in Morocco. General Nogues is resigning and getting out in order to smooth the way for deGaulle and Girard to agree on future political policies for the "Fighting French." It is said that General Nogues has shown Nazi sympathies in the past, which have not pleased General deGaulle.

Corps Hearquarters requires an all-day and all-night extensive guard in Rabat. This, plus our own requirements, is an added burden to those who must provide the personnel while occupied with their training duties. We have been rotating the guard from unit to unit, but this is unsatisfactory because the assigned individuals have no personal interest in their extracurricular jobs. They are always unfamiliar with their guard duties which have to be explained in detail with each change of the guard.

Officers are being taken from their principal duty of training to serve on courts and boards, conduct investigations, and perform temporary duty away from camp.

We have no satisfactory arrangements to receive and dispatch personnel coming to and departing from the Division.

The Headquarters Company already has its hands full feeding, clothing, equipping and transporting headquarters personnel. So I am creating an organization in the Division to be designated "The Special Company." To it will go all jobs that are a harassment to company and battalion commanders, such as those mentioned above. It is to be a flexible organization in both strength and duties. Lt. Colonel Miller Ainsworth will command it.

Thursday, June 10, 1943

General Dawley sent for me today, said he wanted to talk to someone. He is having disciplinary troubles with the 1st Armored Division, General Ernest Harmon in command. The officers and men of the Division have just returned to this area from fighting in the Tunisian theater, and they feel that they own the town. They have been ganging up on the Corps MPs in Rabat, and trouble is in the air. Dawley tells me that unless there is an immediate change in the attitude of both officers and men of the 1st Armored Division, he is going to relieve General Harmon and send me over there to put the "screws on" and straighten them out. I consider this a distinct compliment.

Received a letter from General Desre expressing his thanks for courtesies during his visit. The French speak and write in a most courteous and genteel manner.

More than three hundred trucks and trailers are required by higher headquarters from the 36th Division to haul rations from Casablanca, Morocco, to Mateur, Tunisia, near Bizerte, a distance of more than one thousand miles, for the great mass of German and Italian prisoners of war who were recently thrust upon us as a result of Rommel's surrender.

On the return trip, the trucks will be loaded with prisoners of war who will be placed in barbed wire enclosures at Casablanca until they are sent by sea to their final destination, probably the United States.

It will require several round trips to get them all to the Moroccan port. It would be much easier to ship the prisoners from Bizerte to their final destination, except for the fact that there is little food for them in Tunisia. Nor are any ships scheduled for that port. The food and scheduled ships are at Casablanca.

In addition, we must send a large number of troops to Casablanca to guard and care for the prisoners as they arrive. All this immobilizes the 36th Division.

Because of the long continuous hauls, two qualified drivers per vehicle are required in order that one may rest while the other continues to drive. In addition, there must be guards, transportation officers and NCOs. The maximum number of vehicles have to be made available for this job, and each organization is required to furnish its pro rata share of men and trucks.

This means, of course, that what is left of the Division will have to squeak along with some inexperienced drivers and a paucity of vehicles which, in turn, demands a lot of rearranging and doubling up. An inconvenience, but a necessity.

Colonel Thomas J. Shryock, Executive Officer of the 36th Division Artillery, does not like this and is not cooperating with my staff. He did not turn over the pro rata share of trucks from the artillery until I went to Artillery Headquarters and personally ordered him to do so. He wanted to determine what the pro rata share of the artillery should be, but I did not permit him to change the allotment which I had checked before I approved it.

General Cowles was absent. I did not see him, and I doubt very much if he knows what Shryock is doing.

Sunday, June 13, 1943

On the evening of the 11th, my staff arranged a birthday party for me at the headquarters mess tent, and invited General Dawley and his Chief of Staff, Colonel Gibson, as guests.

Today I received an invitation from General Desre to a cocktail party held in Casablanca yesterday. The mail was so slow that it required five days to arrive here, a distance of 65 miles. I regret this incident greatly, since RSVP was requested. I took special pains to explain to General Desre.

Tuesday, June 15, 1943

This evening, Colonel Kerr, Lt. Colonels Steel and Hal Reese and I went to the home of Monsieur and Madame Benet-Demec in the Medina (the Arab section) in Rabat for dinner. They have a very attractive European style home with a hillside garden that overlooks the river and part of the Medina. The Arab homes have no windows or openings onto the street other than the entrance, a strongly bolted door through the exterior wall. All rooms open onto a courtyard, the whole so arranged that no one can see in and no one can see out.

From the elevated garden of the Benet-Demec home one was able to look into a few of the Arab family courtyards from above. In one yard a group of young girls was carding and spinning wool yarn. Storks' nests were on nearby chimneys, and in each nest were two young storks, about two-thirds grown but still too weak to fly. I am told that these storks will depart in about a month for Europe, some going to Norway, some to Holland and Denmark. After six months they will return again to Morocco.

Saturday, June 19, 1943

Yesterday I visited the prisoner of war cage about 25 miles southeast of Casablanca. One hundred and fifty of our trucks have just brought back 1500 Italian prisoners with their baggage from Tunis. About 25,000 prisoners of war, mostly Italian, are inside the barbed wire enclosure. I have about 750 men there from the 36th Division, and I arranged to have them relieved by a battalion from the 141st Infantry because I prefer to lose one complete battalion rather than have every battalion depleted and under strength.

Monday, June 21, 1943

Shortest night and longest day of the year. I attended a tactical exercise by a battalion of the 141st Infantry this morning. It was a daylight attack supported by artillery. The artillery fire was useless, and the infantry made several vital mistakes. If this had been a real attack, the battalion could have been wiped out. I was exasperated and scheduled the exercise rerun for tomorrow morning.

Wednesday, June 23, 1943

I attended a luncheon at the residence of the Governor of Morocco (Resident General De France au Moroc) Mr. Puaux, in honor of General Wayne Clark. Several French Generals, General Dawley, Brigadier General Frank Allen and myself were guests along with others. The residence is surrounded by a beautiful garden of vividly colored flowers, perfectly trimmed hedges, and clean, straight, inviting walks. The residence, itself, is quite spacious; the rooms are especially large; and the ceilings are especially high. Floors are inlaid with marble; on the walls are silk and satin tapestries; all furniture is upholstered in silk and embroidery.

A company of native soldiers provide the necessary guard and service. When I drove up to the dismounting portico, a big Berber soldier, dressed in a spotlessly white uniform patterned after the native Arab costume, opened the door of the automobile. A line of soldiers, dressed in the same native uniform, standing about 3 feet apart, was posted along each side of the way to the entrance. The soldiers presented arms as I stepped from the automobile and remained at present arms until I entered the doorway of the residence. They were impressive and made a splendid appearance.

Wednesday, June 30, 1943

Today, at 10:00 AM, I officially opened water point No. 1, south of my headquarters. General Lange, Colonel Kerr and Lt. Colonel Steel accompanied me. Lt. Colonel Dillingham, the Division Engineer, was master of ceremonies. It is planned to lay a 6-inch pipe line to carry water from the Bou river to our camp. This water point and pipe line mean a lot for the comfort and cleanliness of our men, since they will now be able to take showers, and there will be an unlimited supply of water for washing clothes. It is a tribute to the resourcefulness and energy of our 111th Engineer Battalion since they had to do it despite the Corps Engineer who would not help in any way.

Monday, July 5, 1943

Last week a corporal of the 141st Infantry came to see me. He wanted to return to the States to get married. He had been living with a woman for about three years prior to his departure for Africa. When he was drafted, he stated that he was married. The woman with whom he had lived had left her husband but had no divorce. Later the corporal was required to make an allotment to his "wife." He did so, and after she had received three months government allowances, he was required to submit documentary evidence of marriage, which he could not do.

Some time ago he came to me in great distress, worrying that he would be put in jail for obtaining government funds under false statements. I advised him to pay back the money his "wife" had received, cancel his allotment to her, have her get a divorce, and then marry in the proper manner. He followed my advice. So last week he received word from his "wife" in Kentucky that she had procured the divorce.

I arranged for him to return to the States to complete the course of events I had advised him to carry out. I sent General Lange to Casablanca to arrange for the corporal to be attached to a guard company which takes German and Italian prisoners of war back to the States on returning transports. Of course, this is all done with the understanding that he will volunteer to return to his regiment after he is legally married.

On Friday of last week I went to Oujda by B-25 bomber with General Dawley. At Oujda we took cub planes to the Battle Training Center at Slissen, not far from Magenta. There we landed on a road and were met by General William H. Wilbur, who is in charge of the school. He had an itinerary arranged for us and took us from place to place to see the different classes of instruction. Although the instruction is valuable, I was disappointed because a great deal of it is elementary in character which our men do not need.

On the way back we stopped at General Clark's headquarters at Oujda. He outlined to us the next period of tactical training to extend to September 15th. He also outlined what will probably be our combat assignment after October 1st. I was dismayed to learn that he intends to commit the sin of dispersing the strength of the Division in the combat assignment, as was tried and found wanting in the initial stages of the Tunisian campaign. I hope the higher commanders will learn their business before long, and stop violating the tactical principles that have been established since Hannibal and all successful commanders who have come along after him.

On Sunday, July 4th, the 143rd Infantry and several other units of the 36th Division took part in a parade in Rabat. I was commander of troops and led the parade. Behind me followed the Sultan's Guard, big black men dressed in bright red Arab-style uniforms. Their band played continuously, and their marches were most inspiring. The Sultan's Guard was followed by a French battalion of infantry. Next came the U. S. Navy aviation personnel from the Port Lyautey air field. The 143rd Infantry was next, preceded by the colors and guidons of all absent units of the Division. This mass of colors was a beautiful sight. The regiment made an excellent impression, and I was well pleased with their appearance and marching.

I received many compliments on the excellent appearance of the men, which I have passed on to the Division.

The 1st Armored Division followed the 36th Division, passing the reviewing stand in a column of single vehicles, 50 to 100 yards apart, at about 15 miles per hour. They made a poor impression. The vehicles were dirty; the men were dirty; and the noise was deafening. Most of the spectators left when they saw only a long column of uninteresting tanks and trucks approaching.

After the parade, the dignitaries, including myself, assembled at General Dawley's mess for luncheon. Generals Clark, Dawley, Harmon and several French generals made a point of seeking me out and telling me how well my troops did in the parade.

Today, along with selected officers of the Division, I witnessed a demonstration in which several planes dropped different types of incendiary bombs to show their effect. In addition, a platoon of tanks moved under an umbrella of 105 mm artillery shells bursting about 30 feet above and beyond the top of the tanks. Two shells burst on the ground among the tanks. There was no damage whatever to the tanks nor the crews.

After this demonstration, the VI Corps Headquarters mess served luncheon in a grove of cork trees south of Port Lyautey. Our artillery band played during the meal. Generals Clark, Dawley, Harmon and I were seated together at one table. Clark told me that an operation is being planned for the Fifth Army to take place this fall.

This evening, selected officers of the 36th and 1st Armored Divisions and I attended a lecture by General Harmon dealing with his battle experiences. He introduced his lecture by saying, "My talk has to do principally with the stupidity of the high command. I say stupidity, because there were times when the higher commanders were stupid as hell." He outlined the operations of the American II Corps through Tunisia and the part taken by the Armored Division. His talk was full of dry humor and criticism of the high command which pleased his audience. He was quite entertaining, but we did not gain much in the way of professional knowledge.

One hundred and twenty-five officers of the Division have departed to attend the Battle Indoctrination Course at Slissen for three weeks, a course which I consider quite elementary for our people. I hope none of them is killed or injured during that training. Generals Clark and Wilbur, who are instigators of this, should realize that we are beyond such training.

Friday, July 9, 1943

Watermelons again. This morning a French farmer and three Arabs came to see me. They claim damage to their watermelon fields. I visited the fields and found that some soldiers of the 143rd Infantry, on maneuvers last night, raided the fields and destroyed a great number of melons. Texas soldiers just can't resist watermelons! They carried away all kinds—green, ripe, large, small. They also damaged the vines by trampling them. In accordance with Articles of War, I required the 143rd Infantry to pay for them.

I directed that the Frenchman be paid the full amount of the damages he claimed, since they were just. I allowed only one fourth of the claims of the Arab farmers because they greatly exaggerated the amount of their loss. Afterward, the French farmer gave me a bottle of his most precious wine which he was saving for the Day of Victory.

Tuesday, July 13, 1943

Last Saturday morning I sent some men from the 143rd Infantry to put out a forest fire 18 miles northeast of Division Headquarters. On arrival they radioed that the burning wreck of a crashed B-25 had set the woods on fire. I visited the scene and found the plane completely destroyed. Three gruesome, charred bodies were smouldering within the wreckage. Apparently none of the three had an opportunity to use his parachute, which indicates that the plane was near the ground when trouble developed.

I may now record that this Division was included in the list of troops for the invasion of Sicily which took place on July 10. It was removed from the list, transferred to the Fifth Army in May, and sent to Rabat to assist in guarding the Spanish-Moroccan border in case of an attempt by Germany to send an airborne force there. This change was made at the request of General Montgomery. He asked that a division with battle experience be substituted for the 36th. The 1st Division took our place. I note from the news bulletins that the landing met with no great resistance and is going according to plan. I regret that lack of combat experience kept us from the invasion—but I am glad to know there is one Commanding General who thinks experience is important.

Wednesday, July 14, 1943

Today I saw the parade of French troops in Rabat in celebration of Bastille Day. I was seated in the grandstand which was in rear of the reviewing stand. On the reviewing stand from right to left were General Dawley, The Sultan of Morocco, The French Governor General of Morocco, and Lt. General Lescruex. Each arrived with an appropriate military escort. First was General Dawley with an escort of half-track reconnaissance cars; business-like but not spectacular. A French band rendered the necessary honors. Next came General Lescruex who commands all French troops in Morocco. His escort consisted of a squadron of native cavalry and a mounted band; smart, neat, alert. The horses were of Arabian stock and beautiful animals. Next came the Governor General, Mr. Puaux. His escort was also native cavalry, similar to that of General Lescruex. Last came the Sultan with an escort of native cavalry; black men dressed in red, with shining equipment; a beautiful sight.

After these preliminaries, a group of French officers and enlisted men were decorated in front of the grandstand in a very impressive ceremony. Then came the parade with the Sultan's Guard of infantry and artillery (horse) in the lead. They were spectacular in their bright red uniforms (Arab style pants) and colorful turbans. They were Berbers and marched perfectly. Each man was as black as the ace of spades and completely self-confident. They were magnificent.

Next came several battalions of infantry in various native and French colonial uniforms. They marched perfectly. When a battalion of Goumiers went by in perfect step, in black robes, obsolete American helmets, absolute confidence showing in their faces, a French General who sat on my right remarked to me, "Those men are devils." They looked it. I am told that the Italian and German soldiers fear the Goumiers who do their best work by killing stealthily at night and carrying back to their comrades the left ear, left thumb or the nose of their victims. I was impressed by the many tanks, armored cars, tank destroyers, jeeps, trucks, radio sets, anti-tank guns and machine guns of all types now in the possession of the French and displayed in the parade. All of this equipment is from the American army.

The Fifth Army has set up a Tank Destroyer Training Center at Sebdue with Lt. Colonel John W. Casey as commandant, and our 636th TD Battalion as school troops. All of the TD Battalions that have been in the African campaign and two French TD battalions are at Sebdue. They have new M-10 T.Ds. with 3-inch guns instead of the 75 mm guns on half tracks which were no match for the German armor. Our 636th, as school troops, gives all types of instruction: tank driving, maintenance, and gunnery, both direct and indirect. German tanks and equipment captured in the area near Cape Bonn are at the school for experimental firing and penetration tests. The officers and men of the 636th are working throughout the long summer days to make themselves proficient and to command the respect of those whom they teach. Each platoon leader is expert in artillery fire methods and the gunners on the 3-inch guns, due to their practice as instructors, are outstanding in speed and accuracy.

Thursday, July 15, 1943

Last evening my Aide and I attended a dinner given by Monsieur Jean Costedoat-Lamarque, The Controller Civile de Sale, at his residence in Sale.

The Controller met me at the gate and escorted me to his house. It was surrounded by a high stone wall with one gate which was guarded by a sentinel, a Goumier. The residence is surrounded by a spacious lawn and an orchard of banana, orange, lemon, almond and peach trees. The house is an elegant European style home. A guard of honor of Goumiers was in formation to receive me. Others present at the dinner were the Controller's wife and daughter, aged 14; his cousin and her husband from Algiers;

Colonel Garrison, commander of the U.S. airfield at Sale, and Lt. Colonel Sweat, liaison officer from the Fifth Army.

After dinner, the Controller presented to me a Goum of long service who had been awarded eight decorations for valor in the French army. He was near retirement age and was said to be the best tea brewer in Sale. We went out into the garden, and the tea brewing began with great ceremony. The warrior-brewer was seated under a palm tree on a rug surrounded by his silver utensils, with an assistant nearby. He heated the water kettle over a charcoal brazier and prepared his brew of tea, mint and sugar, tasting it from time to time to be certain that the taste and temperature were just right. When the proper brew of the tea was accomplished he adroitly poured it into relatively small-mouthed glasses from a distance of three or four feet from and above the glasses without spilling a drop. This was a real art, and his skill proved him to be an old hand at tea brewing.

Wednesday, July 21, 1943

General Dawley sent his Chief of Staff, Colonel Gibson, to the Division today. I placed him on temporary duty as commander of the 141st Infantry. Colonel Werner, the present regimental commander, is to go to Corps Headquarters as the Deputy Chief of Staff. This has been done to give Gibson some experience with troops so that, as Corps Chief of Staff, he may more fully appreciate the effect of Corps orders on the troops who must carry them out. Werner, in order to give Gibson a free hand, goes to learn some of the problems that Corps Headquarters has to contend with. I think Gibson will learn a great deal, if he makes a real effort.

Sunday, July 25, 1943

The 143rd Combat Team departed from Marmora Forest for Arzew today for additional training in landing on hostile shores.

Near Rabat
Monday, July 26, 1943

Yesterday afternoon, accompanied by Colonel Kerr, Lt. Colonels Crowther, Steel, McShane, Ives, Major Travis, Chaplain MacCombie, Corporal Swartz, I went to the home of Monsieur Lamarque to witness a chess tournament between a group of prominent Arabs and the two best chess players of the 36th Division, MacCombie and Swartz. This tournament was arranged by the Controller who is not a chess player but likes to entertain. He and his wife had gone to considerable pains to please their 60 guests who included Arab officials and players, several French families and ourselves. Some could speak only their own language; others could speak two languages, but none could speak all three. When I wanted to talk to the Arabs, it was necessary to have two interpreters: one English-French, the other French-Arabian.

Our host had put up a typical Caid's circular tent with an underlining of many different colored panels sewed together. Underneath, on the thick green lawn, were arranged in a pleasing manner, ottomans, stuffed cushions, chairs and tables. Under a palm tree a short distance from the tent, the uniformed tea makers were seated on a rug with their utensils and materials. Willis Bell, my orderly, and John Clay, my chauffeur, took their stations in the shade seated near the rug, and remained there observing activities and having a good time until we departed.

The chess games started promptly. Our two players lost their first games. They were a little nervous at the start because the Arabs reverse the king and queen position. After they adjusted to the Arab way, they settled down and at the finish our players had beaten all their opponents. The games were interesting to watch because the players were of professional caliber and good sportsmen. The Arabs took their defeat like the gentlemen they are. Servants passed tea, chocolate, beer, wine, cookies, and cakes from time to time during the five hours they played.

During the afternoon, one Arab guest asked me if I would like to visit the old Arab university in Sale. I accepted, and a party of officers and an interpreter drove through the dirty streets of Sale to the ancient building which was erected in the 14th century and has been used as a college for hundreds of years. At the present time it is being restored.

The students sit on the floor around the teacher; their living rooms are five by eight feet cubicles that look like prison cells; no light, no ventilation. The mosque was nearby, but our guide would only let us look in because all unbelievers are forbidden to enter.

We saw the minaret from which, at sunset, the Muezzin calls the Moslems to prayer. I heard him calling when I was in Rabat and felt transported into another world. The weird, pleading, wailing, reverent voice just at dusk seemed so different from anything

I had ever heard before.

While walking back from the college our guide arranged with a good friend of his to invite us into his home. We were amazed at the splendor of this Arabian house. The walls and floors and ceilings were inlaid with one to two inch squares of vividly colored tiles predominately of white and blue, but many were red, yellow, and green. On the ceiling gold predominated. Electric lights made them sparkle. The curtains and tapestries were of elaborately embroidered silk and satin. A patio with flowers and a fountain was surrounded by living quarters. Each room we saw was long and narrow. Along the walls were long, thick, wool-filled divans with red and cream colored satin coverings. Beds were at each end of the room on platforms about five feet above the level of the floor.

I was told that this Arab home, which obviously belongs to a wealthy man, had been in his family for hundreds of years. The present owner is a descendant of an old commercial family, and each generation has added something to the beauty and splendor of the home.

We were invited to tea and I accepted. While we were seated on the ottomans and divans, drinking tea and eating cookies, I could catch a glimpse of the women of the household peeping at us through shutters and from around corners. The Arab women hide whenever a non-Moslem enters their home. Their faces must not be seen, but their curiosity tempts them to peep from a safe distance.

A part Negro servant girl served the tea. I was told that the servants in a wealthy Arab home are virtually slaves, never change, and grow up to become the servants of the younger generation. These servants or slaves are not restricted and may run away if they like, but they seldom do because they have a secure and happy life with their welfare and personal needs assured by their Arabian masters.

The chess tournament and the visit to the Arab home was an experience we will never forget.

After we went through the main gate of the old wall around Sale, on our way back to camp, we passed a Moslem funeral procession. The corpse, wrapped in a white robe, rested on straw on a litter-like crate. This was carried by four men who supported it on their shoulders. There seemed to be no formation. The mourners, all men, followed along at a fairly rapid step, surrounded the litter and chanted hymns. Nobody, other than the mourners, seemed to pay the slightest attention to the funeral procession. Moslem custom requires burial before sundown of the day of death.

The 141st Combat Team departed for Arzew today to join the 143rd for additional amphibious training. Not much of the Division is left here. There is something in the wind. Looks like the German threat across Spain to Spanish Morocco has diminished.

Saturday, July 31, 1943

Yesterday I flew to Gibraltar in a Navy Catalina plane. This was my first visit to Europe since 1919. We arrived at Gibraltar at 9:45 AM and departed at 7:45 PM. Captain Lord, Liaison Officer stationed there by the U.S. Air Force, was especially kind to us. He gave us almost all of his time and drove us about in a jeep. We drove through the many tunnels where the hospital, machine shops, barracks, and storage vaults for gasoline, oil, ammunition, food and water are all housed inside the Rock. The place is truly impregnable, and I am impressed by its great military strength.

The town with its narrow, winding streets and small shops was colorful with its mixed population of English and Spanish. There were many Indian stores where souvenirs could be bought at high prices. I bought Julia a gold filigree Toledo brooch and bracelet to match.

Just received word that we are to get ready immediately for field operations. Apparently we are going to be used in some contemplated operation against Italy. The Division is packing and will start moving to Arzew tomorrow.

Algiers
Wednesday, August 4, 1943

I have been so busy during the past ten days attending to military matters that I have not had time to comment herein.

On Saturday evening, July 31st, I, as an official guest, accompanied by Colonel Kerr, Lt. Colonel Harry Steel and my Aides went to the home of the Pasha of Sale for an Arab dinner. A guard of honor was lined up along the narrow passageway leading from the street to the home. The Pasha and his staff were at the entrance to greet me, and we were ushered into a large, colorfully decorated room.

The Pasha spoke only Arabic, and I could speak to him only

with the help of Mme Lamarque who translated my English to French. Another guest translated from French to Arabic. I am not sure that my thoughts reached the Pasha as I intended because sometimes the interpreters had to struggle considerably with words, and a time or two, when I tried to say something humorous, there was no reaction.

The Pasha's home was elaborately furnished, spotlessly clean, and most comfortable with beautiful ottomans and divans. When I arrived at 8:00 PM, I noted that some of the guests had attended the chess tournament at the home of Monsieur Lamarque. There were several distinguished Arabs and a number of French officials and their wives, including Monsieur and Madame Lamarque. After several minutes of conversation, there was a ceremonial washing of hands and then the Pasha led the way to the dining room. We were seated in four groups, five or six in a group. We sat on cushions around tables which were about four feet in diameter, a foot high, and inlaid with colored wood. There were napkins to use as bibs but no table cloths. A servant dressed in bright colors stood at attention at each table. At a signal from the Pasha, each servant disappeared and returned with the half carcass of a roasted sheep on a large silver tray and placed it on his table. Before taking any of the food we had to say aloud in unison "With the permission of God," while the Arabs said "With the permission of Allah." The Pasha started eating and we all followed suit, pulling off pieces of mutton with the three first fingers of the right hand. The left hand is used by the Arabs to answer the call of nature and hence must never be used to touch food.

The meat was good, but the Pasha insisted on pulling off rare choice pieces and passing them to me as the specially favored guest at his table. I dislike rare mutton so I had a difficult time getting them down, but I did not wish to offend him.

As a climax, the Pasha reached into the carcass and hauled out the kidney which he passed to me as a special favor. It looked raw to me. Madame Lamarque noted my hesitation and told me that I would offend the Pasha if I did not eat it. Offense or no offense, I just could not do it. I had to decline, but the Arab on my right at the table ate it. Madame Lamarque and the interpreter carried on a serious conversation with the Pasha in an effort to explain my discourtesy, but I do not know what they said.

After the roasted mutton came roasted sections of back bone of some large animal with slices of quince on top. The quince was good, but I did not taste the meat.

Next came a tray with roasted whole chickens, one for each guest. They were delicious, but some job to eat with one hand. Next was a chicken liver pie in a silver container about four inches deep and about 14 inches in diameter. I ate some with my fingers which was just like eating a juicy apple pie with one hand. It was only fair.

The next course was couscous. It was a mound of coarse ground boiled wheat with a depression in the center filled with a highly seasoned meat and gravy stew. It was a slimy mess to eat with one's fingers, but it tasted good.

This was followed by cantaloupe cut into bite-sized chunks. Afterward, we had watermelon cut in the same manner. They were delicious. Then came fruit—grapes, peaches, apples and plums.

We wiped our right hand on chunks of bread, which was quite a job single-handed.

After the meal, we retired to a drawing room which was elaborately and comfortably furnished. As soon as we were seated, a servant appeared with a pitcher of water, soap, a towel and a silver waste bowl. He set the waste bowl in front of me, handed me the soap, poured the water on my hands while I washed them, and handed me the towel with which to dry them. He did the same for each guest.

Thus cleansed, conversation was renewed while an expert brewed tea in the center of the room. I had been told that one must drink three cups of tea after dinner and then depart. But I forgot this and lingered on for some little time after the third glass. Everyone was waiting for me to leave, but I didn't realize it. Finally, Madame Lamarque said to me, "We cannot stay longer. We must go." Then I arose, and accompanied to the door by the Pasha and his staff, we all departed.

After I had thanked him, and bade him good night, he said to me in Arabic, which had to be translated, "I wish you and your soldiers happiness and an early victory." I replied by wishing him and his people good health, long life and prosperity.

On Sunday, August 1st, I traveled in a convoy with seven staff cars from Rabat to Oujda. Enroute we visited the native quarter of Fez which was most interesting. The dirty, winding streets were shaded with a cane matting which breaks the rays of the sun, and were so narrow the laden burros had to move through single file.

Along the sides were small shops in which almost anything could be bought: meats, vegetables, fruits (all covered with flies), rugs, brass articles, slippers, leather goods, silks and satins. The merchants, wise to the ways of the American, were asking four to five times the true value. I saw nothing I wanted.

At Oujda I was invited to spend the night at the villa of General Gruenther. Next morning, along with Clark and Dawley and several staff officers from the Division and VI Corps, I boarded a plane for a two hour flight to Algiers. The remainder of the convoy proceeded to Port-Aux-Poules, which is five miles east of Oran, on the sea.

Algiers is a modern French city, a little Paris. We went immediately to the Headquarters of the Fifth Army which is set up in a boys' school vacated for the summer. I was interested in the outdoor washing facilities the boys use. It was a long trough fitted with individual tin basins, each beneath a cold water faucet. The waste was dumped in a brick-lined ditch. I used these facilities during our planning session and found that, while they were crude, they are perfectly adequate. General Dawley and I lived at the Villa Bel Aire, a more comfortable place.

It has been a disappointment to me that we had no combat in North Africa—but at least the Division has had some intensive training which will have its effect when the troops are confronted with the enemy. I have every confidence that the 36th will distinguish itself when we reach the beachhead in Italy.

CHAPTER NINE

Landing at Salerno

Port-aux-Poules, Algeria
Monday, August 9, 1943

The 36th is to see action at last. It is to be given an opportunity to demonstrate its fighting ability.

At Division Headquarters we immediately went to work planning our next operation. I and my staff had conferred with the planning sections of the Army, Navy and Corps staffs at Algiers and had prepared the basic plan for our part in the coming combat mission. There was mutual understanding. The job was done in four days under pleasant and harmonious circumstances.

Three possible landing sites were discussed during the first days of the study—north of Naples, the Port of Naples, and Salerno Bay. There were certain obvious advantages to each. North of Naples was discarded because our air capabilities could not provide a certain and effective support. The Port of Naples was finally discarded because its wrecked condition made it impossible to arrive at clear-cut landing procedures.

Salerno Bay was the site selected. Decisions were made regarding the number and locations of the beaches upon which we are to land; and the number and type of supporting troops to be attached to the Division. With the Navy we discussed the ship space available for the invasion and allotted that space to the best advantage.

All these major decisions having been made, Clark and I returned to our respective command posts, leaving the staffs to work out the minor details. Meanwhile, Division Headquarters had moved to a point near the sea about eight miles northeast of Port-aux-Poules.

My counterpart in the Navy is Rear Admiral John L. Hall who is responsible for getting us on the beaches. We have established most cordial relations. He is always helpful and cooperative and complies with any request I make, or gives convincing reasons why he cannot.

The day after I returned from Algiers I conferred with him on his flagship USS **Samuel Chase.** We had a very satisfactory conference.

On my way back I thought of Admiral Hall's spotless uniform

and clean, orderly ship, and compared them with my soiled, un-pressed uniform and my windswept camp on a field of dust three inches thick. In war, the Navy never misses a meal, a bath nor a bed.

Wednesday, August 11, 1943

I have been making final detailed plans for our tactical opera-tion and for combat-loading of our ships. I have placed General Lange in charge of loading plans. Clark is going to send General "Mike" O'Daniel to my headquarters to assist me in loading the transports and in any other way I desire. Mike is full of ideas and energy and will be a real help.

We have to distribute our vehicles and equipment among a number of convoys which will sail from African ports at inter-vals of one or two days. The first convoy to sail must be combat loaded. Part of this convoy will be loaded here at Oran. The other part will be loaded at Bizerte, some 600 miles east of here. Succeeding convoys must be loaded in such a way that vehicles and equipment will arrive in Salerno Bay or Naples in the order in which they will be needed as our beachhead expands. A change in loading plans of one ship makes many changes necessary on other ships.

I am impressed with the extent of the beachhead I am expected to secure. The distance from Agropoli around to the bridge over the Sele River along the high ground is about 25 miles. How-ever, if we can get possession of Mt. Soprano and certain key points near Ogliastro, Guingano, Capaccio, Albanella, Altavilla, Mount Chirico, and the Sele River bridge at Highway 18, we will control the road net and prevent ground observation of the beach-head by the Germans. Consequently, these key points will be our ultimate objectives in securing the beachhead.

In order to preserve security as well as to expedite planning, I have brought all planning officers from their units to Division Headquarters and placed them in a sealed-off area where they are not to be disturbed by matters not relative to our tactical plans. Only G-3 and myself are to have access to them during planning hours.

Since the 16th Panzer Division is defending Salerno Bay, I expect tanks to be used against us rather early, so I am providing for some artillery and antitank weapons to be put on DUKW's and taken ashore by 5:00 AM. Division Artillery and tank units are scheduled to arrive on the beaches at intervals throughout the morning so that a strong antitank defense will be in place by 10:00 AM.

A couple of British military police have arrived carrying a locked chest containing geographical information about the area around Salerno Boy. This will be of special value to the regimental planners for it is up-to-date and includes air and ground photographs. The British intelligence service is more active and thorough than our own and operates in peace as well as in war.

Friday, August 13, 1943

We have been going full speed in preparing plans for our amphibious operation. The loading plans are being prepared in detail by the staffs of the three combat teams and the transport quartermasters. The plans involve the combat loading of the Division and attached units on the assigned ships, unloading them in proper combat order from the transports into landing craft, and delivering them at the proper beaches at the proper time.

In theory, this is a rather simple matter. However, after our plans are completed and in the process of being written, transports are added; the capacity of some ships is found to be different than reported; or the number of vehicles to be loaded is increased because of demands for more and more space by the Corps and Army staffs, who do not seem to know what they want.

The stupidity of some of the higher staff officers is appalling. Some are unreasonable and some are just plain ignorant and incompetent. They want the Division to secure and hold, in defense, a perimeter of 25 miles. Yet, they want me to take off combat vehicles to make room aboard ship for cameramen and newspapermen with their vehicles. They force me to change my troop lists after we have made up our boat waves and landing plans. I have to be more stubborn than anyone else, and I have to be on the alert to keep some of my own unit commanders from hogging more space on the ships than allotted them. Luckily, our relations with the Navy officers are most cordial and we understand one another.

We are having a difficult time contacting some of the commanders of units that are attached to the Division for this operation. These consist of shore engineers, antiaircraft units. chemical warfare companies, attached artillery, tanks, and DUKW companies. All of them are on the distribution lists for orders, but some have not reported in and we do not know where some of their headquarters are located.

I attended a cocktail party at General Clark's villa in Mostaganem last Tuesday, the 10th, and again last evening. The first one was for four senators: Chandler, Barkley, and two others whose names I've forgotten. Chandler, an obvious politician, talked ceaselessly and criticized without regard to facts. I had to send all soldiers in the Division who are from Kentucky to Mostaganem so he could make a political speech to them. I see why military commanders view politicians as a nuisance in the theater of operations.

But the party was not a complete bore for I saw and had a visit with Paul Paschal who is Assistant Division Commander of the 45th Division. Paul is one of my very best friends. We served together in the 30th Infantry of the 3rd Division in Europe in World War I.

There are tricks in all trades. When we were at Cape Cod, one of our medical officers tried to transfer out of the Division, obviously to avoid going overseas. He did not succeed and has been with us until recently. Primer, Division Surgeon, had been keeping an eye on him to see that he remained with us. But now Primer is embarrassed. His charge has flown. The doctor was injured, not seriously, in what appears to have been a staged accident with a French civilian vehicle. He then arranged to have himself admitted to the base hospital, where with the connivance of someone, he was classified as eligible for return to the United States for medical reasons and promptly loaded on a vessel for home. When Primer learned this, he tried to get him off the ship, but the red tape was too involved. Although the doctor finally has evaded our vigilance and wangled his way back to the comfort of the States, we are glad he is gone.

Tuesday, August 17, 1943

Another hectic day. After having made a number of loading plans, we were notified today that we will receive three additional ships, LSTs. But we do not know how much space on each will be available to us.

This means that we will have to take vehicles and equipment off loading lists for ships previously assigned to us and place them on new lists to be prepared for the additional LSTs. Then we must replace the vehicles and equipment on the original ships: rearranging, relisting, regrouping, replanning.

The transport quartermasters are frantic, waving their hands and violently expressing frustration. My sympathies are with them. My "pick and shovel" planners are taking a beating, but most of them are doing so with resignation. Some men, noted for their calm dispositions and sense of humor, become quite irritable after having their schedules changed several times. I, while trying to maintain an attitude of patience, am exasperated. But it is all to no purpose. The changes continue. We need the patience of Job.

In the midst of all this we received orders from Army to modify all insignia on vehicles and guns by painting a white circle around the present white star. This is a War Department directive. Nevertheless, to require this change at this time under these strained conditions is just plain harassment by higher headquarters. Then too, today we must send to Algiers for loading on convoy D-7 those vehicles which we cannot load on convoys D and D-2, and we do not yet know what vehicles cannot be loaded on convoys D and D-2!

Major Ernest Rambo has set up an "assembly line" for waterproofing the engines of the vehicles which will accompany the landing wave of the combat troops. These engines must be able to operate in shoulder deep water so that when the Navy LCVPs dump the vehicles and men, the vehicles can be driven ashore. But, we don't know how many vehicles will be available to accompany the landing wave.

General Teddy Roosevelt called on me in camp yesterday. He has been with the 1st Division in all of its operations and landings to date. He told me that our situation was quite normal for they went through the same harassment and inefficiency when they loaded for Sicily in July. Confusion, misinformation, and lack of information bedeviled them also. He got a kick out of seeing us go through the same thing.

The patience, cheerfulness, energy, spirit, and sense of humor of Colonels Martin, Forsythe, and Werner are ideal, and I am fortunate to have men of their type in this hour of chaos.

Admiral Hall and General Dawley visited my headquarters in camp yesterday. We discussed many difficulties, came to no conclusions or decisions. None was required.

Tuesday, August 24, 1943

General Sir Harold Alexander, who commands the British Fifteenth Army Group, arrived at Mostaganem today, and I attended a luncheon Clark gave in his honor. Generals Dawley, Ryder and Omar Bradley were guests, also. After the luncheon General Alexander and party visited the 143rd Infantry, which was assembled in formation west of Port-aux-Poules, near the highway. He walked around the troops, asked a few questions of various officers and men in ranks, and then spoke briefly to the assembled officers. His talk was complimentary and encouraging, and I believe he was sincere.

Afterward, I discussed with him my plan of action for the Division in the forthcoming operation. He was well pleased with it. His only concern was the lack of adequate antiaircraft protection during the first three or four hours after daylight. I am also concerned about this, but it is the best we can provide and at the same time take care of other more important requirements. I am well pleased with the plan as a whole. At the conclusion of General Alexander's visit, Clark complimented me for having a well-disciplined Division.

I continue to receive many disconcerting crackpot proposals for changes in my loading and operating plans which I fight to keep from being adopted. Some of the proposals are: fire a 155mm howitzer from a DUKW while cruising in the Bay, to support the landing; switch the chemical battalions from D-2 to D after they have started to load; fulfill demands by higher headquarters for additional space on specific ships after passenger lists are completed and all space is crowded; place Engineer Shore Battalions on the ships assigned to the 143rd Infantry Combat Team while the loading of the Combat Team is under way.

We are required to take along a lot of heavy bridge equipment and grappling hooks to remove barbed wire, all of which, in my opinion, will never be needed.

I am required to provide three "flying jeeps," each equipped with a long distance radio set, and manned by two officers and driver. They are to land early, rush off into the unknown, and report back in code what the enemy is doing; as if we wouldn't know. They won't get very far. I wonder who gave birth to this idea.

When the ships were practically loaded, the Air Force demanded that their demolition bombs be put aboard. I refused to take them. Most of the ships are overloaded with personnel, and the bombs will take up space where our men are to sleep. Bombs loaded on deck will confuse our debarking schedules and, when unloaded onto the beach, our men will have to handle them and clear them out of the way. The bombs can just as well follow on a later convoy since they will not be needed until an air landing strip can be prepared; two or three days after we hit the beaches. Some bombs were actually sneaked aboard, but with the help of Admiral Hall I succeeded in having them removed.

Mike O'Daniel "acquired," by various means, as many DUKWs as possible for use in carrying 105mm howitzers ashore. He even "acquired" from Army Headquarters a DUKW on which is mounted a shack housing the radio set over which Clark plans to give the world a play by play broadcast of the invasion. General Gruenther, Clark's Chief of Staff, insists that Mike return that one—which he will do with some embarrassment.

Wednesday, August 25, 1943

Omar Bradley visited my headquarters today and made a number of helpful suggestions based on his experiences in the Sicilian invasion. He also pointed out some troubles that can be expected on the landing beaches.

I was an instructor at the Army War College when Bradley was a student there, and I am aware of his outstanding ability as a soldier. I was pleased to have the benefit of his experience. He states, among other things, that there will be confusion regarding our landing schedules and that it is absolutely imperative that each individual know thoroughly where he is to go for reorganization after arrival on the beach. I, of course, am aware of this, but I am pleased to have my expectations verified by his experience.

Saturday, August 28, 1943

Today we had a rehearsal of our landing operation. This was only a partial test. It was not the kind of all-out rehearsal that I would have liked, but an all-out rehearsal was not possible. Time did not permit and sufficient naval transportation was not available. The personnel of the Division was put aboard ships, but only a limited number of vehicles were loaded. It was little more than a repetition of landing exercises we previously experienced during training, but, in this case, we tried to visualize ourselves on a hostile beach.

Signal communications were poor and must be improved. Troops were landed on wrong beaches at wrong times. This was the fault of the Navy, and they promise to do better hereafter. Maybe. I set about immediately to correct errors and I believe that I have done so.

Monday, August 30, 1943

I held a conference with all regimental commanders, all battalion commanders, and all commanders of separate units from the Division and from all the other troops that are attached to it for this operation. I went over my plan in detail so that all will be familiar with it. Generals Dawley and Lucas were present part of the time.

Tuesday, August 31, 1943

At 9:30 AM I attended a conference at Fifth Army Headquarters at which Eisenhower and all the higher ranking officers were present. Each presented his plan for his part of the whole operation. The Air Force promises great things. At the conclusion of Air Marshal Tedder's presentation, George Patton, who sat beside me, leaned over and said, "Don't believe a damned word he says. If you see any friendly air before the third day you will do well."

Eisenhower visited the Division this afternoon. Each unit formed in line on the highway near its bivouac. Since he had to drive many miles to see all the troops, he reviewed them while standing in a moving jeep. He was in a jovial mood and complimentary of many units, critical of none.

Wednesday, September 1, 1943

I went to Bizerte to talk to unit commanders of the 36th who are to sail from there and to explain to them their part in the whole plan.

Thursday, September 2, 1943

I have been very busy during the past eight days trying to bring order out of disorder and confusion. Our planners have been working day and night to meet the schedules demanded by the transport quartermasters and the skippers of the ships. It is bad enough when changes occur prior to combat loading, but when they are ordered by higher authority after combat loading begins, with last-off in the hold of the ship and first-off still on the dock, something has to give and essential combat equipment has to be crossed off the loading list for that ship. When this had to be done, I chose to cross off communications vehicles and leave them for later convoys.

When I refused to load the demolition bombs on D convoy a few days ago, Lt. General Ira Eaker, from Eisenhower's headquarters, went over my head to Admiral Hall. Hall told him, "If Walker says the bombs are not to be loaded, they will not be loaded. I furnish the transportation. He decides what, and how, equipment is to be loaded."

Eaker then took the matter up with Eisenhower who called the three of us to his office in Algiers. Eaker, as spokesman, presented the problem to Eisenhower who said, "I am not going to decide this. You three get into the corner of the next room, come to a decision, and let me know what it is."

There wasn't much discussion. We already knew each other's views. Hall would carry the bombs if I would load them. I would not load them unless Eisenhower directed me to. Hall agreed with me. Eaker was outvoted. We filed back into Eisenhower's office where Eaker reported the result.

Eisenhower decided, "That settles it. The bomb's don't go on D convoy."

Hall and I went back to our commands. One day wasted.

An additional number of observers, cameramen, newsmen, and military-government personnel have joined the Division at the last moment. I hope they will have favorable news to report. I am confident of success.

> NOTE: These military government people were responsible to the military commander for the administration of the civilian population in the combat zone and for the maintenance of law and order. They accomplished this by establishing provisional governments, appointing local officials and supervising their actions.

The corporal I sent back to the States last July 5th to marry the woman he had been living with prior to entering the Army will not be with us. He has not returned to the Division and never will. It is possible that he had himself assigned to the

Corps Area Service Command near his home, but it is also possible that he got lost in the replacement stream.

Friday, September 3, 1943

Although we will not sail for a few days, the Division, plus all the troops attached for this operation—some 23,000 in all —are going aboard the transports at Oran and at Mers-el-Kebir, nearby.

Half of my staff is aboard the USS **Funston**. I and the other half will sail on the USS **Samuel Chase**. This is Admiral Hall's flagship, but it is also a transport which will carry its full capacity of troops and equipment. Hall has provided my party with comfortable quarters and invited General Cowles, Colonel Kerr and me to be guests in his mess.

I surveyed the whole area and visited the troops on some of the ships. They are crowded, but the voyage will be short and they will not be too uncomfortable. There is great activity everywhere, but everything is going smoothly, thanks to our carefully prepared plans.

Saturday, September 4, 1943

Dawley and I called on Clark at Mostaganem for a last visit before departure. Clark says the Italian resistance will be negligible; that our own paratroopers will be dropped in Rome; that the Italians will surrender when we approach them; and that the coast defenses are manned by Italians who will not oppose our landing. This would be good news, but it still remains to be seen whether or not it is correct.

At sea
Sunday, September 5, 1943

A beautiful Sunday. About noon the ships of D convoy began to move, one by one, out of the harbor at Oran. By 5:00 PM all were in formation and we were headed for Bizerte where the rest of the convoy will join us.

Now every officer and man will be told everything about our plans and intentions. Everybody is in high spirits and pleased to be taking part in an important landing operation.

I expect to meet at least one German armored division in the Salerno Bay area. One is there now, the 16th, and another may be sent there from the north by the time we arrive next Thurs-

General Walker s h a k i n g hands with General Clark. General Eisenhower in front seat and Admiral Hewitt in back with Clark. General Dawley standing on extreme left. 36th Division CP, Salerno, Italy, September 15, 1943

Pvt. Thomas A. Pastorino of New York, 131st Field Artillery Battalion, with relatives he met in the town of Glevano, Italy, where he was born. September 27, 1943—U.S. Army Photo

The ruined town of Battipaglia, Italy. November 3, 1943—U.S. Army Photo

How deep was the mud? December, 1943—U.S. Army Photo

White phosphorous shells fired by 155th Field Artillery Battalion, 36th Division, in support of attacking infantry. Mont Lungo, December 11, 1943 —U.S. Army Photo

Pack train moving over the rugged and roadless country near Venafro. 504th Airborne Infantry Regiment attached to the 36th Division. December 12, 1943—U.S. Army Photo

Chaplain Robert E. Alspaugh, 1st Battalion, 141st Infantry, during the evacuation of American dead from San Pietro to the 36th Division cemetery at Marzanella, Italy. December 13, 1943—U.S. Army Photo

Woman kisses hand of Col. William Martin of the 143rd Infantry, 36th Division, after Germans were driven from San Pietro. December 17, 1943
—U.S. Army Photo

day morning. The attack on the toe of Italy by the Eighth British Army may draw more German troops into reserve positions in the Salerno Bay area.

I am confident of success if the Navy will put my artillery and tanks ashore at first light (daylight) as I have requested. We are not loaded for combat as I would like. Corps and Army have placed too many restrictions on me regarding ship space and have forced me to make many confusing and disorganizing changes. All this has put my combat loading plans into some disorder. I can foresee confusing situations that may materialize on the beaches. If we have time to get untangled before anything hits us, we still can do our jobs, but my artillery and tanks, which are on ships at Bizerte, must be ashore by daylight or soon thereafter.

Admiral Hall had previously installed on the **Chase** the communications equipment I need to use enroute. He will make every effort to do whatever I want him to do to assist our landing, and assures me that the Navy will put my troops ashore according to schedule. I am not so confident.

For awhile I watched the ships as they formed the convoy, and then, relieved of harassment and looking forward to a few days of rest, I went below for a nap.

I have already fought the Battle of Salerno Bay in my own mind. We are committed to the plans; there's no turning back. It's just a matter of each doing his job.

Monday, September 6, 1943

My ship is one of many gliding along in perfect formation over the smooth sea. The troops are enjoying their rest; lounging about on desk, sleeping in the warm sunshine, playing cards, and cleaning their weapons with utmost care.

I visited various units aboard the **Chase,** observed their classes of instruction, and talked to a number of men and unit commanders. All know what they are to do and where they are to go after they hit the beaches.

Our Special Service Section has scheduled entertainment on each ship for each night we are at sea. The first performance on the **Chase** was this evening. The men crowded every bit of deck space, perched on landing craft and other equipment, and hung onto ropes and superstructure. The comical skit, produced by "volunteers," lasted about an hour and was very funny.

Tuesday, September 7, 1943

This evening our convoy passed the other part of D convoy at Bizerte. It was in formation, motionless, waiting for us to pass. We slowed down to let it fall in behind and join us. Each ship is trailing a captive balloon to protect it from German dive bombers. The whole convoy steaming eastward along the African coast toward the western tip of Sicily is a magnificent sight. As darkness came on I stood on the bridge of the **Chase** and watched as it plowed on into the night. We are now in the war zone. Anything can happen.

Wednesday, September 8, 1943

This is another calm, ideal day. There is not a ripple on the sea.

At first light this morning I looked out the porthole of my stateroom toward the east and could see more than a hundred ships of different types and capacity moving along as if on parade. They were another convoy carrying the British X Corps which will land north of us in Salerno Bay. We slowed down to let them pass and then followed along the northern coast of Sicily.

Our convoy is in four columns surrounded by a ring of destroyers, with three cruisers playing watchdog.

I hope we have fair weather and another ideal day tomorrow for our work in Salerno Bay.

Admiral Hall and I discussed whether or not to put down a preliminary naval bombardment on our beaches tomorrow morning prior to the hour of landing. The ships will be some ten miles off shore when we debark. I studied the latest air photos of the beaches and surrounding ground and could not find any organized defenses within our sector. There is a three-gun artillery battery opposite our beaches, but our intelligence reports it to be obsolete Italian property and unmanned. It is within rifle range of our first waves ashore, and if there are any gun crews, they will be quickly driven off by our infantrymen. There are a few old emplacements back from the beach, but there are no appropriate targets for Navy gun fire, and I see no point to killing a lot of peaceful Italians and destroying their homes.

The 16th Panzer Division is in the area but will not be strong in any one sector, especially along the beaches.

The British who will be landing to the north, will have a

naval bombardment for some time before we hit the shore. The Germans will assume the main landing is there. Our landing may not be discovered until we are ashore. Our first waves should get ashore as a surprise and quickly move inland. If our tanks and artillery are landed on schedule, they will be there for support. By the time the Germans are ready to counter attack, we will be ready for them.

Navy spotting parties are with the third or fourth waves and will be ashore soon after daylight to direct fire on targets beyond the range of our own weapons. A preliminary naval bombardment near the beaches might not be coordinated with the time of landing of the first waves, and confusion might result in the dark, especially if some of the rounds fall short. I do not think that a preliminary bombardment before the actual landing at 3:30 AM will be helpful, but I do count upon effective Navy fire to be directed by the several Navy spotting parties later. Hall and I, therefore, agreed there would be no preliminary bombardment.

The ship's news (Chase) quotes a dispatch from Zurich which says that a landing of American and British troops is expected in the Naples and Salerno area. I am not surprised at this because there must have been many enemy agents in Oran and Bizerte who had only to keep their eyes and ears open to know everything about our preparations and intentions.

Another message just received indicates that the Italians will ask for an armistice soon after we succeed in landing. I hope this is true, but I have my fingers crossed.

Reese, and one of my Aides, Captain Fred Stallings, spend two hours a day in my stateroom, together with two radio operators, perfecting the radio procedure they will use after they get ashore. They will be driving one of the so-called "Flying Jeeps."

I went to see the craft which the Commanding Officer of Troops had assigned to me and my staff for debarking tomorrow morning. It was next to the prow on the starboard side. First, it would have to be lowered to the water. Then its passengers would have to climb down a long rope ladder from a height equivalent to a three or four story building to get into it. I had had some practice in this business, but I thought of the older members of my party who were not in the best physical condition. They had had no practice in climbing down a long rope ladder, which puts a real strain on the muscles of the forearm particularly. I could imagine them getting themselves, their weapons, and their bulky, burdensome equipment tangled up in the ropes, their arm muscles exhausted. Casualties were possible.

I explained my misgivings to the CO of Troops, who very promptly transferred my party to another craft that could be occupied before being lowered to the water.

Everyone is cheerful and confident. I have taken special pains to insure that everyone is fully informed of his part in the operation. We have frequent boat drills and have studied various mechanical procedures in order to become more familiar with them. I expect the Division to do well. Our plans are complete, and it is only a matter of executing them.

Willis Bell and John Clay came to my stateroom today and packed my cot, blankets, four-day emergency rations of bitter chocolate bars and a few toilet articles. They were placed in my jeep which is now on deck and scheduled to be on shore at about the same time I arrive there.

I did not go to bed but I did lie down a time or two with my clothes on. A lot of orderly activity started at about midnight. Everyone had a "Last Breakfast," and soon thereafter, when called by the loudspeaker, the leading waves began to assemble at their debarking places. From the main deck I watched the leading waves leave the ship, then I lay down for another "catnap."

Salerno Beachhead, Italy
Thursday, September 9, 1943

The Division began landing on the Salerno beaches west of Paestum early this morning in fair weather. The shore was divided into four sectors, from north to south, known as Red, Green, Yellow and Blue beaches. At least two nights before, Navy frogmen had determined the exact location of the four sectors on the shore, and just before the leading wave was to land they marked the four beaches with lights which conformed in color to the designated beach and which guided the landing craft to their proper sector.

The leading waves of the 141st Combat Team, landing on our right, were on Yellow and Blue beaches at 3:30 AM and, as I expected, part of the 16th German Panzer Division was there to meet them. They had to do some very hard fighting. Some of our artillery, on DUKWs, was ashore early enough to be of great assistance, but even they were not landed in scheduled order, and single guns had to be organized into provisional batteries as they came ashore. One platoon of infantry was dropped into the sea while being lowered from its transport, causing some casualties. One wave crossed through another on the way to the beaches, causing some confusion and delay.

The Navy spotting parties were landed early, with the 3rd and 4th waves, for the purpose of knocking out German guns and tanks at long ranges. I expected them to get into operation immediately after landing. But they did not do so because their radios were soaked while coming ashore. Hours elapsed before they really got going. The first Navy fire in support of the 141st Infantry, where it was most needed, was not delivered until about 9:30 AM and then in small volume. The losses of the 141st for the day were far greater than those for the remainder of the Division.

The 142nd Combat Team, on our left, was not put ashore on its proper beaches, Red and Green, in all cases. Some waves were landed north of Red Beach. To avoid the German light artillery fire falling on the beaches, a few Navy steersmen turned their landing craft around and put out to sea, temporarily, before unloading their personnel. This caused confusion and the regiment was behind schedule. But, since the resistance it encountered was not as great as that in front of the 141st, its advance troops, moving north and northeast, were some three miles inland by 10:30 AM.

The 143rd Combat Team was in reserve, and its first wave was landed at about 7:30 AM, approximately on schedule. It came ashore over Red and Green beaches, following the 142nd, and moved promptly to its assigned positions.

Part of my staff (18 officers, 10 enlisted men) and I, in an LCVP, each carrying enough equipment for a pack mule, were lowered into the water from the top deck of the **Chase** shortly after 5:00 AM. At the same time, men, loaded down with 75 to 80 pounds of weapons, ammunition and other equipment, were laboriously climbing down rope ladders into waiting craft.

Our steersman, a sailor, promptly steered our craft to join a group of similar boats moving in a circle nearby, waiting for the full complement of its landing wave. Eventually, at about 5:30 AM, our circle straightened out and, as we headed for

Red Beach some 12 miles away, we could see ahead of us, and off to our right, many waves of LCVPs, each wave in column, moving at full speed toward the beach.

About half way to shore, we passed an enemy marine mine, floating near us. Our steersman had to do some maneuvering to miss it. It was about 2 feet in diameter with many horns, each about 6 inches long, projecting perpendicularly from its whole outer surface, a percussion cap on the end of each horn. This was a warning that our Navy had not been able to remove all enemy mines from our landing area, but we had no losses from mines.

While still a mile or so from the beach, I saw off to the south several of our LCMs, LSTs and DUKWs moving aimlessly about. They were carrying artillery and tanks that should have been ashore assisting the infantry, but I was helpless for there was no way to get word to them. Besides, they were under control of the Navy and not subject to my orders. I didn't know what the Navy personnel was waiting for, unless they thought the Germans were going to run away and leave the beaches free from all risk. They should have taken their chances and unloaded on schedule. I could only hope that this failure to do so would not be serious.

As we moved on in, I could see that the beach in front of me was clear of equipment and troops. Some troops, which I took to be part of the 143rd Infantry, were landing on and crossing the beach to the south under light enemy artillery fire.

We were headed directly toward one of our antiaircraft balloons about 100 feet high and anchored some 50 feet from the waterline. A few enemy artillery shells were falling in front of us. From nowhere and quite unexpectedly, a German plane appeared, diving and shooting at the balloon. While my attention was attracted to the plane flying away and to the balloon falling in flames, our steersman unloaded us into waist-deep water, still some 75 feet from the shore. He was in a great hurry. Before we could wade to dry land, he had turned about and was gone. The time was about 7:55 AM.

The beaches were wide, long, and ideal for our purpose. There was very little activity on them. The shore engineers had not yet put down any mesh matting for the vehicles to cross. I expected them to have these roadways ready much earlier. German land mines, if any, were not removed, for the sand had not been disturbed except by shell holes.

There were no real obstacles, only a few patches of old barbed wire here and there which presented no difficulty. I looked for "Mike" O'Daniel who was in charge of Red and Green Beaches, but did not see him. I wanted to ask him how things were going, but I knew he was busy and on the job wherever needed. I also looked for troops of the 142nd Infantry but none were in sight. It required only a glance to note all of these things.

We rushed across the beach through the artillery fire. I led my party inland, about a mile and a half, along the north side of the ruins of the ancient Greek town of Paestum toward a section house on the railroad. The railroad had been designated as the line upon which the infantry was to reform, untangle itself after the confusion of landing, and prepare to continue on to its objectives.

No Italians nor their animals were to be seen. Doors and windows of houses were tightly closed; all were locked or barred; curtains and blinds were drawn. The area seemed abandoned. We felt quite unwelcome, but, of course, we didn't expect a welcoming committee.

As we hurried along we passed two abandoned enemy radios still receiving messages in German. Here was an opportunity, perhaps, to pick up some helpful information. My hopes sank when I found that none of us could understand German. The abandoned sets, however, indicated that our 142nd had surprised the German radio operators.

When we were passing the ancient Temple of Ceres and I saw the ruins of Paestum, I had the unpleasant feeling that we were desecrating sacred ground. A little later we were moving across a field of bright red tomatoes, and I noted that they could be a possible supplement to our emergency rations of bitter chocolate. I was chagrined to find myself, surrounded by antiquity and in the midst of battle, thinking of my stomach.

There was no small-arms fire, but German artillery gunners, on the hills to the east and along the railroad to the south, amused themselves by shooting at us as we moved along a stone fence toward the section house. Primer was slightly wounded. Carl Phinney and Charles threw themselves on the ground when a shell burst near them. I shouted for them to come to the stone building where we were protected. They had run about 25 feet when another shell burst on the exact spot where they had been lying. They are now living on borrowed time.

I had about 10 minutes at the section house to survey the area in all directions. I could see no activity by our own troops but was confident they were carrying out the missions assigned because I heard small arms fire from various directions where the troops should be. Since there were none of our troops along the railroad, I assumed that they had passed over and to the east of it. I could see sun flashes off a number of vehicles moving about on the level ground two miles or so to the southeast, but I could not be sure they were ours. Maybe they were German. I learned later in the day that they were German tanks which had been firing on the 141st Infantry and the two south beaches, Yellow and Blue.

When the German artillery stopped firing at us, we followed the railroad north toward a large quadrangle of buildings which, during the planning at Oran, I had selected from an air photograph to be my command post. Each of us was armed, fully prepared to take care of ourselves in case we ran into a German patrol. Actually, we constituted a combat patrol ourselves.

We came upon a culvert under the railroad which was walled up at both ends with concrete building blocks, without mortar. It had been done recently and looked suspicious to me. It might be occupied by Germans. By words and by pounding on the wall I directed any person inside to come out. There was an outburst of weeping and wailing. An Italian family had taken refuge there, and the women and children were terribly frightened. Although I do not know a word of Italian, I do know some Latin, and I got the impression they were saying prayers. I am sure they thought we were going to kill them. First out was the father, followed by the mother, two teenaged girls and six-year old boy. They were extremely relieved and happy when I waved them back to their nearby small farm home.

As we approached the farm buildings I had selected for my command post, the owner, C. Vannulo, and his family, all dressed in their very best clothes, came out to meet us. In a most friendly manner they welcomed us to occupy the buildings, one of which turned out to be an especially large tobacco warehouse. Among the racks of drying tobacco we set up my Command Post and were ready for business in a matter of minutes. Almost immediately the unit commanders began reporting, in person, their progress and locations.

I told Colonel Martin to push east and get possession of the road along the western side of Mount Soprano, which was in about the center of our sector. And I urged Colonel Forsythe to get possession of the bridge over the Sele River, at the northern part of the sector. I cautioned General Cowles to set up his antitank defense for the whole area as fast as the proper weapons came ashore. He told me that he was already doing so. All this was in accord with my original plans. I was just "pushing." I felt that I ought to be doing something.

The situation was somewhat vague due to a lack of communications. Some of the radios had been unavoidably drenched and damaged. But we could not use them anyway. It would be foolish to tell our enemy what we were doing by sending messages in "the clear." To encode and decode was too slow. Distances were not great. Messengers on foot or in a jeep were faster. The few jeeps we had were in constant use.

My vehicles were not with us. Both were destroyed by artillery or mines while being driven over the beach. Private Bay, the driver of the jeep, was killed. Sergeant Bell, who was driving the reconnaissance car, and who came ashore later in the day, was not hurt, merely a scratch on his leg, but Colonel Kerr's orderly, Private Draper, who was riding with Bell, was severely wounded.

We had been in the tobacco warehouse only a short time when Colonel Ives, who was observing from the top of one of its towers, reported 13 German tanks moving from the north toward the landing beaches. They were west of us, between the railroad and the beaches. I hurried out and saw 5 or 6 of them, only 300 yards away bearing down on some of the 143rd Infantry which was in reserve. Part of the 151st Field Artillery Battalion, 34th Division, which had been attached to the 36th Division for the landing, had just arrived in position and was concealed nearby. The gunners began firing at the tanks east of Highway 18 at a rapid rate. General Cowles took part in this and even helped lay one of the guns. (See Appendix A.) Within a short time they knocked out four of the tanks, and the others fled. Captain Wiley Stem's Cannon Company of the 143rd was in on this affair and got at least one tank. The crews of the four tanks were made prisoners. Some were very badly burned, because each tank burst into flames the instant it was hit. I watched this duel from the flank. It was thrilling.

During this duel, the German tanks and our artillery were firing at each other across a road. At the moment of maximum fire, I saw, to my amazement, one of our DUKWs moving along the road at full speed directly into and through the field of fire. It was carrying the radio set for use in communicating with Army Headquarters aboard the **Ancon** out in the harbor. I had sent Carl Phinney to the beach to find the radio set and bring it to my Command Post. Phinney and the driver heard the firing but did not know what it was all about until they were in its midst. It was only by a miracle that the DUKW was not hit and the men killed.

Some of the original group of 13 German tanks extended their attack west of Highway 18 toward Red Beach and killed or wounded some of our men who were debarking at the time. O'Daniel, who was in charge of that beach, quickly put available guns into action and repelled the attack. I am told that his guns got two tanks, which means 6 of the 13 German tanks were destroyed.

Later, Ives discovered another group of 10 tanks near the same spot, approaching from the same direction. Again there was a similar duel. Three tanks were destroyed; others were hit and damaged. Those able to get away, fled.

We gave the German tanks a real beating on our whole sector, knocking out at least eleven. I keep my own tanks, antitanks and antitank guns in concealment where they have an advantage over any German tanks that approach our infantry. I don't believe in sending armored combat vehicles out into the open to be an easy target and to be destroyed when the enemy has a good antitank defense, as in this case. We let the enemy tanks come to us.

The German tank attacks were by small groups, each group acting on its own initiative and not supported by infantry. These were piecemeal attacks and quite to my liking. From about 10:00 AM on, our troops were sufficiently protected by antitank weapons to take care of this kind of threat.

The German tanks could have caused us a lot of trouble if they had attacked in mass formation at an early hour. However, we were favored by the terrain which is crisscrossed by canals and abounds in other obstructions so their tanks had to move cautiously.

Another advantage. The first shot at a tank would usually

cause a great cloud of dust to envelope it and blind both the driver and the gunner. They were helpless because they were not accompanied by infantry. Once they came within range of our antitank weapons they were disposed of easily.

Antiaircraft units, antitank units, artillery, tanks, and supplies have been arriving on the beaches all day long.

I was pleased, and also relieved, at 12:30 PM, when Lt. Colonel Joseph S. Barnett's 3rd Battalion, 143rd Infantry, got possession of the northwest section of the road which circles the base of Mount Soprano. He was able to move on southeast to the village of Capaccio and set up road blocks on the far side of the town. This meant that the Germans to the south of us could not use the road to join those north of us except by going completely around the mountain to the east and then north. The 3rd Battalion captured several German patrols at its road blocks.

During the late afternoon the 601st Tank Battalion and the 645th Tank Destroyer Battalion arrived. Both are from the 45th Division. I sent one company of the 601st to assist the 141st Infantry, which was having trouble on the south flank. The remainder of those two battalions was posted on the north flank near the Sele River and was directed to cooperate with elements of the 142nd Infantry already there to repel any German attack on our left (north) flank.

The Germans blew up the bridge on Highway 18 over the Sele just before dark. Later, the 645th Tank Destroyer Battalion surprised a group of 4 German tanks moving within its area, destroyed 2 and the other 2 quickly surrendered. It is my opinion that these 4 tanks were lost and confused in the dark and wandered into the area of the 645th, unknowingly.

At about 8:00 PM the 36th Engineer Regiment arrived. It is posted near Highway 18, north of Division Headquarters. Tomorrow morning it has the job of clearing out any enemy that may be in the area west of Highway 18 and south of the Sele River.

All other combat units moved to their assigned positions immediately after landing, in accordance with my plan for the initial deployment of the Division. By midnight the greater part of the combat elements were ashore and in combat formation on an outer perimeter of some 12 miles and a radius of approximately 4 miles, prepared to move forward to final objectives and to receive a counter attack.

Dawley visited my Command Post in the afternoon. He made

no suggestions and appeared to be pleased with the way our deployment was going.

Friday, September 10, 1943

Early this morning the 141st Combat Team advanced to and occupied all of its initial objectives. The German commander of that sector, south of Mount Soprano, realizing that his troops were isolated when the 143rd took possession of Mount Soprano, withdrew during the late afternoon yesterday and last night. This greatly facilitates our defense of the beachhead. Now, our principal attention is directed to the area north of Mount Soprano and south of the Sele and Calore Rivers. Nevertheless, I have an outpost south of the mountain and will keep it there until the British Eighth Army comes up from the south.

Combat Team 179, 45th Division, arrived this morning and is posted astride Highway 18 to protect our left flank and prevent any German crossing of the Sele River. It is supported by the 191st Tank Battalion and the 645th Tank Destroyer Battalion already there.

Combat Team 142 took up positions in the vicinity of Albanella.

Under the command of General Miles Cowles the 36th Division Artillery, with the 151st Artillery Battalion attached, is in selected firing positions prepared to fire on German troop concentrations with special attention to the Mount Soprano—Albanella—Altavilla —Calore River areas.

Antiaircraft units are installed to protect the beaches.

Our own troops now on the beaches in reserve or in the forward areas are disposed so that any attack by German paratroopers will be met immediately.

We are busy getting communications established, mostly by messengers; distributing equipment and vehicles as they come ashore; becoming familiar with the terrain, especially the road net; establishing supply arrangements; and perfecting antiaircraft and antitank protection. All of which was well understood and provided for before we left Africa.

Today Clark and Dawley visited my CP in the tobacco barn. Clark directed Dawley to take command of the units of the 45th Division as a part of the VI Corps and protect the left flank of the 36th. This was a change in command arrangements. Before we embarked at Oran, I had been told by Clark that I would be in command of all troops south of the Sele River during the first three days, but responsible to him.   However, I have no objection to the change.

The enemy has not materially interfered with our landing.   My plans are going well.   The beaches are free from enemy artillery and machine gun fire.   I am pleased.

Like Georgie said, there was no cover provided by our Air Force.

Saturday, September 11, 1943

From the moment I stepped ashore I wanted possession of the high ground in the vicinity of Altavilla because it gave the Germans an excellent view of Salerno Bay and our whole area. So, early this morning the 142nd CT sent motor patrols to Altavilla and north thereof to contact and report any enemy in that area; to establish liaison with similar patrols of the 45th Division north of the Calore River; and to follow up patrols by occupying the high ground north and east of the town.   Altavilla, as its name implies, is nestled on the side of Hill 424 near the top.   Its houses, built of stone, are hundreds of years old.   Its streets are narrow, winding and steep.

Patrols occupied Altavilla at noon.   Later, Lt. Colonel Gaines J. Barron's 1st Battalion, 142nd Infantry, moved into the town, meeting only minor opposition.   The other two battalions were in position south of the town, near Albanella.

I discussed the tactical situation with Dawley and Troy Middleton, Commander of the 45th Division, at about 1:00 PM.   Dawley told me that the 179th Combat Team, 45th Division, was advancing northeast, between the Sele and Calore Rivers, to join up with the 36th left flank on the Calore north of Altavilla. Patrols are to maintain liaison between the two Divisions.

Trigger-happy gunners of our antiaircraft units shot down two Spitfires this morning while they were coming in to land on the new airfield.   A real tragedy.   I told Colonel Wilson, who commands the attached antiaircraft units, that I wanted no more firing on friendly aircraft; that his gunners must hold their fire until planes are definitely recognized as German.   Later, two squadrons of P-38s, 31st Fighter Group, landed on the improvised field at about 1:00PM.   No casualties reported.

At about 2:00 PM Clark and Dawley came by my CP and explained the arrangements for bringing in additional troops as reinforcements.

Major Shield, British X Corps, arrived at about 3:00 PM. He brought information about the situation of the British landing north of the Sele River and took back a report of our situation. I am told that he and his driver were captured this evening just after crossing the Sele.

At about 4:45 PM our 155th Field Artillery Battalion observed and shot up a group of 25 German tanks north of the Calore River. According to the report, 11 were destroyed, 3 immobilized, and the remainder retreated toward the northeast.

Late in the afternoon, Brigadier General W. H. Wilbur brought oral orders from Army Headquarters to send one battalion combat team to reinforce Darby's Rangers on the mountain northwest of the City of Salerno. I gave this job to the 1st Battalion, 143rd Infantry. It moved to Red Beach and will be transferred in landing craft to Maiori tonight.

At 6:30 PM I moved the forward echelon of Division Headquarters from Vannulo's tobacco warehouse to a house near a large spring about 1½ miles to the northeast.

We are now in possession of all our final objectives and have proved that the German tanks are vulnerable and unable to breach our antitank defenses.

Sunday, September 12, 1943

Early this morning the Germans began infiltrating around the battalion on the Altavilla position. At 9:15 AM I went to see Dawley and explained the situation to him. He directed that I reinforce the battalion at Altavilla and occupy the high ground north and east of the town and connect with the right flank of the 45th Division along the Calore.

I gave the job to Colonel Martin. He is to use the 143rd Combat Team, less the 1st Battalion now with Darby's Rangers and less the 2nd Battalion in Division reserve, with the 1st and 3rd Battalions, 142nd Infantry, attached. He is to be supported by Company A, 751st Tank Battalion and the 155th and 132nd Artillery Battalions. I ordered the 636th Tank Destroyer Battalion, in process of debarking, to support this attack by bringing up its guns as they became available. O'Daniel, who was no longer needed on the beaches, reported to me at 1:30 PM and I sent him to assist Martin in every possible way.

It took considerable time to issue the necessary orders and to

The Salerno Area

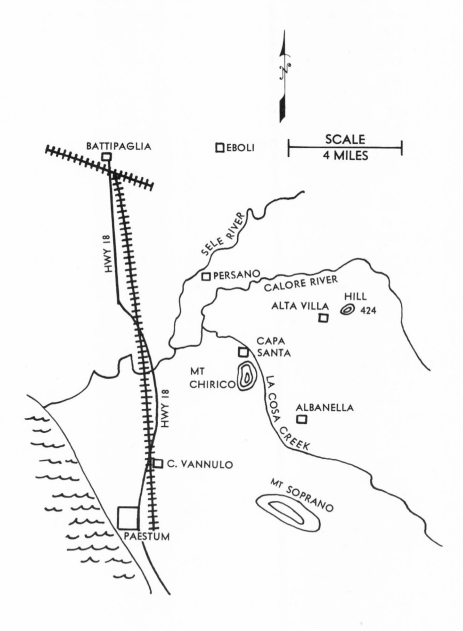

BATTIPAGLIA

EBOLI

SCALE
4 MILES

HWY 18

SELE RIVER

PERSANO

CALORE RIVER

ALTA VILLA

HILL
424

CAPA
SANTA

MT
CHIRICO

LA COSA CREEK

ALBANELLA

HWY 18

C. VANNULO

MT SOPRANO

PAESTUM

assemble and deploy the troops, especially since the 3rd Battalion, 143rd Infantry, had to march several miles.

In the course of the day I checked our antitank defenses with General Cowles to reassure myself that we could take care of any German tanks that might appear north of the Sele and in the area bounded by Albanella—Altavilla—Calore River—La Cosa Creek.

At 3:00 PM two air officers from Army Headquarters called at my CP to discuss plans for dropping units of the 82nd Airborne Division to reinforce our beachhead.

At about 4:00 PM Dawley told me to send one infantry battalion to the low ground between the Sele and Calore Rivers, facing northeast. He pointed to the position on a map, indicating the front to be about 1½ miles long and about 1½ miles east of Persano, from coordinates 905185 to 923170, to cover the gap between the 45th Division on the left and the 36th Division on the right.

> NOTE: Map Reference: Campagna sheet 198 IV Italy 1:50000, Geographical Section, General Staff, No. 4229. Published by War Office 1941, Second Edition (Coloured) 1943 (England)

I was a little surprised at this because I understood that a regiment of the 45th Division was advancing between the rivers and was protecting our left flank. Dawley stated that units of the 45th Division would be just across the Sele River opposite the left flank of the position the battalion is to occupy.

I told Martin to send his 2nd Battalion, which was in Division reserve, because it was nearest and would have only 5 miles to march. I went to see the battalion commander, Lt. Colonel Charles Jones, explained what he was to do, and told him not to expose his men to enemy observation after getting into position.

At 4:30 PM an Italian civilian reported 40 German tanks were on the road in the vicinity of the town of Cosa La Croce, some 20 kilometers to the east. Observation and bombardment by air was requested because these tanks are an excellent target for it. Nothing happened.

Late this afternoon, the Germans stepped up their attack on the high ground at Altavilla. The 1st Battalion, 142nd Infantry had a tough time and were finally driven out of the town. At 7:30 PM I checked the plans for retaking the lost ground with Generals Wilbur and O'Daniel, Colonels Martin and Forsythe, and ordered Martin to move his command into position during the night and to retake Altavilla tomorrow morning. Wilbur has been temporarily assigned to my headquarters by Clark.

It is taking more time than it should to issue orders, assemble units, and transmit information because we cannot use radio in the clear and have only a small portion of our motor transportation. This applies principally to arranging offensive action. Defensive arrangements have been built up as units arrived and are now complete.

Monday, September 13, 1943

This was a bad day for the Division. At about 9:00 AM Dawley ordered me to send two battalions of the 141st Infantry north of the Sele River to fill a gap between the 56th British Division and our 45th Division. This gap had never been closed by British troops, and the Germans were threatening to occupy it. I sent the 141st CT (less one battalion to remain on our south flank) and substituted the 133rd FA Battalion for the 131st FA Battalion because the latter was in position on the south flank and if moved would have to be replaced. This made only one move necessary for the artillery. Since the highway bridge over the Sele is destroyed, Werner's command had to cross on the railroad bridge. North of the Sele the CT was shelled by enemy artillery and had to switch to a road nearer the coast. They arrived at their position at about dark and reported that they were being eaten up by mosquitoes.

At about 5:00 PM, a report was received that the 2nd Battalion, which Dawley sent yesterday to fill the gap between the Sele and Calore Rivers, was being attacked; that the greater part of the Battalion had been captured; and that the remainder had fled. At first I jumped to the conclusion that this was a disgraceful performance. But as more and more information became available, I changed my mind.

For one thing, the 45th Division, west of the Sele River, was repulsed in its effort to advance, and a gap of some 2 miles or more existed at Persano, leaving the Battalion dangerously isolated and exposed. As a result, strong German forces of armor and infantry struck the Battalion from both front and rear simultaneously. Being without adequate antitank weapons, and being too distant from its own artillery to receive effective close support, it was quickly overwhelmed, with a loss of some 500 officers and men, including the Battalion Commander who was captured. The 132nd FA Battalion, in position south of the Calore, under Martin's command, attempted without success to stop the movement of enemy tanks through the gap at Persano.

Secondly, when Dawley told me to send the 2nd Battalion between the rivers, I did not know, and Dawley did not tell me, that the Germans had defeated and driven off the 179th Combat Team, 45th Division, the day before on that same ground. As a result, I did not warn Jones that he was going into territory where the Germans· had already been victorious.

After the defeat of Jones' Battalion and encouraged by their success, some of the German tanks and infantry, making reconnaissance in force, moved south from Persano, and a few succeeded in crossing the Calore River. However, they withdrew about 7:30 PM when they ran into our antitank defense organized by General Cowles. This consisted of the 36th Division Artillery plus the 151st Field Artillery Battalion; the 636 Tank Destroyer Battalion; and two companies of the 751st Tank Battalion. The artillery of the 45th Division took part in this action and did an outstanding job.

At about the same time, 6:40 PM, other German Infantry in considerable strength crossed the Calore north of Altavilla and was passing around the left flank of the 3rd Battalion, 143rd. This looked like trouble, and I went to see the situation. I met Martin at his improvised CP, together with O'Daniel, "Pete" Green, and CO, 751st Tank Battalion. Their troops were being attacked on both flanks and were about to be enveloped on the left. Since there were no other Division troops available to support the attack, there was only one thing to do. I told Martin to cease his attack and get his command together behind La Cosa Creek to avoid being surrounded. Then I went to explain the situation to Dawley. He ordered the 36th Division to organize and defend a position between the Calore River and Mount Soprano with La Cosa Creek as the front line, about 8 miles long. It was late in the day, about 9:00 PM, and the position had to be reconnoitered and occupied during the night.

I divided the Division front into three sectors and placed a brigadier general in command of each sector because the various troops, except the infantry, are not accustomed to working together, and I want everything possible done to be ready to meet an attack by daylight tomorrow.

General Wilbur's task force, consisting of the Cannon and Antitank Companies 143rd, 2nd Battalion of the 36th Engineers, one company 636th TD Battalion, Co. A 751st Tank Battalion, is to defend a 2-1/5 mile sector from the junction of the Calore River and La Cosa Creek to Carruli on La Cosa Creek (Map coordinate 918120).

General O'Daniel, with a task force consisting of 143rd Infantry (less detachments), 2nd Battalion 141st, to be returned from the British sector, 3rd Battalion, 142nd, is to defend the approximately 2 mile sector from Carruli to a stream junction southeast of Majuri (Coordinate 918120 to point 920095).

General Lange with a task force consisting of one company, 636 TD Battalion, one company 751st Tank Battalion, and the 1st and 2nd Battalions 504 Parachute Infantry (to arrive during the night), is to defend the 4½ mile sector from the stream junction southeast of Majuri to Tempe (Coordinates 920095 to 970062). Colonel John Forsythe will command this sector until Lange can come up from Blue and Yellow Beaches where he has been on duty.

The 2nd Battalion, 142nd, is to remain near map coordinate 970060, 1½ mile south of Albanella, to protect the right flank and be prepared to counterattack toward the north on Division order.

The Division Artillery is to take positions west of La Cosa Creek to support the defense and be prepared to fire in the sector of the 45th Division east of Highway 18.

The elements of three battalions which have had the greatest losses are to be assembled and reorganized in the rear of the position north and south of Biagia in reserve.

The 111th Engineer Battalion is to bring in wire, mines, and tools and assist all units with the organization of the position.

I have, available for this job, 4 battalions of infantry, the 2nd Battalion of the 36th Engineers, the Division Artillery, the 151st Artillery Battalion of the 34th Division, a battalion of tanks, and a battalion of antitanks. All in all there are some 88 guns of all types to support the defense; quite ample.

Information received from our Reconnaissance Troop indicates that the enemy is concentrating in the area Controne—Castelcivita—Corleto—Roccodaspide. Requests were made to the Air Support Command to maintain observation of this area and to bomb some

40 German tanks reported east of Castelcivita on the road to San Angelo. However, the latter request was refused by the Air Support Command. They said they could not find the tanks.

Tuesday, September 14, 1943

Early this morning I checked our defenses and am well pleased with the progress made. The part of the front between the destroyed bridge on Highway 18 at the Sele and Capa Santa Hill is principally within the zone of the 45th Division. Nevertheless, I feel compelled to assist in its defense because, if it should be penetrated, my left will be outflanked and I will have to face to my rear.

There is very little concealment near the river, between the bridge and Capa Santa, where troops can be posted to prevent a crossing by direct fire. General Cowles and I do not wish to expose our tanks and TDs to systematic destruction by posting them continually in the open where they will have to be if they are to fire directly on an attempted crossing. For the same reason this area is not suitable for defense near the river by infantry. So the tanks and TDs are being posted back from the river under concealment, with observers well forward where they can see any enemy approaching from the north and east.

Firing positions are being selected and prepared in advance to be ready for any possible attacks. If enemy tanks appear, the appropriate firing positions will be occupied. It is not my intention to completely stop a crossing. Some may get over on this side, but they will be disposed of by our antitank weapons. Artillery observers are posted so they can bring fire on any German infantry or tank concentrations along or beyond the Sele, the Calore or La Cosa Creek, covering an arc of more than 180 degrees.

German tanks may possibly make a stab between Mount Soprano and Dafensa Monti Hill. If they should, a company of our tanks is posted there in readiness.

The 504th Parachute Infantry under command of Colonel R. G. Tucker dropped in last night without casualties. Steps had to be taken to prevent them from being mistaken for the enemy because all our troops had been alerted to keep a sharp lookout for a possible German drop, and I did not want trigger-happy gunners shooting our own paratroopers in the dark. All ground units were notified and officers of antiaircraft and machine gun units were ordered to stay with their guns during the night until the drop was completed. Our ground crews were not to fire until orders to do so were given by company commanders in each case.

I have assigned the paratroopers in Division Reserve near Majorano, behind the right flank. They look like excellent soldiers, are in high spirits and fully informed of what they are to do.

With these arrangements, my command is quite confident that any German attack anywhere along our front, which will have to cross open ground, will take a severe beating. In fact, the Germans will be using poor judgment if they should attack with tanks in small groups as they have been doing.

I am told that the staff of Clark's Fifth Army Headquarters was thrown into a panic a night or two ago, after they occupied the Bellelli Villa because of a wild battlefield rumor that they were about to be run over by German tanks. Of course, they had no business being so close to the front, but the rumor is they were there because it was the most spacious and comfortable villa in the area. In their enthusiasm for comfort, they overlooked the tactical situation.

Anyway, early today Army Headquarters, which has moved south from the Bellelli Villa (I am told some went back to their ships), is apprehensive about its own security and has ordered me to send one tank destroyer company and one infantry battalion to guard it. I was also directed to post one company of TDs to guard Corps Headquarters. There is no necessity for this, but I will send to Army Headquarters two platoons of tank destroyers from their positions in reserve and one of the infantry battalions that has had heavy losses. They will still be in reserve.

I will send to Corps Headquarters a company of TDs now being landed on the beaches. This will not weaken our defense to any important degree, but it indicates that higher headquarters does not know that my troop dispositions insure its security automatically and that special arrangements are not necessary. Our defenses are ample to meet the situation.

At 12:40 PM the enemy formed for attack opposite our north flank and south of the Calore River. Army ordered naval gunfire on this concentration. OK by me, but not necessary. Our TDs and tanks plus supporting artillery took care of this without Navy help, but we needed more infantry and I brought up the

1st Battalion, 141st Infantry, to strengthen the position.

Our 636th TD Battalion is doing excellent work. It is credited with the destruction of 7 German tanks yesterday and 12 today. Today one TD alone destroyed 5 tanks and one refueling truck by firing only seven rounds. German tanks in front of them do not have a chance. (See Appendix B.)

Clark arrived at my CP at about 2:00 PM and seemed quite worried. Without any preliminary discussion of the tactical situation, and in a rather irritated and disappointed manner, he said to me, "What has gone wrong with the 36th Division?" He was referring to our reverses between the Sele and Calore Rivers and at Altavilla and implying that we were not doing well.

I replied, "Nothing has gone wrong with the 36th Division. Everything is all right." Everything was all right. We had no business sending that battalion off by itself between the rivers northeast of Persano. Its failure was not entirely its fault. The Altavilla affair was really a reconnaissance in force. It met with greater resistance than I expected, but we are prepared at all times for any counterattacks the Germans may make. There are no breaches in our position. I don't think Clark understands this.

Army Headquarters should know what is going on because my operation and intelligence sections keep VI Corps informed, and VI Corps, in turn, reports to Army, but these reports are not always up-to-date because of our fast-changing situation. My headquarters has complete and timely information. The prisoners we are taking give us an indication of what is brewing behind the German front. The Division staff and my combat troops are anxious and alert, of course, this being their first battle, but they are confident and feel superior to the Germans.

Anyway, his visit was very short, and he departed after telling me that the Navy was going to bombard the town of Altavilla. I wondered why.

I do not see how the destruction of buildings and the killing of civilians in Altavilla is going to help our situation, especially since Clark does not intend that we move forward from our position in cooperation with the bombardment. There are probably some of the enemy in Altavilla, but they will take cover and protect themselves as soon as the shelling begins. A few of them might become casualties. Anyway, the greater part of the German force will be on the high ground outside the town.

After the bombardment, the town can still be occupied by enemy troops.

My views were not requested, and I did not volunteer them.

At 4:30 PM the 155th and 132nd FA Battalions reported they were firing heavy concentrations on some 25 tanks west of Altavilla and 9 tanks south of Altavilla. The Germans took a beating, lost a lot of tanks and withdrew. Our losses were practically nil. In the meantime, I alerted a battalion of the 504th Parachute Infantry and some units of the 142nd Infantry for possible counterattacks, but did not need them.

Today, at frequent intervals, I received messages from both Corps and Army Headquarters directing, "Not one foot of ground is to be given up." "There must be no retreat," etc., all of which gave me the impression that Clark and Dawley were needlessly worried about our ability to repel a German attack.

Late this afternoon, I recalled General Lange from his duty at the beaches and directed him to take command of the south sector at once and insure that it will be ready for a possible attack tomorrow morning. Colonel Forsythe had been in command of the south sector and has done well, but I felt that I should have a brigadier general in charge of each sector.

Wednesday, September 15, 1943

Early this morning I went to check the Cosa Creek defenses. Enroute, I came upon General Lange and his party in bivouac and just getting up. We discussed my instructions of the night before. He admitted that he had not complied with them because, he said, he was worn out and needed a rest. Everybody was tired and needed a rest. I could not avoid comparing his actions with those of Generals Wilbur and O'Daniel, and Colonel Forsythe. All of them had been up all night on the 13th and 14th and had done excellent work. I concluded that I would prefer one of them for my Assistant Division Commander and told Lange that I intended to make such a recommendation to the Corps Commander, which I did.

While I was away, General Alexander, Clark, and Air Marshal Conningham visited my CP at about 8:15 AM. Coloner Kerr explained the situation to them, but they made no comment. Kerr complained to Conningham that our Air Support Command had not cooperated with us as we would have liked, whereupon Conningham, with some show of authority, said he would take care of that. I don't think any orders he may give will make any difference.

Lieutenant Gutting, Company K, 143rd, reported that what was left of his company came out of Altavilla last night, having spent Monday and Tuesday in the town, surrounded, and under continual enemy attack. They were there yesterday afternoon during the naval bombardment but were well protected by stone walls and buildings. This was a surprise because reports since the 13th indicated none of our people were in the town.

Wilbur is assigned to the 36th Division as Assistant Division Commander. General Lange has been relieved. Colonel Forsythe is taking over command of the south sector.

The 505th Parachute Infantry and the 325th Glider Infantry, in LSIs, arrived on the beachhead. Last night a parachute battalion was dropped near Avellino behind the British front, some eighteen miles north of Salerno City. Since both ourselves and the British are on the defensive, I don't think the paratroops will be in action very long after landing, for they are not going to get any help and will be strictly on their own.

Thursday, September 16, 1943

Last night the 45th Division on our left flank advanced and extended its front from the Calore across the Sele and northwest beyond Persano.

This morning Dawley ordered me to retake Altavilla. The 504th Parachute Infantry with one company of 636th TD Battalion will advance from the south along the high ground during the night to capture hills 315 and 424.

About noon 40 German tanks were reported to be on the eastern slope of the ridge, a kilometer southeast of Altavilla. We had to get rid of these before the advance of the 504th tonight. So concentrations of artillery were placed on them and naval gun fire was requested. We also asked our Air Support Command to bomb them, but, as usual, our request was refused, Air Marshall Conningham, notwithstanding, because, they said, one of the reconnaissance planes had been over this area previously and had not seen any tanks. Undoubtedly these are the same tanks that have been in the Castelcivita area for the past 4 days but have kept themselves concealed from our air reconnaissance. A later report revealed that our artillery bombardment had scattered them but they may be in a position to counterattack the 504th tomorrow morning.

I have moved my CP to a group of buildings at Guimenteria. (Map coordinate 880078).

Friday, September 17, 1943

The 504th Parachute Infantry occupied hill 315 early this morning but soon thereafter Colonel Tucker reported the enemy was heavily shelling his position. Later he reported that the enemy was bringing up reinforcements for counterattack and that he was having heavy losses.

General Ridgway came to see me and asked for the 180th Infantry Regiment to reinforce Tucker's command. Army Headquarters refused this but VI Corps directed Tucker to hold out until night, then to return to the vicinity of Albanella. Later, Tucker's troops found the going easier and occupied both hills 315 and 424. He was told to remain there overnight.

This afternoon Eisenhower, Vice Admiral Hewitt, Clark and Dawley visited my CP and discussed the situation. All were cheerful. They had nothing in particular to say, no instructions, no criticism of me.

I have just received the following letter:

"HEADQUARTERS FIFTH ARMY"

"Dear General Dawley:

"As your Army Commander, I want to congratulate every officer and enlisted man in the Fifth Army on the accomplishment of their mission on landing on the western coast of Italy. All the more splendid is your achievement when it is realized that it was accomplished against determined German resistance at the beaches. Every foot of our advance has been contested.

"We have arrived at our critical objective; our beachhead is secure. Additional troops are landing every day, and we are here to stay. Not one foot of ground will be given up.

"General Montgomery's battle-proven Eighth English Army, our partner in the task of clearing the German forces out of Italy, is advancing from the south and in a matter of hours its presence will be felt by the enemy. Side by side with this Eighth Army, the Fifth Army will advance to occupy Naples, Rome and other cities to the north and to free Italy from German domination.

"I am highly gratified by the efficient manner in which the US VI Corps and the British 10th Corps have worked side by side in mutual support, each being proud to serve by the side of the other. Their performance has justified the confidence placed in them by the people of the United Nations. They know that we shall drive on relentlessly until our job is done.

"I desire that the contents of this letter be communicated to all ranks of your command.

> Sincerely yours,
> Mark W. Clark,
> Lieutenant General, USA,
> Commanding."

1st Ind.

"Headquarters VI Corps

"To: Commanders, all units and organizations.

"The receipt of this letter is a matter of intense satisfaction to me. To you who have made such a commendation possible belongs the credit. **Carry on. We are on the way.**

> E. J. Dawley,
> Major General, U. S. Army,
> Commanding."

I am sending it on with the following endorsement:

"HQ 36th Div.

"To: All Units

"I deeply appreciate the fine fighting spirit of every member of the 36th Division and their excellent achievements since our initial landing."

At 8:00 PM Lieutenant Quail, 5th Division of the British Eighth Army, arrived at my headquarters with a message from Major General Bucknal regarding the location of the elements of the Eighth Army which is coming up on Highway 19 to join us. They are now at Montesano, about 25 miles south.

CHAPTER TEN
Rebuilding The 36th

Salerno Beachhead, Italy
Saturday, September 18, 1943

The Germans have withdrawn from our front. They began moving out last night. It looks like the battle for the beachhead is over. We are regrouping and reorganizing while moving forward to Highway 19 and Sere. The men need good food, good water, a chance to clean up and a good rest.

This operation has given my men a greater confidence in their ability to destroy enemy tanks. From day to day, during our fighting, I could sense a growing assurance among all with whom I discussed our situation, both officers and enlisted men, that the manner in which the Germans employed their tanks in the open made them almost perfect targets and relatively easy to destroy.

The Division did well, and I am pleased.

Sunday, September 19, 1943

I have heard, but not from Clark, that he was alarmed for some reason when we were in defense along La Cosa Creek, and ordered the Navy to prepare to evacuate the 36th Division and attached troops from the beachhead. He never discussed his uneasiness with me, nor did he ever discuss with me the detailed disposition of my troops and their missions. He may have talked to some of my subordinate commanders. It is my opinion that he was uneasy because he did not know that I had adequate antitank defenses from the very beginning.

Before we went aboard ship at Oran, I had published in orders that under no circumstances would anyone, regardless of rank, commandeer another person's vehicle after landing on beaches. I did this because only a few vehicles would be taken ashore on the first day and each vehicle was assigned to a very definite and important job. Both my vehicles were destroyed on the beaches while coming ashore. They were to be used for messenger service and to take me over the area so I could keep abreast of the tactical situation as it developed. I was handicapped by their loss because it was more difficult to visit the various units after they were ashore. I had to use members of my staff as messengers.

On the morning of the 10th, Phinney, the Division Quarter-master, who had been "here and there" the previous day as one of my foot messengers, delivered a jeep to me. I asked no questions. Later I drove to the bridge over the Sele on Highway 18 to visit the battalion of the 142nd CT in that area, where I talked with Lt. Colonel Miller Ainsworth. Later he told me the sequel to my visit. He said that after my visit he met Colonel Martin. Ainsworth asked him why he was walking, since each regimental commander was authorized to have a jeep. Martin replied, "Some son-of-a-bitch stole my jeep."

Ainsworth replied, "General Walker has your jeep. He was talking to me a while ago, and I saw the 143rd identification on it."

I did not steal Martin's jeep, but I did have a good trans-portation officer. When I next saw Martin he had another jeep. I kept his. Circumstances alter cases.

Monday, September 20, 1943

The British 5th Division is moving up on our right to the town of Sere. The 3rd, 34th, and 45th Divisions are pursuing the retreating Germans. The 36th Division is in Army Reserve.

I flew over what was once the town of Battipaglia. It is a complete wreck. I am told that the Navy had the principal part in its destruction. A town on a map makes an excellent target for the men of any fire direction center. It can be hit every time, and the flying debris and dust prove the fact and give the observers and spotters a feeling of pride and accom-plishment. Actually, such destruction adds little or nothing to improvement of the tactical situation and is seldom justifiable.

When I returned from an inspection of the area late this afternoon, I found this note from Dawley on my desk: "Goodbye to you and your fine Division. Mike." I could make nothing out of it other than that he had been relieved as Corps Commander. I was distressed and wondered why.

I met Dawley in the Philippines in 1913, when we were on field maneuvers; he in the Artillery and I in the Infantry. I have been associated with him since on several occasions. I have a high regard for his professional ability.

Two or three days ago he sent me the letter of commendation he had received from General Clark. I have searched the Salerno operation for a possible clue to his relief. I can find some tactical mistakes of a minor nature by the troops of my command. For these, I, not Dawley, am responsible, but neither Clark nor Dawley has made any adverse criticism to me, personally, of my conduct of the operation. However, I can recall these incidents that might unfairly have contributed to his relief:

One was the disaster that befell the 2nd Battalion, 143rd Infantry. When Dawley gave me his instructions to move that battalion to a position between the Sele and Calore Rivers, Troy Middleton, commanding the 45th Division, was present. He arrived before I did. He heard the instructions.

When Dawley indicated the front line of the area the battalion was to occupy, and stated that the right flank of the 45th Division would be on the left of the battalion across the Sele, Middleton made no comment. I presumed that he and Dawley had discussed my instructions prior to my arrival. I have served previously with Middleton when we were both instructors in the tactical section of the Infantry School. He was one of my regimental commanders in the 36th Division at Camp Blanding, Florida, and I have a high regard for his ability as a soldier.

When Dawley finished his instructions and Middleton did not make any comment, I presumed that the information I had received regarding the 45th Division was correct and reliable, and passed it on to my regimental and battalion commanders. Actually, the right flank of the 45th Division was two and a half miles to the southwest of the point indicated by Dawley to me. The result was the disaster the next day. I know that commanders are sometimes misinformed. I should have been more cautious and should have had my staff ascertain the location of the 45th Division. All three of us are equally responsible for this unfortunate misunderstanding of the facts: Middleton and Dawley for passing along unverified information, and I for not having it checked.

There was another incident on the 17th when Eisenhower, Clark, Dawley and Admiral Hewitt visited my Headquarters. They asked me to explain the situation, and I did so in broad terms, but they didn't pay much attention to what I was saying. When I finished, Eisenhower turned to Dawley and asked, "How'd you ever get the troops into such a mess?"

From Dawley's explanation it was obvious he wasn't aware of my pains to insure tactical control and coordination. He never did explain that there was no "mess." I was about to make this point when Eisenhower changed the subject, so maybe he wanted to hold Dawley responsible for a "mess" that didn't exist.

Later on the same day, Clark, Dawley, Ridgway and I, with two jeeps, drove to the town of Albanella to look over the ground where an attack was being planned by Ridgway's paratroops. I rode out with Ridgway, but Clark asked me to ride with him and Dawley on the way back. They got into an unfriendly discussion, and Dawley intimated that he did not approve of some of the things Eisenhower and Clark had done. He referred to them as "boy scouts." Clark was quite upset and remained silent most of the way back to my headquarters. After Dawley and I got out of the jeep, Clark drove off in a huff, leaving Dawley with me. I wondered why I had been invited to ride with them for I was never included in the conversation. Maybe Dawley's remarks on this occasion had some bearing on his being relieved.

> NOTE: After the war, I was told by a reliable source that Dawley was relieved because General Alexander, on visiting his headquarters on the beachhead, had noticed that Dawley's hands shook when he was explaining the situation. This caused Alexander to conclude that Dawley was too unsteady for combat command, and he recommended to both Eisenhower and Clark that he be relieved. If this was the reason, it seems to be unjust to Dawley for he handled his job as well or better than Clark handled his.

Our losses to date are 250 men killed. There are about 850 wounded and about 700 missing, bringing the total loss to about 1800 men. For this type of operation, the number of killed and wounded is not excessive, but the number of missing is far too great. Almost all the missing are prisoners of war captured by the Germans from the 141st opposite Blue and Yellow beaches on D-day; from the 142nd at Altavilla on the 12th and 13th; and from the 2nd Battalion, 143rd, northeast of Persano between the Sele and Calore Rivers on the 13th.

On the first day of the invasion I chose a site near the tobacco barn for our cemetery. The task of supervising the burial of our dead men was the unpleasant duty of the Division Chaplain, Herbert E. MacCombie.

There, German prisoners of war dug a trench 6½ feet wide, 5 feet deep and about 60 feet long. A second parallel trench was started when the number of dead required it. Bodies brought to the grave site were laid, side by side, along the trench. Each was searched for personal effects, which were tied into a bundle, marked with the man's name and organization, and delivered to the Graves Registration Service to be sent eventually to the next of kin. This searching of bodies was a gruesome business since they were in various stages of decomposition and lay in eerie, grotesque postures.

Each soldier wears two identification tags (dog tags) on a tape around his neck. One of these was removed from the body, the other was buried with the body. After all proper records were made, the body was wrapped in a bedsack or other material and laid in the trench. At the head was placed a wooden cross about 1½ feet high and about a foot wide, improvised by our Engineers from material found in the area. On this crude, unfinished, temporary cross was tacked the second identification tag. A chaplain conducted a short burial service for each individual. Earth was shoveled over the dead, while at the same time the trench was being extended to receive more bodies.

When, as sometimes happens, no tags were with the body, burial was suspended until all possible means of identification were exhausted: Personal effects, organizational markings, laundry marks, locality where found, identification by survivors, etc. If the investigation, which was made of record, failed to identify the body, it was buried under a cross marked "Unknown."

There was an MP at the site but the German prisoners made no attempt to escape. I think they considered themselves lucky to be out of the war. The use of prisoners for burying the dead may be irregular, so they were used only two days until bulldozers were available.

After the battle of Altavilla, Chaplain MacCombie selected a second burial site near that town. There were many bodies in and near the town which had to be buried without delay for the stench was nauseating. The 141st searched the Altavilla area, and the 142nd and the 143rd searched Persano and the area between the Sele and Calore Rivers.

A representative of the Graves Registration Service, recently arrived, has selected a third site for a permanent cemetery. This means disinterment and reburial by the GRS. It would have been helpful if the GRS representative had been with the Division during combat.

Tuesday, September 21, 1943

I have received many reports of gallantry from platoon, company, and battalion commanders, and I must see that the men receive awards in keeping with their deeds. I am proud of my command for they have given their very best on all occasions. That is all any commander has a right to expect from his troops.

The Texas flag that Governor Stevenson presented to the Division at Camp Blanding, Florida, in 1942, has been brought ashore and I intend to display it, along with the United States Colors, the 36th Division flag and my own 2-star general's flag in front of my tent. All four are on ten foot staffs which can be pushed into the ground. They will be on display during fair weather from reveille to retreat and will provide a bright cheerful sight amid our drab surroundings.

Of course none of them will ever be carried in battle unfurled. During the Civil War, it was considered absolutely necessary by both Union and Confederate troops that their colors or standards be kept flying in battle. Whenever a color bearer fell, it was deemed an act of gallantry and honor for a nearby soldier to seize the staff and raise the fallen flag. The presence of their unfurled colors was an encouragement to the fighting men, and cheers usually followed its reappearance. Also in those days, men of opposing armies sometimes stood in full view of one another and shot each other down. But times have changed. Concealment and surprise are two very important tactical principles today. Unfurled colors would violate both and have no place on the modern field of battle.

Lt. Colonel Paul W. Dillingham, Division Engineer and Commanding Officer of the 111th Engineers, and Major Oran C. Stovall, his Executive Officer, came to see me this afternoon. They had a problem to discuss. Stovall did most of the talking. He stated that he felt that Dillingham had not handled the 111th Engineers in the best professional manner during our recent battle and that, as a result, the morale of the Battalion was low. He cited a number of specific instances to support his statement. Dillingham agreed that the specific instances, as stated by Stovall, were true. After interrogating both parties I concluded that Major Stovall had the greater knowledge of the capabilities and tactical employment of division engineers. I placed him in command of the 111th Engineers by virtue of which he became Division Engineer.

One of three Bailey bridges (80 feet, double-single, capacity 40 tons) constructed over a stream between Venafro and San Pietro by the 111th Engineer Battalion to support the San Pietro attack. November, 1943

Troops of the 504th Airborne Infantry Regiment move past an immobilized American tank. San Pietro, Italy, December 17, 1943—U.S. Army Photo

Chow time. Battery A, 155th Field Artillery Battalion. Mignano, Italy, December 19, 1943—U.S. Army Photo

Well-camouflaged German pill box. Mont Lungo, December 26, 1943 —U.S. Army Photo

Left to right: Generals DaPino, Walker, Keyes, Truscott and Harmon. Minturno, Italy, December, 1943

Generals Walker and Wilbur, Colonel Kerr. Christmas Eve, 1943, Presenzano, Italy

General view of San Pietro on side of Mt. Sammucro after the battle.
—U.S. Army Photo

Company G, 141st Infantry, in hasty defense after the capture of Mt.
Trocchio. January, 1944—U.S. Army Photo

Altavilla, Italy
Wednesday, September 22, 1943

I issued the following memorandum today:

> "Our Division has completed its first baptism of fire. It
> has the unique honor of being the first American division to
> land on the mainland of Europe during this war. It likewise
> is the first American division to make a landing against German
> opposition. We all can be proud of the results obtained, for the
> Division accomplished its mission.
>
> "Our pride in what we and our comrades have done, must
> not, and I feel sure will not, blind us to the fact that we have
> much to learn. During the days that follow, it is my desire
> that every officer and man of the Division shall try to do
> his individual job more carefully, more thoroughly, and with
> a more aggressive spirit.
>
> "To those of our comrades who have given their lives, we
> bow our heads in silent appreciation of their brave deeds
> and pay homage to them as worthy Americans.
>
> "You have done well and I am proud of you."

Our D-12 convoy has arrived off shore, carrying equipment we
had to leave behind in Africa. Our kitchens are loaded on trucks
and will go directly to their units, as soon as they are off the ships.
These will be welcome, for our troops have not had a hot meal
since debarking on the 9th.

The Special Company which I organized while we were at Rabat
in Africa has been doing an excellent job under command of Lt.
Colonel Charles H. Dobbs. It is a kind of catch-all organization
with a semi-permanent cadre of officers and enlisted men who
perform the administrative functions of the combat units and give
company officers more time for training. It remained in Africa
to receive replacements which had not arrived when the Division
left for Italy; to care for, ship and deliver all equipment left behind, including some 20,000 barracks bags and 2,000 vehicles.

Army Headquarters is worried about the possibility of a German
parachute drop on top of it. The Army G-3, Colonel Brann, phoned
and directed that one battalion of infantry be stationed near Army
Headquarters at once. The 2nd Battalion, 142nd Infantry, under
Lt. Colonel Sam Graham, got the job. It is to provide parachute
defense for the Headquarters at night. During the day it is to be
available for such training as I may prescribe. Since the Battalion
is on the alert through the night, I shall prescribe no training in

the daytime.

Friday, September 24, 1943

We are in camp in an assembly area some 7 or 8 miles square west of Altavilla, not far from the Calore River. The men are in pup tents. I have a command tent as an office. A large number of soldiers from various units, including our own, are wandering around the area. Bob Ives and the MPs are establishing straggler lines with fixed posts and patrols to collect all soldiers who do not have passes and return them to their own units.

I am doing all I can to get organized, equipped, and trained for the next operation which probably will be an offensive against a German defense.

Clark told me that he saw Fred Jr. a few days ago and that he and his battalion were doing well with Darby's rangers. I am pleased to hear this, especially from Clark.

I was through Altavilla again today. Buildings are destroyed, streets are blocked with debris, and the stench is still there. The bombardment of this village, full of helpless civilian families, was brutal and to no purpose. The people are very poor, very ignorant, very religious, and all of them, in the midst of their wreckage and sorrow, have a haunted terror in their faces along with an expression of helplessness. Such is war! May the time come when wars will be no more.

Saturday, September 25, 1943

Clark visited me today and laid down a plan of action for the 141st Infantry Combat Team to make an envelopment by sea, landing in the Pompeii area. Mike O'Daniel is to command the force. This operation must receive very careful study and planning in order to succeed. The Germans will be well prepared to defend the beach, and the landing must be timed to coordinate with our forces advancing toward Naples. I don't want any more of my men isolated and defeated.

Lt. Colonel McShane, G-3, has gone to the hospital with a nervous breakdown. Lt. Colonel Steel, my G-4, is also in the hospital. Lt. Colonel Crowther, G-2, is also sick. Just when I need them most, they get sick. Good soldiers are supposed to take care of themselves and not get sick.

The British X Corps has been directed to take Naples, but I don't think they will do it very soon. Maybe, if they have several weeks to get there, they will succeed, for they are very slow and deliberate and do not take their operations as seriously as we do.

Monday, September 27, 1943

Steel and McShane are going to Africa, sick, and will not return to the Division. I will miss them. I will replace McShane by Fred, Jr. Fred is a graduate of the Command and General Staff School at Fort Leavenworth and is the best qualified officer in the Division for G-3. There are those who will yell "nepotism," but let them yell. If I did not think that he were the best qualified officer for the job, I would not put him there.

Steel has been an outstanding, efficient officer—one of my best. He was a very hard worker, an optimist who was eager and able to do any job I gave him. I will replace him with Carl Phinney who has been doing an excellent job as Division Quartermaster under Steel's supervision.

Some of our men are not responding to the instruction which is based on lessons learned in this last operation. They are not taking their current training seriously enough, and they are going to suffer needless casualties because of their indifferent attitude. They think the war is over and they should be allowed to rest.

Yesterday I laid a wreath on the grave of one of my soldiers at each Division cemetery, during special memorial services conducted by Chaplain MacCombie. Our losses were greater than those of the Germans, due, in my opinion, to our inexpertness.

Yesterday I went back and took a more leisurely look at the ruins of the ancient temples at Paestum than I did the day I came ashore. They were built by the Greeks about 500 B. C. The stone pillars are in a good state of preservation. This was an important center of civilization before malaria caused its abandonment. If Admiral Hall and I had agreed to lay down a preliminary bombardment on the beaches, it would have undoubtedly leveled these antiquities to no purpose.

Forsythe, 142nd Infantry, reported that one of his self-propelled gun carriers ran over a land mine in its bivouac area east of La Cosa Creek and was demolished. Two men were injured. An examination of the ground revealed three other mines near the same place. They are American mines. Stovall, Division Engineer, is making an investigation to determine who placed the mines in that area during our defense of the Cosa Creek position and, through just plain negligence, left them there without marking them. Wouldn't it be wonderful if everybody did his duty.

Clark tells me he is sending an artillery colonel to the Division to command the 142nd Infantry, and he is taking Forsythe to Army Headquarters. He says Forsythe is too old for his job.

In my opinion, Clark's real reason is he wants to give one of his friends a regiment. There is no cause to relieve Forsythe. I find no fault with the way he has done his job. It is quite irregular for an Army commander to prescribe, arbitrarily, who shall command regiments in a division.

Three officers are not performing up to standard and I am going to reclassify them. One, a major, has been on a special assignment for two months, but has made no real effort to learn his job. He does not control his section and his services are unsatisfactory.

A captain in the same section consistently failed to follow instructions and at times deliberately acted contrary to instructions, while reporting that the instructions were being faithfully carried out.

Another captain, an organization commander, has already been relieved. He had no command ability and could not be relied upon to perform duty that required initiative. All have had more than a fair chance to prove themselves worthy of their jobs. They don't have what it takes.

The Division has received so many replacements for both officers and enlisted men that only about half the personnel is now from Texas.

We had a severe storm last night which continued for two hours. The rain came down in sheets, and there was no letup in the thunder and lightning. One man of the medical corps was killed by lightning only 200 yards from my tent. Today, many of our headquarters personnel, who were careless putting up their tents, are trying to dry their bedding and equipment. Many of them relearned, through pain, that they must pitch their tents properly and dispose their equipment inside, if they wish to survive surprise storms without soaked baggage.

Friday, October 1, 1943

I will long remember this day. General O'Daniel, my aides, and I started off in one jeep from the Division CP, near Altavilla, to go to the front, south of Naples, to visit Fred's 1st Battalion, 143rd Infantry, now with the British.

When we drove through Battapaglia we were appalled at the complete destruction of this old town by our own Navy. There wasn't a single building intact. The town can't be repaired; it will have to be rebuilt. We could smell the dead bodies buried in the rubble.

I'll never order the destruction of a simple native village unless it is organized for large-scale defense. And in that case, no civilians will be there because they will have been ordered out by the enemy defenders.

We followed Highway 18 to the town of Salerno. The buildings near the railroad yards were completely wrecked by allied bombings before the British landed. The Italians were standing around looking at their ruined homes in bewilderment, but even in the midst of destruction and grief, they were friendly toward us.

From Salerno we turned onto the road to Naples. I saw two or three British and several German tanks destroyed along the road, but there was no evidence of heavy fighting, such as discarded empty shells and cartridge cases, fresh trenches, abandoned equipment, battlefield litter or graves. I saw two British and two German graves between Salerno and Naples, all of which is positive evidence that the Germans retired voluntarily and were followed, not pushed, by the British.

We passed through New Pompeii and saw the bell tower, which is a thing of beauty. There was not a war scar on it, yet, the buildings near it were hit and damaged. The town stores were open, but had nothing in them other than wine and souvenirs. We also took time for a quick tour of Pompeii which was spared by both the Germans and the Allies. From here I had an excellent view of Vesuvius and the smoke drifting skyward from the crater. We noted the wall of ashes that marks the limit of excavation to uncover the destruction caused by the eruption some 1800 years ago. I felt that I was treading on historic ground as I walked along the streets and looked into the homes which were destroyed before Christianity was accepted in Italy.

We came upon a column of British tanks and soldiers moving along the road toward Naples. We passed by them one tank at a time. I was pleased to note that the British MPs were on the job and would not allow double banking. We saw group after group of natives displaying Italian flags. They threw bouquets at the soldiers, begged for biscuits, clapped their hands, and held their fingers up to display the V for victory.

At Torre Annunziata, we saw more destruction by artillery and had an opportunity to look over the ground where our 141st Combat Team was, at one time, alerted to have made an amphibious landing. That ground would have been unfavorable for an attack by us. Fields of fire would have been short in range and restricted in width. There is a great deal of cover and concealment for the German defenders, and many stone walls, ditches, and buildings which would obstruct the movement of tanks and vehicles. Thank the Lord we did not have to make that landing. It was a rather stupid concept, and, fortunately was discarded, since, even if successful, the tactical advantages to be gained would have been practically nil.

I also had an opportunity to look over the mountain range where Fred's battalion has been engaged since September 12 with Darby's Rangers. It is rugged and they must have had very rough going. 1 met Major David M. Frazior who told me that Fred's battalion was at Torre del Greco. There, a soldier told me the battalion was at Santo Giovanni, a place on the map in the suburbs of Naples. We passed through the streets of Torre del Greco which were filthy with garbage and litter, the natives unconcerned.

We went on beside a British tank column through Portici to Giovanni. There I found Fred with his battalion halted in the midst of a British tank column. He said that he had been attached to a British armored brigade, having been detached from the 82nd Airborne Division which was going to occupy Naples. This was a disappointment to him and to me. I do not like to have any of my units attached to a British command because our people are more aggressive and will expect close, prompt support by artillery and tanks, which they may not get. Fred also said that he had light casualties to date, two officers and seven men killed.

A few minutes later I met General Clark and asked him to let the battalion go into Naples with the 82nd Division, but he refused. He said they had to go to the British armored brigade; that he would release the battalion as soon as he possibly could; and that the 36th would probably move to the Naples area about the middle of next week, the 6th.

I went on into Naples to the square of Garibaldi which had just been occupied by the troops of the 82nd Division. There I met General Ridgway and talked to him for a few minutes. He promised to return my division transportation, now with him, as soon as he receives his own from the convoy now in Salerno Bay.

I was impressed with the complete destruction of the railroad yards and piers. Both are a total wreck. As we passed along the streets, mostly deserted, small groups of Italians, here and there, would smile and clap their hands. I believe they were pleased to see the Americans in their city.

The regular municipal police were operating under direction of our American Government representatives. They were obviously cooperating in every way and were assisted by armed Italian soldiers. The sight of a great city like Naples with wrecked buildings, deserted streets and bewildered people was very depressing. There was no food in sight, and I do not believe there was much on hand in the few homes still occupied.

At 3:00 PM, we started back to the 36th Division, retracing our steps. At Pompeii I procured two Italian national flags which I shall keep as souvenirs of this day. A group of girls was standing on the street with bouquets ready to throw at passing tanks. I stopped and signaled for a bouquet. Several came running and gave each of us some yellow flowers. Near Torre del Greco we passed large groves of oranges and English walnuts. I had never seen English walnuts growing before. A little girl threw some walnuts fresh from the tree, into our jeep.

It is depressing to see the Italian children, most of whom are dirty, sickly and undernourished. Captain Stallings broke a piece of D-ration chocolate into several parts and gave it to some children crowded around our jeep. Those who did not get any were disappointed, and one or two cried real tears. I think it would be right and proper to take Hitler and Mussolini over Europe, show them the destruction and misery they have brought upon their own people, and then behead both of them with a dull axe.

All along the route there were groups of discharged Italian soldiers, three or four together, trudging along toward their homes, sitting beside streams bathing their tired feet, helping farmers harvest their puny crops in exchange for a meal, or begging rides on Allied military vehicles. They reminded me of the descriptions I have read of the return of the defeated Confederate soldiers to their homes at the close of the Civil War.

Thursday, October 8, 1943

Yesterday I visited Fifth Army Headquarters at Naples where

it is located in a large grove. There, in a conversation with Clark he told me that John Lucas is to be the new commander of the VI Corps. Although I was not looking forward to it nor expecting it, Clark did tell me back at Oran that I would be the Corps Commander if anything happened to Dawley. I am satisfied where I am.

Clark also told me that the Division is to move to the town of Nola under Lucas' command.

I met Lucas first at Fort McKinley in the Philippines in 1912 or 1913 where he had just joined his regiment after graduation from West Point. Not long ago he and I were Brigadiers in the 2nd Division at Fort Sam Houston. I was Assistant Division Commander and he was commander of the Artillery Brigade.

I visited the 1st Battalion, 143rd Infantry, occupying an abandoned barracks in north Naples, and told Captain Alvin Newell, Battalion Adjutant, of the proposed move. Some replacements for the Battalion had just arrived and were rather low in spirits. I talked to many of them and tried to cheer them, but I did not make much headway. One man complained that he had been trained as an artilleryman and that he now was being put in a mortar platoon in an infantry company.

I told him that there was some reason for his complaint but that our needs were for men in the infantry; that the artillery had no vacancies; that we employ men to the best advantage where needed for the good of all; that it is impossible to train men back in the States in the exact numbers for the various skills that must be replaced overseas; that the basic training he received as an artilleryman is similar to that received by other soldiers; that he will soon learn the techniques of the mortar and will be well-qualified for his assignment. He listened but was not satisfied. What he really wanted was to get out of the infantry.

The Germans had set a number of time bombs at various places in Naples and these have been exploding during the past ten days. Two exploded at the city post office building, one inside and one outside under the street. About 20 American soldiers were killed or wounded, and many Italians, who were working inside, died. This is contrary to the rules of war adopted at the Geneva Convention. Only a cruel, brutal and treacherous person would do such things because nothing tactically is gained. I drove past the post office in my jeep about 20 minutes before the explosion.

We have had a great deal of rain and mud during the past two days, and many enlisted men are quite miserable because they will not take proper care of themselves in bad weather. About 1800 sopping wet replacements arrived at night during the rain. There was not a dry spot anywhere for them to lie down, and their equipment was drenched. To top it all, a truck carrying 25 of them to their assigned units slid down an embankment in the rain and dark, turned over on its side and threw them out into the mud and water. It was a mess, but fortunately no one was seriously hurt. Their cheerless and uncomfortable introduction to their new Division will remain in their memories for a long time.

Mr. Trace, our Red Cross representative, has a doughnut machine. Two Red Cross girls are making 4000 doughnuts per day, which is a real help to the morale of the men. The girls live at one of the evacuation hospitals and go to their work from there. The Red Cross people are very cooperative and are doing everything they can to make the life of the enlisted men a little more bearable.

At my conference today I told the staff that the Division is to go into Army reserve and is to move to a bivouac area northwest of Nola. The route that we are to follow is through Salerno, Avellino and Nola. The movement is under the direction of the commanding general, VI Corps. The arrangements for the movement, that is, the schedule for columns and serials, will be arranged by the Corps Headquarters Staff at Avellino. Our G-3 and our Transportation Officer will send representatives to stay there and assist in working out details for the movement until it is completed. In addition, a reconnaissance of the road from Salerno through Avellino to the bivouac area must begin today to determine the practicability of using that road and the need for any special guides or military police posts at narrow or dangerous places. I want to know if it is a two-way road all the way, and if there are any narrow bridges or fills.

Our G-1 will have charge of the assignment of unit bivouac areas within the new Division area. He will take representatives of each unit with him. On his way he is to stop at Corps Headquarters and get the definite location of the Division bivouac area.

I would like to begin this movement, if satisfactory to General Lucas, on Monday; the trucks to take one serial up one day, return the next day, and go back the third. One regimental combat team will be moved on Monday, one on Tuesday, one on Wednesday and the remainder of the Division on Thursday.

Any supplies now being unloaded at Naples should be held there until Sunday and then sent to the new area. After the conclusion of this movement the Quartermaster will move our extra baggage and property to the new area for storage as soon as the roads and trucks can be made available.

Nola, Italy
Tuesday, October 12, 1943

The Division is moving to our new bivouac area today.

A few days ago I gave orders for a German motorcycle and small scout car, in possession of some men of the Headquarters Company, to be turned in to the Army Ordnance motor pool. They had been damaged and abandoned by the enemy. The men who found them spent a lot of time and energy fixing them so they would run, on the assumption that they would keep them for their own use. To this I had no personal objection, but Army directed me to send them to the motor pool.

The possessors grew angry when they received the order and deliberately destroyed the vehicles with an axe. This was malicious destruction of government property, in violation of the Articles of War, an offense that cannot go unpunished. I ordered the two officers who allowed the destruction to take place in their presence to be punished under the provisions of AW 104 and to be sent back to the States for discharge. I ordered the three noncommissioned officers who took part in the destruction to be reduced to the grade of private and transferred to a rifle company.

A few days ago I had to approve the death sentence of a soldier who refused to leave the ship with his platoon when we landed on September 9th. It is very hard to approve the shooting of a man even when he is guilty of the very serious offense of misbehavior before the enemy, but I had no other course. It is my duty to the government, to the other men of the Division, and to their relatives and friends to approve the sentence of the General Court Martial when the evidence supports the charge. The Articles of War are mandatory. Of course, he will never be shot because higher authority, which has the final approval in sentences of death, will commute his sentence. They always do.

Tuesday, October 19, 1943

It is a damp, wet, rainy, and unpleasant day, an example of what we are in for in Italy.

At one time last August, when we were in Algeria planning this invasion, serious consideration was given to making our landing on the beaches northwest of Naples instead of at Salerno Bay. Yesterday I looked over that area and found especially strong defenses consisting of trenches, pill boxes, concrete gun emplacements, and barbed wire entanglements, all organized and mutually supporting each other. I thank my lucky stars that we did have to land in that area. We would have had very tough going indeed.

I have talked to Captain Carl R. Bayne and Lieutenant Julian Quarles regarding their parts in the action of the 2nd Battalion, 143rd Infantry, and their subsequent escape. Their statements verify my views of what happened to that battalion on September 13th between the Sele and Calore Rivers.

A limited and hurried reconnaissance was made just before dark on the 12th, and the battalion arrived on the site during the night. A tentative deployment for defense was made upon arrival, but there was some confusion in the defenses on unfamiliar terrain. After daylight, the deployment was improved, and the men were told to keep themselves concealed.

At about 9:00 AM, a German force of some 5 or 6 scattered tanks accompanied by a few foot troops, perhaps not over a company, suddenly appeared as a complete surprise, bearing down on the left rear of the battalion. It had come across the Sele River, through the gap between the battalion and the 45th Division, and was followed by a much larger force. Since no enemy was expected from this direction, confusion followed. The battalion was routed and some 500 men were captured, including the commanding officer, Lt. Colonel Charles Jones.

When news first came to me of this disaster, I was greatly disappointed because, on the spur of the moment, I assumed that the battalion had been negligent and had put up a poor fight. Without full details, I made some uncomplimentary comments which, later on, I regretted for they were not justified. As a result of my talks with Bayne and Quarles, I am convinced that the battalion was not entirely at fault. We had no business sending them over there, misinformed and without antitank protection. This was their first deployment in their first battle.

Friday, October 22, 1943

Yesterday I made a reconnaissance of the forward area in the battle zone north of the Volturno River. All the bridges are one lane which creates traffic bottlenecks.

The British pay little attention to camouflage. I was not surprised at this.

There was no bombing of the front line troops from the air by Germans, indicating that they have to economize on planes and use them for more remunerative targets.

The VI Corps has moved on and we are now in the II Corps. Major General Geoffrey Keyes, much my junior, but nevertheless my new Corps Commander, paid me a visit today and discussed probably future plans for employing the 36th Division.

Tuesday, October 26, 1943

I visited Headquarters Fifth Army at Caserta to discuss with Clark the probable future operations of the 36th Division. Nothing definite.   He is considering an amphibious operation to envelop the German west flank.   The lack of necessary landing craft, the difficult terrain, the poor road net together with possible isolation of our forces by German demolitions, make the project most difficult, and I hope he does not order it until more favorable conditions exist.

Lest someone get the impression that all I do is scribble in this book I am recording here the edited notes made by my Aide of my activities yesterday, October 25th, which is typical of all my days when the Division is not in the front line.

"Chief of Staff and G-3 conferred with Commanding General at 0740 regarding inspection of Division by II Corps.   Brigadier General O'Daniel telephoned CG at 0745 re tactical exercises and the proposed amphibious employment of the 141st Infantry. Major General Keyes arrived at CP at 0750 to observe division activities. CG and General Keyes went to 143rd CP at 0810 and CG returned at 0850.   Division Ordnance Officer conferred with CG at 0900, concerning priorities of resupply for ordnance material damaged or lost during recent fighting.   CG left CP at 1050 and went to Naples to attend a ceremony at the University where the honorary degree of Doctor of Political Science was conferred on Lt. General Clark.   CG returned to CP at 1200 and conferred briefly with Major General Keyes at 1230 re progress of the inspection by II Corps.   The Ordnance Officer brought a rifle, equipped with a telescopic sight, to CP at 1300 and advised CG that the Division has been issued 20 of them for the use of snipers. G-1 conferred with CG at 1330 concerning approval of recommendations for awards and promotions of several officers. C/S and Judge Advocate conferred with CG at 1345 regarding action to be taken on several court martial cases. Lt. Colonel McMurtray reported to CG at 1400 from Army Headquarters where he has been on duty as liaison officer. G-4 conferred with CG again at 1430 regarding supply problems. G-1 conferred with CG again at 1445 regarding decorations and promotions. CG and Brigadier General Wilbur left CP at 1500 to attend a II Corps inspection team critique at Fianura and returned at 1745. Artillery Commander conferred with CG at 1900 regarding personnel and equipment problems."

Thursday, October 28, 1943

I have four lieutenant colonels who are not performing their duties satisfactorily. I would like to replace them with regular army officers, since regular officers know proper military standards. These officers mean well; they do what they think is a good job, but they are handicapped because they do not have a clear concept of the standards they should be striving for. Two of them would work better under direct supervision rather than as battalion commanders. But where am I going to get any regular officers with experience? There are none, so I must train them within the Division.

I am authorizing visits to Pompeii, and in addition am sending 20 percent of the command to Naples each day. I have arranged for 14 combat officers who need rest to be sent each week to the Excelsior Victoria, the officers' rest hotel at Sorrento. I want everybody to enjoy these recreational opportunities before we go back into the front lines.

General Keyes and his inexperienced staff have been making an inspection of the 36th Division and made a number of comments regarding deficiencies which are already known to me. Our motor maintenance, military courtesy, and care of equipment are below par, which is always the case after battle. The troops feel that they are entitled to a rest and a temporary letup in the usual disciplinary routine. We have not come back to our usual standards as rapidly as we should, and I shall take steps to correct these deficiencies. Correcting deficiencies is a never-ending procedure.

Some people at higher headquarters seem to think that the periodic rapid marches of four miles in one hour, which they have prescribed and which we are making, are great builders of stamina. They are no such thing. They are unnecessary and undesirable. Every time we have to make one, the Division loses some of its older and better NCOs. We will never have to make any such marches anyway. In the forward areas the Germans won't let us; in the rear we'll use trucks to transport troops. Ordinary marches are all we need to keep in good physical condition.

Yesterday, Lt. Colonel J. Trimble Brown, Regular Army, whom I had never met, came from the Fifth Army Headquarters to see me. He said he would like to be assigned to the 36th Division and to an infantry battalion; that he was bored with his unimportant duties at Army and wanted to get away from there. He said that he had been in command of an infantry regiment in the African campaign and told me the details of his being relieved, in which I saw no justice. He was asking to get away from the comforts of Army Headquarters and to take up the duties and hardships of a battalion commander, which no one would do unless he wanted to fight. I told him I would find a place for him in the Division. He went back happy.

Wednesday, November 3, 1943

Yesterday, I visited the 3rd Division at the front and had lunch with the Division Commander, General Lucian Truscott. He has a private mess for himself, his Chief of Staff and his Aide.

General Keyes has his own private mess, also. I prefer to have my General Staff at my table in the mess for all officers at headquarters. Both Keyes and Truscott have equipped either trucks or trailers for living quarters. I am satisfied with my tent. I expect to have a gasoline heater when it gets colder and will then be quite comfortable. In my command tent, an auto headlight connected to a truck battery provides light. My observations at the front will help the 36th Division in its future mountain operations: the best type of packs for men to use for carrying supplies; the most practicable rations; the best use of assault battalions; transportation problems and methods of road repair; the laying of wire and use of radios; military police procedures; and the care and use of pack animals.

Our 111th Engineer Battalion under Major Oran Stovall has been doing an excellent job helping, along with other engineers, to clear the port of Naples of debris and sunken ships.

Thursday, November 4, 1943

I visited Army Headquarters at Caserta and talked briefly to Clark. He stressed the need of discipline and speed in our next operation. Discipline and speed are always to be stressed. Our speed will be determined by what the Germans do and how well we do.

Keyes visited my headquarters and explained his plan of operations when the II Corps, consisting only of the 36th Division, takes over its assigned sector next week. He makes it appear quite intricate, but it is really quite simple.

I asked General Gruenther, Clark's Chief of Staff, to assist me in obtaining an outstanding artillery officer to replace General Cowles, who is sick in the hospital and will be sent back to the States. Colonel Shryock, Executive Officer of the Artillery Brigade, is in line for the position and hopes to get it, but I will not give it to him. He has not been cooperative with the Division Staff, and considers himself untouchable in all matters within the Artillery Brigade.

Capua, Italy
Sunday, November 8, 1943

I visited General Ryder at his Command Post today. The men of that Division, the 34th, are undergoing a lot of hardships but are pushing on regardless. They are having an average of 20 men killed per day. The average number of wounded is about 70 per day. The infantry is advancing over rugged mountains where supply and signal communications are very difficult. Pack animals are being used to assist in supply. The weather conditions—rain, mud, cold—are very trying.

Tuesday, November 10, 1943

I had a long talk with Colonel Shryock, now acting CO, Division Artillery, regarding the low standard of discipline in the artillery. Now he is properly impressed with the necessity of improving discipline.

Thursday, November 12, 1943

Lt. General Courtney H. Hodges visited me at my Command Post north of Capua yesterday. He is visiting the Italian front to gather training ideas for the troops composing his Army which is being organized in the United States.

I told him that it is the same old story; individual discipline and leadership training must not be neglected. One must constantly check on orders to see that they are carried out as intended. Inexperienced junior officers and NCOs have to be taught to assume responsibility for their own men and to punish them when they need it.

Most youngsters, in their first job as leaders, do not have the courage to say "no" or to hurt peoples' feelings when necessary. They are unwilling to be spoken of in uncomplimentary terms. They have to learn that this goes along with the job. If left to their own devices, they will try to get along as one big happy family. In battle this costs lives. This lack of discipline and leadership results from inadequate training, insufficient time to thoroughly learn assigned lessons, improper disciplinary training, and poor leadership on the part of unit commanders whose weaknesses are emulated. Bad habits acquired during basic training in the United States will have to be corrected the hard way by repeated costly battlefield experiences. I told him that, in my opinion, this applies to all trainees no matter where they come from. Of course, I was not telling him anything he did not already know.

I was delighted to see Courtney. When I first came into the Army, way back in 1911, as a green second lieutenant of infantry, and joined my first regiment, the 13th Infantry at San Antonio, Texas, he was one of the senior second lieutenants. He had attended the United States Military Academy, but had flunked out. He came into the Army as a result of an examination for civilians, as I had. He saw that I needed help and took me under his tutelage. He looked after me like a father during those first weeks, introduced me to all the intricacies (in those days) of a shavetail's life, watched over my performance, generally kept me in line. This was a trying time for me, and I have never forgotten his help. From San Antonio, the regiment went to the Philippines where our friendship continued. George Marshall and Hap Arnold were First Lieutenants in the 13th at that time. Sometime later, Arnold went to the Air Corps. I have served with Courtney many times since. Our last service together was at the Army War College when he was a student there. Courtney is a grand person. He is no genius, but I know he will do well as an Army Commander. I wish he commanded the Fifth Army.

CHAPTER ELEVEN
Breaking the Bernhardt Line

Mignano, Italy
Tuesday, November 16, 1943

The Division is relieving the 3rd Division on the front line.

Last night, in spite of the darkness, I observed the movement of the 142nd and 143rd CTs into their forward areas. They were on time, silent, and in good order. I spent the night at my CP north of Capua and discussed several matters with Colonel Kerr. Upon my return I found that the CP of the 3rd Division had been shelled during the night. One shell killed the 3rd Division Provost Marshal and wounded several others. Another shell struck just outside a tent in which Lt. Colonel Crowther and Captain Clark Wren were sleeping. They had been sent from the 36th Division to arrange details for the relief. Shell splinters and fragments tore through their tent, making many large holes above and below their cots. Miraculously, neither was touched.

Wednesday, November 17, 1943

I took over command of the 3rd Division sector from General Truscott at noon.

Thursday, November 18, 1943

The 36th Division has been relieving the 3rd Division on the front between Mounts Cesima and Camino, northwest of Mignano on Highway 6. We completed the relief in four nights and the men did an excellent job. This has been a most trying operation because it has rained day and night. The men are soaked to the skin, and their uniforms are covered with mud up to their waists. They are cold and have no opportunity to dry their clothing or have hot meals. It is very dark at night, and trucks and jeeps mire down on stretches of bad road and on bypasses. Beyond the limit of vehicular travel, all front line battalions have to be supplied by men who carry what is needed by hand up the side of the mountain through the mud and rain. I visited all our regimental CPs, observed the nature of the terrain, and noted how difficult our position is compared to that of the Germans. They are on the heights above and look down upon our front and flanks which gives them a marked advantage.

NOTE: This was the very strong and well-coordinated defensive
position which the German Command designated, "The
Bernhardt Line." It was held in depth and was firmly
fixed onto the mountains and many defiles in the area.
It consisted of mutually supporting strong points established on the many tactical features which the mountains,
valleys and gullies provided. Its defensive arrangements
were well-concealed and were very difficult to discover.
The Bernhardt Line was not a delaying position. It was
a covering position for the Gustav Line and was stronger
than the Gustav Line in its mountain areas.

Truscott told me that the Germans had been shelling his CP
each night for the last ten nights, but he had done nothing about
it. I did not take over the 3rd Division CP but placed my CP 500
yards to the east, out of direct German observation, to avoid exposing my staff to nightly shelling and casualties, even though
this move made extra work for the Signal Company. In this
location there are four caves. General Wilbur, Colonel Kerr and
I sleep in one, the general staff sleeps in another, and the special
staff sleeps in another. The caves are dry and provide shelter
from shell fire and bombings. I have taken pains to camouflage
all troop areas and to prevent fires and smoke which may be
visible to the Germans. I have instituted action to procure 12,000
combat suits, 6,000 pairs of leather gloves, and 2,000 gasoline
space heaters for the men in the front positions.

Clark and Keyes visited my CP today. They have ants in their
pants and want to get going now that they have a "fresh" Division
in line. I am working on a plan to comply with their wishes. The
job will be difficult if the Germans choose to make it so.

Our engineers and signalmen have been going day and night.
They surely take a beating. In spite of all the discomfort and
hardship, the morale of the Division is excellent. We have had
several killed and wounded.

Seven Germans deserted to our front line yesterday. They were
wearing summer clothing, were wet and cold, and their morale
was very low. They were quite willing to talk freely and answered
all our questions. They said they were sick and tired of the war,
had had nothing to eat for two days and were through with it.

Major General Templer, who commands the 56th British Division on my left flank, called with Clark later today, and we
discussed plans for possible operations on our fronts and ways of
cooperation between our divisions. Templer was not enthusiastic

about doing anything on his part, but quite enthusiastic about following up any successes I could attain. I shall cooperate with him in every way possible, but I don't think he is going to do anything except talk.

Friday, November 19, 1943

Still raining and muddy. The troops are wet and some of them are in mud up to their ankles.

Several "sightseeing" generals came to see what the front looks like. General Wilbur took them up to the CPs of the 141st and 143rd where they could see the location of our front lines. They were satisfied with this and have gone back to their jobs able to say that they have been at the front.

To prevent being bombed, I have taken pains to conceal our location from air observation. At night a few shells have been falling on the low ground across the road but none directly in the CP area. More rain and deeper mud today. Temperature at 1:00 PM, 59°.

For dinner today we had stewed rice and tomatoes, salmon croquettes, diced carrots, bread, gravy, hot chocolate, and bread pudding. This is the regular ration issued to all messes, but I have especially good cooks who know how to make the most of what is issued. However, the men who are doing the fighting on the mountain sides will have to subsist on the C or K rations.

To make sure each man in the Division will have a Thanksgiving dinner, turkeys are being kept in cold storage until units now in line can be relieved and returned to the rear.

I believe my Division mess is probably the finest in the European Theater of Operation and certainly the best in the Fifth Army. This is principally due to the imagination, dedication, and outstanding ability of S/Sgt. Cloyd Abruzzo, Technical Sgt. Ben W. Bonam, S/Sgt. Glen "Big Daddy" Gooch, Tech. 4 Clarence "Goat" Heard, S/Sgt. James C. Kirschner, Tech. 5 Woodrow W. Knippsa, Technical Sgt. Erba L. Shook, PFC Maxwell Maddox, Tech. 4 Leon McClouskey, Technical Sgt. Charles Buntin, and PFC Robert H. Brashers.

Yesterday twenty-one prisoners were taken by the 142nd Infantry.

Sunday, November 22, 1943

I visited General Templer, 56th British Division, on my left.

He explained his plan to take the Mount La Difensa hill mass in cooperation with my Division. I am quite certain that, although he promises great things, he will do little to help us in the operation directed by Army Headquarters. He says that he must have starlight after two days of fair weather to do his job at night. I am amazed that a division commander would set such a condition to govern the date for starting our operation. I will go on the assumption that I shall receive no help from him.

Tuesday, November 23, 1943

Generals Alexander and Clark were here for lunch. I took them up to see the front. While enroute, we were stopped by shell fire. We got out of the jeeps, and Alexander led the way to a rise of ground beside the road to look at the German positions. While there, five German shells fell near us; the second one, 50 feet in front; the third one, 50 feet behind. I expected the next one to strike exactly where we were standing, since we were in full view of the German artillery observers, and apparently one of them had a "bracket" on us. But, it did not. None did any damage. Alexander, in true British tradition, paid no attention to any of the shells, but Clark and I took full notice of each.

Thursday, November 25, 1943

Thanksgiving Day. I had a conference with my staff and subordinate commanders and went over, in detail, plans for the capture of the Mount La Difensa-Mount Maggiore mass.

Many of my men are developing trench foot because they are not able to dry their feet, socks, or shoes for days at a time. This condition will grow worse before it gets better. One way to dry their socks is to wrap them around the waist next to their bodies.

We are having too many losses by shell fire because our people are careless about concealment of bivouacs and movement near them. They know that the German observers are looking down on them from all directions, but they do not realize that carelessness by some individuals means casualties for others. Our losses are twice what they should be.

Wednesday, December 1, 1943

I have been very busy today checking on final arrangements for my plans to attack and capture Mt. Maggiore. The Germans are in a strong position, and this is not going to be an easy job

Prior to Attack of Bernhardt Line

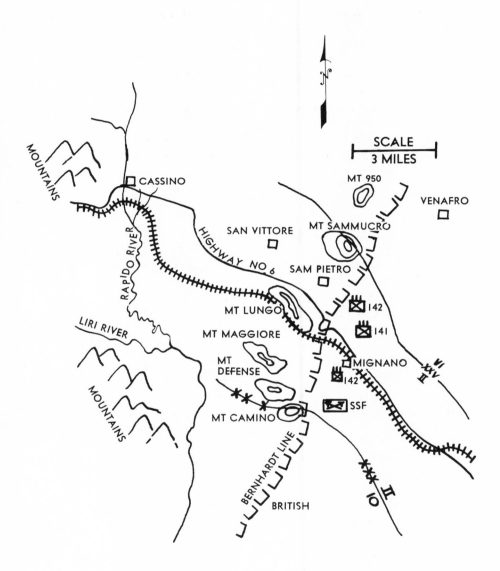

SCALE
3 MILES

MOUNTAINS

CASSINO

MT 950

VENAFRO

RAPIDO RIVER

SAN VITTORE

MT SAMMUCRO

HIGHWAY NO 6

SAM PIETRO

142

LIRI RIVER

MT LUNGO

141

MT MAGGIORE

MT DEFENSE

MIGNANO

142

VI

MOUNTAINS

SSF

MT CAMINO

BERNHARDT LINE

II

10

BRITISH

because of the conditions under which we will have to fight and supply ourselves. Everything has been done to coordinate the whole operation, and I see every reason for success. Effective artillery fires have been arranged to support the infantry attack.

Brigadier General DaPino, Italian Army, and four of his staff officers arrived at my CP at noon today on their way to the front to look at Mt. Lungo and the vicinity where an Italian brigade may have to fight later.

The Commanding Officer of the 3rd Ranger Battalion completed his advance on the town of San Pietro yesterday. His battalion is attached to this Division, and Keyes ordered me to order him to make a reconnaissance in force. I would never have ordered it myself. When you know where the enemy is—which we have known for some time—and his strength, there is no point to making a reconnaissance in force. I don't know what Keyes expected to accomplish by ordering it, since he was fully aware of the situation in front of him. I assumed that the Battalion Commander knew enough not to get his outfit out into the open and get it shot up. He had 11 killed and 19 wounded, mostly by artillery fire, while trying to cross open ground in attack formation. Of course, he obtained no more information than we already had. Nor did he punish the Germans. A needless sacrifice to poor judgment in ordering it, and to poor leadership in the manner of execution.

Speaking in general, a reconnaissance in force is a limited attack, but in this case where we already know the enemy's strength and location but where, nevertheless, an order from higher headquarters directs a reconnaissance be made in force, an attack by a lone battalion in broad daylight over relatively open ground is improper and costly. A better procedure would have been to push forward combat patrols under cover and concealment, and support them by reinforcements, if and when they should be successful.

Thursday, December 2, 1943

This has been a busy day with last minute arrangements for tonight, and with visitors galore. The following news correspondents and photographers visited my CP, just in time for lunch: John Lardner, **Newsweek**; William H. St. Meman, **Chicago Daily News**; H. R. Knickerbocker, **Chicago Sun**; Lt. S. R. Shepard, Army Pictorial Service; Robert Capa, **Life**; Sannow, **Universal News**; Bert Brandt, **Time**; George Hicks, NBC **Blue Network**; N. W.

Bigart, **New York Herald Tribune;** Major Bruce Low, 15th Army Group; and Lt. Wilson, INC, AF HQ.

The Army and the Corps Commanders and C/S Fifth Army also dropped in for lunch and expressed wishes for our success.

Friday, December 3, 1943

This morning the 142nd Infantry under Colonel George Lynch and the Special Service Force under Colonel Frederick which is now under my command attacked and captured Mt. La Difensa and Mt. Maggiore. Tough going. The rain and mud were very bad. The men climbed up the mountain slopes and cliffs last night and slopped through muck and water, soaked to the skin and muddied from head to foot. Nevertheless, the attack went according to plan. The rugged mountain slopes together with the bad weather make supply difficult. One man out of three must carry on foot and by hand supplies to their positions. At night it takes 8 hours for a man to make the trip of five miles from the nearest point a jeep can go. We are in the process of organizing a mule pack train to go where jeeps can't go. But there are some places where even a pack mule cannot go. Few American troops have ever had to fight under more difficult conditions in any war.

Saturday, December 4, 1943

General Vincenzo DaPino, commander of the 1st Motorized Group (Italian), along with his Chief of Staff and other staff officers, unit commanders, and Major Campello, liaison officer and interpreter, arrived at my CP at noon for lunch and a conference regarding plans for the relief of the 141st Infantry by the 1st Motorized Group, preparatory to an attack on Mount Lungo by the Italian unit. This is probably the first Italian unit to be committed to action on the Allied side. I get the impression that this unit has been hastily put together; that the Commander and his Staff are not professionally prepared for a combat mission; that, principally for political reasons, Clark wants me to use them.

Sunday, December 5, 1943

All objectives of the Special Service Forces (SSF) and 142nd Infantry have been taken. This ends the first phase of my plan. I made a personal reconnaissance over the combat area in an artillery observer's plane. In my next phase, which Corps has approved, the 1st Motorized Group (Italian) is to take Mount Lungo, the 143rd Infantry under Colonel Martin is to take San Pietro and the summits of Mount Sammucro, and Colonel Tucker's paratroopers are to take the heights north of Mount Sammucro.

Another conference with General DaPino. I don't think he has much enthusiasm for his job.

We tried to supply the 142nd Infantry on Mt. Maggiore by air today. The first attempt was a failure because out of five packages dropped, two were lost and two fell into the German positions, so only one was received by our men.

Jack Rice, AP photographer, and Ernie Pyle were here for lunch.

Tuesday, December 7, 1943

I had luncheon with Keyes and the Crown Prince Umberto at Keyes' mess. I wonder what went through Umberto's mind when his food was served on china with the royal crest, probably from the royal palace in Palermo.

The Prince, who may someday be the head of the Italian government, is an alert, intelligent, cultured man. I believe he has unusual common sense and good judgement, and he impressed me very favorably. Many photographers and newsmen were present.

Wednesday, December 8, 1943

The 1st Motorized Brigade (Italian), the 143rd Infantry, and the 3rd Ranger Battalion attacked to capture Mt. Lungo, San Pietro, and Mt. Sammucro. The Italians advanced in vulnerable formations, were beaten back with heavy losses by a German counter attack, and were completely demoralized. The 143rd captured Hill 1205, the prominent summit of Sammucro, but were stopped in front of San Pietro, where the Germans were in strong defensive positions protected by barbed wire and mines. Its losses were quite heavy. The 3rd Ranger Battalion got on Hill 950, its objective, but was later driven off.

During these battles, I was visited by all the brass hats in the theater. Crown Prince Umberto, Assistant Secretary of War McCloy, Clark, Keyes, Sultan, Eagles, Paschal, Meyer, Rooks, McCreery, Alexander, Templer, etc., etc., etc. I had a difficult time attending to tactical demands with all these tourists coming and going. Photographers and newsmen were numerous, also. All of them must be received courteously and made to feel welcome. However, they are in the way.

Monday, December 13, 1943

Just finished giving orders for an attack to be made on the 15th. The plan definitely does not suit me, but I can see nothing better to do under the circumstances. The terrain is mountainous and very rugged; the level ground is a sea of mud; and the men are wet, cold and miserable. But, if this attack goes as planned, the Division will receive the praises of both the Corps and the Army Commanders. They would give almost anything for a big success.

Clark told me that in view of the demoralization of the Italian Motorized Group on the 8th, I must give them a battle mission which they **cannot fail** to accomplish.

Colonel Lynch, who commands the 142nd, came in yesterday literally plastered with mud, and wet from head to foot. I arranged for him to have a bath, three good meals, and tried to get him some new clothes, but failed.

Visitors are arriving in greater and greater numbers at meal time. Even Ernie Pyle likes our food, although he does not like to associate with officers above the grade of captain. The food we have is the same that is issued to all troop messes. My Mess Sergeant and cooks know how to make the best of it.

I have decorated many men of the Division since we have been in line. I have them assembled in small groups, four to eight, at some convenient point in the area, and go there to meet them.

I visited the 2nd and 3rd Battalions, 143rd Infantry, in the front line east of San Pietro. They have had heavy losses. I brought out with me, in my jeep, a man who had had most of his hand shot off by a machine gun. He had lost a lot of blood and was very weak. I hurried to the nearest first-aid station where he was given a transfusion and a bowl of hot soup. If he gets back to a hospital soon, and he should for an ambulance was waiting, he will survive.

I pinned a Silver Star on Captain Peterson, 636th Tank Destroyer Battalion, while he was passing my CP enroute to a Clearing Station. He was wounded in the head by a mine, but throughout the night he continued to move his tank destroyers into position where they will be ready to support the attack to be made on the 15th.

Monday, December 14, 1943

My Aide keeps terse notes of some of the things I do each day. An edited copy of his notes for today reads:

"Corps Commander, General Keyes, telephoned at 0745 to receive reports of patrolling last night. General Wilbur, Assistant Division Commander, conferred briefly with CG at 0800. Major Stovall, Division Engineer, discussed operations of his battalion with CG at 0820. CG discussed prime movers for 57 mm guns and care of pack animals with Major Rose at 0900. CG telephoned Colonel Tucker, 504th Parachute Infantry, at 0915 to briefly discuss the present situation in his area.

"Colonel Carl Phinney, G-4, discussed problems regarding supply of artillery ammunition with CG at 0930. At 0945, word was received that Colonel Richard Werner was wounded in a dive bomb attack on his CP at 0930. General Wilbur conferred with CG concerning a possible replacement for Colonel Werner who will go to the hospital. Colonel Walter Hess, CO 36th Division Artillery, arrived at CP at 1000. Lt. Colonel Stark, II Corps Headquarters, arrived at Division CP at 1015 to attend a conference composed of General Wilbur, Colonel Hess, Lt. Colonel Harry P. Stark and CG, regarding supply of artillery ammunition and employment of Division and Corps Artillery in the current operations.

"Lt. Colonel Wyatt, 2nd Battalion, 141st Infantry, arrived at CP at 1100 to confer with CG and General Wilbur. Upon the recommendation of General Wilbur, CG placed Lt. Colonel Wyatt in command of the 141st Infantry, and General Wilbur telephoned Lt. Colonel Price, ExO, 141st Infantry, to inform him of this change. Lt Colonel J. Trimble Brown, 1st Bn 141st, called at CP at 1300 to confer with CG regarding the coming operation. Corps Commander called at CP at 1500 and went over the Division plans for the coming operation."

Friday, December 17, 1943

The Division has been engaged in battle since noon on the 15th to capture San Pietro and Mt. Lungo. Yesterday the 142nd Infantry carried out its attack on Lungo with skill and speed, and had possession before noon. The regiment advanced across the valley between Mt. Maggiore and Mt. Lungo before daylight and struck the German position on the right flank and rear just at first light. Lt. Colonel Sam Graham and his men of the 2nd Battalion did a grand job. It was done exactly as I planned it and has broken the forward position of the German defense.

The Italian Motorized Brigade moved forward to occupy the eastern part of Lungo after the 142nd had already taken the remainder of the mountain. They were successful, as ordered.

ar, the 143rd, assisted by the 141st and a company of tanks,
taken San Pietro, but the troops have made heroic efforts
so. The losses before the town have been heavy. Many
ued had to be abandoned within enemy lines. Some may
out in no man's land for days. This is bad, and is one of the
misfortunes every soldier hopes to avoid.

We have no proper terrain for employment of tanks. The approaches to San Pietro from the east are covered with terraced
vineyards, unsuitable for tanks, but General Brann, G-3, Army,
made a special trip to my CP before the attack to tell me that
Clark wanted me to use tanks in this operation because there are
many tank units in the theater that have not done any fighting. I
explained this to the tank commander, Lt. Colonel Felber, and told
him to take a look at the area, prepare the best plan he could for
no more than a company of tanks, and write the paragraph to go
into the Division Field Order for its employment, which he did.
The only way he could use them was straight down the road leading to the town, where they could be disposed of, one at a time,
by German antitank gunners, and where they could not help our
infantry. He lost several tanks, but very few men.

The Corps and the Army Commanders have made frequent visits
to my headquarters during our fighting. They try not to meddle
in my affairs as Division Commander, but they do. They are not
able to appreciate the very difficult conditions under which the
front line infantry is serving, and often get the jitters and become
alarmed over incidents of minor importance. Their jitters have
prevented me from relieving my troops by rotation for rest from
time to time, because they insist on keeping more troops in the
line than are necessary. I have told my staff not to pass on reports that will alarm higher headquarters without first obtaining
my approval.

German planes bombed the vicinity of my CP yesterday. Several
bullets and shell fragments from Corps antiaircraft guns struck
about us. Danger from our own anticraft gunners is greater than
from the German planes. For protection, it is necessary to have
some holes in the ground to jump into when our own antiaircraft
begin firing. A bullet from friendly troops punctured one of the
tires on my jeep.

Sunday, December 19, 1943

Colonel Martin's 143rd took San Pietro on the 17th and our

troops now are west of the town.

General Eisenhower and his Chief of Staff, Major General Bedell Smith, Clark and Keyes visited my CP today for luncheon and to look at the German positions in our front. I took them to a point on Highway 6 where they had a good view of San Pietro, Mt. Summucro, and the German positions west thereof. At one point, while Eisenhower was looking across the valley, he said to me that he would like to see an artillery concentration put down on San Pietro which is a pile of ruins. I was surprised at this. Perhaps Eisenhower thought the Germans were still in San Pietro. Maybe he just wanted to see the dirt fly. Bedell Smith overheard his statement and told me in a subdued tone not to pay any attention to Ike's directive.

Clark and Keyes do not understand why we were so long in taking San Pietro and the western slopes of Mt. Sammucro. The answer is quite simple. The Germans were in well-prepared defensive positions. They had an advantage over us. To get them out took time.

Captain Walter L. Ford, a psychiatrist with the Medical Corps, has been here for some time as an expert on the emotional disorders of soldiers. We have orders that he is to testify at every court martial where the accused is charged with a major offense, to inform the members of the court whether or not the accused is responsible for his own acts. If Captain Ford testifies that he is not responsible, the accused goes free.

Ford has had no experience with soldiers nor with the conduct of a battle. He arrives at his conclusions by interrogating the accused, going back into his life as far as the man can remember. As a result of this one-sided investigation, Captain Ford goes before the court and in almost every case presents some incident of mental unhappiness in the accused's life that has unbalanced his normal thinking as evidence that the accused should not be punished.

So I had to talk with him. I explained that by far the greater number of soldiers do not want to run the risk of being killed in battle; that, to avoid this risk, a few would rather be in the guard house awaiting trial, and thereafter, serving sentence, than to be in the fighting area; that they lay their plans with care and intelligence to accomplish their purpose; that this is one of the most serious conditions with which officers and NCOs of small infantry units in combat have to deal.

I suggested that he would learn as much or more about the true emotional conditions of the accused soldier by interrogating his company officers and NCOs as from the accused. Also, I said that he should not overlook the fact that the company commander, being responsible for the good order and discipline of his unit under the dangerous and trying conditions of battle, must maintain his unit at the maximum strength and handle minor offenses on the spot; that he is dependent on the military courts for assistance in maintaining good order and for punishment of men whom he cannot handle on the spot.

I pointed out that there are three types of men who run away from battle: (1) Those who do so deliberately because they refuse to do their duty. This type should be tried and punished, if found guilty. (2) Those who have done their duty well in the past but have been under the strain of combat too long, until their nervous system breaks down and their self-control is gone. This type should be sent to a rest area under quiet and peaceful conditions until they are completely recovered. (3) Those who do not have the physical courage or strength to withstand hardship and danger. Men of this type are a liability to a combat unit and should be transferred to other duty.

The company officers and NCOs know their men and, generally speaking, will protect men in types two and three. The men they send to the courts for trial are those who deliberately run away or deliberately commit other offenses because they will not do the duty of which they are fully capable.

Ford listened patiently to my lecture and as he departed said, "You have told me some things I did not know."

Wednesday, December 22, 1943

This is about as miserable a day for the troops as one can imagine. Several units are moving to new positions this afternoon. I regret the hardships they must endure tonight. Wet, muddy, cold, and hungry, they will go into a camp in the mud and rain without rest or sleep. They have been going for 35 days.

Now the Germans are defending every mountain, and we will have to fight for every inch of ground. In front of us is another strong German defense.

The higher commands pay little or no attention to the hardships of the men. They set up schedules of progress to be made from day to day, but they do not consult the German soldiers, who are defending the positions in our front. The Italian campaign will not be finished this week, nor next. Our wasteful policy or method of taking one mountain mass after another gains no tactical advantage, locally. There is always another mountain mass beyond with the Germans dug in on it, just as before. Somebody on top side, who has control of the required means, should figure out a way to decisively defeat the German army in Italy, instead of just pushing, pushing, pushing.

The destruction of villages, homes, private property and public utilities goes on continuously. The destitute Italians, homeless and ragged, whose relatives have been killed in their homes by both German and American artillery, present a pitiful sight. There is no punishment too great for the tyrants and insane persons who caused this war.

Day before yesterday, Major Green and Captain Swank delivered a truck for my use, a truck fitted as an office and quarters. The truck is authorized and was converted for my use by the Division Ordnance Company, the 736th. It has a bed across the front end, a clothes closet, wash stand with a 30 gallon water tank, desk, telephone stand, chest of drawers, and electric lights which can be connected to the headquarters generator. This truck was made without my knowledge, and presented to me as a surprise. I appreciate the gift, and the spirit behind it, especially since it's getting colder and wetter each day. This will be better than a tent, but since I am already set up for business in my command tent and have quite comfortable sleeping quarters in my cave, with Wilbur and Kerr for congenial companions, I shall not occupy the truck until we move from here.

Captain Henry T. Waskow, CO Company B, 143rd, was killed on the slopes of Mt. Sammucro on December 14, during the operations to take San Pietro.

> NOTE: Ernie Pyle, war correspondent, was with the 36th Division at the time, and wrote one of his famous war stories, "Captain Waskow," based on the love and devotion expressed by the men of Waskow's command.
>
> By courtesy of, and with permission of, the **Temple Daily Telegram**, Temple, Texas, I reprint here Captain Waskow's letter, written to his parents and relatives prior to the battle.

CAPTAIN HENRY T. WASKOW
HIS LAST WILL AND TESTAMENT

"Herewith my last will and testament:

"Greetings:

"If you get to read this, I will have died in defense of my country and all that it stands for—the most honorable and distinguished death a man can die. It was not because I was willing to die for my country, however—I wanted to live for it—just as any other person wants to do. It is foolish and foolhardy to want to die for one's country, but to live for it is something else.

"To live for one's country is to my mind to live a life of service; to—in a small way—to help a fellow man occasionally along the way, and generally to be useful and to serve. It also means to me to rise up in all our wrath and with overwhelming power to crush any oppressor of human rights.

"That is our job—all of us—as I write this, and I pray God we are wholly successful

"Yes, I would have liked to have lived—to live and share the many blessings and good fortunes that my grandparents bestowed upon me—a fellow never had a better family than mine; but, since God has willed otherwise, do not grieve too much dear ones, for life in the other world must be beautiful, and I have lived a life with that in mind all along. I was not afraid to die, you can be assured of that. All along, I prayed that I and others could do our share to keep you safe until we returned. I pray again that you are safe, even though some of us do not return.

"I made my choice, dear ones. I volunteered in the Armed Forces because I felt it my duty to do so. I thought that I might be able and might do just a little bit to help this great country of ours in its hours of darkness and need—the country that means more to me than life itself—if I have done that then I can rest in peace, for I will have done my share to make this world a better place in which to live. Maybe when the lights go on again all over the world, free people can be happy and gay again.

"Through good fortune and the grace of God, I was chosen a leader—an honor that meant more to me than any of you will ever know. If I failed as a leader, and I pray God I didn't, it was not because I did not try. God alone knows how I worked and slaved to make myself a worthy leader of these magnificent men, and I feel assured that my work has paid dividends—in personal satisfaction, if nothing else.

"As I said a couple of times in my letters home, 'When you remember me in your prayers, remember to pray that I be given strength, character and courage to lead these magnificent Americans.' I said that in all sincerity and I hope I have proved worthy of their faith, trust, and confidence.

"I guess I have always appeared as pretty much of a queer cuss to all of you. If I seemed strange at times, it was because I had weighty responsibilities that preyed on my mind and wouldn't let me slack up to be human like I so wanted to be. I felt so unworthy, at times, of the great trust my country had put in me, that I simply had to keep plugging to satisfy my own self that I was worthy of that trust. I have not, at the time of writing this, done that and I suppose I never will.

"I do not try to set myself on a pedestal as a martyr. Every Joe Doe who shouldered a rifle made a similar sacrifice—but I do want to point out that the uppermost thought in my mind all along was service to the cause, and I hope you all felt the same way about it.

"When you remember me, remember me as a fond admirer of all of you, for I thought so much of you and I loved you with all my heart. My wish for all of you is that you get along well together and prosper—not in money, but in happiness; for happiness is something that all the money in the world can't buy.

"Try to live a life of service—to help someone wherever you are or whatever you may be—take it from me, you can get happiness out of that, more than anything in life.

HENRY T. WASKOW"

Saturday, December 26, 1943

Yesterday was not a very Merry Christmas for the people of Italy and the world. I went to visit the three infantry regiments during the morning and decorated some 40 men who earned awards during the current operations. A Silver Star or a DSC is an inadequate award for their achievements, but they are the only rewards I have to give. It is marvelous the way the men keep going under the existing conditions. They are wet, muddy and dirty, but their spirits are excellent.

Where it was possible, a good Christmas dinner was served to the troops. Other troops, now in the front line, will get their Christmas dinners as soon as they come out of line.

Our headquarters mess had an exceptionally good dinner yesterday. Roast turkey, dressing, gravy, whipped potatoes, stewed cauliflower, fruit salad, hot rolls, butter, cake, coffee, and three kinds of pie: apple, custard, and chocolate. This was not a special for Division Headquarters. It was the regular Christmas ration, and all messes could have had the same, if their cooks had taken pains to prepare it.

During dinner a lieutenant and three enlisted men from the 434th Antiaircraft Battalion, now attached to the 36th Division, came by and, as a surprise, played and sang several appropriate numbers. We enjoyed the music and showed our appreciation. The hope was expressed by many that next Christmas would be

Company G, 141st Infantry, dug in for attack or defense. January 15, 1944
—U.S. Army Photo

Pig sty serves as protection for the 143rd Infantry Message Center. Rapido
River, January, 1944—U.S. Army Photo

Note sparcity of concealment for American forces on the east side of the Rapido River. Liri River in foreground.—U.S. Army Photo

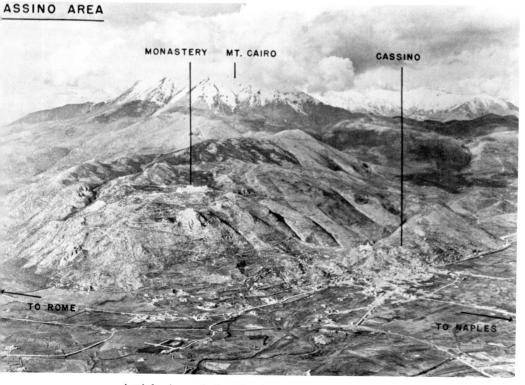

ASSINO AREA

MONASTERY   MT. CAIRO   CASSINO

TO ROME

TO NAPLES

Aerial view of the Cassino area.—U.S. Army Photo

Smoke screen used to conceal the advance of the 143rd Infantry and
tanks to the edge of the Rapido River. January 22, 1944
—U.S. Army Photo

Soldiers of the Reconnaissance Company of the 636th Tank Destroyer Battalion
clearing mine fields. January 30, 1944—U.S. Army Photo

Lt. Col. Harold Reese, right, talks to German soldiers during truce on Mt. Castelone. February 14, 1944

General Walker about to decorate men of the 36th Division. Presenzano, Italy, December, 1943—U.S. Army Photo

spent under peaceful conditions.

Keyes sent me a fifth of whiskey as a Christmas present. I'll keep it around and probably give it away later to someone who can use it.

Plans are being worked out for the relief of the 36th Division by the 34th. I will be glad to get the Division back where the men can have a bath and clean clothes. Snow is beginning to collect on the higher mountain peaks, which will add to our present adversities.

A couple of nights ago an AP photographer came to my cave and asked permission to take a picture of its interior. I sent for Hal Reese and we opened some of our Christmas packages while sitting on my bunk, so the photographer could take his pictures. At his request, I sent him to Army Headquarters in a cub plane where he can have his photographs developed and radioed to the States in time for inclusion in next Sunday's newspapers.

Alife, Italy
Saturday, January 1, 1944

We were relieved by the 34th Division on December 29 and 30 and went into bivouac in the San Angelo—Alife—Piedmonte area. We have a lot of work to do to get cleaned up and equipped for future training.

Yesterday we had lots of rain, and last night and today we have one of the worst rain, wind and snow storms I have seen strike a tent camp. The wind blew down all our tents, and the cold rain and snow soaked everybody and everything. Since the mess tents were down, nobody had breakfast. However, in spite of the storm, the cooks prepared a good New Year's dinner which they served at 3:00 PM. My new command post truck was a great help during the storm, and I was able to take some others in with me.

Many new officer replacements arrived last night in the rain and spent a very unhappy night and day. They and their baggage are soaked. This storm recalled to my mind the terrible wind storm we had at San Joaquin, Mexico, on Christmas Day, 1916. Then, our camp was wrecked and it took us two days to get back to normal. Because of losses, only about 40% of our personnel are from Texas.

Thursday, January 6, 1944

This morning I sent two staff officers to Naples for a day or so to check the rest facilities which Bob Ives arranged for our junior officers at a Swiss tourist hotel, the Pensione Mueller. I want a quiet place where our tired and deserving officers may go for a few days' rest. Infantry officers will go first, but I hope to give all staff officers an opportunity to spend some time there before we go back into line. Our enlisted men already have an excellent rest area at Caserta.

The temperature last night was below freezing; puddles are covered with a thin film of ice.

I received a letter of commendation from Keyes today for the job the Division did between November 15 and December 30. Mostly "baloney."

Although we are in a rest area, I directed the Division Engineer, Oran Stovall, to prepare a topographical study of the town of Cassino, the Rapido River, and the area on this side of the river, just in case we may need that information.

Saturday, January 8, 1944

Yesterday I received another new command truck fitted with bed, desk, upholstered chair and sofa, clothes closet, chest of drawers, wash stand and large mirror. This office truck was made in Naples by the 13th Ordnance Company in accordance with a directive from Army Headquarters. Similar ones are being made for each division commander in this theater. It is all anyone could wish. It has two sets of lights; one is attached to the truck battery, the other can be hooked up to any generator. It is heated either by a gasoline stove or by a hot air system connected to the truck engine and radiator. Wilbur calls it a palace. He falls heir to the one I have been using.

I visited several troop areas yesterday and found that the men had been heating some tents by burning gasoline in open cans. Of course, the inside of the tents were black with soot from the open flame. The heat given off by a tomato can full of burning gasoline, even if there were no smoke, is not worth the trouble. Company officers should not permit this procedure for it is akin to birds fouling their nests.

I told them to stop such foolishness, get some soap and water, and wash the inside of their tents. Good gasoline heaters have been issued, but not enough for one in every tent. The men will have to double up to keep warm.

While the Division is in this rest area, I have been giving a lot of thought to a possible plan for crossing the Rapido River just in case we have to do it. My experience at the Marne River against a German crossing in WWI taught me to appreciate the difficulties for which preparation must be made. There are rumors that some Division will have to cross it, but nothing official.

Since the Battle of Salerno, the Germans have been fighting a delaying action, giving up ground only when forced to do so. By slowing down our advance, they have gained time for their engineers to fortify a defensive zone across Italy, known as the Gustav Line. This line, one hundred miles south of Rome, extends from the Tyrrhenian Sea along the Garigliano and Rapido Rivers, northward across mountains to the Adriatic.

The sources of the Rapido River lie in the mountains some 35 miles from the Tyrrhenian Sea. Collecting its tributaries near the base of the mountains, including the icy waters from the snow-capped Mt. Cairo, the Rapido flows south some 10 miles past the town of Cassino and across the Liri Valley to its junction with the Liri River. This junction forms the Garigliano River which continues on some 15 miles to the sea.

Highway No. 6 crosses the Rapido River at Cassino and continues up the Liri Valley to Rome. The Liri Valley itself is about 5 miles wide and about 20 miles long, walled in by mountains on both sides. Its entrance is blocked by the Rapido River. At the center of this entrance lies the village of San Angelo on the west bank of the Rapido.

The Liri Valley is the only practicable route to Rome for tanks and supply vehicles in an advance beyond the Rapido. Elsewhere along the Gustav Line, where the ground is mountainous, the Germans need fewer troops, but at the entrance to the Liri Valley they have placed their strongest fortified defense which includes the unfordable Rapido as an obstacle. Obviously, the Germans intend to fight a defensive battle there.

Our Intelligence officers have been going all-out to keep up-to-date regarding the progress and development of the Gustav Line. Information from aerial photographs, prisoners of war, Italian civilians, and eyewitnesses of German troop movements and fortifications is plotted on Intelligence maps which are issued to the troops every ten days by Fifth Army Headquarters. These maps show, in detail, the location and extent of the field fortifications. By comparing the latest map with the previous one, the German organized defense buildup during the preceding ten days is clearly revealed. These maps have been issued periodically since November.

I'll swear, I do not see how we, or any other Division, can possibly succeed in crossing the Rapido River near San Angelo when that stream is included within the main line of resistance of the strongest German position.

Sunday, January 9, 1944

Stovall has been investigating possible engineering problems involved in crossing the Rapido. He reports that there is an appalling lack of basic engineer supplies in the Fifth Army area. The standard unsinkable footbridge, designed and needed by infantry troops for crossing rivers, does not exist in Italy.

He discussed the engineer problems with Colonel Gallagher, II Corps Engineer, and Colonel Wilson, Assistant Corps Engineer. They considered several plans of attack across the river and discarded them all as unsatisfactory. They agreed that any attack north of Cassino will be blocked by mountains. They looked upon the Liri Valley as a muddy bottleneck, guarded by an organized defense behind an unfordable river, without suitable approach routes or exits. Stovall contended that any attack made north or south of Highway 6 would create an impossible situation and end in failure and result in the loss of a great many lives. Gallagher and Wilson were not opposed to his views.

CHAPTER TWELVE
Crossing The Rapido

Alife, Italy
Wednesday, January 12, 1944

We have orders to go back into combat, and I have been quite busy disposing of some delayed administrative and disciplinary matters. I held a conference at 1:00 PM with staff officers and unit commanders and went over plans for moving the Division from our present rest area near Alife into the Mt. Porchia—Lungo—Rotondo area, and for taking over the sector east of the Rapido, now occupied by the 6th Motorized Infantry of the 1st Armored Division.

I am impressed with the efficiency and expertness of the Division Staff and commanders of all units of this Division. They constitute a smoother working team and have a greater esprit de corps than that of any division in which I have ever served. Because they remain on the same job month after month after month and do not come and go as in a regular army division, they have a personal interest in each other. They have the Division standard operating procedures down pat. For this movement I did not issue any formal written orders. I need tell them only the what, the when, and the where. They know the how, and work together for the good of all. There is no bickering, no jealousy, no discord.

Mt. Rotondo, Italy
Thursday, January 13, 1944

The forward echelon of Division Headquarters moved to a new CP on the southeast side of Mt. Rotondo, approximately 1½ miles north of the town of Mignano, in preparation for the impending operations. We have orders to push forward to the Rapido. As yet, no official word that we are to cross it. However, I strongly suspect we will have to cross it and in my conversations with Clark and Keyes I have mentioned the difficulties involved. They do not want to talk about them.

Friday, January 14, 1944

Tomorrow, the 141st (Wyatt) reinforced by the 753rd Tank Battalion (Felber) is to attack and occupy the Mt. Trocchio area, the northern half of our sector. I went over plans with Wyatt and Felber. We don't expect any great resistance, but we are prepared for it. Martin's 143rd will advance and occupy the southern part of our sector—on the left of the 141st.

Saturday, January 15, 1944

As a result of the successful attacks made today by the 141st and 143rd Combat Teams, we are now on a front of some five miles, along the Rapido where it flows south across the Liri Valley. In fact, we are looking west straight up the Liri Valley and are confronted by the strongest defenses on the Gustav Line. The situation looks bad for us.

Mts. Trocchio and Porchia are in our sector and stick up sharply out of the otherwise rather level ground which slopes gently toward the Rapido River, becoming flat and low about a mile this side of the river. Trocchio is a rocky mass that provides the only good observation point within our area.

Except for a few isolated patches, there is no suitable cover within a mile or more of the river where troops may be concealed during daylight. So I have to station units from two to five miles back from the river and maintain outguards and patrols along the river at night. The greater part of our area is a deep, thick mud, three to four inches deep for men and six to ten inches deep for vehicles. There are no hard surfaced roads for loaded trucks and heavy vehicles.

Our patrols report that Germans have planted mine fields at all of our suitable approaches to the river.

On their side, the Germans have organized a formidable defense. The unfordable Rapido alone is a major obstacle. It is from 40 to 50 feet wide, from 8 to 12 feet deep, with vertical banks 3 to 4 feet on both sides. The current is quite swift, about 4 miles per hour. The temperature of the water is estimated to be a few degrees above freezing. There are no bridges.

It is quite clear that the German main line of resistance consists of a series of strong points on the higher ground some 300 to 800 yards back from and roughly parallel with the river. These consist of riflemen, machine gunners, mortar crews, anti-tank crews and tankers. Some are behind concrete; others are dug in, protected by barbed wire. They command all the ground between them and the river, as well as much of the ground on our side. They protect each other by the interlocking fires of their weapons. Trees and brush have been cut down to improve their fields of fire. Outguards are posted along the river to give warning, in case we should attack, and to prevent our reconnaissance patrols from crossing the river at night.

Artillery of various types is emplaced in rear of the strong points. These are arranged in depth and are able to bring down concentrations on our troops wherever exposed. In addition to artillery, the German rear area contains local infantry reserves, antitank guns, tank units, and service units. The high mountains on both sides of the Liri Valley extend right up to the Rapido and provide ideal observation stations from which, through their high-powered telescopes, the Germans are able to examine in detail our whole area from front to rear. It must be assumed that this whole German defense is controlled by an effective communications system which includes the observation stations on the mountains west of Cassino and south of the Liri River.

The German troops opposite us are experienced in battle and led by professionals who know their business.

Sunday, January 16, 1944

An amphibious force under the command of Lucas is to land some 60 miles up the coast near Rome on the night of January 21/22. Today, in cooperation with that landing, I have some very ambitious orders from II Corps.

The 36th Division, in the south zone of the II Corps, is to cross the Rapido on the 20th and establish a bridgehead some 4 miles wide and 3 miles deep, as far as the town of Pignataro. When the bridgehead is established and bridges over the Rapido are in place, the 1st Armored Division is to pass through us, attack up the Liri Valley toward Rome with the hope of going all the way to join Lucas' beachhead.

The 34th Division on our right, in the north zone of the II Corps, is to make a demonstration on January 20th to divert attention from our attack, and then act as opportunity offers.

Corps artillery will support us. Corps engineers, tanks, tank destroyers, and other units are to be attached to the Division.

On January 20th, the III Air Support Command is to bomb the German strongpoints and troop concentrations opposite us.

I can't imagine how a demonstration by the 34th Division will cause the Germans to ignore us. The air bombing is not correctly timed because it allows the Germans time to recover before my attack. Both will only serve to alert the Germans.

This is going to be a tough job and I don't like it. There is nothing in our favor. Again I explained the difficulties to both Clark and Keyes and suggested that a greater chance of success could be had by attacking north of Cassino where the Rapido is fordable and the German defense is weaker. I do not look upon the mountains in that area as impossible obstacles. There, a coordinated attack can be made by a greater initial attacking force, in daylight, with greater surprise, and on a wider front, with the missions of seizing Mt. Castellone, cutting Highway No. 6 west of Cassino, and outflanking the German defense between Cassino and the Liri River.

It seems to me that such an attack, properly planned and executed, promises greater success and fewer losses than a frontal attack on the strongest part of the German defense where, because of German mine fields and limited crossing equipment, we are confined to a few crossing points and where we will have to build up, under fire, a coordinated attacking force by infiltration west of the river, immediately following the disorganization of crossing. Clark and Keyes were not interested. They do not understand the problems and do not know what I am talking about.

Monday, January 17, 1944

We have to cross the Rapido in the San Angelo area. But how? The equipment available for crossing is unsuitable. The improvised foot bridges—planks lashed to rubber boats—will be heavy and clumsy to carry by hand to the river. The larger rubber boats are heavy and cumbersome. They will easily be punctured by shell fire and will be difficult to launch and use as ferries because of the high banks and swift current. The wooden boats are heavier than the large rubber boats and more difficult to launch in the swirling water. We have had no practice in launching this type of equipment under Rapido River conditions. The little instruction the 143rd and 142nd had some weeks ago in launching boats on the placid Volturno is of no help here, where skill and teamwork is necessary under most difficult conditions.

Even when there is no opposition, it is no easy job to launch one of the heavy wooden or rubber boats on the Rapido as a ferry. Four or more men on our bank will have to hold onto a rope tied to the prow of the boat while others, holding onto the side of the boat, ease it down onto the swift current.

This must be done with care and skill or the boat may be swept downstream by the strong current. While the men on the rope hold the boat in place, others must climb down into it. Then they will paddle it across to the opposite bank while the men play out the rope as needed. If the men do not hold onto the rope, the boat will be swept downstream at twice the speed of a man walking.

While the paddlers hold the boat in place, the men must scramble up the opposite bank. They will carry with them a second rope tied to the prow. Then the men on the two ropes will pull the boat back and forth for use as a ferry. Each of the heavy rubber boats will transport 24 men. If it were possible to maintain 6 to 8 ferries of this type, it would be possible to put an infantry company across the Rapido in minutes; a battalion could cross in an hour or so.

But, when the time comes to handle this equipment at the river, the alerted Germans will bring down concentrations of fire from artillery and small arms onto the river banks. Havoc and chaos will follow, resulting in disruptions of formations and confusion due to the loss of leaders.

The expected damage to our crossing equipment means that we must hold some of it in reserve at the beginning.

Due to lack of time, the Engineers will not be able to do a satisfactory job of clearing mines. The removal of mines is a tedious, time consuming, and dangerous operation. Six or more men, close together in line and on their knees, face the suspected mine field. Using bayonets, they probe into the ground as they move forward, inch by inch. By holding the bayonet at an angle of about 30 degrees, the tip will strike a mine without exploding it. The mine is then carefully uncovered and the fuse removed. The sides of the cleared lanes must be outlined by white tape or manila rope, even though the German outguards may be able to see them. When this work has to be done at night, as in this case, mines may be passed over and casualties can occur.

The limited crossing equipment and the few narrow lanes to the river force us to cross at a limited number of points—bottlenecks.

Even when our troops get across the river, they are nowhere, for there can be no success until they are in possession of most of the strong points of the German position. Our men must form for attack immediately after they are across, just when they are at their greatest disadvantage.

In the midst of fire and confusion, how can the disorganized troops build up a fighting formation by infiltration on unfamiliar ground with no known landmarks to establish location and direction? How can proper control be exercised when leaders are casualties and units are separated? How can artillery effectively support such a situation and keep the German defenders down within their fortifications when our artillery ammunition is restricted to little more than enough for a preparation of 30 minutes? There are no satisfactory answers.

I will have to make the crossing at night because we cannot possibly succeed in broad daylight when our formations will be in bottlenecks under perfect German observation. I, and everybody else, know we are violating an important tactical principle. Night operations must be simple.

But, there is no way in the world to keep this operation simple. We are undertaking the impossible, but I shall keep it to myself; however, my staff and regimental and battalion commanders are no fools.

I feel the way I do because I commanded the 1st Battalion of the 30th Infantry, 3rd Division, at the Marne River on July 15th, 1918. On that day, the 10th German Infantry Division of about 10,000 men made an attack across the river. In good defensive positions along the Marne, my battalion of 1200 men turned the Germans back, disorganized them, confused them, and slaughtered them. There I learned the great advantage that defenders of an unfordable river have over the attackers. I was particularly impressed because my men were fighting their first battle against veteran German soldiers.

It appears to me that the defeat of the Germans on the Marne on July 15th, 1918, is about to be repeated in reverse on the Rapido in January, 1944. Nevertheless, I shall do everything in my power to succeed.

Our reconnaissance patrols are having great difficulty getting across the Rapido at night because of enemy fire from machine guns and mortars and because the rubber boats are unsuitable for crossing. The current is too swift. The boats capsize in the swirling water. Small shell fragments puncture them, making them useless. Last night 5 of 7 boats used by the patrols of the 141st Infantry were lost.

The Rapido Area

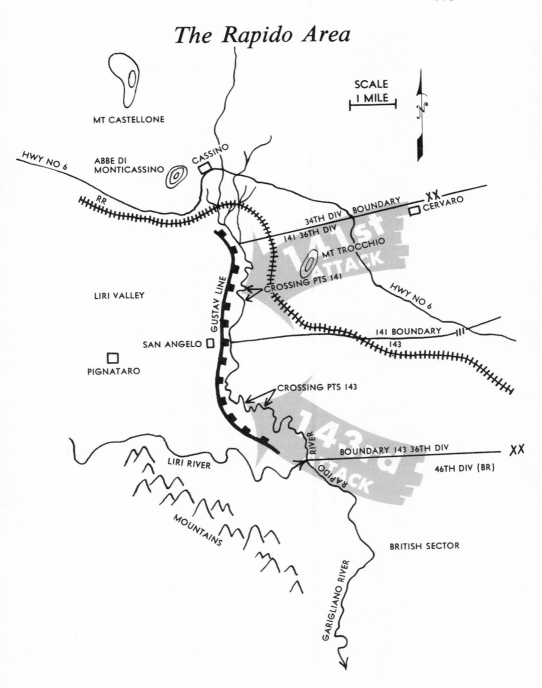

MT CASTELLONE

HWY NO 6

ABBE DI
MONTICASSINO

CASSINO

SCALE
1 MILE

RR

34TH DIV BOUNDARY

XX

CERVARO

141 36TH DIV

MT TROCCHIO

141st ATTACK

HWY NO 6

LIRI VALLEY

GUSTAV LINE

CROSSING PTS 141

141 BOUNDARY

143

SAN ANGELO

PIGNATARO

CROSSING PTS 143

143 ATTACK

BOUNDARY 143 36TH DIV

XX

LIRI RIVER

RAPIDO RIVER

46TH DIV (BR)

MOUNTAINS

BRITISH SECTOR

GARIGLIANO RIVER

Division Field Order No. 42 was distributed to the command today, but General Wilbur, the Division Staff, the Combat Team commanders and I have been discussing its contents since the 16th. (See Appendix C.)

I am sending the 141st Infantry, with two engineer companies and a chemical warfare company attached, to cross the river north of the village of San Angelo, and the 143rd Infantry, with similar attachments, to cross south of San Angelo. The 142nd Infantry is in Corps reserve and not available. Each regiment will have 30 pneumatic rubber boats, about the same number of heavy wooden boats, and four improvised footbridges. After the infantry is across, engineers are to construct two pontoon treadway bridges. Corps and Division artillery is to put down a 30-minute preparatory bombardment and try to neutralize the German positions.

The actual crossing is to begin at 8:00 PM, three hours after sunset. This will allow time, between dark and 8 o'clock for the troops to assemble and carry the boats and footbridges a mile or so to the river. The boats cannot be stored nearer the river because there is no concealment there. They must be hand carried because the noise of trucks grinding through the deep mud will alert the German outguards.

After 8 o'clock there will be 11 hours of darkness, during which the infantry will have to get across, form for attack and seize a good portion of the German line of strong points soon after daylight, in order that the bridge sites will be free from small arms and mortar fire. If the infantry cannot do this, the bridges cannot be emplaced. If the bridges cannot be emplaced, our infantry on the German side of the river cannot be supported.

Tuesday, January 18, 1944

I talked to five Lieutenant Colonels of Infantry who arrived today for duty with the Division. They are replacements for battalion commanders who have been killed, wounded, or are sick. All of them are over 35 years of age, and one is close to 50. Some have never commanded an infantry battalion even on maneuvers. Evidently, the personnel section of the War Department doesn't realize that battalion commanders must be young and aggressive and must also be the best trained and most experienced officers available. Certainly, very little thought has been given to this matter when officers such as these, who are quite willing to do their best, are flown over here to step in and command infantry battalions in combat.

With battalion commanders of this type, casualties of the men will be greater, and they themselves are quite apt to be killed, wounded, or reclassified before they learn the names and characteristics of their subordinates.

It is not a good thing to bring inexperienced battalion commanders in from the outside during combat. It is far better to promote our own officers to battalion leadership. They have the experience and energy and know their men. They also have esprit de corps and, because of their proven ability, deserve to be promoted within their own organization. This applies to every unit in the Division.

Thursday, January 20, 1944

The weather is improving. No rain since January 1st, but the fields are muddy. I hope the good weather continues.

The 111th Engineers, working during the last three nights, have cleared lanes through the mine fields to the river and marked them with tape. This is dangerous work, especially at night, and they have had a number of casualties. The lanes are too narrow because we have not had time to widen them.

Tonight the 36th Division will attempt to cross the Rapido River opposite San Angelo. We have done everything we can, but I do not now see how we can succeed. On top of everything else, Army has rushed us into this mission too fast. We should have had ten days instead of three to get ready. But even with adequate time, the crossing is still dominated by heights on both sides of the valley where German artillery observers are ready to bring down heavy concentrations on our men. The river is the principal obstacle of the German Main Line of Resistance.

I do not know of a single case in military history where an attempt to cross an unfordable river that is incorporated into the enemy's main line of resistance has succeeded; so according to history, we may not succeed. The mission should never have been assigned to any troops and, especially, when both flanks will be exposed when we get across.

General Hawksworth, 46th British Division, now on my south flank, came to my CP this afternoon to express his great disappointment for the failure of his Division to cross the Garigilano River last night and seize the heights so that he could protect my left flank. His failure, under more favorable conditions than our own, is an omen of the future, and makes it tough for my men who now have none of the advantages his crossing would have provided.

I was called to Corps Headquarters to explain my plan, as set forth in Division Orders, to General Keyes and his Staff. They listened intently. On the large battle map, I pointed out the mission assigned to my troops and explained in general terms the difficulties involved. This was no time nor place for me to dwell upon my real feelings. I let them know that I was doing everything possible to succeed. The type of questions asked by a few persons indicated that they do not understand the intricacies of the task before me.

Clark talked to me on the phone this evening and sends his best wishes; said he was worried about our success. I offered no encouragement. I think he is worried over the fact that he made an unwise tactical decision when he ordered troops to cross the Rapido River under these adverse conditions. However, if we get some breaks, we may succeed. But they will have to be in the nature of miracles.

General Wilbur will be at the CP of the 141st Infantry during the battle. At about 3:00 PM I went to the CP of the 143rd Infantry with the intention of remaining there during the attack. But I found that Martin and some of his staff had gone forward to join his battalion commanders and to supervise their crossing. By remaining at the 143rd CP I would be out of contact with both Martin and Division Headquarters except by telephone. So I returned to my CP where I would be better informed and where I could better influence the course of the battle. Actually, I will have little influence on the battle because everything is committed; I have no reserves; use of artillery ammunition is restricted; and I have no freedom of maneuver.

Friday, January 21, 1944

The attack last night was a failure.

As soon as it was dark both regiments proceeded to carry out their part of the operation. A cold dense fog hung over the river and visibility was near zero. The crossing was preceded by a heavy artillery preparation which began at 7:30 PM and ceased at 8:00 PM. After the preparation, our artillery continued to fire on selected targets.

The 141st Infantry, in the right (north) sector, assigned the 1st and 3rd Battalions to cross at two separate points.

The 1st Battalion used the rubber boats. It was delayed because the carrying parties, while enroute to the river, were disorganized by enemy shell fire and part of their equipment was destroyed. The rubber boats were clumsy and awkward to carry in the mud, fog, and darkness. The tapes, marking cleared lanes, were not visible and their locations were not known, unless one would stoop down and grope for them. After a time, the tapes were trampled into the mud or destroyed by enemy artillery. Confusion followed. The guides from the 19th Engineers lost their way. None of the rubber boats were successfully launched because of the swirling current, the high vertical banks, and the continual German fire. Eventually, all boats were destroyed or carried downstream.

The 3rd Battalion was to cross by means of the improvised footbridges. It was also delayed while enroute to the river because of destroyed equipment and confusion due to casualties. By 4:00 AM this morning, it had successfully emplaced the one and only footbridge which had not been destroyed.

The 1st Battalion, all of its boats having been lost or destroyed, was permitted to use the only remaining footbridge. Companies A and B, and part of Company C, succeeded in crossing and advanced over the low ground in uncoordinated, independent, and separated groups. Soon after daylight, these groups were pinned down by overwhelming fire. They made no further progress.

By daylight, Lts. Roscoe and Artimovich, with ten men of A Company, were as far as the barbed wire which surrounded one of the German strongpoints. Artimovich, CO A Company, and most of the men were killed there. Miraculously, Roscoe and two men were not hit. Later in the day they returned by swimming the frigid river. The current swept them a long way downstream, but they were finally able to grab onto some roots and get out of the water. Behind a small building not far from the river, they built a fire to dry their clothes and warm themselves. This small building was an aid station under the charge of Captain Cunningham, a medical officer of the 141st. Here he treated the wounded and others who had swum the river.

The 3rd Battalion of the 141st did not cross because the only footbridge was destroyed by continuous German artillery and mortar fire even before all of the 1st Battalion was across.

In the left (south) sector, the 143rd Infantry planned to cross at two separate points. The leading elements procured their boats, improvised footbridges, and were led to the river by guides from the 19th Engineers.

The 1st Battalion, 143rd, arrived at the river on time. Enroute it received rather light artillery fire, but there was some confusion due to the clumsy loads and mud and because of the darkness and fog. It began to launch the rubber boats immediately upon arrival at the river and started Company C across. The artillery and mortar fire which had been falling on the crossing area was increased, and by the time Company C was across, all the boats were destroyed or lost. Major David M. Frazior, the Battalion Commander, sent for more boats and most of the Battalion was across by 6:00 AM. It was unable to make any important progress. It had to defend itself from the beginning and was forced into a pocket with its back to the river. After daylight, it was fired on continually at short range by German tanks and self-propelled guns in hull down positions, and by small arms and mortars. It was completely overwhelmed by this fire and could not be supported by other troops on our side. Being in the open with little or no protective cover, it was about to be wiped out when the battalion commander ordered what was left of it back to our side of the river. It recrossed on the one remaining, but damaged, footbridge.

The 3rd Battalion, 143rd Infantry, had difficulties while enroute to the river. Guides from the 19th Engineers, assigned to lead the carrying parties, lost their way in the darkness and fog and wandered into a mine field. The mines and artillery fire caused a great many casualties and destroyed most of the rubber boats. The disorganization and demoralization which followed could not be effectively controlled. Much time was lost in reorganizing. The Battalion Commander found it to be impracticable to rely on rubber boats and decided to use the footbridges. But the continual bombardment of the crossing site and the continual loss of leaders and equipment prevented any real progress. Only a few had crossed by daylight when the battalion was ordered to return to its original assembly area.

Keyes, with some of his staff, came to my headquarters at 10:00 AM and directed that I make another attack at once; that we cross the Rapido and start building the heavy vehicular bridges immediately after the assault boats are launched. I told him that I had ordered the attack renewed at 9:00 PM tonight. He directed that I attack as soon as possible, preferably before noon, because, he said, the sun shining in the eyes of the German defenders would make it more difficult for them to observe our operations.

His Chief of Staff, Colonel Francis M. Willems, carried a clip board upon which a number of lines and arrows had been drawn to indicate what we were to do. Anybody can draw lines on a map; that doesn't require brains nor tactical ability. But it does require knowledge, skill, discipline, and many other good qualities to figure out, in detail, with reasonable accuracy, the difficulties that lie in the way, and just how and when and with what the difficulties are to be overcome so that success will result.

I realized that neither Keyes, nor those with him, understood the situation nor the problems. I explained that no real gains had been made in the previous attack, that several hours were required to reorganize and prepare for a renewal. The various infantry units had to prepare new plans, issue the required orders, and procure the required crossing equipment. All this would take time.

But he was impatient, in a determined mood, and insisted upon the attack before noon. I felt like saying that battles are not won by wishing, while ignoring the facts, but this was no place to court insubordination. He said that since some elements of the 141st Infantry were west of the river there was every reason why their success should be augmented by a second crossing, to be initiated at once. I explained again that there had been no success by either regiment; that even though some elements of the 141st were across the river, they were disorganized, fighting for survival from whatever cover they can utilize, isolated between the river and the main German defensa with no support nor signal communication; that smoke and haze and restriction on artillery ammunition prevented effective artillery support.

Nevertheless, having been directed in positive terms to initiate the second attack at once, I informed Keyes that his orders would be carried out as soon as I could confer with the 19th Engineers, who are responsible for improvising footbridges and procuring rubber boats to replace those lost last night. I assembled the staff, conferred with them and the two regimental commanders, Martin and Wyatt, and set 2:00 PM as the hour for the attack.

I and everyone else knew that the necessary arrangements could not be accomplished by that time, but 2:00 PM was as late as Keyes would permit. Later the hour was postponed to 3:00 PM and again to 4:00 PM.

The impatience of Corps Headquarters and its repeated prodding to get the attack launched prevented further postponement. Neither regiment was completely prepared at 4:00 PM. Nevertheless, the artillery preparation was put down at that time; much of the ammunition was wasted. The stage was set for another failure, a repeat of last night.

The stupidity of some higher commanders seems to be profound. I agree with General Harmon that "There are times when the high command is stupid as hell." When I heard him say that back in Africa, I thought it amusing. Not today. It's too close to home.

Saturday, January 22, 1944

Yesterday the Division made its second attempt to cross the Rapido, using crossing equipment that had been brought in during the afternoon.

Soon after the artillery preparation, the 1st Battalion, 143rd Infantry, began to cross. Immediately, enemy artillery and mortar fire began falling on the crossing site. As before, the boats and footbridges were gradually destroyed or lost so that each succeeding group had less equipment than the preceding one. Companies A and B did not get across until 6:35 PM, a half hour after dark. Part of Company C was across by 11:00 PM. The remainder never did get across.

The Battalion made no progress west of the river. It was subjected to continual fire that caused a gradual and further reduction in the strength of the units which had already been depleted by the first attack. By daylight the Battalion Commander and the commanders of Companies A, B and C were either killed or wounded. The Battalion was pinned down on flat ground with little or no protection. Being unable to advance, and losing men to no purpose, the Battalion was ordered by the regimental commander to return the best way it could, to the east bank of the river to reorganize and await instructions.

The 3rd Battalion arrived at its crossing site at 4:30 PM. Smoke was placed along the river to conceal its approach. Nevertheless, some prearranged German artillery and mortar fire came down on the Battalion while carrying its crossing equipment to the river. It was more fortunate than the 1st Battalion. Compaines I, K and L crossed the river in rubber boats after which the first footbridge was put in place, and the entire Battalion was across by 6:30 PM. It came under searching machine gun fire immediately. Casualties were continuous, but it made some progress. It silenced some of the German machine guns in its zone of advance. By 9:00 AM this morning, ammunition was running out and had to be resupplied. This could not be done effectively because of exposure to grazing machine gun fire and artillery and rocket fire, which, in greater intensity than formerly, was placed on the troops and crossing sites from 9:00 AM to 10:00 AM. As a result the position was untenable.

When the 2nd Battalion, 143rd, approached the river it was met by guides from the 19th Engineers who led it astray. Much time was lost hunting for the footbridge. Eventually, Captain Volheim, from the 3rd Battalion, guided it to the footbridge and across toward the right flank of the 3rd Battalion. By 8:00 AM Companies E and F had advanced only 200 yards from the river. By 1:00 PM both the 2nd and 3rd Battalions were repulsed and driven back to the east side.

While I was visiting Lt. Colonel Denholm, commanding the 2nd Battalion, this afternoon, the Germans shelled his CP. It was harassing fire, but three of the shells fell close enough to throw dirt on us.

Losses in killed, wounded and missing for both attacks are reported by the 143rd to be a total of 969 officers and enlisted men.

In the north sector, the 141st Infantry was not ready to launch its second attack at 4:00 PM. Its troops had been through a severe battle. Missing leaders had to be replaced. Previous difficulties had to be discussed, and improvements made. Movement within its area in daylight was exposed to German observers. It was not in as good condition after the first attack as the 143rd.

I sent General Wilbur to the CP of the 141st to assist the Regimental Commander in every way possible to prepare for the second attack. After a review of the situation with Wyatt and members of his staff Wilbur decided, correctly, that no attack would be launched until proper arrangements could be made.

At 10:00 PM, when the 2nd Battalion, 141st, began to cross; the German artillery and mortar fire was as intense as the night before.   Losses and destruction followed.   The same conditions prevailed as existed in the first attack.   Rubber boats were punctured and lost.   By 1:00 AM most of the 2nd Battalion was across. By 3:30 AM most of the 3rd Battalion was across.   By 5:00 AM both battalions had managed to advance past barbed wire, 200 to 600 yards from the river, where they were forced to dig in and seek protection from all kinds of fire, which was being continually directed at them after daylight.   Because of the smoke, which was put down to conceal movement, close artillery support was ineffective.   Signal communication with the east bank did not exist; hence there could be no coordination of our infantry and artillery efforts.   The need for ammunition, food and water could not be met.   The wounded could not be evacuated.

At about 4:00 PM the Germans launched a counterattack, taking advantage of the smoke and haze which partially concealed their movements.   These initial counterattacks were repulsed.   But by 5:00 PM the battalion commanders and executive officers of both battalions, and all company commanders except one, were either killed or wounded.   The Germans surrounded and captured most of the remaining men; however, the sound of the American weapons was heard intermittently until 10 o'clock tonight.   None has been heard since.   Because boats and footbridges have been destroyed, any survivors will have to swim the river.   Some, who tried it earlier, were overcome by the cold water and drowned. Both regiments will try to recover their wounded tonight.   I do not know how this can be done.

The 141st reports their losses as 76 killed, 333 wounded, and 641 missing.

Keyes kept himself informed of the progress of events all day. Late this afternoon, when he became convinced that the second attack was a failure, but that some of the 141st Infantry were still holding out across the river, he directed that the 142nd Infantry, which was in Corps reserve, be returned to the control of the 36th Division and that a third attack at 2:30 tomorrow morning be made, using only that regiment.   The regiment had only a few hours before dark to make the necessary reconnaissances and preparations.   The 19th Engineers were hard pressed to provide boats and bridges the 142nd needed.   We have never had enough.   The time allowed is insufficient, as it was yesterday. The stage is being set for another disaster.

Once again, I pointed out to Keyes the disadvantages, but again they received no consideration. Just because some men of the 141st were across the river and were pinned down on the other side did not mean success in the slightest. There cannot be even the beginning of a successful crossing until a considerable portion of the German main line of resistance is occupied and held by us, so that heavy bridges can be put in place for supporting troops to cross. Not even a dent has been made in the German defenses.

Nevertheless, in support of his decision to make another attack, he made the ridiculous statement that the Germans are "groggy;" that their morale is low; that all that is needed is another "blow" by a fresh regiment to turn them out of their position; that it may be that they are already preparing to withdraw. This was wishful thinking. The Germans have received no "blows" during the past two days, but we have taken several from them. Their morale is high. Their positions are reinforced. It is silly to say they are "groggy" and are thinking of withdrawing.

As soon as I was given the positive order to launch a third attack tomorrow morning, I notified Colonel George Lynch, Commander of the 142nd, and other commanders concerned.

I sent Wilbur to help the 142nd get organized for its attack. The following is a note he sent to me:

> "Smoke and fog all day, hence no daylight reconnaissance of adequate nature. Bridge cannot be started until 142 is well over, hence cannot be completed tonight with attack at 2:30 AM. Equipment for crossing is sufficient for three footbridges only. Last night we started with five. The Bailey Bridge group is loathe to put up the bridge under fire. The German garrison has been reinforced, hence purpose at least partly accomplished. In my opinion an attack **tomorrow** night is indicated."

I agree that if there must be an attack, tomorrow night, not tomorrow morning, "is indicated." I did not send Wilbur's note to Keyes because I had already explained the difficulties to him and he had ignored them.

Amidst preparations being rushed to meet the crossing time, Keyes, having conferred with Clark, phoned me and rescinded his order for the attack, adding, "You are not going to do it anyway." I cancelled the attack immediately. Another disaster avoided.

Keyes' insulting remark implies a charge of disloyalty and disobedience. Such a charge is baseless and untrue. I have done everything possible to comply with his orders.

CHAPTER THIRTEEN
The Aftermath

Mt. Rotondo, Italy
Sunday, January 23, 1944

The battle for the Rapido is over. It will long remain in my memory. Two of my regiments were wrecked there. Thank God, Keyes finally changed his mind and cancelled the third attack.

Yesterday at about 4:00 PM a mesage was brought to the CP of the 141st Infantry by Private Manella, Medical Corps, who was captured across the river on the 21st and was released to deliver the message. The translation follows: "To the English Commander: The German Commander desires that the English Commander grant a three-hour truce for the purpose of caring for and removing the English wounded. It is desired that the time of the truce be disseminated. The German Commander."

Wyatt suspected some form of deception or ruse and ignored the request. Under the circumstances, I can't think of a ruse that would result in any particular tactical advantage to the German Commander. The most that he could gain would be to capture a few stretcher bearers. Wyatt should have taken advantage of the opportunity to recover his wounded, especially so since the time for the truce was left to him.

NOTE: Here is Manella's statement of January 22, 1944, which he signed after having received help in describing ground locations on a map:

"My name is Private Savino Manella, ASN 32885684. I am an aid man attached to Company A, 141st Infantry. I crossed the river with Company A on the morning of 21 January at about 5:00 AM. I crossed at coordinates 868168 and proceeded inland to the road which runs between coordinates 862167 and 862171. We received mortar fire on our boats when we were crossing the river. While we proceeded inland, mortar fire fell around us close to the river. The farther in we got the less there was of mortar fire. As soon as we ran out of the mortar fire, we ran into the machine gun fire. The company stopped on the east side of the road (this is the road described in the above coordinates) and started digging in. We knocked out three machine gun nests that I know of. We knocked out the machine gun in front of us, but the machine guns from the flank and the one from the left rear continued to fire on us. There were a lot of casualties. Lt. Phillip G. Poteet (SIC) was in charge of my platoon. We started taking the wounded into the house which was located at 862167 (this was determined on a photo map) because of the heavy mortar fire, also because of some hand grenades which were being thrown at us. We moved the wounded into the farm house.

"At 12 noon, the Germans started closing in on us. At about 12:30 PM we were captured by the Germans. There were about 20 of us taken prisoner. I don't know how many dead or wounded there were, but there were plenty, all out in the field around the house. The road referred to above has a high bank on both sides. The Germans have emplacements dug into the embankment in which they have their supplies and CPs. I remember seeing lots of German machine gun emplacements, but I can't point out exactly where they are located. Yesterday afternoon, 21 January, at about 2:00 PM, more Germans with machine guns started coming into the CP. I don't know how many German soldiers there were, but there were new ones coming in. They looked clean and had not been fighting yet, I could tell that. They had a lot of grenades which they shoot from the ends of their rifles just like our rocket launchers. This morning they were bringing in more ammunition and more machine guns around the CP. When they left the house, they moved toward the river from the same direction that I came in. There were still more German troops coming in this afternoon when I left. There were about 25. They were mixed up—rifle and machine gun men. There was a lot of moving around that CP and I saw a lot of fresh soldiers. They gave me the message which I delivered and when they gave it to me they said they wanted to pick up the English wounded and their wounded, too. The Germans have a lot of trenches dug."

Clark and Keyes came to my headquarters today for lunch and conference, and were not in a bad mood. I invited them into my command truck, along with Wilbur and Colonel Walter Hess. The operations of the preceding two days were discussed primarily along the lines of General Clark's initial question to the effect, "Tell me, what happened up here."

The conversation was not one in which there was any attempt to blame anyone for the serious check which the Germans have given our operations. In fact, at one point, Keyes made a statement generally to the effect that, from the information available before the operation, it had seemed to him to be a worthwhile operation. Clark at this point interjected the remark, "It was as much my fault as yours."

I asked Wilbur to verify their statements in writing, over his signature. Clark and Keyes may attempt to refute their remarks.

Clark has now decided to attack with the 34th Infantry Division over the high ground north of Cassino, which is what I suggested he do a long time ago and what he should have done in the first place. There the river is fordable and not so strongly defended. An attack can be made in daylight, with a greater chance for surprise because the troops can be concealed prior to the jump-off, and a greater force can be employed on a wider front with better coordination since no boats or bridges are required. The attack can be made in the direction of Mount Castellone to seize the high ground, cross the mountain ridge, cut Highway No. 6 west of Cassino and outflank the defenses blocking the entrance to the Liri Valley. But, this will be more difficult now that the Germans have been alerted.

Carl Phinney, Division Quartermaster, "stole" a kerosene heating stove for my truck. Unit commanders in the forward areas who need them most—they are smokeless and usable in a blackout—and for whom they are intended, have to steal them from staff officers in higher headquarters, in the rear, who do not need them.

Monday, January 24, 1944

Lt. General Devers, from Alexander's headquarters, and Keyes visited my CP at about 3 this afternoon. They asked a lot of questions. Devers wanted to know if I had given orders for my men to carry unloaded rifles when they crossed the Rapido. I told him, "No." He said some of our wounded, now in hospitals, had made such a report to his interrogators.

When Devers left my truck and was walking to his jeep, Wilbur, who apparently had been waiting for the opportunity, stopped him and engaged him in conversation. Wilbur was saying some things that Devers did not like, for Devers' face became flushed. He kept moving toward his jeep as Wilbur followed along, still talking. Devers climbed into the jeep, but Wilbur put his hands on the vehicle, determined to make Devers hear him out. Devers nudged the driver to move on, but he hesitated, apparently not being in the habit of driving off in the midst of a conversation. However, after the third or fourth poke by Devers' riding crop, the driver pulled away.

I do not know what it was all about, but I distinctly heard Wilbur say, "The whole trouble is that you people in the rear do not know what goes on up here." Under the circumstances, something may come from this conversation.

Tuesday, January 25, 1944

I have orders to conduct demonstrations along our front. I also have orders to be prepared to cross the Rapido again, if the 34th Division attacking on our right is successful. The two are inconsistent. If we are to be ready for another crossing, we must begin now to remove mines on this side of the river. I authorized Carl Phinney to buy some sheep for Major Stovall who wants to use them, as an experiment, for clearing Schu mines and trip wires.

At about 10:00 AM today Captain Joel Cunningham, medical officer of the 141st Infantry, went to the near bank of the Rapido with an ambulance, parlied with a German officer, and requested that he and his medical personnel be permitted to evacuate our dead and surviving wounded west of the river. The German commander agreed to a two-hour period provided both sides withhold all fire into that area. I approved the agreement, and notified the 143rd to recover its dead and surviving wounded, also.

Captain Kaplan, medical officer of the 143rd, crossed the Rapido, and after conferring with a German officer, set the time for cessation of fire opposite the 143rd from 3:15 to 5:30 PM. But our people did not wait for the officially agreed time. As soon as the agreement was approved, they began ferrying our dead and wounded. The German soldiers joined our men and assisted in the evacuation. They were reserved, but friendly. Some spoke English. They joined in conversation, and along with other topics, stated that they thought our soldiers, during the second attack, should have surrendered when they were initially surrounded and cut off from returning to the east bank; that by continuing to fight they only brought casualties onto themselves with no hope of success.

II Corps Headquarters was about to be notified that these arrangements had been completed, when a Corps staff officer phoned and informed G-3 that a "feinting" operation had been directed to be made within the Division sector by armored units, all under Corps direction and control. They were to proceed to two areas on high ground in the sector of the 143rd Infantry. From there they were to "maneuver around," exposing themselves to the view of German observers to attract attention. During this maneuvering, the tanks were to fire from various positions on selected targets across the river. All this was supposed to give the Germans the impression that another attack was about to be launched by us.

This was a most unusual way to conduct a "feint," and since one of the target areas was where the 143rd was collecting wounded, it was also quite disconcerting. All this "feinting" business was supposed to assist the 34th Division, attacking north of Cassino, by drawing German reserves to our front. Just how? The Germans, secure and confident, in their strong and battle-tested positions behind an unfordable river, would recognize this as an amateurish attempt at deception for the tanks cannot cross the river; and therefore there would be no reason to reenforce their position. A feint or deception must be subtle and give an impression of a real attack.

Since the armored units were already moving into the Division area, the situation regarding the collection of our wounded was explained to the Corps staff officer and he was told that the tanks now enroute must be turned back. Uncomplimentary remarks passed back and forth. "Does the 36th Division know there is a war on?" This was countered by a comment that the "pop-gun" affair as ordered was useless, would appear ridiculous to the Germans, and would not help the 34th Division in the slightest. Other comments followed. The upshot was that several liaison officers were sent by Division to intercept the armored column and turn it back.

Later, the 143rd asked for an extension of time. The Germans agreed and all units of the Division were notified. The Corps, however, not being yet notified of the extension of time, phoned again. The armored units were again entering the Division area, but the "demonstrations" and firing would be postponed until 5:30 PM, the hour originally set for collection of wounded to cease. More strong words flew back and forth. In the end, the armored column was turned around the second time and disappeared eastward.

I was amazed that the higher authority would plan, direct, and carry out such an operation within the combat area of a Division without any prior ground reconnaissance or coordination with the activities of units already located within the area involved, and with no advance notice. It is contrary to combat principles and very confusing for high authority to arrange and direct an operation within the combat area of a division, without coordination and without consulting the proper persons at the division head-quarters.

While all this was going on, the two regiments, working as rapidly as possible, brought back some 60 bodies and only 7 surviving wounded. The wounded had lain within the German minefields and barbed wire, exposed to the cold January weather, for 4 days, with no food or water except what they carried with them when they crossed the river. Prior to the cessation of fire, they had not been approached by friend or foe.

The great loss of fine young men during the attempts to cross the Rapido, in violation of good infantry tactics, is chargeable to wishful thinking.

Today, I received two messages by our own homing pigeons from across the Rapido. One in English: "Everybody is giving up pig-wounded. I may as well do the same unless I die first. 3rd Bn 141st Inf." This message was probably written by a German soldier, since there was no fighting west of the Rapido after 10:30 PM on the 22nd.

The other, in German: "Americans of the 36th Division: Herewith a messenger pigeon is returned. We have enough to eat and what is more, we look forward with pleasure to your next attempt."

The Germans are having fun at our expense.

Wednesday, January 26, 1944

Clark has just informed me by telephone that he is not satisfied with Colonel Martin as a regimental commander and he is going to assign him to the job of training replacements. He is sending me Lt. Colonel Paul D. Adams, whom I do not know, from the Special Service Force to command the 143rd. Martin is not perfect. He has not done as well as I would like, but he has done nothing, nor failed to do anything, during past operations that would justify relieving him from command of the regiment.

The Division has been directed to make daily demonstrations on this side of the river. We are supposed to frighten the Germans. The Germans know, as do all good soldiers, that if we were going to make an attack, we would not make an ostentatious display of our intentions.

Thursday, January 27, 1944

Corps conducted a demonstration of its own this afternoon in our sector with tanks firing into the German positions. These tanks stationed themselves in the midst of the installations of the 141st Infantry. The result was that after·they were gone, the

German artillery placed counter battery fire on the tank locations, and destroyed two of the M-7 weapons of the Cannon Company of the 141st, killed one man, and wounded another. This time the "feinters" sneaked in without letting anybody know of their intentions. The "demonstration" did more damage to us than to the Germans.

Friday, January 28, 1944

Received another pigeon message from the Germans this morning. It was written in German on the 26th and is an indication of what they believe is real wit and humor:

"To the 36th Division: You poor night watchmen, here is another pigeon No. 2, back so that you won't starve. What do you plan in front of Cassino, with your tin can armor? Your captured syphilitic comrades have shown us the quality of the American soldier. Your captains are too stupid to destroy secret orders before being captured. At the moment, your troops south of Rome are getting a kick in the nuts. You poor nosepickers. The German troops."

I sent a letter of appreciation to Martin, and am sending him and Wyatt to Sorrento for a week's rest, beginning today.

The attack of the 142nd Infantry, now with the 34th Division, north of Cassino, is not going well. They were ordered to attack this morning in a piecemeal manner without being given time for proper reconnaissance.

We are maintaining a token defense on this side of the Rapido. If the Germans should cross the river and attack us, we would have a job on our hands. I have too few troops to withstand a serious attack. But, there won't be any. The Germans have no place to go.

Stovall reports that Company A, 111th Engineers, lost six men last night in mine clearing operations at the river. He also reports that yesterday, in the hope of exploding personnel mines, Lieutenants Bill Dold and Jim Mueller, T-5 Frank Conversano, Staff Sergeants Ed Haynes and James White, together with two natives, all dressed like Italian farmers, drove 230 sheep along the river in broad daylight for a distance of three miles without alarming the Germans, but when they turned the sheep around to start back over the same route, the German outguards fired at them. No one was hit. The sheep were abandoned for the present. A few mines may have been exploded but the experiment did little good.

Saturday, January 29, 1944

Around 9 o'clock this morning, Clark telephoned to say he was leaving Headquarters and wanted me to meet him on the road near the little village of Mignano. I wondered what was up his sleeve, and suspected it would not be pleasant. Sgt. Clay, my driver, and I started out in my jeep and kept driving until we met Clark coming our way. We got out of the jeeps, greeted each other, and shook hands. Clark walked down the road, indicating that I should follow him, and when we were out of hearing of anyone else, he said he was concerned about the Division; that its morale was low; and that he was going to make some changes.

I told him its morale was low because a great many officers and men who had been received as replacements since Salerno had not been indoctrinated with the Division spirit due to the lack of time, and that the low morale was due principally to recent reverses and heavy losses of leaders in the lower units.

Clark didn't accept this view. He said the low morale was due to a lack of good officers in key positions. He said I would have to replace General Wilbur, Assistant Division Commander; Colonel Kerr, my Chief of Staff; Colonel Werner, 141st Infantry; and my two sons, Fred, Jr., G-3, and Charles, my Aide. This was a blow.

Clark had no fault to find with any of these officers and did not point out any deficiencies, except to say that Wilbur was a bad influence in the Division. Wilbur knows his business. Back at Salerno, Wilbur, a graduate of the Military Academy, was highly praised by Clark when he urged me to accept him as my Assistant Division Commander.

I told him that all these officers were satisfactory to me, and that I wanted to keep them. He said I had not surrounded myself with strong key officers. This was just an excuse to make scapegoats of them.

Clark said he had been asked why he permitted my two sons to remain in the Division contrary to orders. That's a subterfuge because they were assigned by War Department orders.

Then he told me he was sending Frederick of the Special Service Forces to take Wilbur's place.

I asked him what he was going to do with my people whom he was relieving. He did not tell me. Then I asked him to send them to the States on rotation. He said he could send some of them to the States, but that it was difficult to do this with colonels.

The conversation ended when he told me to think over the reassignment of my officers and see him in a few days. I'll see him Monday.

Just a few days ago he had directed that Colonel Martin, 143rd Infantry, be relieved. Now he has removed my Assistant Division Commander, my Chief of Staff, my Operations Officer, another regimental commander, and my Aide.

This is a very sweeping change and clearly shows that either he or Keyes is convinced that I do not have the ability to select capable personnel as my assistants, or that they are trying to cover up their stupidity in ordering the Rapido River crossing. Obviously there is some kind of collusion against the Division. I will have to notify all these officers of their pending reassignment, a most unpleasant task.

Sunday, January 30, 1944

Because of the hardship under which the Infantry is, and has been, serving I have directed that each infantry regiment shall send 28 men each day to the enlisted men's rest area at Caserta for three whole days of rest. This means that each regiment will have 140 men absent from duty; going to, and returning from Caserta. The regimental commanders do not like this, claiming that they need every man for defense against possible German attack. If I were in their places I might feel the way they do. But I am not in their places and the Germans are not going to launch any serious attacks. They are too busy at Anzio. It is important that we improve our morale. God knows, the doughboys need a rest and a change of scenery.

Monday, January 31, 1944

Early this morning, I went to talk with Clark at his Headquarters. I told him Wilbur and Werner had gone to the hospital and that I would like for him to send Fred, Jr., back to the States because Fred feels that he will be handicapped in the Italian theater. Clark said he would do so. He did not know what assignment he would give Kerr.

I've done a lot of thinking since Clark relieved my key officers contrary to my wishes. By staying with the Division, I am hurting the officers and men. When a commander becomes persona non grata at higher headquarters, his men suffer. The officers Clark removed were in no way responsible for the Rapido fiasco. Werner wasn't even there. But, they are being used as scapegoats. This is a great injustice to the Division. If they want a scapegoat, they should "can" me.

NOTE: By permission of Harper and Row, Publishers, Inc., the following is quoted from "The Battle for Italy" by Major General W. G. F. Jackson, British Army:

"Many Americans had criticized Montgomery's careful, methodical preparations for a major river crossing. Eighth Army's ponderous buildup of guns and ammunition, its careful reconnaissance of the enemy positions, its deception plans and its rehearsals all seemed old-womanish.

II (US) Corps approached the Rapido as if it was attacking enemy rearguards as had been the case on the Volturno. Through no fault of its commander or men, 36 (US) Division lacked the time needed for the careful preparation of what should have been regarded as a major set piece battle. They should never have been asked to carry out this attack on a major German position behind a river obstacle with only five days to prepare. The blame must rest with those who allowed the tyranny of Overlord to dominate the tactical as well as the strategic battlefield. 46 (Br) Division's attack on II (US) Corps' southern flank towards Saint Ambroglio fared no better than 36 (US) Division's. Its assault brigade managed to get just one company across the river and the attack was wisely abandoned. In the final battle of Cassino, 36 (US) Division's task was just accomplished by a whole British Corps supported by 1,000 guns after two months careful preparation and in hot spring weather which enabled men, tanks and guns to move freely over the open fields. One US division with five days' preparation, attacking in mid-winter, stood no chance at all. Unfortunately the commanders were not to know this at the time. The toughness of the Germans in defense with winter on their side was still underestimated."

Tuesday, February 2, 1944

I received a letter from Colonel Werner, who is in the hospital.

"My Dear General:

"Your letter thanking me for my services is the finest reward I could have expected to receive. I shall treasure it always as one of my finest possessions.

"General Walker, you have exerted a lasting and profound influence over the men of the Division. Your insistence on the simple, homely, old-fashioned American virtues was a refreshing return for many men to the things that gave our country its sound beginning.

"To me, and thirteen thousand men of the 36th Division, who made the invasion, you will always be, without regard for

Presentation of medals to approximately 130 men of the 36th Division by General Clark. Maddaloni, Italy, March 11, 1944—U.S. Army Photo

T/Sgt. Charles E. Kelly of P i t t s burgh, Pennsylvania, Company L, 143rd Regiment, receives the Congressional Medal of Honor from General Clark. March 11, 1944— U.S. Army Photo

Hungry Italians waiting for left-over food and garbage from a 36th Division kitchen. Maddaloni, Italy, April, 1944—U.S. Army Photo

General Walker decorates men of the 142nd Infantry. Maddaloni, Italy, April, 1944

A timber trestle bridge in the mountains of Italy constructed entirely of native material by the 111th Engineer Battalion.

Sgt. Everett W. Bastion, Company E, 143rd Infantry, and comrades patrol for snipers near Velletri. May 27, 1944—U.S. Army Photo

36th Division Command Post near Cisterna. May 28, 1944—U.S. Army Photo

Ambulances of the 111th Medical Battalion and scout cars of the 36th Reconnaissance Troop pass over a stream filled in by the 111th Engineers. May 28, 1944

who has commanded in the past or who may command in the future, "The Old Man, our Division Commander.

Sig/ RICHARD J. WERNER
Colonel, 141st Infantry"

Cervaro, Italy
Saturday, February 5, 1944

The Forward Echelon of Division Headquarters moved from the foot of Mt. Rotondo to several damaged buildings in the town of Cervaro.

Sunday, February 6, 1944

Wilbur, Kerr, Werner and Martin are gone.

I doubt if any Division in the United States Army has ever been treated as The 36th has been in this case. There has never been an instance, to my knowledge, where an Army Commander has arbitrarily thrown out the key men on the Staff and the principal commanders of a Division without any charges against them. I shall have no opportunity to say who will replace those taken away because Clark is going to fill these vacancies himself. I have had nothing to say as to who will be my Chief of Staff for Clark has sent me one of his own choice for that job.

Of course, I know that Clark would not act in such a manner, if he intends to continue me in command of the 36th. Hence, there is only one inference I can draw, and that is that I am marked for relief from command of the Division as soon as Clark can find an easy way to do it. My replacement apparently has not yet been selected, and since so many key officers are being replaced all at once in the Division, it is inconvenient to kick me out at this time. I feel that I have but a month or so in my present position.

I do not understand why men go into the National Guard and give their time to qualify as officers, when they know that they are going to be discriminated against and mistreated, if and when a war comes along. No wonder the National Guard dislikes and mistrusts the Regular Army. As a matter of fact, the patriotism, ability, and devotion to duty of the officers and men of the 36th Division are on a par with those of any other division in which I have served, be it Regular Army or National Guard. And, I am not prejudiced.

I have had quite a struggle with myself over this unheardof procedure because the spirit of the Division has been given a severe blow. The older officers and men are going to resent this arbitrary replacement of their commanders, whom they greatly admire. I gave each of those departing a letter of appreciation. Each told me that he prized that letter more highly than a Legion of Merit.

Colonel Vincent and Lt. Colonel Fred Sladen have reported for duty; Vincent as Chief of Staff, Sladen as G-3. I have discussed with them the manner in which they are to perform their duties. I shall help them in every possible way for I do not blame them for the manner in which they happened to be assigned here.

Tuesday, February 8, 1944

Yesterday, General Teddy Roosevelt and General Monsabert paid me a visit at my CP at Cervaro. Monsabert commands the French 3rd Algierian Division on my right flank, and Teddy is the American Liaison officer at his headquarters. We discussed the tactical situation and plans for an attack to be made by both Divisions on the night of 10/11 February. Our ideas were in complete accord. Both Roosevelt and Monsabert are experienced officers and good tacticians, and it was a pleasure to talk sense with someone who knows his business.

Wednesday, February 9, 1944

I received an order today directing the Division to make an attack to capture the mountain tops west of Cassino. The Division is very weak as a result of the Rapido fiasco and incapable of any sustained all-out attack. Every indication is that the Germans are going to reinforce and hold their position in front of us—Cassino. They are not worried about our beachhead at Anzio. They can take care of that any time, and at their leisure, unless it is reinforced.

The Germans dropped about 30 shells into my CP area this afternoon. One shell was within 10 yards of the mess tent. Later this afternoon they threw a smoke shell into the yard just north of the building in which my staff and I are located, and a high-explosive shell a little later. I figure they have ranged in on us and will shell us tonight.

I visited Lt. Colonel Van Pyland's CP this afternoon with my Aide and saw Pyland's tank destroyers put a concentration on a nebble-werfer position and on some houses where German tanks were concealed. Tonight I see three tanks burning within the German lines. Pyland had knocked them out.

Cairo, Italy
Thursday, February 10, 1944

They did shell my CP in Cervaro last night. No damage of any importance. I, accompanied by my Aide, my G-1, G-2, and G-3, in three jeeps moved to my forward battle station here in Cairo, to be in touch with the attack we are to make at dawn tomorrow.

Friday, February 11, 1944

We did not succeed in our attack at dawn this morning. I am required to expend weak units on missions that demand strong and vigorous execution. All three regiments in this Division are greatly depleted. The remnants are holding their positions on top of the mountain under trying conditions of combat and weather.

Saturday, February 12, 1944

Beginning at about 4:00 AM the Germans put down one of the most intense artillery preparations on Cairo and neighboring areas that I have been in since the German artillery bombardment at the Marne on July 15, 1918. More than 2,000 shells fell in the Cairo area between 4:30 AM and 6:30 AM. I knew that this was a preparation for a counter attack on our position on Mt. Castellone, and warned our artillery and infantry to expect an attack at dawn. All our wire lines were blown out soon after 4:30 AM. The Germans did attack at dawn in force. Our troops, the 142nd Infantry especially, were ready for them and met them with rifle, machine gun and mortar fire.

Our artillery concentrations, previously prepared, were called down on them. Hand grenades were used freely. I could hear the small arms fire at the top of the mountain above me, nine-tenths of which was our own. This continued until about 11:00 AM, when it died down. I knew then that our troops had won. It is reported that over 200 German dead are lying in front of our positions. Our losses are light.

Brigadier General Robert I. Stack, who succeeds Wilbur as Assistant Division Commander, and whom I never saw or heard of before, came to the forward battle station this forenoon, and I placed him in command of the sector. Later I returned with my party to the CP at Cervaro.

Cervaro, Italy
Sunday, February 13, 1944

A German with a white flag came up on Mount Castellone this

PM with a request from his commander for permission to pick up and bury his dead. I granted permission for them to do this between 8 and 11 tomorrow morning. Keyes tanks cannot get up on this mountain.

This afternoon, Lt. Colonel Aaron Wyatt, Werner's replacement in command of the 141st Infantry, was killed and Lt. Colonel Price was wounded when a German shell made a direct hit on their CP in a house in Cairo. Both were ideal officers, and Price was a great help to the regiment; he knew the personnel because of his long service in it. When Price came by my CP on his way to the hospital, I gave him the fifth of whiskey Keyes gave me as a Christmas present. He was pleased to get it and sampled it immediately.

The 142nd Infantry is still in position on top of Mount Castellone. Temperatures are below freezing, and the men have to subsist on cold, canned "C" rations. They have no heat. They have my deepest respect. No soldiers anywhere have had greater hardships than those of this Division since last November 15th.

Monday, February 14, 1944

When the Germans, under the flag of truce, arrived this morning to pick up their dead, they asked for an extension of one hour, which I granted. Later today they asked to continue the work tomorrow at the same period. This I refused since an attack is being made tonight by the 7th Indian Division on our left flank to capture the monastery mountain and Cassino.

I am recommending the 142nd Infantry for the President's Citation, but I don't think Clark knows enough about the situation and the splendid fight the regiment went through on Castellone on February 12th to approve it.

Major General Monsabert called on me at my CP this afternoon. When I told him that more than 200 German dead had been picked up in front of our positions by the Germans under a flag of truce, he said, in French, "Congratulations. Magnificent! You now have partly evened your losses at the Rapido."

Tuesday, February 15, 1944

I have the following note from Andy Price:

"General Walker:
"I am in ward 9, 36th General at Caserta. Have had most of the fragments out now and no bones are shattered. I am

doing all right. Sorry I had to let you down in a pinch. My regard for you is next to worship. I do want the letter from you, more than anything.
Sincerely,

Sig/ Andy Price
Lt. Colonel, Inf."

A day or so ago I issued an order prohibiting the Red Cross girls, who have been distributing doughnuts and other Red Cross supplies to soldiers in our forward areas, from going into the zone of German artillery fire. I feel responsible for them, and I do not want any of them killed. They did not like this order and came to see me. They want to be free to go anywhere they choose, and do not want to be thought so precious that they may not go where anyone else in the Division may go. I rescinded the order. They went away happy.

From my CP I watched the bombing of the Benedictine Monastery on the mountain top above Cassino. It was bombed four times. The first salvo partly struck the monastery; other bombs fell on the positions of the 4th Indian Division on Hill 593, 1,500 yards from the target, causing 40 casualties in that command. Great clouds of smoke and dust arose, completely concealing the monastery and vicinity for ten minutes. In the afternoon, a bombing group made an almost perfect hit on the monastery and did great damage.

An escaped Italian stated to one of my staff that there were about 500 civilians, men, women, and children, and eight monks in the monastery where they had taken refuge from Cassino. He said that no German soldiers were stationed in the monastery; that only one German medical officer visited it occasionally to treat some of the sick Italians; that no weapons were in the monastery, but some were placed outside about 200 yards away. The casualties among the civilians must have been great.

This monastery is the site of the origin of the Benedictine order, which dates back to 500 AD, and the present building dates from 1600 AD, so I have been told. This was a valuable historical and religious monument which should have been preserved. The Germans were not using it, and I can see no advantage in destroying it. No tactical advantage will result since now the Germans can make as much use of the rubble for observation posts and gun positions as of the building itself. It makes little difference, anyway, whether the Germans used the building for observation posts or gun emplacements, since the mountain top on which the building stands serves the same purpose.

If I had had the decision to make, I would have prevented its destruction. To date, I have ordered my artillery not to fire on it. Hereafter, whenever I am offered a liqueur glass of benedictine, I shall recall with regret the needless destruction of the Abbey Di Montecassino.

Friday, February 18, 1944

Yesterday, three news reporters and one photographer came to my CP at Cervaro. They asked me many questions about my views on many tactical orders that have been issued by the higher command—Clark and Keyes. I avoided personalities, but answered their questions frankly. They promised to use the information I gave discreetly and were especially interested in our attack across the Rapido, the heavy losses there, and the reasons for failure. They were also interested in the present policy of keeping divisions in the line undergoing losses until the greater number of officers and men are casualties, which makes it difficult to absorb and train the large number of replacements needed to bring a division back to full strength. They expressed their concern with several of the policies cf the high command.

The New Zealand Division made an all-out attack to take Cassino and Monastery Hill. The only thing they gained was possession of the railroad station on the low ground south of the town, which is more of a liability than an asset. They failed to gain any ground south of Hill 593, near Monastery Hill, or in the town.

Monday, February 21, 1944

I have learned from reliable sources that my "enemies" have been doing a lot of talking at II Corps and at Army Headquarters in Caserta. They have done me and other officers of the Division a lot of harm. Sooner or later their false gossip will be revealed. But by that time many injustices will have been done.

The record of the 36th would satisfy any intelligent observer. The "enemies" of the Division do not know, or do not want to know, that the 36th has been given the three hardest jobs in the Fifth Army: Salerno, the Mt. Maggiore-Mt. Sammucro position and the Rapido. Cassino Heights was also tough.

Then, too, some Regular officers cannot see anything but mediocrity in a National Guard Division. There are some people who just don't like anything from Texas, and yet our personnel, at this time, is only about 25% from Texas.

Also, I have been impatient with staff officers of higher commands who harass my Division with impracticable directives which I have to counteract. When I tell them that their "bright" ideas will not help, and why, they do not like it. So, they do not like me. They are like big flies buzzing about a horse struggling under a heavy load. They bite him in many places to help urge him on, but they only make it more difficult for the horse.

It would be much better for everybody concerned if the young whippersnappers would conform to ordinary staff procedures and operate within the boundaries of their responsibilities.

So, I attribute this unfavorable gossip to ignorance, prejudice, and ambition.

Mr. Lewis, Miss Curry, and Miss Decker, all Red Cross people with the Division, came to Cervaro today to hand out doughnuts to men of the 36th Division and stopped by my CP for supper. They wanted to come "up front" where again they could see and hear some of the war. Our doughboys will laugh at the intimation that Division Headquarters is "up front."

Thursday, February 24, 1944

I had a short visit with Clark at his CP near Presenzano. He seemed worried, said losses at the beachhead near Rome were fairly heavy; 16,000 to date. That is a very heavy loss indeed, equivalent to one whole division. He said he was going to build an all American Fifth Army. "The British are so complacent," he said.

I visited the rest center at Caserta. I went through the place and was pleased with the facilities. Good mess, movies, library, writing rooms, reading rooms, warm water baths, barber shop, dormitories, bedding furnished, game rooms, post exchange, dental clinic, and new clothes for old. It is a good place for front line infantrymen to spend three days. All the labor is done by hired Italian civilians—kitchen police, scrubbing, policing of barracks and grounds; everything.

Enroute to Cervaro I visited our cemetery where already more than 3,000 American soldiers are buried. Depressive.

Friday, February 25, 1944

Today, Clark stopped by my CP in Carvaro, still noticeably worried. Called his CP on my phone and became quite irritated when he was told the lines were busy, and yelled at the switchboard operator, "This is General Clark, cut in on the line and do it now." He asked me to take him up to the top floor of the building my staff occupies, where he looked at Cassino and the Abbey Di Monte-cassino through my field glasses. He remarked, "I don't see why they can't take the Monastery and Cassino. Bombing the Monastery was a mistake. It is now an ideal place to fortify."

This is correct. It was a mistake. Anyway, one must recognize a desirable quality in his character when he will admit his mistakes. By doing so he will eventually learn.

Maybe it would be better for all concerned to have someone of experience, who possesses greater tactical ability, in Clark's position.

When Clark told me there were not enough replacements for both the 34th and 36th Divisions, I suggested that he fill up the 34th first since they have already gone to the rear area for reorganization. If he will do this, the 36th will have more time for training and rest, which we need. Clark said we might have a whole month out of line. We can accomplish a great deal in that time if we are let alone. We have many new officers and NCOs who have to be made familiar with their new jobs.

There is some uncertainty as to who is going to relieve our infantry regiments on Mt. Castellone tonight. Clark says the French will do it. General Monsabert says they will not do it because he does not have enough troops—only two infantry battalions. Again, impossible missions are being assigned to the troops. How long, pray, will it be until the high command learns that assigned missions must be within the capability of the troops and that victories are not won by wishful thinking.

I have received the following letter from Colonel William Martin:

"Dear General Walker:

"You are, no doubt, informed as to my new assignment as Director of Training at the 2nd replacement Depot. Upon my arrival here I found many interesting angles having to do with the administration and training of replacements with which I was not familiar. Most of my time has been spent so far becoming acquainted with my new job and planning ways and means by which I hope to overcome some of the obstacles, and enabling me to increase the efficiency of the replacement when he arrives at his assigned combat unit area. If I can help any at all, I will feel that my efforts will not have been wasted.

"When I left the Division I was naturally feeling rather bad since I am unfortunate enough to have in my make-up considerable sentiment and I had, through the years, allowed myself to feel that I was a part of the heart and soul of my regiment and my Division. During the 27 years that I have served the military all my time was served in the 36th, or in elements which later went to form the 36th when it became a Division. I have never worn a shoulder patch other than the T-patch. I surely did hate to cut them all off. Four commanding Generals have guided the destiny of the Division during my service there.

"You will please forgive me, Sir, if I say to you that never have I known a Division, every officer and man, to hold their commander in higher respect and confidence, nor had the deep feeling of affection that the 36th has for you. You have been strict, firm, hard when necessary, but always fair, just and right. I shall always be grateful for the privilege of having served under you, and in leaving your command I carry with me memories that will always be among my most priceless treasures.

"Of course, I will follow the success of the 36th with great interest as it goes forward to Victory. My best wishes will be with it always and I predict for it many more outstanding achievements to add to its already glorious record.

"Please accept my warmest personal regards.
Sincerely and respectfully,
Sig/ W. H. Martin."

After the unfair manner in which Martin has been treated, he shows a real determination to carry on and give his best wherever he may be. Under similar circumstances, some officers would let their wounded sense of justice adversely dominate their interest in their job and devotion to their duty.

CHAPTER FOURTEEN
Preparation for Special Mission

Alife, Italy
Thursday, March 2, 1944

More rain—this is the eighth successive day of rain. We are now reorganizing and training for a special mission.

Blair Moody, correspondent from the **Detroit News,** visited me and asked some questions regarding military tactics in general. He said that he did not know anything about tactics and if I would explain some of the basic principles it would help him in his work. I gave him as much information as possible in one hour. But knowing the basic tactical principles is like knowing the alphabet: they are no help unless one knows how to put them together. He asked permission to talk to some of the Division personnel regarding their battle experiences and said that anything he wrote would be presented to the censor. I approved.

I visited General Ryder, 34th Division, at his CP. Keyes and Major General Willis Crittenberger came there during my visit. I had not seen Crittenberger since his recent arrival from the United States. He started in by telling Ryder and me that everybody back home knows the 34th and 36th Divisions are doing the fighting in Italy; that the headlines of the newspapers in the States are full of deeds of the 34th and 36th. This, of course, is applesauce, with perhaps a grain of truth. Crittenberger will go places. He always knows what to say that will be pleasant to hear.

Friday, March 3, 1944

Keyes stopped by my CP at about 9:00 AM. We were sitting alone under the overcast sky on a couple of metal folding chairs, the kind used at funerals. Since he seemed to be in a receptive mood, I told him that there had been a number of incidents, since the Rapido mess, in which Clark and Devers unjustly have shown no confidence in me; that as a result, I am on the defensive and find it difficult to do my best work; that I have no desire to work for persons whose confidence I do not have, for confidence is a mutual condition that must work both ways. I told him quite frankly that I think these incidents are part of a scheme to make the Division and myself a scapegoat for the

Rapido fiasco.

I also stated that if Clark and Devers and he really have no confidence in me, then, for the good of the Division, the sooner I am relieved as its commander, the better. I told him that I don't deserve to be relieved; that I am doing my job better than any other person can do it, but that I cannot continue to do good work while I and the Division personnel are treated unfairly.

I didn't hold back. I let him know what had been gnawing at me ever since Clark relieved my officers. I am fed up with the whole damn mess.

Without the slightest hesitation, Keyes replied, "You should not be relieved now. First you should get the Division into a good state of efficiency during this period of rest, and after the next operation, which should be a success, you can be reassigned without any feeling on the part of your superiors that you have not been successful."

This was equivalent to saying, "We are going to 'can' you alright, but we are going to do it with kid gloves, and when we are ready."

The facility with which he came up with his plan convinces me that he had this means of getting rid of me in his head before he came here. I do not think that he would have made such a suggestion unless he had talked it over beforehand with Clark and, perhaps Devers.

I asked him if he could guarantee that the Division would be given a mission it could accomplish, rather than an impossible one such as the crossing of the Rapido. He did not answer my question, but said, "The very fact that you are commanding a National Guard Division means you have two strikes against you from the start." This was more discrimination. I was getting angry. Further conversation would be pointless. I had no more to say on the subject.

National Guard and Reserve Divisions are not allowed to go overseas until they attain Regular Army standards. The 36th was in training in the United States for 2 years and 3 months. It has the same equipment; its training has been just as effective; and its personnel is just as well, or better, qualified as the personnel of any regular division. Its replacements in both officers and enlisted men have come from the same sources as those of a regular division. But because it originated in the National Guard there are certain Regular Army officers who will always carry a prejudice against it. I served in the 3rd Division in World War I, and the 36th is better than the 3rd was then, or is now.

Blair Moody told me that he could not mention my name or my Division in his dispatches. The Army censor told him that I am known as a general who is in the habit of making wide envelopments, and that if the Germans knew I was in Italy, they would expect wide envelopments and would be able to counter them, and thus prevent my success. Of all the silly reasons; imbecilic! The Army censor is either an ignoramus or he takes Moody to be a fool. The Germans have known that I am in Italy since last September 9th, and I am not addicted to any one form of attack. If I am permitted to have my way, any attack I make will depend upon the tactical situation in which the division is involved at the time.

I told Moody the real reason why my name is withheld is because Clark does not tolerate any competition in the news. News items must refer to "General Clark's soldiers" or to "General Clark's Fifth Army." Of course, if reporters should use the names of the division commanders, people back home would not be interested in the name of Lt. General Mark Wayne Clark. They would prefer to follow news of the divisions in which their men are serving.

Went to Caserta yesterday. Saw Andy Price and Lt. Potts at the 36th General Hospital, and Colonels Kerr, Werner, Forsythe at rear echelon, Fifth Army. All of them looked happy. Price and Potts are getting along well with their wounds. I sent letters of appreciation to Lt. Colonels Harris and Cox, and Major Rambo. They are returning to the States on rotation.

Our plans for training for our next operation are going well. I do not know just what our job will be but it will involve combat in mountains.

Saturday, March 4, 1944

Sometimes soldiers do things that are amazing. Last December when the Division was relieved by the 34th Division, three men of the 141st Infantry were abandoned, unknowingly, on top of Mount Sammucro. While their battalion was there it was supplied partly by pack mules and partly by men laboring up the mountain under heavy pack boards. This was a grueling and time-consuming job.

In order to maintain the fighting strength of the battalion, the required number of pack men were procured from units in reserve. A group of recently assigned replacements, directly from the States, were temporarily bivouacked in the service area of their regiment. This group was "easy pickins" for the regimental supply officer.

On the day prior to the relief of the regiment, 2nd Lt. Howell, now in the hospital, who had been impressed into this unpleasant duty, organized a detail of five men from these green replacements, loaded them down with special items, and turned them over to Lt. Spiva who led them up to the top of the mountain. Enroute, two men became exhausted and were sent back to the service area; their loads deposited alongside the trail. When the remaining three arrived at the battalion supply dump, they were also exhausted, and Spiva ordered them to stay there until he should return the next day. Unfortunately, Spiva was severely wounded on his way back to the service area. He was immediately removed and sent to the hospital. He is still there.

When Lt. Spiva did not return, the three recruits at the dump, Sneall, Hall, and Simmons, having been taught back in the States that " orders are orders," became confused and bewildered. They stayed on, and on, and on, subsisting on the food in the dump. They were discovered a few day ago, in good health and spirits, by members of the 3404th Quartermaster Company, who were engaged in salvage operations, searching for and collecting all useful supplies and equipment abandoned on fields of past battles.

I have not talked to the three men, but I am sure they didn't have an easy time, for they were there two months in midwinter living under such makeshift shelter as the dump could provide. The weather was real tough at times and their meals must have been extremely monotonous. How bored and miserable they must have been by days of tedium! But I suspect that their plight was made bearable by the thought that they were not risking their necks alongside their buddies. If they had had field glasses, they could have witnessed quite a show, at the Rapido and at Cassino, for they were sitting on the best observation point in the area. Of course, they will not be punished. Unwisely, but obediently, they were carrying out their orders as they knew them.

Maddaloni, Italy
Thursday, March 9, 1944

We are now in a new area near Maddaloni, not far from Caserta; moved here on the 7th to be nearer our mountain training area. Yesterday, I received orders to alert one combat team to be ready to move on 8 hours notice to exploit the break-through of the New Zealand Corps which is to make an attack at Cassino soon. There will be no breakthrough, and there will be no need for the combat team of this Division. But, of course, I shall alert it.

While passing through Caserta, I stopped in front of the post exchange while my Aide, Lt. Kelley, went inside to make a purchase. On the street I saw three little boys, bareheaded and barefooted, begging from soldiers passing by. One of these boys attracted my special attention. He was not over 4 years old, small for his age, and very dirty. His clothing was ragged and insufficient for the chilly weather. His hollow eyes, pleading face, emaciated little body, suffering written all over him, but especially on his face, made him an object of pity. Searching my pockets I found two pieces of candy and a stick of chewing gun. I got out of the Packard, walked over to the little fellow, and gave them to him. His hands were filthy dirty; his nose was running. He took them and ran off, delighted. He is one of millions in Italy who are underfed and underclothed.

At meal time, groups of women and children, dirty and hungry, gather about our messes with empty tin cans in their hands, pleading, begging, fighting to get into line for the garbage and any leftover food. There is never enough garbage or leftovers to go around so some receive nothing in their tin cans. The smaller children are pushed aside by the older ones and often get nothing. Their disappointment is great and they often cry. Most of them, however, have older sisters or brothers who share with them. One cannot help feeling sorry for them. Our soldiers are impressed by the great number of young Italian children everywhere.

Saturday, March 11, 1944

At 2:00 PM today a ceremony was held for decorating personnel of the Division. Tech Sergeant Charles E. Kelly, 143rd Infantry, received the Congressional Medal of Honor. Two DSCs were awarded, and 150 Silver Stars. Clark landed by cub plane in front of the troops and pinned on all decorations himself. He also made a short talk to the troops and paid compliments to the Division and to me. A surprise.

Many photographers as well as newspaper reporters were present. The cameras were grinding and clicking all during the ceremony. Afterward it was discovered that I was in 95 per cent of the movies and press pictures. This, so I am told, will force Clark to release my name to the press for news going to the United States. He will be reluctant to do this, but he has made the occasion one of national importance and members of the press tell me that he will have to release my name. We'll see.

Maddaloni, Italy
Monday, March 13, 1944

Devers stopped at my CP near Maddaloni yesterday and asked about my need for replacements. He also stated that the investigation, by General Clarkson, regarding shortage of ammunition and unloaded rifles at the Rapido, showed that there was nothing to the report. Devers seemed in a very friendly mood, and I felt reassured after his departure.

I talked to a number of men in the 141st Infantry today. They were in fine spirits. If we can get our replacements soon and have time to absorb them, we will do well in our next combat assignment.

I have been informed that, after 48 hours of deliberation at Fifth Army Headquarters, my name was released today by the Army censor for news items and photographs. This would make a good news story in itself.

Wednesday, March 15, 1944

Yesterday, with Carl Phinney, I visited Naples. I saw Lt. Colonels Griffith and McCall, Colonel Lawley, and Brigadier General Hamblen. These officers live in complete comfort in villas. As far as their comfort is concerned, there is no war. Last Monday evening Phinney and I had dinner at the Royal Palace in Caserta as guests of Colonel Forsythe. Such luxury! Paintings, tapestries, rugs, furniture, tableware, bar, chef, service. They do not know that a war is on, except from hearsay.

Colonel Shryock was there; was unfriendly; spoke to me about his imagined unfair treatment in being transferred out of the Division to Chief of Staff of the Rome Municipal Government

Command. I released him at the special request of General Crain. I hear he has been spreading a lot of evil talk about the Division.

Sometimes I think that those who feel they are unappreciated have a compulsive desire to tear down other people. Shryock would have been a better officer if only he could have realized that he was a member of a team along with other officers in the Army and that one just must not be a "loner."

Saturday, March 18, 1944

Last night, with A. B. Crowther, Carl Phinney, and Lt. Kelley, my Aide, I attended the opera "Cavalleria Rusticana" at the Royal Opera House in the palace at Caserta, which we all enjoyed. The opera was of one act and vocal and orchestral selections followed. I was also interested in the opera house itself. Five tiers of boxes extend around the whole of the theater from one side of the stage to the other side. The main floor was not large. The interior is decorated with paintings and gold in a very attractive manner. This opera house was used exclusively by the King and his Court 100 years ago. The orchestra was perfect—the singers were first class.

A Colonel W. N. Gillmore was assigned to the Division yesterday, without my knowledge, for duty as Executive Officer, Division Artillery. This was done by Brigadier General Lewis, Chief of Army Artillery. I wanted Lt. Colonel John Garner as Executive Officer of the Artillery. Clark is undoubtedly behind this invasion of the Division, also. Garner has been in the Division more than 25 years and is well-qualified for the job. Just when he has a chance to be promoted, some other less deserving person is shoved in ahead of him. Of course, he will not like it. Neither do I.

Sunday, March 26, 1944

Last Wednesday, the 22nd, accompanied by Wick Fowler and several officers of the Division, I went to the Salerno beach to go over the scene of operations of the Division on last September 9th. Fowler intends to write a series of articles for his newspaper, the **Dallas Morning News**.. When we arrived at Pompeii, I noticed a few black cinders scattered on the ground and asked an Italian who could speak English what they were. He told me they were cinders from Vesuvius and had been falling since last Tuesday. After we had gone on eastward I noticed that the ashes and cinders were thicker.

Finally, after we had gone about three miles east of Pompeii the ashes were so thick on the road (10 to 12 inches) that the larger American and English trucks and native vehicles had stalled, causing a traffic jam.

A big, dense, black cloud of smoke hovered over us and Vesuvius. Cinders were falling about us like hail. One about two inches long and an inch thick struck Colonel Garner on the nose, knocking off some of the skin. The whole area looked like it was covered with black snow. The growing crops were buried. Members of every family were on top of their houses shoveling off the cinders to prevent the flat roofs from caving in. I saw some roofs that had collapsed.

An Italian, employed by the American Red Cross, told me that the ashes had ruined the crops for this year, but that next year the crops would be better than usual because the ashes would fertilize the soil. The ashes gave off a slight odor of gas, and after we had been stalled for a couple of hours, our throats and nostrils were raw.

The people who are dependent on their fields for food were distressed. Some were crying silently. A religious procession passed us. Two men in front, carrying a patron saint, were followed by about 100 women, in double column, who were chanting prayers to the Lord to bring an end to the curse of Vesuvius. Many of them were weeping. I wish I could have taken a picture of them.

It took us five hours to get through that traffic jam. We arrived at Paestum at 10:00 PM. The ashes and dust from Vesuvius covered the ground as far south as the Sele River. We stopped for the night at the Neptune Restaurant, near the old Greek ruins. This was a famous restaurant where tourists stopped in peacetime, but it is now a billet occupied by 12 MPs, who moved out to let us have the place. Lt. Colonel Dillingham, formerly with the 36th Division, was in command of the area, and he went to great length to make us comfortable.

Next day, Tuesday, it was raining, but we went over the battlefield, beginning at the beach. I had the movement of each infantry battalion followed from the beach to its final invasion objective. An officer from each battalion explained its operation on the ground, pointing out locations of various incidents. I showed Fowler my route to the CP at the tobacco warehouse; the tower from which Ives saw the German tanks approaching; where the two tank attacks took place near the CP; and the positions our troops held at Altavilla. On our return, the Salerno-Naples road was closed and we had to detour. I enjoyed the trip, even the ashes.

At 4:00 PM, accompanied by Bob Ives and Lt. Kelley, I visited the 36th General Hospital and awarded a Silver Star to Sergeant Hardaway and a DSC to another NCO. The hospital was crowded with seriously injured soldiers. As I walked through the various wards, I was greatly impressed with their sacrifices and noted that those with missing arms and legs were in the majority. Yet they were cheerful. Hardaway had lost both his legs at the Rapido. Pinning a Silver Star on the shirt of a legless man occurred to me as ridiculous; it certainly is an inadequate reward. However, he seemed appreciative. When I think of the foolish orders which unnecessarily cause deaths and broken bodies, it makes me feel like crying "HALT!" Men who do the dirty job of fighting and bear the greater hardships are looked upon by some people in rear areas as so much hay or ammunition. I suppose it has to be so. It is a curse we have upon us. In war one cannot be sentimental beyond a reasonable point. If one is, one must not show it outwardly. But for God's sake let us, who are the commanders, prepare ourselves for our jobs and use our brains in a manner that will defeat our enemy with the least number of losses.

I stopped to see Hal Reese who is in ward 10, 36th General Hospital, recovering from pneumonia. He showed great emotion when I stopped by his bed; he was so glad to see me. He wanted to know if I was all right and still with the Division. He said he would get well because I had come to see him; that he had been very sick and had expected to die on two occasions. He wanted to talk to me about many things. He is not allowed to have visitors and I knew I should not stay long. I must go back and see him again tomorrow.

I stopped to witness some training exercises by the 143rd Infantry. The instructors are taking their work seriously and are doing a good job.

Monday, March 27, 1944

Paid a visit to Hal Reese at the hospital. He seemed improved yesterday, and is in much better spirits.

General Hess, my artillery commander, stopped by to tell me how much he enjoyed his rest at Sorrento last week. He deserved it.

Bell, my orderly, came back from Caserta "for a square meal;" his words. He had gone to Caserta for a four-day rest. I think he is a little homesick. I miss him when he is away and will be glad when he returns.

The reorganization and training of the Division is going along quite well. Everybody is busy, and I sense a serious attitude on their part toward their work.

Wednesday, March 29, 1944

Accompanied by Lt. Kelley, I visited the front of the 88th Division and the CP of the 351st Infantry in a stone quarry east of and not far from Minturno. That front is especially quiet. The bridge on Highway 7, over the Garigliano, is being smoked constantly during the day. The purpose is to prevent the Germans from adjusting fire on the bridge and destroying it, and from interdicting traffic over it. Very few vehicles pass over it during the day. The smoke is put down within 50 yards of the bridge and serves to pinpoint its location to the German artillery observers.

The Germans can see vehicles before they enter the smoke cloud, and can calculate their time of arrival at the bridge; thus the Germans can take pot shots with artillery at vehicles on the bridge if they wish. A little planning can arrange things so that the bridge need be used only at night. So why the puny bit of smoke? The Germans are laughing at us again.

Saturday, April 1, 1944

I have prepared a roster of 15 field officers to be returned to the United States on rotation during the next year. I have given preference to age and service among those who have performed their duty well.

Last night somebody stole my jeep parked in front of the Division movie in Maddaloni. I had permitted Warrant Officer Hampton and Private Tychsen to take it to town to the show. They left it parked in the street without removing the distributor rotor which I told them to do.

Keyes is coming to the Division today to award the Legion of Merit to 1st Lt. Roger L. Gutterman, Reconnaissance Troop. It seems to me that the Corps Commander should confine his pinning of decorations on people in his own Corps troops. Everyone knows that Keyes had nothing to do with the award.

Tuesday, April 4, 1944

I pinned one DSC and fifteen Silver Stars on officers and men of the 142nd Infantry at a simple ceremony arranged by Colonel Lynch and Bob Ives. Wick Fowler was present and used the occasion as a basis for a news item to his paper.

This evening I pinned a Silver Star on a lieutenant of Battery A, 132nd FA Battalion, who did spendid work as a forward observer on Mount Castellone. The Battalion Commander, John (Pete) Greene, turned the whole battalion out for the ceremony which was a spendid thing for him to do. I had supper with him afterward. Pete is an outstanding artillery commander. All his officers and men have great respect for and confidence in him. So do I.

Wednesday, April 5, 1944

This afternoon I witnessed an artillery demonstration by the 133rd FA Bn for our recently arrived officers and men. It was well done, but was quite simple. It consisted of laying down a creeping barrage in front of an imaginary line of advancing infantrymen. Suitable for beginners. Keyes and members of his staff were present and seemed to be pleased.

This evening I talked to Lt. Puckett, 142nd Infantry, about his case. He was an NCO in the 15th Infantry when I was in command of that regiment at Fort Lewis in 1939. He has been in trouble several times. His last offense was to go AWOL with a jeep. He was gone less than 24 hours. He was tried by General Court Martial, found guilty, and sentenced to forfeit $50 of his pay per month for six months.

After talking to his regimental commander and to Puckett himself, I decided to reduce the sentence to $25 per month for three months. He has done excellent work in combat, is a good field soldier, and I feel that he has learned his lesson and will settle down and behave himself. At least he said he would. I am willing to encourage him by reducing his sentence.

Thursday, April 6, 1944

A recent replacement came to see me today. He said his company commander and the NCOs were mistreating him. They told me he falls out on hikes after the first halt and claims his legs will not carry him any further; the doctor said there is nothing wrong with him. He is a malingerer. The government has trained him, fed him, clothed him, paid him and his dependents on the assumption that he will take his place alongside his comrades in battle, but all is wasted on this man. He will run away as soon as the fighting starts. The sooner we get rid of him the better.

I have finally received official permission to take over the Pensione Mueller, Piazza Mergellina 43, in Naples as an officers' club for the 36th Division. For some time I have been sending 21 junior officers there per week for rest and relaxation. The place is neat, clean, quiet, and comfortable. Mueller, the proprietor, is Swiss. He formerly catered to tourists.

Easter Sunday, April 9, 1944

Attended church services this morning by Chaplain Lehne. Joined in communion—Lutheran ritual. Last evening I attended a dance given by the Special Troops in the Ball Room of the Royal Palace at Caserta. This was a beautiful setting. The flowers were cut off their stems and wired onto other stems, saving the buds for later blooming.

Miss Coyle and Miss Mary Tiverti, two nurses from 36th General Hospital at Caserta, where Hal Reese is a patient, had dinner at my mess today. Hal has been telling them that the food served in their hospital is terrible; that I have a good mess; that they could learn something about preparing food by eating a meal here. Our meal was a good one which pleased them. After the meal I had Mess Sergeant Shook explain to them how he prepares whipped cream, brown fried potatoes from dehydrated potatoes, custard pie and scrambled eggs from powdered eggs. He convinced them that to be a good cook, one must be willing to work and give thought, study and care to the subject. They told me that they did not think the information would help much because the hospital cooks were not interested in their jobs.

Forino, Italy
Monday, April 10, 1944

Division Headquarters moved today from Maddaloni to Forino, south of Avellino. I, accompanied by Bob Ives, traveled to Forino by way of Naples and Salerno in my Packard sedan. I stopped by Replacement Center No. 6 at Naples to pin a medal on Sergeant Charles Kelley. The personnel officer presented a different Sergeant Kelley whom I had to disappoint. The Commanding Officer was very apologetic and embarrassed as he should have been. I sent for the proper Sgt. Charles Kelley and found that he had departed for Africa and the States by plane the day before.

Sometime after the smoke cleared away at Salerno, I approved a recommendation for a Medal of Honor for Corporal Charles E. Kelley, Pittsburgh, Pennsylvania. He is the first soldier in the 36th Division and Fifth Army to receive that medal. Army Headquarters has been giving great publicity to his citation, being careful not to mention the 36th Division. I am amused and not at all surprised to learn that Kelley has been taken over by Army Headquarters as a "Fifth Army Hero," given the title of "Commando," and is now being returned to the States to advertise the exploits of "General Mark Clark's Fifth Army." Well, such things happen.

I stopped by Pensione Mueller to inspect the place. Herr Mueller served us a special drink, cherry flip, and Frau Mueller served us an excellent dinner. Both said our officers are well-behaved, and the officers stated that they were delighted with the comforts of the place during their week's rest there. I bought two big iron padlocks from Mueller for locking my jeep and command car while they are parked.

An enlisted pilot and a mechanic of one of my fleet of ten reconnaissance planes were killed yesterday. They banked before they had adequate speed and altitude. This accident was due to carelessness. I have noticed that enlisted men take too many chances as pilots, reflecting the typical American attitude toward danger.

Forino, Italy
Saturday, April 15, 1944

Major General "Sandy" Patch and Brigadier General Brann,

G-3, Fifth Army, visited my CP today. Brann explained to me the probable mission of the Division in the next operation. If it turns out to be what he says, we can and will do the job; however, I don't place much faith in his plans materializing as stated.

I have appointed a committee consisting of Lt. Colonels Crowther, Carl Phinney and Bob Ives to study the question of whether a memorial to the 36th Division should be placed in Italy. If so, where, what, how?

Our mountain training area here is better for our purpose than the previous one.

Tuesday, April 18, 1944

I spent the morning with the 2nd Battalion, 143rd Infantry, Lt. Colonel Gualden M. Watkins, commanding. Since he is a replacement and has not been with us very long, I discussed many tactical principles with him. He is pretty much set in his ways, but I think I gave him some new ideas that will be helpful to him. He finds it difficult to permit or encourage his subordinates to act on their own initiative. He wants to direct every move they make. I have told him to change his ways and encourage personal initiative on the part of each soldier, as well as each officer. He says he is going to do this.

Thursday, April 20, 1944

This evening I attended a dinner in Naples given by Major General Arthur Wilson at his billet in honor of the Crown Prince Umberto. Generals Devers, Patch, Eaker, Edwards, Johnson, Keyes, Grey, Immel, and several others were there. The billet is an expensively constructed, furnished, and decorated home of some wealthy person, requisitioned for Wilson, who commands the port at Naples. Many Italian servants were in evidence. Certainly, no general officer who lives in such luxurious surroundings can feel that he is participating in a war. For Arthur Wilson, this is a vacation, not a war. In my opinion, the procedure is improper, unbecoming a senior officer of the Army, and should be stopped. His quarters should be ample and suitable, but not luxurious. Clark, Keyes and division commanders are living in tents or trucks.

The approach to the entrance of the villa was lined with spick and span MPs. There was considerable fanfare as each guest arrived. Very impressive, but also very unnecessary except for the Crown Prince and Devers. A great deal of fuss was made over the Crown Prince upon his arrival, but I noticed that after he had been introduced to everyone, he was left to talk to the junior officers. I felt that he was neglected and talked to him for some time while drinks were being served before dinner. He remembered our meeting near Mignano last December, just prior to the attack by Italian troops attached to my Division at the time. Their attack was a fizzle, but we didn't mention it. He is quite interesting, has a pleasing sense of humor, and, I feel certain, is quite capable, being blessed with good judgment. He talked sense, no pretense, no BS. Refreshing. After the dinner he graciously consented to autograph my place card which is a likeness of an Italian Lieutenant General's cap, of the type which the Prince wears.

We were seated according to regular army rank. I sat on Lt. General Dever's left. Lt. General "Sandy" Patch was on my left. Major General Keyes, my Corps Commander, but much my junior in regular army rank, was seated far down the table. He may have felt embarrassed.

Saturday, April 22, 1944

Lt. Kelley and I attended a ceremony at which Lt. General Juin presented awards for gallantry to units and individuals of the 3rd Algerian Division which is commanded by General Monsabert. This impressive event, staged within the historic ruins of Pompeii, with Vesuvius as the backdrop, is another example of the ability of the French to excel in patriotic ceremonies. We arrived from Forino on time only because we drove too fast over the autostrada and went at once to the ancient market place opposite the amphitheater. There, the French troops were already in formation. They looked smart, neat, proud. They were wearing American uniforms, but they had dressed them up a bit. After the smartly dressed band played **The Star Spangled Banner, God Save The King,** and the **Marseillaise** with proper military formality, Juin began awarding the decorations. He read the citations himself and pinned on the decorations, assisted by his Aide, however, as his right arm is lame.

An American aviator acted very unwisely during the award of decorations by stunting and diving toward the spectators, pulling out of the dive just in time to pass overhead and miss the startled crowd. Typical American roughneck stunt to spoil the solemnity of the occasion.

Following the awards, the spectators moved to the inside of the famous old amphitheater. The troops then marched in review through the amphitheater to inspiring martial music. The cadence was 120 steps per minute. They marched by as platoons, each a rectangle, 6 columns, 9 ranks, with a full step, giving the impression that they were going somewhere; in contrast to American soldiers who sometimes pass the reviewing stand taking short steps as if walking on eggs.

After the impressive review, which took place in the arena where some two thousand years ago gladiators were fighting lions, General Monsabert invited me to have luncheon with him and General Juin at a table at least 100 feet long, laid under a beautiful arbor just across the street from the entrance to old Pompeii.

I was seated on the right of Countess de Laure, a Russian by birth who had married a wealthy Frenchman now deceased. She inherited his wealth and has fitted out several hospitals for the French Army at her own expense. Her son, a 1st Lieutenant, is Aide to General Albert Gruenther. The Countess could speak only a little English and I could speak no French, so there was no conversation. Unfortunate! To my right were several French generals. One was a Brigadier whom I had met in North Africa. He kept up a continual chatter with the Countess which was interspersed with laughter. All this made it impossible to hear or join in the conversation with a British Brigadier and Keyes who sat across from me and were the only other persons present who spoke my language.

The first course was roasted mutton chunks (six or eight) on a wire spit—rare, smoky black, unseasoned, unpalatable. I ate one but could eat no more. We were being served a Moroccan barbecued luncheon, and I knew I was "in for it." Next came a plate of couscous swimming in soup. This would not have been bad if the green beans, okra, cabbage, etc., in the soup had been cooked. They were nearly as raw as when they came from the garden. I could eat only the liquid broth.

General Monsabert kept insisting that I eat more, but I could not. Next, a waiter brought in a whole roast sheep on a large tin platter. Monsabert undertook to carve it, but finally gave up. A French Brigadier took over and gave us an example of clumsy carving fit for the dog kennel. He had a dull knife, but he cut off and pulled off large hunks which he waved about with a great display of success. He gave me a whole hind leg. It was quite rare, dripping blood and made me half sick. I protested. He insisted. If there is anything that is impossible for me to eat, it is rare mutton. Monsabert must have sensed my feelings for he gave me his plate, took charge of the hind leg, carved it into many pieces and passed it around to those on his right. I was thankful for this. After the remains of the carcasses were removed, we were served raisins, almonds, apples and oranges. Wine was served throughout the meal. After the luncheon, which began at 12:30 and ended at 2:30, I accompanied Juin and Monsabert to the amphitheater where musical entertainment was provided in honor of Juin, the senior French general. This was poor, and we departed after a few numbers. The guard of honor for Juin was smart, attentive, alert, and seemed to bob up unexpectedly at different places as the General moved about within the area.

All in all, I thoroughly enjoyed the occasion and shall long remember it.

Yesterday, Colonel Ives brought to the mess an Italian Count who is going to help us obtain a piece of land near Paestum for a memorial to the 36th Division. He is quite well-to-do, considers himself quite apart from the native Italian peasants, has no sympathy or interest in them, and blames them for their present condition of poverty. It is my opinion that they are ignorant and helpless and are the victims of the State, the Church, and the large landowners.

We are getting ready for a real knockout blow to the Germans in our front. I talked to many officers and men of the 141st and 142nd yesterday, and they all feel that we are in better fighting condition now than at any time since landing on the shore of Salerno Bay. I agree with them, and I feel that we are going to give a grand account of ourselves in the next operation.

Monday, April 24, 1944

This morning I witnessed an exercise by two infantry battalions; an attack up a mountain and progress along the mountain top, phase by phase, for 48 hours. The 2nd Battalion, 141st Infantry, was one and one half hours late at the line of departure and was too greatly dispersed and strung out.

If this had been the real thing the attack would have failed. Colonel Johnson, the battalion commander, is new, never has been in combat, and has a great deal to learn. I would much prefer to fill the vacancies in the Division by promoting deserving persons who have been with us through the past year. Nothing can hurt the morale of experienced and deserving personnel more than to bring people from the outside who do not know their business. But higher headquarters does not appreciate this and forces people onto us whom we do not want. We have to do the best we can under the circumstances.

Tuesday, April 25, 1944

Keyes visited the Division at Forino to pin four DSCs on men of the Division. I much prefer to do this myself, but he insists on doing it so he can show himself to the troops. Most of the officers and men are not interested in him at all. After the war they will forget him and his staff completely. Their interest, now and after the war, lies with the men of the 36th Division.

I saw the movie, "This Is The Army," tonight on the open-air screen in the bivouac area of the 111th Medical Battalion in Forino. It was better than the stage show I saw some time ago at the Royal Theater in Naples.

Thursday, April 27, 1944

I visited General Hospital No. 36 at Caserta and pinned a Silver Star and Bronze Star on Chaplain Lehne who has been through some very gruesome experiences in this war. He has been on duty at the Division Cemetery ever since we landed in Italy and has given every dead soldier of the Division an individual burial service under very trying conditions. The burial place of soldiers killed in a war is very depressing.

Enroute home I stopped at Pensione Mueller (36th Division Officers' Club) in Naples. Had a grand lunch; inspected the premises; talked to some of the officers there. Everyone is delighted with the place and is happy to spend a week there. Herr Mueller gave me another bottle of his precious wine which he has had for 15 years and which he says cannot possibly be obtained anywhere else.

Friday, April 28, 1944

Clark visited the Division today in the Forino area. He seemed very friendly; spoke to many officers and men; looked through many bivouacs, kitchens and motor parks; and observed some of the training activities. He had lunch with me at my headquarters mess. While at the bivouac of the 155th Field Artillery Battalion, Clark approached a group of men being instructed by a sergeant. The sergeant, speaking to Clark said, "General, we have had a question puzzling us for some time. We have been instructed to salute whenever an officer approaches us, no matter what we are doing. Now, suppose a man is shoving a shell into the gun when an officer approaches. Should he drop the shell and salute?" A damn fool question.

Clark ignored his impertinence by answering, "Whenever in doubt, salute, and you will always be right."

Those within hearing distance smiled, as if to say, "Fools can ask questions wise men cannot answer."

Clark told me he did not know what was holding up his recommendation to the War Department for a Distinguished Service Medal for me for my planning and successful landing at Salerno Bay. Said that he was going to hurry it up. I hope he does because I would like to have that medal, not so much for that service, but because it is proof that my conduct of that operation received the whole-hearted approval and appreciation of the Army Commander.

I know that I, my staff, and my troops did a spendid job. From the time that my Command Post was set up at the tobacco barn, I was constantly considering possible threats and making dispositions to be prepared to meet them. I knew at all times where my combat troops were posted, what their missions were, and what they were doing. I visited them as frequently as my duties would permit. I conducted what may be termed an offensive-defense; that is, I pushed units out to extend the perimeter of the beachhead while, at the same time, I had to be prepared for attack upon our positions. I did everything that any capable division commander would have done. If Clark thinks I deserve a medal, I will be pleased to receive it.

It is my opinion that no officer above the rank of lieutenant colonel should be eligible for the award of the Medal of Honor or the Distinguished Service Cross. What can a colonel or general do that is above and beyond the call of his duty? Being commanders or staff officers, their ordinary duty embraces self-sacrifice, extraordinary exertion in an extreme crisis, dynamic leadership in a decisive moment. It is impossible for them to qualify for either of these medals for valor, unless they are equipped with a weapon, enter the fight alongside the enlisted soldier, and put up a better performance than he does. If and when they do this, they are not attending to their own business. The Distinguished Service Medal is their proper reward.

When he departed, Clark told me that he had had a most enjoyable day; that he was pleased with the caliber of the officers and men; that he felt we will do well on our next assignment. I agree with him.

Saturday, April 29, 1944

I visited the Signal Company in its bivouac and inspected its area and some equipment. The personal appearance and military courtesy of the men of the company are below standards. I have noted some improvement recently since the former company commander returned to the States. Lt. Wells promises that he will bring the company up to standard, and I hope he will make some progress. He has a difficult job because most of the men in the company are technicians and are working where he cannot personally supervise them. Also, being technicians, they feel that as long as they do a good job, they should be relieved from the tedious requirements for good order and military discipline.

When men are up at all hours of the day and night, laying wire, looking for breaks in the lines, manning and repairing some equipment, coding and decoding messages, in the rain, mud, and cold, doing their utmost to keep the signal net of the Division in full operation, they are not particularly enthusiastic about their personal appearance and military courtesy. I can understand their viewpoint. However, these trying conditions of service do not exist now. At present, the Division is in a training area and now is the time for the company to improve its disciplinary standards.

Major "Red" Morgan, 141st Infantry, was promoted to his present rank about a month ago and recently went to Naples to celebrate with some of his friends. They all drank a little too much and tried to enter an officers' club after closing hours.

An MP on duty at the entrance refused to let them in. Morgan protested, voicing the opinion that combat soldiers ought to be respected and granted some exceptions, especially by their non-combatant brothers in the rear who have never heard rifle fire. He took out his hunting knife (all officers in the Division carry them) and began to clean his fingernails, saying at the same time, "I ought to use this knife, but I won't."

The MP told him to put the knife away or he would take it away from him. With that Morgan slugged the MP, was arrested and placed in confinement.

Red got in touch with me and asked me to get him out of the guardhouse. I arranged for him to be returned to his regiment. Next day, Clark called and directed me to take appropriate disciplinary action against Morgan for his misbehavior, implying that I should try him by a General Court Martial and report back the action I had taken. I do not want to try him by court martial.

I have Morgan's story. He says he had too much to drink, recalls the incident only hazily, and regrets his misconduct. He is one of my very best combat officers, and in view of his splendid record I have arranged for him to apologize to the MP. I will then administer a reprimand, but I shall try to word it in such a way that it will be more in praise of his achievements in battle than in censure for his misconduct. I hope this will end the matter.

If the MP had had a sense of humor, he would have realized that Morgan had too much to drink, would have handled him accordingly when he moved to strike him, rather than treat him as a person trying to beat up an officer of the law. Morgan's actions in getting out his knife and cleaning his fingernails while saying, "I ought to use this knife, but I won't," should have brought a smile or laugh from the MP instead of resentment and hostility. I am sure one of my own MPs would have taken benevolent charge of Morgan and kept him out of the clutches of the law.

Sunday, April 30, 1944

Today General Joyce, British Army, paid me a visit and was my guest for luncheon. He and General Stack are preparing a phony amphibious landing exercise under direction of Fifth Army Headquarters, using unit radio sets in an effort to deceive the Germans into believing that we are preparing for a landing on the shore somewhere north of Rome. The Germans are expected to intercept our messages, decode them, and fall for the deception. Maybe they will be fooled, but I doubt it. If we really meant business, we would maintain complete radio silence and would not be sending messages broadcast in code for our enemy to pick up. All professional soldiers know this, including the Germans.

I am having a meeting with my unit commanders to discuss various phases regarding our mountain training. I do not want to leave a single stone unturned to insure our success in our next operation. If Clark does not change his mind, we are going to attack over the high ground between the Liri Valley and the sea. This will be a different kind of fighting than we have had in the past because the Germans will not have an organized defense as they had in the mountains in the San Pietro area last December.

Lt. Colonel Brewster, former Surgeon of the Division, was transferred to the Headquarters of the VI Corps last July, when Dawley was Corps Commander, with the understanding that he was to be assigned as Corps Surgeon and be promoted to the rank of Colonel. He has not been made Corps Surgeon, nor has he been promoted. After 10 months service with the Corps, during which he has become convinced that no opportunity for increased responsibility or promotion will be given him, he requested that I attempt to get him back to the Division.

This I did because I consider Brewster a most able Division Surgeon, superior in many ways to some regular army medical officers because he takes greater personal interest in the welfare and comfort of the sick and wounded, and sees to it that they get the best available medical attention. In this he does not spare himself.

Today he reported to me for duty; happy, cheerful, relieved, and glad to be back home. He has been at the beachhead near Rome for 100 days, subjected to shellfire each day. He needs a rest and I am sending him to Sorrento next week. He told me that he would rather serve under my command than under the command of any other general officer he knows. This was no "applesauce." I think I have had enough experience to know the difference between flattery and sincerity.

Chaplain MacCombie returned to the Division last week from a hospital in Africa. He was quite sick when he left the Division

Pfc. Edward J. Foley, Company C, 143rd Infantry, checks and double checks his rifle. Velletri, Italy, May 29, 1944—U.S. Army Photo

A destroyed German anti-tank gun at the edge of Velletri believed to be the gun that killed Lt. Col. Harold Reese. June 1, 1944

German prisoners being interrogated at the Command Post of the 141st Infantry. Velletri, Italy, June 1, 1944

Prisoner taken by the 1st Battalion, 141st Infantry. Velletri, Italy, June 1, 1944

Men of the 141st Infantry, 36th Division, riding tanks into the outskirts of Rome. June 4, 1944

General Marshall and General Walker discuss the tactical situation. Near Grossetto, Italy, June 18, 1944

Left to right: Generals Walker and Marshall. Sgt. Adaysh, General Clark. Near Grosseto, Italy, June 18, 1944—U.S. Army Photo

Major General Niedermeyer, commander of the 162nd German Division which was destroyed north of Rome by the 36th Division.

Final review for General Walker. Requested by the men of the 36th Division. Salerno, Italy, July 7, 1944

last December and has been in one hospital after another since. He, too, was glad to be back home where he has cheerful friends with whom to associate. He said the life in a hospital in Africa is nerve-racking because they are full of discarded colonels and lieutenant colonels who are pleading one ailment after another in order to stay in the hospital as long as possible. I am not surprised at this. I was in a hospital at Contrexeville, France, for a few days during WW I and observed the same thing. Some officers, not being enthusiastic about getting back to their units on the fighting front, sought operations in succession. They would have an appendectomy, followed by a tonsillectomy, or anything to stay in the hospital as long as possible.

This afternoon I assembled all subordinate commanders at my CP for a conference on our next operation with the II Corps. I explained that our mission is to advance some 16 kilometers across a mountain range to get in the rear of, and finish off, the German 91st Division now in the vicinity of Formia. The height of the mountain mass is approximately 4000 feet. We have been doing some special training for this job, and I feel confident that we shall have a great success, if we are assigned a proper objective, and if the attack is properly timed.

Monday, May 1, 1944

I am impatient with some of the company officers because of their poor training methods. Today I witnessed training in the 1st Battalion, 142nd Infantry, in scouting and patrolling. It was very inefficiently done, and the instructor used little or no imagination. There was little effort to prevent noises resulting from talking, walking on leaves, and rattling equipment; no real thought given to choice of routes that provided the best concealment; no preliminary examination of houses, ridges, groves, where Germans might be in observation; no explanation of how to protect themselves from being ambushed or fired on at short range; no alternative advance by part of a patrol while the remainder covers and protects it by fire.

I explained all this to the new company commander. He gave me the impression that he had only a hazy idea of these elements of the subject. Yet an operation is pending in which good scouting and patrolling will be a very important contribution to our success.

No wonder I become impatient with them, and yet I know that we can never attain perfection because our losses have to be replaced by persons who are the best available, although some of them will lack the experience and knowledge needed to do a good job. But I take comfort in the thought that while they may be weak in some respects, they are strong in others.

Tuesday, May 2, 1944

Accompanied by Lt. Colonel Fred W. Sladen, my new operations officer, and Carl Phinney, I went to visit the Anzio beachhead now under command of Major General Lucian Truscott. We departed from the Naples dock area at 7:00 AM in a fast PT boat. General Mike O'Daniel, who now commands the 3rd Division, was also a passenger.

The skipper showed no concern for the Germans. He skimmed along the enemy shore within artillery range. I searched the shore through my field glasses but saw no signs of life. We were not shot at. The trip required 4 hours. As we approached Anzio, we noticed that the area occupied by friendly troops was covered by a haze produced by many smoke projectors distributed throughout the occupied area. As a result, observation of the harbor area by the Germans was almost impossible even from an airplane. We were met at the dock and were taken in a jeep to VI Corps Headquarters where I met General Truscott. He had just returned from a five-day rest at Sorrento.

Truscott explained his plan of operations and the mission for the 36th Division. Having spent the past several weeks preparing ourselves for an attack on the 91st German Division over the mountain mass near Formia, we now find ourselves assigned to a different kind of job at Anzio. We are to exploit a successful attack to be made by the 1st Armored and 3rd Infantry Divisions.

General John L. I. Hawksworth, who now commands the British 1st Division, and I were guests for luncheon at Truscott's mess. In the afternoon, Truscott's Aide took all three of us in a jeep over the area to see the sectors held by the Special Forces (Brigadier General Frederick), by the 34th Division (General Ryder), and by the 45th Division (General Eagles), and to see the bivouac area that will be assigned to the 36th Division when it arrives at the beachhead. From the observation post of the 34th Division, I was able to view the terrain over which the 36th Division may attack.

I had supper with Eagles and General Paschal, with whom I enjoyed a personal visit. That evening we returned to the CP of the VI Corps and went over the tactical plans for our possible employment.

Wednesday, May 3, 1944

This morning I went over the artillery plan of operation for the whole beachhead with Brigadier General Carl Baer, and over the antiaircraft warning system and defensive fire system with Brigadier General Townsend. Both systems are well-organized and are functioning smoothly and efficiently.

Qualiano, Italy
Thursday, May 4, 1944

Moved my CP from Forino to Qualiano and spent many hours catching up on my official paper work. I have my staff do as much of the paper work as possible, but there is some that I have to do myself, such as approving or disapproving court martial sentences, promotions, decorations, awards, and transfers of certain personnel.

Friday, May 5. 1944

I attended a conference at Headquarters Fifth Army for all general officers who are to take part in the coming operation of the main front. Plans were explained in detail and Clark made a rather unusual statement. He said that he is under pressure from above (Alexander) and from below (Keyes and Truscott) regarding the employment of the 36th Division, and that he does not want any more pressure exerted from below. Keyes' face showed dissatisfaction, but he said nothing. Can it be that personal relations between Clark and Keyes are not any too harmonious?

Saturday, May 6, 1944

I attended a conference at Headquarters II Corps near Piedmonte. Nothing new developed regarding our future employment. I know what we are to do either in the II Corps or in the VI Corps, and I am getting ready to do either one. If we have a chance to do something sensible, we will succeed. I hope our assignment is with the II Corps, Keyes, because we are better prepared for that job.

I sent Colonel George Lynch and "Jazz" Harmony to the beachhead by cub plane to look over the terrain so they will be informed, if and when their regiments go to that area. Both pilots, not paying any attention to business, lost their way and came in to shore near the mouth of the Tiber, in German-occupied territory. They realized their blunder just in time, turned south, and skimming the sea, arrived at the beachhead, but not until all the anti-aircraft, navy, and air forces at the beachhead had been warned to hold their fire, if two cub planes should come in from the direction of the enemy. They were lucky that they were not shot down. All this because the pilot in charge, Captain Murray, was not paying attention to his business. There is absolutely no excuse for their getting lost.

I have used up most of today on my paper work and correspondence. Wick Fowler, **Dallas Morning News,** had dinner with me last night. He is with us to write stories about the Division for his paper. The Army censor does not permit him to mention the organizations of the men he writes about.

I will now read a few more pages of **Lee's Lieutenants,** Volume II, loaned to me by Carl Phinney. I enjoy reading of the men of Lee's Army of Northern Virginia, especially when written by Douglas Southall Freeman, a man who is historian, orator, and master of rhetoric. I have heard him lecture to the students at the Army War College on many occasions during the years I was an instructor there. His subjects always had to do with some phase of the Army of Northern Virginia, for he knows that Army and its operations almost as well as General Robert E. Lee did.

Monday, May 8, 1944

I visited the headquarters of the 141st and 142nd Regiments, the 155th FA Battalion, and the 636th Tank Destroyer Battalion. Had a long talk with Harmony (141st) about problems to be expected in our next operation. He has had no battle experience, but is enthusiastic, and I expect his regiment to do well. I told him that the 141st used to be the best saluting regiment in the Division, but now it is the poorest. He said he would correct this. We will see.

Lynch (142nd) invited me to witness a demonstration of firing antitank grenades from a machine gun which had been fitted with a grenade launcher. The greatest range was 375 yards, farther than one can be projected from a rifle. The men seemed very enthusiastic about their modification, but I doubt if it will be of much value in combat because of the maximum range. Machine guns will seldom be that close to enemy pillboxes during an attack. In mountains, machine guns with launchers may be of value in firing from higher to lower elevations, but this is really the job for the infantry mortars.

A letter from a mother:

> "Dear Sir:
>   Please listen to a mother. My son who is a Private in the 143rd Infantry, he was wounded the 11th of December in the left leg, was put back on duty the 11th of March. I can see by the writing my son don't seem normal either physically or mentally. Please General You send me boy home Please don't have him kill do something about it you are such a big man hear me please. I am so worry about my boy I am afraid of loosing my mind. He is a World War veteran orphan only a few teeths left going on 32 years please Mr. send me home my boy I thank you."

This is just one of many such letters that I receive from the mothers of the men in the Division. Every time I read one, something pulls at my heartstrings.

NOTE: The soldier survived the war.

Tuesday, May 9, 1944

Lt. Colonel A. B. Crowther is leaving us today to return to the United States. He is quite happy for the opportunity to get back home. He was inducted into the Army as a Lt. Colonel with the 36th Division on November 25th, 1940, hence is serving in his fourth year as Division G-2. He has done outstanding work during his service and deserves to be promoted. Some officers who were 2nd lieutenants in November, 1940, have gone up to lieutenant colonel. I have no vacancy in the Division to which I can promote Crowther, so he is stymied here. I have given him a letter of appreciation and intend to recommend him for the Legion of Merit. He has performed all his duties in a superior manner, and I will miss his cheerfulness and loyal support.

I have given considerable thought to many recommendations recently received for Silver Stars and Bronze Stars. I approved many, but also disapproved many. While some of the acts described were meritorious, they were not sufficiently outstanding to warrant awards. I realize that this business of awards is very unsatisfactory. Many who deserve awards never receive them.

Many who do not deserve awards do receive them.

A lot depends upon the language used to describe the act upon which the recommendation is based. An outstanding act of gallantry, if insufficiently described, may be disapproved. An act of just ordinary duty, involving no more than ordinary performance in a dangerous situation, if glowingly described, may be approved. After all, I have to be governed principally by the language used, although I try to visualize the act itself as I would describe it. This is unsatisfactory, of course, but it is the situation under which we have to work.

Thursday, May 11, 1944

Clark came to the Division near Qualiano to pin a number of decorations on persons in the Division. I met him at the landing strip at 9:15 AM where he arrived by cub plane. We went directly to the place for the ceremony. The band and a composite battalion were already in place. After the appropriate three flourishes and **General's March,** Clark spoke briefly to those present through a loud speaker. In well-chosen words he praised the Division, made some complimentary remarks about me, and spoke of the future employment of the Division, saying that it would be held in Army reserve to be used at a critical stage of battle. This is, of course, a position of great responsibility and a compliment to the Division.

Afterwards, he pinned a DSM on me, saying, "It gives me a great kick to have this opportunity to pin this medal on you. You have done and are doing a grand job."

Gracious words. I am, of course, greatly appreciative of this award which was instituted by Clark last December when the Division was in the midst of successes and when my reputation stood high with him. I have not stood so high in the estimations of Keyes and Clark since the Rapido catastrophe.

After the troops passed in review (they looked exceptionally well), the many officers of my staff and the unit commanders rushed up to congratulate me. They were really pleased to have my services recognized.

CITATION
Distinguished Service Medal

"FRED L. WALKER (03029), Major General, Army of the United States. For exceptionally meritorious service in a position of great responsibility as Commanding General, 36th Infantry Division, in the Fifth Army's invasion of Italy in September 1943. General Walker planned the landing of his Division and attached units on the beaches of the Gulf of Salerno, Italy, and coordinated the action of all units in such a manner that the entire force performed as a cohesive team. The disposition of the Division and the tactical order of landing, determined by General Walker, with exceptional foresight, were of major importance in the success of the invasion. General Walker went ashore with the leading elements of the Division to control operations personally and to make the decisions necessary for the accomplishment of the Division's mission. For a period of twelve days, he fought and maneuvered his forces in one continuous and unrelenting operation in the face of determined enemy resistance, successfully terminating the operation by driving the enemy from all the territory in his Division's sector. General Walker's exceptional foresight in planning and his superior handling of the forces at his command contributed importantly to the securing of the Fifth Army's bridgehead on the continent of Europe. Entered the Service from Ohio."

I accompanied Clark back to the air strip where he took off immediately for another ceremony for the 509th Paratroop Battalion. Enroute he said that he was being pushed from above (Alexander) to commit the 36th Division in the Anzio beachhead. He implied that he would rather employ the Division on the southern front.

After delivering Clark to the landing strip, I returned to the same field for another ceremony in which I passed out a number of Silver Stars, Bronze Stars, Good Conduct ribbons and Combat Infantry Badges. I made a few remarks to the troops to let them know that their hard work and efficient services as mechanics, signalmen, truck drivers, supply men, and others, are appreciated by me.

This evening I attended a dinner at the villa housing the rear echelon of Division Headquarters, at San Prisco, given in honor of Irving Berlin. He has a very pleasing personality, is easy mannered, and is a good conversationalist. We posed together for a picture for one of the enlisted men.

The dinner table was arranged on the patio and was in the form of the letter T, for Texas. The table was decorated with a number

of bouquets; the food was superior.   The ice cream was the first I
have eaten since I left the States.

At the conclusion of the meal, Hal Reese, who acted as toast-
master, introduced Berlin who made some appropriate remarks.
I was then introduced, but I pointed out that a soldier never
creates anything that will live after him, whereas, in the case
of our guest, he would leave songs and music that would live
forever.

I had the members of the band who wear the Combat Infantry-
man's Badge stand while I explained that they were both musicians
and soldiers.   I described their hardships as litter bearers on
Mount Maggiore last December when they were attached to the
142nd Infantry.

Later, Berlin, accompanied by the band, sang some of his famous
songs. Jon Forte, the musician in the band who composed the
song, "Somewhere in Via Roma," gave me an autographed copy
after it had been played and sung for Irving Berlin.   I appreciate this.   Berlin autographed my place card and, at his request,
I autographed his.   This was a most delightful evening, and a
welcome change of environment.   I had Berlin taken back to
Santa Maria, a short distance from San Prisco, where his show,
"This Is The Army," is now playing.

In a few days we will be back in battle. I do not know for
certain whether we are going to Anzio or are going to cross the
mountains with Keyes. It makes very little difference because
the Division is well trained for either mission. We are prepared
for anything!

CHAPTER FIFTEEN
Breakthrough at Velletri

Qualiano, Italy
Friday, May 12, 1944

The long expected attack by the forces on the main Italian front was launched at 11:00 PM last night. Progress up to 4:00 this afternoon is as planned. The Germans have put up strong resistance.

In this war, Headquarters sends us visitors even on the verge of battle. Marlene Dietrich and her show played at the 36th Division bivouac today. She and her party had luncheon at the Division Headquarters Mess. Everyone who could find a camera was snapping her picture. She arrived wearing a GI wool cap and OD unionalls. She was no sooner out of the sedan, which I had sent to Naples for her, when she spotted Colonel Brewster, ran over to him and threw her arms around him. She then explained that the Colonel, while he was on duty at VI Corps, had given her sulfa drugs when she was sick and had brought her "back to life." Everyone thoroughly enjoyed this demonstration, and Brewster did not object.

At luncheon, Miss Dietrich sat on my left and talked interestingly of her experiences since coming to Italy to entertain the troops. She had all of us sign an American dollar bill and gave each of us a card with her picture and autograph. Three other entertainers were with her: one comedian, one singer, both men; and one woman comedian. They made it a point not to say or do anything that might draw attention away from Miss Dietrich.

I saw the show at 1:00 PM. The stage was a rough lumber platform. Two trucks, one on either side, formed the exits and entrances and housed the loud speakers and dressing rooms.

When I arrived with my camp chair, I took a seat about 30 feet in front of the stage in the midst of the crowd of enlisted men who were seated on the ground.

After the show, which was for the Special Troops, Miss Dietrich and her party went to the area of the 141st Infantry for another performance before some four thousand men. Later she and her party were guests for supper with the men of Company K, 141st. The cooks had prepared an excellent meal for the occasion. She and her party took mess kits, got into line, received their chow in a soldierly fashion, sat on the ground and ate with the men. Afterwards, Miss Dietrich called out the names of the men as she distributed the mail from home. One after another came up to receive his letter from her.

All members of the troupe told Captain Nykiel, my Special Services officer, that this was one of the most delightful days they had had since leaving the United States. When he told them that the men attending the shows today would be fighting in ten days, they were surprised. They said they had been entertaining service troops in rear areas, but that they much preferred being with the combat soldiers. Miss Dietrich asked Nykiel to express "to your general" her thanks for, and appreciation of, the opportunity to visit the 36th Division. The feeling was mutual.

At 3:30 PM I attended a decoration ceremony by the 143rd Infantry at which I awarded to some 35 officers and enlisted men the Silver Star. Prior to pinning the medals on the men, I made a short talk to the entire regiment as it stood at ease in formation. I praised their past achievements, expressed my appreciation for what they have done, and pointed out trials to come. Brigadier General Walter Hess, commanding the Division Artillery, and Lt. Colonel Ives, my G-1, both told me that my remarks were inspiring to everyone.

Sunday, May 14, 1944

I visited the command post of the 85th Division today to learn the situation at the front, to get a good look at the battlefield area, and to see the terrain preparatory to possible employment of the Division in that sector. I found the 85th and 88th Divisions are making splendid progress; better than planned.

I have received orders from Clark, who phoned me, to have the 36th Division ready, within 24 hours after notice, to move and load on ships now in Naples harbor. I told him that my artillery, now committed north of Minturno, cannot do this unless I am given exclusive use of the coast road and the bridge on the Garigliano River.

I had to enter a protest to Army Headquarters today to prevent the II Corps from moving the 636th Tank Destroyer Battalion across the Garigliano River and beyond Minturno. Keyes had been told by Army Headquarters not to move it, but he was going to do so anyway. As a result of my protest, it was not moved. You can't always trust the higher command. You have to watch them all the time to keep from being imposed upon.

I had lunch with the Headquarters Battery, 36th Division Artillery, in the ancient castle of Minturno which was built 200 years before Christ. The town is on a steep hill. The main street through the town is about 16 feet wide and the side streets are only about 8 feet wide. Many of them are really stair steps. The buildings and streets reminded me of those in Fez, Morocco.

Tuesday, May 16, 1944

I pinned the Silver Star Medal on about 50 men of the 141st Infantry at a ceremony in which the whole regiment was formed in line. I praised it for its past achievements. Included was the following statement:

"Historians have pointed out the hardships of General Washington's troops at Valley Forge as an outstanding example of what soldiers can endure, but the hardships which you suffered last winter while fighting on the mountain heights, which you were required to occupy, surpass those of the Continental Army at Valley Forge. Historians also point to the storming of Chapultepec by General Scott's troops, to the assaults on Lookout Mountain and Missionary Ridge by soldiers of General Grant, and to the charge of Pickett's Division at Gettysburg as outstanding examples of soldierly courage. But the soldierly qualities which you displayed during two days and nights at the crossing of the Rapido last January, your heroism, loyalty and devotion to duty, and your determination to win against the unsurmountable defenses of the enemy never have been and never will be exceeded."

I gave them a summary of the situation now in front of the Fifth Army where 3,000 prisoners were taken, including one regimental commander and his staff and eight battalion commanders. I explained to them that it was a distinct honor for the 36th Division to be placed in Army reserve in this critical operation; that the Division would be committed to battle at a critical time and critical place within the next ten days to deliver the "knockout."

The regiment passed in review after I pinned on the medals. The men looked grand and powerful passing in massed formation by companies, marching in perfect step, bayonets fixed, and rifles slung over the right shoulder. I congratulated Harmony on his fine ceremony and regiment. He replied, "We are ready to do whatever you order."

Wick Fowler has arranged to give news items about us direct to the United Press and Associated Press representatives in Naples so that they can be cabled immediately to the States. I will let him use my command car and driver to travel over the area and procure the stories that will be of interest to the people in Texas.

I am expecting orders for the Division to move into combat at any moment.

Thursday, May 18, 1944

This has been a busy day. Our plans for loading the LSTs for movement to Anzio have been completed and all troops, including the Division Artillery and the 636th TD Battalion are ready to move to the loading area.

Captain James H. Blake, Commander of the Division Headquarters Company, came to see me at my direction. He has reduced one of his men from sergeant to private for what I consider a minor offense. I went over the case in some detail with Blake, who is a relatively new replacement, and pointed out that NCOs, like the rest of us, do make mistakes once in a while, but that they should not be arbitrarily "busted" unless they are not capable of handling their jobs.

A mistake now and then must be expected. Then, too, an NCO, if married, has a family in the States which he is supporting by allotment, and when he is "busted" for a minor mistake, his family loses much of this allotment and undergoes additional hardship. If an NCO is not qualified to do his job, "bust" him and do it promptly, but don't "bust" him just because he made a minor mistake. He is human. We all make mistakes. Blake said he would restore the man's former grade.

Anzio, Italy
Saturday, May 20, 1944

Yesterday I flew in a cub plane to the Anzio beachhead. The Division, less the rear echelon, will assemble here on the 22nd and be in reserve, a place of honor. It will be used after the main attack starts.

Last night I was the guest of General Truscott at the house in Nettuno where he has his quarters. He spoke very complimentarily of me and the Division, and he feels confident that we will do well any job he gives us. He is quite junior to me, but as long as he commands the Corps, I shall do all in my power to carry out his orders. I respect him for he knows his business.

After going over the plans I received from Truscott yesterday, I believe the Fifth Army has a good chance for success. I still feel that more immediate and profitable results would have been attained if, on last Wednesday, the 17th, the 36th Division had been put into battle on the south front, attacking through the 85th Division. We could have gone over the mountains rather rapidly and without much German opposition.

I issued the necessary instructions to insure that the action of the 36th will be coordinated with the action of the Corps.

Sunday, May 21, 1944

I took a look all along the front from a cub plane and afterward went up front in my jeep, but could see very little from the ground. I could see Cisterna and Cori, two towns now in the enemy's possession, which may be in my zone of attack. I did become more familiar with the road net.

Tuesday, May 23, 1944

At 5:54 this morning, the VI Corps in the Anzio beachhead began its drive to the north to break through the German defenses, interrupt the German supply lines, and join up with the other Fifth Army troops which have broken out on the Cassino front and are approaching from the south.

The 3rd Infantry and the 1st Armored Divisions are making the initial attack. This is the first really organized German position either of these Divisions has encountered during this war. The 36th has made two attacks against organized positions: the Mt. Lungo—San Pietro area and the Rapido. The German defenses at Salerno were not organized.

I am watching, with interest, the progress of the two Divisions. Now they have their toughest job to date. When they bog down, we shall take over.

Clark visited my headquarters yesterday but had very little to
say. Just wanted to know if the 36th was all set to take up the
attack when ordered. I told him we were ready. He spoke un-
complimentarily of the British Eighth Army and said it was
making an attack of minor proportions, with one Canadian Division, to capture Pontocorvo on the southern front. I said that the
Eighth British Army will never have a better opportunity for
success than to attack now. He agreed. Our own 85th and 88th
Divisions, and the French troops under General Juin, on the
southern front, have done a magnificent job to date.

Wednesday, May 24, 1944

The attack by the 3rd and 1st Armored Divisions here in the
beachhead is going slowly, too slowly. They have had 24 tanks
knocked out, and six of their TDs have been destroyed; most
of them by mines, I am told. The losses of the 30th Infantry,
3rd Division, have been heavy. The going is tough. The 142nd
Infantry and the 636th T D Battalion have been taken away
from me by the VI Corps and placed in Corps reserve. I hope
the Corps will not fritter them away or use them to replace
elements of the battered 3rd Division.

Our troops on the southern front are making progress and
are now 30 miles south of us. I am watching developments so I
can intervene with the least delay when orders reach me.

Near Velletri, Italy
Thursday, May 25, 1944

Accompanied by Bob Ives and Kelley, I visited a part of Cisterna while the troops were still mopping up. On an open field
near the outskirts of town I saw five American tanks that had
been knocked out by two concealed German antitank guns. The
guns were dug into the ground at one corner of the field so
that their muzzles were only about 4 inches above the surface.
In order to conceal muzzle blasts, the crew had spread several
water soaked gunny sacks beneath the muzzles. The Germans
had stayed with their guns as long as possible because this
opportunity to knock out American tanks was one they wanted
to make the most of. Concealed, the gun crews had picked our
tanks off, one by one, as they lumbered across the open field,
not more than 300 yards away. This was about as stupid a

trick on the part of the tank commander as one can imagine. There was concealment on both sides of the open field which the tanks could have used for their advance. I wondered what fool had ordered those tanks to cross that open field during battle.

Like the horse cavalry, tanks should come out for the "charge" only when their enemy is out of ammunition, or running away, or demoralized, or too weak to resist. In the face of an antitank defense, tanks had better stay in close support of their own infantry and not go running off by themselves across open fields. The 36th Division has no fear of enemy tanks. We know how to fight them. We proved that at Salerno.

I received a letter from Gus Rosenberg of Brownwood, and from Walter Humphrey of Temple, asking my cooperation in raising funds to build a memorial to the 36th Division. Each wants it in his own city. I shall avoid taking part in either effort, for I would like to see it placed on the beaches at Salerno Bay.

I have been informed that our troops, advancing from the southern front, have joined forces with our troops about 5 miles south of the original beachhead boundary. Good news.

My Advance Command Post in now in a group of ruined dairy farm buildings about 2½ miles northeast from Cisterna, before the town of Velletri. The Germans have not been firing any artillery at us since our arrival here, although this is an ideal artillery target.

Friday, May 26, 1944

I visited the combat area of the 141st Infantry which is holding a part of our front and found the truck-drawn antitank guns supporting the regiment deployed in the regimental rear area, where they could not protect the front line infantrymen. I gave instructions for them to be moved much farther forward.

"Jakie" Devers came by for an informal visit.

After dark we relieved the 1st Armored Division in the front line south and east of Velletri. We have the mission of holding along our front. We are not to become involved in serious combat, are to be ready to withdraw on short notice, and move promptly to exploit a breakthrough anywhere on the VI Corps front.

Saturday, May 27, 1944

Held a conference attended by Colonels Adams and Harmony, their operations officers and the Division General and Special Staffs, to go over plans for possible future missions. We are prepared for almost anything.

There is a possibility that we may be employed in conjunction with the attack of the 3rd or 34th Divisions. They are not making any real headway, have been pretty well battered, and I don't want to relieve either one. It is beginning to look like there is not going to be any breakthrough for us to exploit. I prefer George Washington's theory—avoid fighting your enemy where he is strong; fight him where he is weak.

I made a reconnaissance of the front occupied by the 143rd Infantry. Patrols have not recently met any strong resistance on this front.

I asked Stovall to determine whether a temporary road can be made over Mount Artemisio for artillery and tanks. If that area is lightly held by Germans, we may be able to break through there.

Sunday, May 28, 1944

Stovall, after detailed reconnaissance by himself and his staff, reported to me that he can build a suitable road over Mount Artemisio for artillery and tanks.

So, I made another reconnaissance of our front line area in a cub plane to look for evidence of German defenses in front of us and to get a good look at Artemisio. I saw almost no field works. Nor did I see any entrenchments or gun positions. It looks to me like this is the place to break through. I told our air photo section to search our air photos of the area for evidence of any German defenses. It reported very little enemy activity. At 4:30 this afternoon I made another reconnaissance of our front lines by jeep and on foot.

To close the gap now existing between the 141st Infantry and the 3rd Division, I set up a temporary task force under command of Ives, consisting of Co. I, 141st Infantry; Co. A, 636th TD Battalion; and one platoon from the 36th Reconnaissance Troop. He is to move his command north to the Velletri-Guilianello road and act on the defensive.

While I was at the CP of the 1st Battalion, 141st Infantry, this afternoon I found the battalion commander drunk, unable to think intelligently, ignorant of the location of his own troops and the location of the enemy. He was incapable of making a decision. He has been with us only a short while, a Regular Army officer who came to us as a replacement directly from the States. I will not permit such rubbish to remain in the Division. His incapacity has not had a bad influence on his command, however, because his Battalion Executive Officer, Major "Red" Morgan, and the Battalion Staff were on the job, alert, and had the situation under control. The Staff tried to keep him out of my sight.

It is a sorry situation when the government educates an officer at various service schools and pays him over a period of many years, in order to have a competent officer ready to lead troops in battle, only to have him incapacitate himself by getting drunk, especially when his command is deployed for battle. Harmony, who is his classmate, asked me to retain him in the Division. I am surprised that he would even ask such a thing of me.

I have had some other things go wrong. Today a commander of a tank destroyer company refused to obey orders from an infantry battalion commander, to whose unit he is attached. Another recently arrived replacement, commander of a tank company not deployed for combat, was found drunk. He will be punished. What kind of an organization do you suppose these inebriates came from?

Today I saw about 100 German vehicles wrecked along the road north of Cori. Among them were 11 Tiger tanks. Near the scene were about 60 fresh German graves. Our airplanes caught this German column on the road, bumper to bumper, and took advantage of this ideal target to bomb it.

I also passed hundreds of Italians returning home from the German area, having passed through both front lines: old or crippled men; women of all ages and types, carrying and leading babies; and children trying to help their parents, sisters, or brothers. All were dirty; many were ragged and barefooted. Their faces showed that they had suffered. I feel very sorry for them.

May 29, 1944

I didn't sleep much last night. I kept thinking of the advantages and disadvantages of attacking on our own front. The more I thought about them, the more I became convinced that we can break through by striking straight ahead over Mount Artemisio. I worked out a plan in my head to take Velletri from the rear. I explained it to Stack and Slayden this morning, and they like the idea.

Two news correspondents are with the Division for a few days: Graham Hovey, INS, and Ed Johnson, **Chicago Sun.** They have been told that the 36th Division is awaiting a breakthrough and may be sent into Rome. They want to accompany us so they can say that they and the 36th Division captured Rome.

Two Air Force officers just came into my CP to spend five days with our front line Infantry. They are from a unit in Sardinia and are looking for an interesting experience. I hope they will not be disappointed.

At 8:00 PM, Sgt. Clay and I departed for Corps Headquarters where I was to attend a conference of all Division Commanders. The dirt road, full of chuck holes, was crowded with vehicles, and we were enveloped in great clouds of dust. We bumped and worried along, arriving just as the conference was getting started. In the conference room some 60 persons were seated in silence awaiting the "word." A seat was reserved for me in the front row.

There, before an enlarged and well-lighted battle map that covered most of the wall, General Truscott explained his plan and issued his orders. He directed that the 36th Division move to the rear of the 34th Division on our left, tomorrow, and relieve that Division on the night of the 31st. This was bad. That Division is bogged down and has had no real success since it started its attack on the 23rd. The 36th Division was being shoved into another impossible situation. I wanted to propose my plan as a substitute but, at the close of the conference, Truscott was in no mood to listen to a suggestion that would mean cancellation of the orders he had just issued. I decided to see him later.

Upon my return, near midnight, I discussed our mission with my General Staff and blocked out tentative plans for the move. Warning orders must go to the troops tonight.

Tuesday, May 30, 1944

At 9:00 AM I held a conference attended by all unit commanders and Division staff officers, in which I went over my order for moving into assembly areas in rear of the 34th Division several miles to our south. Our movement was to start at noon. I much prefer to break through in front of us, over Artemisio, and take Velletri from the rear (north).

Right after my conference, Truscott came to my Command Post, and after explaining the reasons, I asked him to change our mission and let us go over Mount Artemisio.

He said, "You may have something there. I'll call you back within the hour," and departed.

I held up the movement of the troops, awaiting an answer. When he phoned at about 11:00 AM, he said that he had talked to Clark, who approved the change, and that I should go ahead with my plans. His last words were, "AND YOU HAD BETTER GET THROUGH."

This is a veiled threat meaning: if you don't succeed, you'll be on your way back to the States; the responsibility is all yours; although I approve of your plan and consider it better than mine, I assume none of the responsibility.

I was surprised that Truscott would take that attitude.

I put the staff to work at once to arrange for the change. Counterorders and new orders were hurried to the troops in fragmentary form.

I called a conference of unit commanders and their principal staff officers at 3:00 PM and explained the change in our mission. They were greatly pleased and enthusiastic about our new challenge. Since the troops were already alerted to move and I had prepared orders for the new plan in case I should be allowed to use them, the change caused no confusion.

Our operations for tonight and tomorrow have promise of being spectacular. We are taking chances, but we should succeed in a big way.

Several more newspaper reporters joined the Division today.

Wednesday, May 31, 1944

Stack, G-1, G-2, G-3, and I left the CP at 4:00 this morning and established an advance CP just off the road, under a railroad overpass, a mile or so east of Velletri and within a stone's throw of the extreme forward position where our outguards were posted last night. The 143rd Infantry was marching past as we arrived. I overhead a soldier say, "There's the General over there. We must have a hell of a long way to go."

This is a crude advance CP. We are without shelter, but we don't need any.

The weather is excellent and we are going to succeed. Stovall's engineers are opening a road over Mount Artemisio, and all three combat teams are on the move in enemy territory.

Near Velletri, Italy
Thursday, June 1, 1944

A very busy and eventful day. It seems a week since this morning.

Last night all 20 of us bedded down on the ground, expecting to move forward this morning. I cautioned everyone to keep his weapon close at hand because German patrols or snipers might come into the bivouac during the night.

Before daylight we were awakened by machine gun and rifle fire which seemed to be no more than 250 yards away. However, no bullets were striking in the CP area. Since the three combat teams had already passed beyond us, I thought Germans had infiltrated between my CP and the regiment. Hal Reese and I got everyone together and quickly organized reconnaissance patrols to investigate the source and cause of the firing. It was just dawn. The firing in our immediate vicinity ceased when the patrols were starting to move out and the Germans, if there were Germans, vanished.

While I was going about helping to get everyone up and armed, I came across a man completely covered by a blanket, lying alongside the stone bridge abutment. With some impatience, I poked him with my foot and said, "Get up and get your rifle."

Slowly the face of Ken Dixon appeared. He is a news reporter who had been up most of the night with the 142nd Infantry which had gone forward. Irked and resentful, he said, "I'm a noncombatant. I don't have a rifle." He covered his head, clearly indicating that at the moment he had no interest in a news story.

After a C-ration breakfast, Hal and I walked forward over a part of Stovall's new road to a group of buildings where Harmony's

141st had its CP. It was a busy place with messengers coming and going, wounded being treated, and prisoners being interrogated. I called the Forward Echelon of my CP from there and learned that all was going well. Our troops were meeting very little resistance, except the 141st, which had the job of taking the town of Velletri.

I went forward to the CP of the 1st Battalion, not far away. It was deployed in contact with the Germans. There was small arms fire, here and there, and the battalion was preparing for an organized advance. I went to observe one of the leading companies. The company commander seemed to be taking more time than necessary to get moving, for it was important that the Germans be kept off balance and not be allowed time to regroup and reorganize. I urged him to speed things up and, on my own, undertook to help him by going over to one of his platoon commanders who was getting ready to move out, and said, "Lieutenant, get your men up and get going. Get going."

He looked askance at me and with some impatience, as if harassed, he said, emphasizing each word, "General, I'm going, but I'm not going 'til I get ready."

In other words, he was saying, attend to your business and let me attend to mine.

Was he impertinent, insubordinate, disobedient? Not at all. He has been living under battle conditions since the 26th. He has just been through a grueling fight. He was tense, but confident. He alone was responsible for the success of his men, and he did not wish to be interfered with. He was right. It is not my business to direct platoons. But occasionally I become over enthusiastic.

Several German prisoners who had been brought into the Battalion CP where Reese and I were observing, were a little slow to obey the command to assemble. Acting on a sudden impulse. I kicked one of the slow ones in the behind with the side of my foot. He was most startled and immediately jumped into place. Hal observed that it is most unbecoming of a Major General to kick a German prisoner. I agreed, of course. One of the news photographers with the Division later heard of the incident and asked me to repeat the kicking so he could get a picture of me in the act. I declined. I am not looking for that kind of publicity.

I was with the 1st Battalion, 141st Infantry, all afternoon. It

was on the Division left flank, advancing on Velletri. When
there was a pause in the German fire, Hal Reese and I walked
along the road behind the self-propelled cannon company vehicles
of the regiment while the foot troops moved ahead through the
cane and vineyards on both sides. As we approached the town
of Velletri, the Cannon Company vehicles stopped at a bend in
the road. Hal walked out beyond the bend, in front of the leading vehicle.

In a few minutes, Chaplain MacCombie came to me and told
me Hal was dead. A German antitank shell and a mortar shell
had simultaneously struck near the vehicle and a fragment from
the shells tore away Hal's left side. He died instantly.
MacCombie said the men had carried Hal's body to the courtyard of a small house off the side of the road, but I didn't want
to see it. There was nothing I could do to help, so after I had
overcome my grief, we moved on into Velletri.
I have written the circumstances of Hal's death to Julia, and
asked her to go to Philadelphia immediately to tell Sue. Julia
can get there before the official "Regret" telegram arrives. I
am very, very sorry. I warned him twice not to get in front of
the tanks. He was a grand person. I shall miss him.

Many prisoners have been taken by our Infantry today. The
12th German Paratroop Regiment, Herman Goering Division,
which was in our path must have been completely destroyed.
During the day I received an intercepted message which directed
a German regiment to withdraw and move to the west side of a
stream north of Velletri. It never arrived there. Our troops
were in full possession of Velletri by midnight.

Wick Fowler has been with me all day. When it was over, he
said to me, "I have been told that if I want to be safe I should
stay with a general. I have had enough today. I will never
again follow a general up front." He was joking.

North of Velletri
Friday, June 2, 1944

We have succeeded in a big way. The 142nd and 143rd Regiments climbed Mount Artemisio and the 142nd came in behind
Velletri. This was cleverly done, mostly at night, and resulted in
complete tactical surprise to the German High Command. Prisoners tell us they did not suspect that we had a whole division

in their rear until it was too late. But, the German delaying forces in front of the 141st fought for every foot of ground. Scattered and concealed in the brush and trees, they would lie in wait for our men to walk through the brush toward them. Then they would machinegun our men, run back a 100 yards or so and wait again. But our men knew their business. They would shoot into the brush with continuous fire and then rush in. The Germans who threw up their hands were taken prisoner. Those who tried to run away were shown little mercy. It was a matter of survival.

The Division CP was moved into a damaged school north of Velletri. The Germans have removed their dead, but many dead horses and wrecked vehicles are evidence of heavy losses. Our bulldozers are busy burying the dead animals. Three stray enemy snipers were captured in the CP area this afternoon by headquarters personnel.

We are having success everywhere. This is wonderful. I am proud of the 36th.

However, our success was lessened by an unfortunate accident. Our own air support planes bombed and strafed our own troops this afternoon, killing eight men, wounding twenty-five, and destroying three vehicles. This is a tragedy. Such accidents destroy morale. Inexperienced pilots are careless in identifying troops on the ground. Close support of infantry by air is no help anyway. Our own artillery does a better job. Air support can help best by bombing enemy reserve formations and artillery positions.

During the latter part of the afternoon, Clay drove me back to my advance CP, under the railroad overpass. Later we returned over the same route. At one point, a lone soldier was standing at the side of the road near one of our tanks. He raised his hand for us to stop, and said, "General, the road ahead is mined. I have called some men to remove them. They are on their way. He was Captain Bernis Sadler, 111th Engineers.

This did not sound possible to me. A half-hour before, we had driven over that very section. But, there were the tire tracks on the dusty surface of the road, and there in checkerboard pattern were the mines. I counted 27 circular pieces of macadam that had been removed and replaced, a mine beneath each. How did we escape? The tire tracks proved that we had driven across that mine field without triggering a fuse. This could not happen again in a thousand tries.

Sadler said, "Sir, you were lucky."

I answered, "Indeed we were. But we have been lucky twice. You saved our lives. If you had not been here, we would now be blown to pieces." I thanked him.

Soon the engineers arrived, removed and defused the mines, and in a few minutes we were on our way.

North of Velletri, Italy
Saturday, June 3, 1944

This was a trying day. When I departed from my CP to visit the advancing troops of the 141st Infantry, I told Lt. Colonel David D. Barton, our new Division Signal Officer, to arrange for a telephone to be placed near where I would be. I explained that I would indicate my location by parking my jeep on the side of the road so its two stars would be visible to anyone approaching from the rear. When I arrived at the front battalion area, my driver parked the jeep, and I made certain the stars were clearly visible from the rear.

I found that the battalion, in contact with the Germans, was stopped. It was deployed in fighting formation, but there was very little firing. I had to give some orders to the commanders of the battalion of the tanks and of the tank destroyers because the officers were moving too slowly. We have to push the Germans with everything we have, now that they are on the run, their defenses broken. We are conducting a pursuit, but some of our officers lack enthusiasm. The enlisted men, on the other hand, are eager to go after the Germans. This was a situation when **it was** my business to give orders on the spot, and I did tell them what to do. Nearby, Stack was also trying to get things moving.

I came upon a telephone and an orderly in a small gully. I thought it was for me and picked up the receiver, intending to talk to the regimental commander, Colonel Harmony. Someone was talking on the line, and I recognized the voice of Major Ross Young, Executive Officer of the 141st. He was talking to an officer at battalion headquarters. I listened, hoping to pick up some helpful information. I was amazed and also amused at the conversation which went something like this:

Young: "What's the trouble?" Answer: "The Germans are putting up a real fight to hold the crossroads in front. We're scattered through the woods. Everybody's tired. We've been going now for three days and nights."

Young: "Do you need anything?" Answer: "Not right now."

Young: "Any brass up there?" Answer: "Yes, both Walker and Stack are up here running around."

Young: "Well, don't pay any attention to them. You've got your orders. They won't stay around very long. In the meantime, stay out of their way."

Here I broke in. "Young, is that you?"

"Yes, Sir."

Silence.

"You are not very anxious to get things going up here."

Silence.

"Remember, **you** also have some orders."

Silence.

"Are you still there?"

"Yes, Sir."

"I'm doing your job. You should be up here doing what I'm doing."

Silence.

"Young, you're no soldier. No soldier would drag his feet at a time like this. I'll see you later."

I replaced the receiver and looked up. There, standing at the edge of the gully looking down at me, a broad smile on his face, was Chaplain Bernard J. Fenton, 141st. He had overhead and was amused by my part of the conversation.

The phone I had ordered for my own use never arrived. When I returned to the Division CP about noon and asked for Barton, I was told that he had gone forward during the morning and had not been heard from since. I was greatly distressed for I feared he had driven beyond our lines and was captured. A similar incident happened when I was with the 3rd Division in France in World War I.

My misgivings were well-founded. Barton and his driver had passed my parked jeep and driven on into the fire of the German defenders. Both were killed instantly by a burst of machine gun fire. They, and their jeep, remained in the middle of the road until our troops dislodged the Germans.

Sunday, June 4, 1944

Clark and Truscott visited my CP at noon today. Both were

in a most friendly mood, delighted, happy, and all smiles. Both congratulated me for the Division's breakthrough. Clark said, "I am going to see to it that you and the 36th Division get credit for this in the newspapers back home. You have done a marvelous job."

This announced procedure was quite different from the ordinary course of events. So, in order to waste no time, I sent for Wick Fowler and told him what Clark had said. We were pleased. Now he could wire the full story to the **Dallas Morning News.** In order to save time, I made one of my reconnaissance planes available for him to get his story back to Army Headquarters, for all news stories have to be OKed by the Army Censor.

When he returned, I asked Wick if he got his story off promptly to the United States. He replied, "No General. By the time I arrived at Army Headquarters, Clark had changed his mind, and my story did not get by the Army Censor." So again we get no credit.

I have ordered all three regiments to continue pushing on toward Rome. They are making good progress. Everybody is pleased. However, only a few prisoners are being taken, which is evidence we are not advancing fast enough.

Today I was with the leading battalion of the 141st, left column. Stack was with the other two regiments, right column. My column was held up by a German delaying force at Marino until 1:30 PM, when resistance vanished. The Germans hastily withdrew, hurrying toward Rome. Then we pushed through the town with tanks and TDs leading the way. We crowded the foot troops onto the tanks, and all other vehicles, as tightly as possible, and we traveled along without meeting resistance.

Our road ran into Highway No. 7, the road to Rome, on our left. When my column arrived at the junction, I met a colonel of the 1st Armored Division who had just arrived there, leading his column of tanks. He told my Battalion Commander (Red Morgan) that he had the right-of-way on Highway 7 and that he, Morgan, could follow his column. I told the colonel that we would take the right half of the road, and he could take the left. He did not like this.

I noted that a battery of his artillery was in position, prepared to fire in the direction from which we had come. They had realized just in time to avoid another tragedy that we were friendly troops. Thank the Lord!

The head of both columns were abreast and side-by-side as we moved into the outskirts of Rome. There Truscott joined me and explained that I was outside my sector boundary. I knew this, but I had to use Highway 7 to reach the outskirts of Rome. I moved the column north and turned it toward the city on a main street a half mile north of Highway No. 7.

The Germans were waiting for us. They commanded the street with machine gun and tank fire. We had to advance from house to house. Progress was slow. Four of our dead lay sprawled on the sidewalk.

One of our tanks was hit and burning in the street with the crew inside. Not a pleasant sight. The lieutenant, who commanded the tanks, became hysterical at the tragic death of his men. Shouting and weeping, wringing his hands, pacing back and forth, he cursed the war, his superiors and me. No longer able to command, I sent him with an escort to the hospital. Poor fellow. "Shell shock" is the term sometimes applied to this hysteria.

Artillery began to shell our vehicles which were stopped well to the rear. At first I could not determine where the shells were coming from. Through my field glasses I could see a battery of our friends to the south, the 1st Armored Division. They were in position, their guns pointed right at us, firing on us. Suddenly they stopped. Fortunately, only two of our men were slightly wounded and only three trucks disabled. I have no patience with triggerhappy people.

The German resistance ended an hour or so before dusk. Then the Italian women came into the streets and covered the bodies of our soldiers with flowers from their gardens.

I joined Stack at the Division CP which had been established in a motion picture studio. The 142nd and 143rd Combat Teams had gone into bivouac.

At about 10:00 PM, Colonel Carlton, the Chief of Staff of the VI Corps, called and asked, "Where are you?"

"On the edge of Rome," I said.

"Which edge?"

"Southeast edge."

"Well, everybody is on the near edge of Rome. Nobody is on the far edge. The General (Truscott) wants somebody on the far side of Rome, but everybody is sitting on this side of Rome. He wants to report that the VI has taken Rome. Do you understand?"

"Yes, Sir."

Not a direct order, but an implied one.

All the troops were in bivouac, resting after four strenuous days and nights. Were the Germans going to fight for possession of the city? Were the streets blocked by defended barricades? I did not know. But, I sent out an order for the staff and artillery and infantry commanders to assemble for a conference at 11:00 PM. There, I ordered the Division to resume the advance through Rome.

None of us knew any of the streets. They were a maze anyway, crisscrossing and leading every which way. We had maps of the city, but a map is not much help at night. There were no Italian policemen, no directional signs, no street lights, and no lights in any of the buildings.

My orders were very simple. I designated an assembly area for each combat team about 5 miles northwest of the city, directed each commander to advance through the city to his assigned area with the least possible delay; the Division to advance initially in column of combat teams in the order 141st, 142nd, 143rd; the head of the 141st to pass an initial point at 2:00 AM; each combat team commander to impress as many Italian civilians as necessary to act as guides.

At the conclusion of my orders, Harmony, exhibiting a feeling of helplessness, asked, "How am I going to get my combat team through Rome when I have no route nor boundary?"

"I do not know the condition of the streets within the city; nor do I know where, nor what type of resistance you may meet. We will start out in a column of combat teams, yours leading. You will be free to go where the situation demands. I just want you to get into your assembly area on the other side of the city in the shortest possible time."

My words did not change his attitude.

I dismissed the conference and lay down on my bunk.

NOTE: Such was the day-by-day account of the breakthrough at Velletri. However, it is possible to be so close to an object as not to see it in full perspective.

Therefore, to complete the record I have secured permission from **Military Review**, January, 1963, and from the author, to append here the excellent article "A Classic Stratagem On Mount Artemisio," written by an official Army historian, Dr. Ernest F. Fisher.

Backed by the daily accounts, this summary will give a full picture of the golden moment of The 36th. See Appendix D

CHAPTER SIXTEEN
Pursuit and Stop

Rome, Italy
Mondays, June 5, 1944

At 1:00 AM, I got up and went to see how the 141st was getting along. Harmony, whom I found after a 20 minute search, told me he would be ready to march at 2:00 AM. I then went to the 142nd. There I found the combat team commander, Colonel Lynch, and his staff assembled near the initial point and his troops moving into position preparatory to following the 141st. I went back to the CP of the 141st. No staff; no troops. Harmony said he had not yet found his battalion commanders. I told him to follow the 142nd. Lynch started his march promptly at 2:00 AM, well-supplied with capable Italian guides to show him the way. I accompanied his regiment. It is wonderful to have a subordinate commander who knows how to get results.

At first, as we moved along the dark streets, we could hear people clapping their hands at the windows of the buildings, but we could not see them. Later, when it became evident that the Germans had abandoned the city, men, women and children, in night dress and slippers, came into the dark streets to welcome the Americans. Some ran up and down the column offering wine to the soldiers. Since the Germans had withdrawn, our advance through the city turned out to be merely a night march. Day was just breaking when we crossed the Tiber and passed the Basilica of St. Peter. After daylight, the Italians appeared on the streets dressed for a holiday; women and children threw flowers at the passing soldiers. I am certain they were sincere in their joy.

In order to preserve the energy of the foot troops, I authorized commanders to fill every possible space on vehicles with infantrymen. They were riding on everything that had tracks or wheels. I saw three men riding on the tube of a 155mm howitzer; others were on the trials. I counted 16 riding on a jeep and a ½ ton trailer. Springs and tires suffered, but the whole division was on the western outskirts of Rome soon after daylight. I was with the advance guard.

Just west of the city a well-organized delaying force stopped our advance for several hours. Several of our men were killed there. Lynch and "Pete" Green, 132nd FA Battalion, had their observation post in a villa from which we had an excellent view of the ground occupied by the enemy. But, the Germans were so well concealed that it took us two hours to locate their main positions. After that, Green's artillery and the infantry, working together for about an hour, were able to drive them off. In my enthusiasm, I tried to help Lynch and Green select targets for artillery fire on groups of Germans whom I could see running about from time to time. This, of course, was none of my business and must have been much to the disgust of both of them. I saw an antitank gun firing from a building and asked Green to knock it out. He did. Another German antitank gun destroyed one of our tanks. The Germans fired intermittently on our observation post on top of the house with machine guns and mortars. The driver of Green's jeep was killed by a mortar shell.

The Division arrived on the western outskirts of Rome without its usual signal communications. Because of the resistance in front of the 142nd, it was necessary to deploy the 141st on its right and to place the 143rd in a reserve position. I assembled several staff officers, issued verbal orders which they were to transmit to the various combat team commanders, and sent them off in jeeps. No difficulty. The deployment was made as directed without confusion.

While this deployment was in progress, I went to another elevation where one could see the ground occupied by the Germans. Nearby was what appeared to be an abandoned jail or prison, for there was no one in it and the gates and doors stood ajar. I learned from a native that all prisoners, as well as all keepers, had been turned out this morning by the retreating Germans.

My command post is located in a beatiful home on the west edge of Rome; Villa Panfili, via Aurelia Andica, No. 3, Principi Sr. Doria, Commandant Sr. Cabriotti Giovanni, in case you want to look it up. This was the headquarters of a German General who departed at 2:00 AM at about the same time the 36th Division was entering the eastern edge of Rome.

Three Miles North of Rome, Italy
Tuesday, June 6, 1944

I am told that the 36th Division is the first to pass through Rome with all of its men and equipment. My men are happy and proud of their achievements, and I am proud of them.

When we passed through the city, the streets were pitch black, and we did not really see Rome. As soon as Army Headquarters could get themselves into comfortable billets, an order was issued placing Rome off limits for combat troops.

This is not the way to treat the men who made it possible for the high command to sleep in clean, comfortable beds in hotels they have commandeered for their own use. There are two types of soldiers. First, there are those who fight and endure great hardship. This demands stamina, knowledge and intelligence. It is true that at times, when there are no bathing facilities, these "men of action" are sweaty, dirty and even smelly, but they do what only real men can do. Then there are those who do not fight. They don't like to have combat troops around because, I presume, they give them a feeling of inferiority. So, they order the combat troops to stay away.

Today I received a message from General Marshall, Chief of Staff, in which he personally congratulated me and the Division for our brilliant maneuver which had broken the German defenses east of Rome. I shall publish it to the Division tomorrow.

Bracciano, Italy
Wednesday, June 7, 1944

We are making rapid progress. I visited Lynch at his CP. Many of his men were riding bicycles. He explained that his advance guard had beaten off a German bicycle delaying force a short while before and his troops had pushed them so fast they had to abandon their bicycles which were parked in a nearby woods. He moved his combat team on toward Civitavecchia, meeting almost no resistance, and bivouacked in the outskirts of the city for the night.

The Division is now pursuing the German retreat. This is a similar action to what other Divisions were doing just after Salerno.

Five Miles North of Civitavecchia, Italy
Thursday, June 8, 1944

There is only light resistance in our front, and we are advancing 5 to 10 miles per day, taking some prisoners and losing very few men.

North of Civitavecchia, Italy
Friday, June 9, 1944

Our friends in the G-3 section of the Fifth Army Headquarters are bellyaching each day because we do not advance as far as they would like. If we advance 5 miles, they say we should have gone 10 miles. If we go 10, they say we should have gone 15 miles. This is typical of inexperienced staff officers of higher commands who have never fired a short nor missed a meal.

The G-4 section of Fifth Army Headquarters has fallen flat on its face. We are having a devil's own time to keep ourselves supplied. There are no Army supply dumps. We have to go all the way back to the Port of Naples for food, gasoline and ammunition—a 200 mile round trip. I don't think Carl Phinney has had any real sleep since Rome. We put two drivers on each of our trucks and keep them going back and forth to Naples night and day. The men spell each other at the wheel. We have to keep pushing with everything we have.

It is the Army's business to keep its supply dumps close to our rear so we may give our full attention to the front. But, Army is not doing it. So, today I went back to visit Corps, Army and Port of Naples Headquarters to see what I could do to get some help. Corps could not help At Army Headquarters I was looked upon by the staff as a robber, trying to deprive that sanctorum of its conveniences, or as a charlatan trying to tell them how to run their business. I got nowhere.

At Naples I went directly to see my friend, General Art Wilson. I explained my situation and told him I needed three truck trains (100 trucks) attached to my Division at once. He smiled and said, "Well, Fred, I have the trucks alright, but I have orders not to assign any transportation to anyone without Clark's OK. The Army intends to keep everything under its thumb."

After a pause, he continued. "Clark will hang me if I let you have them without his permission, but I know you need them. I'll tell you what I'll do. I'll give you the 100 trucks. If Clark doesn't like it, I'll get out of it some way. What do you want me to load onto them when I send them up? I'll get them off tonight."

"Gasoline," I answered. "Every truck loaded with gasoline."

I thanked him. It's a real pleasure to do business with somebody who knows how to get things done. I'll have Phinney take charge of the truck trains when they arrive; he'll be looking for them.

I was back at my CP at 5:30 PM. What a day!

Near Tarquinia, Italy
Saturday, June 10, 1944

Art Wilson kept his promise. Today 65 trucks arrived, each loaded with gasoline in 5 gallon cans. Phinney established a gasoline dump near Montalto to supply the Division vehicles. Everybody is happy.

In addition to these trucks, all our units have picked up and repaired at least a hundred vehicles of various types which the Germans abandoned in their haste to get away. We are still picking up some each day, and our mechanics are working around the clock to get them running. These German vehicles, added to our own trains, are a great help in many ways. They make it possible to keep our fast moving units supplied forward from our temporary division supply points. Carl Phinney and his men are doing a wonderful job.

Near Montalto, Italy
Sunday, June 11, 1944

Yesterday, Brigadier General Butler, Deputy Corps Commander, came to my CP and made some uncomplimentary remarks about my Division Engineer. He said my engineers were not "putting out," and had no plans to meet the present situation; that Truscott is displeased at our progress; that we had no trucks available to move infantry forward to meet our possible needs; and made some other silly statements, all of which were unwarranted, unfair, and untrue. Butler is a nuisance.

I am 57 years old today, so the Mess Sergeant baked a cake for me and decorated it with "Happy Birthday" and many candles. We had pork chops, stewed peas, bread, butter, jelly and sliced pineapple in addition to the cake. Bob Ives contributed candy and fruit cake to the menu. Except for the cake and candy, this is the same ration that is issued to the troops when they are not fighting. When they are fighting, they "feast" on canned C and K rations.

After Phinney established his gasoline refilling point for vehicles of the Division—thanks to Art Wilson—our "highly efficient" Army G-4 commandeers it, takes it over as an Army gasoline distributing point, and deprives us of control just when we need it most. This is one hell of a situation when a front line division, engaged in a pursuit, must not only supply itself from the base at Naples, but must, in addition, supply the Army distributing points because the Army is not doing it.

Orbetello, Italy
Monday, June 12, 1944

I am fed up with the theoretical Army Staff. Now the Army Military Police Officer has told my G-4 that we must turn in to Army Headquarters at once all German vehicles we have repaired, are now using, and desperately need. He says Army Regulations require all captured materials to be turned in as government property. True. But, they don't say when. And further, what better use can the government make of them? Combat Regulations stress the need to push the enemy with everything you have while you have him on the run. God deliver me from book soldiers. Could it be that all this harassment is done deliberately to impede our progress and minimize our success? But why?

Today I received a letter from Clark inquiring whether or not I would desire assignment as Commandant of the Infantry School. Here it is, dated June 10, 1944.

"Dear Fred,

"I have received word from General McNair asking as to your availability for assignment as the Commandant of The Infantry School. What are your desires?

"I want you to know my deep admiration for you and the leadership you have demonstrated in this recent battle for Rome. Your Division performed outstandingly, and I am very proud of you. There is a possibility of your Division leaving my control soon. I tell you these things, for they may help you in arriving at your decision. Please know that if the 36th Division were to remain in the Fifth Army Command, of course, I would always feel secure with you at its helm. I realize, too, that you have been overseas for a long time and have had much combat. This opportunity may be a fine one for you.

"Please be frank and let me know immediately your desires, and I will act accordingly.

Sig: Wayne
Mark W. Clark, Lieutenant General,
Commanding

"P.S. Consider all I tell you here as secret not to be discussed with others. I tell you this so as to help you make your decision."

I have been expecting this letter for some time. It is cleverly worded to save Clark's and my faces, and to give the impression of a choice, but there is no choice. It is a reassignment.

It results directly from my conversation with Keyes after the Rapido, in which I requested reassignment if Devers, Clark and he lacked confidence in me, and Keyes' too quick reply that I should be reassigned after the next successful operation of the Division.

It is obvious that, as a result of my conversation with Keyes, my "reassignment" has been "in the works" since the Rapido. Clark must have arranged this with McNair when he was in Washington last April before our breakthrough at Velletri. Otherwise, why would McNair choose me, at this time, from many others scattered all over the world? Clark is not responsible for filling vacancies in the United States. Only in order to carry out a prior plan would he be so solicitous for The Infantry School that he would send a Division Commander engaged in pursuit of the enemy to be its Commandant. Only to carry out a prior plan would an Army Commander "reward" a Major General, whose Division has just broken through the German defenses at Anzio and opened the gates to Rome, by sending him back to the United States.

I do not want to leave the Division, but I will not be sorry to leave this Theater and this Army.

I have no confidence in Clark's ability to select and assign proper missions to combat divisions. The same goes for Keyes. I have already been assigned two impossible missions: one, to cross the Rapido; the other, to butt into a German "stonewall" defense at Anzio. Although the latter was cancelled at my request, I may be given other impossible missions which would unnecessarily kill and maim great numbers of men.

I do not wish to be subjected to more official insults from Clark similar to the one I had to take after the Rapido when he relieved my key officers, over my objections, and without any specific charge against any of them, and then arbitrarily assigned their replacements.

Clark gives his ear to disgruntled former members of the Division now on duty at his Headquarters and accepts them as a better source of information regarding personnel and morale of the Division than I am.

I am sure Clark has confidence in my ability as a Division commander. He just wants to get rid of me. He and his staff do not seek and do not appreciate any suggestions for improving tactics and supply as they affect my Division.

Well! I have bellyached enough. Here, with some equivocation and flattery, equal to that of Clark's, is my reply:

"Dear Wayne,

"Your letter just received, regarding my possible assignment as Commandant, The Infantry School, presented a difficult problem for me to solve. I have decided to accept the assignment.

"I have been with this Division nearly three years. I feel toward it as one feels toward the members of one's immediate family. The members of the Division are devoted to me, personally; they have absolute confidence in my ability to lead them in battle. They have responded with enthusiasm to every directive I have given them.

"They have succeeded in every mission assigned to them except the crossing of the Rapido. Their failure there was no fault of their own. It will be hard to leave these splendid officers and men. In a way, I feel that I am deserting them at a time when they need me most. I know, too, that the people of Texas will be disappointed when they learn of my departure from the Division. However, I am 57 years old today. I am the oldest division commander in the Army.

"I have commanded a Division longer than any other except General Persons. I believe that the feeling of the War Department toward me is that I am too old for combat responsibility. I am not too old for my job, but I cannot convince the War Department of the fact when the claim is made that division commanders should not be over 45 years of age.

"I am troubled about my successor. I am of the opinion that either General Stack or General Frederick would take up where I leave off and carry the Division forward along the lines I have followed. I have only one request. That is that the Division not be given to General Butler. I am certain that he will spoil the present high morale in a short time. He is essentially a staff officer type. I shall regret severing my close association with you in combat. I have enjoyed every moment of my service under your command.

"In view of the above, I desire that I be made available for assignment as Commandant of The Infantry School.

"Sincerely,

Fred"

General Crittenberger assumed command of the IV Corps yesterday, so I will have to educate him and his staff since they have had no combat experience. But I must not let him know I am doing it. This will be the third corps commander and staff that I have had to educate in the capabilities and limitations of the Infantry: Dawley, an artilleryman; Keyes, a cavalryman; Crittenberger, another cavalryman. This is backwards to what it should be. Truscott, even though a cavalryman, knows his business. I like to work with him. We understand each other's language.

Art Wilson, who commands the Port of Naples, called at my CP with Crittenberger. I took them up front. At the time, our troops were advancing along Highway No. 1, meeting minor resistance.

I told Harmony that I am going to relieve him from command of the 141st Infantry unless he does better from here on. He is too slow, lacks tactical skill, and is too theoretical.

I explained to him a day or two ago that he should keep his leading troops off the road and follow along the high ground or concealment along the side of the road when pursuing the enemy. The German delaying forces are not strong enough to cover the whole front. They are practically tied to the roads so they can get away quickly when they have to move. The thing to do is to outflank them, get behind them and cut them off.

Nevertheless, because the Germans had not been firing for some time, he concentrated men and vehicles in a farmyard by the side of the road. The Germans waited until they had a lucrative target, then shot them up with artillery, killing and wounding a number of men and destroying many vehicles. Too bad!

What to do about Major Ross Young, Executive Officer of the 141st Infantry? I have decided, as a result of my conversation with him over the phone last June 3rd, to relieve him. Not for what he said about Stack and me, but because he does not have the aggressive attitude that a Regimental Executive Officer should have. Stack and I know that, at times, we are called all the names in the book to our backs, so there is no point to getting excited just because we happen to hear some insubordinate language not intended for our ears. Young may remain in the Division provided he can find another assignment not involving duty with the three fighting regiments.

General Johnson, Commanding General, Rome Area, visited the Division CP today to tell me that the Hotel Elisio has been rented in Rome for the exclusive use of officers of the 36th Division as a rest hotel, and that a suitable villa has been reserved for the use of general officers and colonels of the Division when in Rome. Some time ago I asked Johnson to find these accommodations for us.

I have been ordered to send Stack to England for a ten-day observation tour. This is a waste of his time. Nothing to be learned in England that Stack and I do not already know. I need his services here. We are engaged in important operations.

The Division broke through the German delaying position in our front today after decisively defeating two battalions of the German 303rd Infantry regiment.

Ten Miles South of Grosseto, Italy
Friday, June 16, 1944

Another letter from Clark:

> "Dear Fred,
>
> "I have a note on my calendar which tells me that today, June 11, is your birthday. Congratulations and many happy returns.
>
> "I believe that every man in the Fifth Army knows what a splendid job you turned in as Commanding General, 36th Division, and how much it has contributed to our success. I shall be grateful to you for your help.
>
> "Let us hope that on your next birthday you can be with your family at home and that our battle here will be over and done.
>
> "With best wishes, I am,"

He is not going to let me forget how pleasant it will be for me to be out of his command. He wants the record to indicate that he is not pushing me out.

I am thankful to General Al Gruenther, Clark's Chief of Staff. I called him and explained why I wanted to hold onto the captured German vehicles. He said, "Keep them. You don't have to turn them in now. Turn them in when you no longer need them."

Whenever I can do business with him, things go well.

The 143rd is stopped until the Engineers can get some bridges over the streams and canals. We must get our tanks and tank destroyers over so they can assist the infantry to advance.

I watched the MP Sergeant George Clanton loading German POWs onto a truck to send them back to the "cage." He is six feet tall, weighs 225 pounds, and was all business. He took them as they came—privates, NCOs, officers—all mixed up. Each one stepped up onto a bench, then onto the truck-bed, then moved to the front of the truck-bed and stood, facing the rear. The prisoners tried to spread out to avoid being crowded, but the Sergeant would make room for more by shoving forward those near the rear end, using all of his 225 pounds.

One prisoner pointed to his officer's insignia as he approached the bench, indicating that he should not have to ride, crowded in with his enlisted men. The Sergeant grabbed him by the arm, yanked him up onto the bench and shoved him onto the truck. When it seemed to me that the truck was fully loaded, I told the Sergeant so. He replied, "Sir, the truck will carry 36 POWs. I always count them."

He loaded on ten more. They were packed so tightly that no one could turn around. However, they had less than one hour to travel to the "cage" and by holding on to one another, they could keep from falling out when going around curves in the road.

I issued the following memorandum because I may be leaving the Division any day now, and I want the men to know that their accomplishments during my command have been appreciated. They do not know that I am leaving:

"It is with great pride that I congratulate you on your magnificent achievements in battle to date.

"Nine months ago you landed on the hostile beaches of Paestum, the vanguard of your country's army, to crash the gates of Hitler's European fortress. In that, your first action of the war, fighting courageouly against well-trained enemy forces of long combat experience, you established the first American beachhead on the European continent, the first to be established anywhere by Americans against the German opposition. For this achievement alone you have a right to feel justly proud.

"Later on, while subject to hardships that have never been exceeded by any troops anywhere, you drove the enemy from his well-organized and stoutly defended positions in the hill masses of Camino and Sammucro; from Mt. Maggiore, Mt. Lungo, Mt. Rotundo and San Pietro.

"You punished him severely. His losses in men and material were great. Through this period of bitter winter weather, under the most adverse conditions of climate and terrain, you maintained a cheerfulness and enthusiasm far superior to that of your enemy.

"Then came your gallant effort on the Rapido. Let us bow our heads in reverence to the fallen comrades who crossed that bitterly contested stream and put up a great, if losing, fight, as great from the standpoint of sheer gallantry and determination as any recorded in the annals of our Armed forces.

"At Cassino and Castellone Ridge you were severely tested. You suffered losses, but you captured vital high ground from the strongly entrenched enemy, and held it throughout the month of hard fighting.

"After a well-deserved rest you were ordered to attack again at a critical time and at a critical place near Velletri, to break the stronghold of the enemy defenses east of Rome. History will record forever your outstanding success. In a week of brilliant maneuvers and relentless assaults on one position after another, Velletri, Mt. Artemisio, Rocco Di Papa, Marino and beyond, you killed and captured well over three thousand of the enemy; routed him from his strong, well-organized positions and drove him across the Tiber in disorder.

"Your brilliant performance on that famous battlefield was a major contribution to the capture of the first European capital to be recovered from Nazi occupation. For your magnificent achievements there, General Marshall sent a personal message of congratulations to you and to me. The German army is still reeling from your blows. The relentless pressure of your attacks will substantially shorten the duration of the war. Your victorious march through the cities of your enemy cannot long be delayed."

South of Grosseto, Italy
Saturday, June 17, 1944

Clark visited my CP today and said, "You and your Division have been doing a grand job."

He also said that I would be transferred home on about July 7th, to be Commandant, The Infantry School; that General Marshall will visit my Division either tomorrow or next day and that he intends to recommend to Marshall that Frederick be given command of the 36th Division. Clark seems to think that Frederick is a world beater. He has not done anything to indicate to me that he is a world beater. He has, however, accomplished every mission assigned to him. Many other commanders have done the same.

There is no doubt but that the War Department considers me too old for combat duty, but since they are taking me out, with Clark's help in pushing me out, I am pleased that it is coming at a time when I and the Division have received the congratulations of all the higher commanders for outstanding success. Any business organization that would throw out an executive who has been outstandingly successful, would be headed for bankruptcy.

Today we are getting ready to attack and break the delaying positions of the German forces in front of Grosseto.

Grosseto, Italy
Sunday, June 18, 1944

Today about 4:30 PM we were preparing to move my CP to

Grosseto when word was received that Marshall, accompanied by Generals Devers, Clark, Handy, Barr, and others were on their way to my CP at Collecchio, south of Grosseto. Our move was temporarily suspended.

Marshall took me aside where he could talk to me alone. He asked me a number of detailed questions regarding the tactical situation, the dispositions of my troops, the strength and fighting habits of the Germans in my front, noted the losses of the Division since Velletri, and congratulated me and the Division.

When congratulating me and the Division, he said, "I think it is marvelous the way you were able to coordinate your supply and other services with your tactical operations and keep moving as rapidly as you did."

I thanked him and told him that I had received his cable of personal congratulations to me and the Division and that we all appreciated it. He said, "But you have done much since then."

I told him that the opportunity I have had and am having to pursue a defeated and retreating enemy seldom comes to a division commander, and that I have tried to make the most of it. I did not tell him what a time I have had to keep the Army Staff from messing up my pursuit.

After our conversation, he and his party went on to the bivouac of the 142nd Infantry, near Grosseto. He told me he did not want me to accompany him to the 142nd because he had "too many people trailing along already." I stayed at my CP during the remainder of his visit within the area of the Division; less than an hour.

I greeted Generals Devers and Handy briefly. I wanted to talk to Clark but did not have an opportunity. All of them congratulated me enthusiastically on my achievements since May 25th. Devers was particularly generous in his praise.

As soon as the Marshall party left the Division area, I moved my CP to Grosseto into an abandoned sanitorium which is a modern building and will be especially suitable for an army hospital later.

The retreating Germans have destroyed all bridges and have mined the passages to them. Our 111th Engineer Battalion is busy removing the mines and filling in the gaps. We do not have the time nor material to construct new bridges, so a bulldozer at the destroyed bridge pushes earth from the road side up onto the solid roadway. When a good big pile is accumulated, the bulldozer pushes it into the gap. After shoving in several piles, the earth is packed down and the gap is passable. Depending on the size of the stream, most of the destroyed bridges are filled within 30 minutes, or less. Corps and Army Engineers later will clear the streams and construct temporary bridges.

Pestalozzi, Italy
Monday, June 19, 1944

I have just received word that the 36th Division will be relieved on June 27th and will then move by water from Civitavecchia to Salerno, where it will pass to the control of Headquarters Seventh Army. This is General Patch. I presume that the Division will be assigned for an amphibious operation which I have just learned is pending. I deeply regret that I will not be with it.

If I had known that the Division was to pass to Patch's Seventh Army and invade Southern France, I would never have accepted Clark's reassignment.

Tuesday, June 20, 1944

I visited the CPs of the 517th, 361st, and 143rd Infantry Regiments. The 517th and 361st are attached to the Division. I noted on the roads much equipment and many destroyed vehicles abandoned by the Germans in their retreat. They also abandoned nine 155mm artillery howitzers. They were abandoned when our observers saw the Germans moving into position and put concentrated fire on them, driving them off in disorder. A German prisoner told me that he heard Colonel Solders (German) give an order last night at Montepescali (now CP 143rd Inf) to his staff to retire toward Florence, delaying as they go; that the next stop would be ten miles to the northeast of Montepescali and east of Highway No. 73. Apparently, we gave the Germans quite a beating yesterday.

Wednesday, June 21, 1944

Today the Division advanced 10 kilometers toward Pisa. An enemy strongpoint delayed our advance seven hours. It was stronger than anticipated and our advance guard had to be reinforced. I would like to be near Pisa before we are relieved on the 27th, but to do this, we will have to go faster. We must push harder.

My CP is in an open field as no suitable building is available. But this is quite all right, since the enemy artillery and air force are of no concern and camouflage is not necessary.

Friday, June 23, 1944

Yesterday Clark came by. Said I would be relieved on about July 7th; that I could take Lt. Kelley, my Aide, Charles as an Aide, and Willis Bell, my orderly, back to the States with me; that he was attaching Frederick to the Division so he can become oriented before he takes over command when I leave; and that he wanted me to "sell" Frederick to the Division.

I told this to Stack, who has done a grand job as Assistant Division Commander, and who is senior to Frederick, and who has had considerably more combat experience than Frederick. He does not like the idea of Frederick taking command, and I don't blame him. Bell was happy when I told him he was going home with me. I have not yet notified the others.

The going up front is slow, too slow. Yesterday, two German Tiger tanks stopped several hundred vehicles, tanks and tank destroyers of the 1st Armored Division almost all day. Last evening, just before dark, two of our patrols knocked out the two tanks. The armored force had been puttering around all day trying to scare the German tanks away. It remained for a half dozen doughboys to do the job for them, while the powerful Armored Combat Command B stood still along the highways, burning up thousands of gallons of gasoline.

I have prepared a message to the Division announcing my departure and will issue it on the 26th day of June. I hesitate to issue it now because I fear it will have a bad effect on the present fighting effort of the troops. I know that all in the Division are going to be disappointed when they learn that I am leaving.

The French commander now in possession of Elba offered to help me by landing 500 Italian commandos on the shore a few miles north of my present position. I sent Ives to Elba in a cub plane to accept the offer. I told him to arrange for the amphibious operation to be made tomorrow night. We will see what happens. They really want to help.

Bob had an experience. When he and the pilot came in to land, there was a lot of running around below, and they did not know whether or not they were going to be shot down. But they landed safely. The French commander received him courteously and was quite eager to join forces with us, but he had little ammunition and no water or land transportation. He wanted us to provide these which we could not do. We did give him some rifle ammunition. It all came to naught.

Follonica, Italy
Saturday, June 24, 1944

Robert Frederick arrived at my CP last evening. He will be here a few days as an observer before he takes over command.

Today I moved my CP well forward to avoid another move tomorrow, because we are advancing about 10 miles per day. We may be shelled by the Krauts before we get out of here, but I don't think so. They are too occupied, with their retreat and with saving as much equipment as possible, to give any attention to a few people and vehicles moving about a division CP.

I visited the 517th Infantry, which was recently attached to us, to get some combat experience, and found the men of the leading battalion in a state of great excitement. The battalion headquarters had received word that a German patrol was on the wooded hill about 1200 yards in front of them. I do not know what they had out forward in the way of security, but everyone had a rifle or a carbine in hand and was expecting to be attacked at any minute, although one could clearly see 1200 yards in any direction. It is strange, but true, that the farther to the rear one is, the greater the excitement when someone cries, "Germans over there."

Sunday, June 25, 1944

The fighting is continuing. I have made it a point to conduct the operation of the Division in a manner that our advance will be as rapid as possible and without excessive losses. I have accomplished this by taking advantage of the terrain to turn the Germans out of position by attacking them on their flanks and rear from high ground; by avoiding direct frontal attacks; by maintaining close artillery support for the infantry; by going after key terrain on high ground; by using trucks to move reserve battalions, thus permitting them to get more rest and less marching; by personal visits to the various commanders; and by taking a personal interest in the activities of all units of the Division. I have bypassed unimportant terrain features and thus saved time.

Hess and Stack both stated to me that they were very disappointed when they learned that I am going to the leave the Division.

General Ryder, 34th Division, came to my CP to say he would like to take over the advance tomorrow morning, if I have no objections. Since we already have advanced over 200 miles and captured over 5000 prisoners, and have been fighting continuously for a month, I have no objections. Neither does anybody else in the Division, even though we won't get to Pisa.

Rome, Italy
Monday, June 26, 1944

I wanted the Division to know that I was being "rewarded" for the breakthrough at Velletri by being sent back to the States, and issued a memorandum today:

"To the Members of the 36th Infantry Division:

"I have been informed that I am to be relieved from command of your Division and that I am to be reassigned to duty in the United States as The Commandant, The Infantry School.

"This is a great disappointment to me for I had hoped to remain with you throughout your combat operations in this war. However, I am appreciative of the battle experience I have had with you and the friendships I have made.

"I have been with you for nearly three years. Your loyalty, devotion to duty, gallantry in action and pride in your Division have been all that any commander could desire. You have enthusiastically responded to every directive I have given you. No soldier can do more than that.

"Your next Division Commander will be Brigadier General Robert T. Frederick. I know you will show him the same loyalty, enthusiasam and confidence that you have shown to me.

"I greatly regret leaving you. Wherever you go, whatever you do, you shall always have my deepest personal interest and my very best wishes."

After the 34th Division passed through us this morning, I assembled the Division preparatory to transporting it to a staging area near Rome. I want every man in the Division to have at least six hours in Rome, so the movement has been scheduled accordingly. The exclusive use of a hotel in Rome has been procured for accommodation of officers of the Division where they will have an opportunity to clean up and rest. The capacity of the hotel is only 65, but by adding cots we can take care of more. I also arranged for a delousing and bath unit and a clothing unit to be installed in the center of the staging area where the men just back from the dirt and filth of the battlefield can have a good bath, shave, haircut and get new, clean uniforms prior to visiting Rome.

I went to Rome this morning and took up residence in the

villa of Sr. D. Virgilio Cordeschi, Via Jacopo Peri 11. This is a very beautiful and comfortable home which Trimble Brown arranged with General Johnson for senior officers. I have invited Generals Stack and Hess; Colonels Harmony, Lynch and Adams; Lt. Colonel Trimble Brown; Lieutenants Kelley and Walker to occupy the villa with me. Trimble is in charge of the villa and has arranged for service and meals.

Many officers spoke to me this evening at the hotel, expressing their regrets that I am leaving the Division. They appeared to be really disappointed. The only real reward I receive for my past three years with the Division are the statements of appreciation from the men.

Wednesday, June 28, 1944

Today was most interesting because I, together with Stack and Hess, Brown, Kelley 'and Charles, visited Vatican City and was granted an audience with Pope Pius XII. The audience was arranged by Chaplain Fenton of the 141st Infantry, who accompanied us.

The Pope was most gracious, spoke to us in English and asked each of us what part of the United States we were from. His Holiness asked me whether the Catholic Chaplains of my Division were setting a proper example for the officers and men, and I assured him that they were. He said he had seen many American soldiers in St. Peter's and on the Piazza of St. Peter's, and he had concluded that American soldiers were very pious. I replied that they are pious and religious men, but that in all groups there are some who disappoint us. He replied, "Yes, yes. I know."

He then told me that we should precede him and his Swiss Guard to the hall where the public audiences are held, and stand to the left of his chair in the place of honor.

The hall was packed with Allied men and women in uniform: Australian, American, British, Canadian, French, Polish, and Red Cross personnel. All eyes were on Stack, Hess and me as we walked down the designated aisle toward the dais. The large crowd was respectfully silent as the Pope, preceded by his Swiss Guard, was carried on a portable chair to the dais. There he took his place on the chair overlooking the assemblage. He addressed the group, first in English, then in French, and gave them his blessing.

When he finished, he first walked over to me, took my hand,

gave me his blessing, and did the same for each of my staff officers in turn. Afterward, he passed along the edge of the crowd, permitting anyone who wished to kiss the ring on his hand. After a few minutes, he resumed his seat in the portable chair and, preceded by his guard, departed in the same manner as he had arrived.

Prior to and after the audience, we were permitted to visit many rooms in the Vatican. I have never seen such dignified beauty—marble, gold, paintings, mosaics, tapestries, furniture, stained glass windows, carpets, altars—all were beautiful beyond description, and perfect. The Sistine Chapel and St. Peter's itself were most impressive. In one room we saw what is said to be the most valuable tapestry in the world. At a distance of just a few feet, it appeared to be an oil painting. It was necessary to examine it closely in order to know that it was really a tapestry.

From persons of every grade and rank I have received expressions of regret at my leaving the Division. Enlisted men, officers, sergeants, lieutenants, majors and captains, especially those of the Infantry, have spoken to me whenever they met me. They are truly sorry I am leaving them. Sometimes my feelings get the better of me for I, also, am sorry to leave them. Some of them speak with appreciation for what I have done to avoid costly tactical maneuvers and to look after the welfare of the enlisted men. This is my greatest reward. Perhaps the greatest that can come to one who has carried the responsibility of command of men in battle.

Friday, June 30, 1944

I have received letters of commendation from Clark, Truscott and Crittenberger, and a letter of appreciation from Colonel Paul D. Adams. Each praised the 36th Division and my leadership for accomplishments to date. Each expresses regret at my departure. I know that each is sincere except Clark. There is no letter from Geoffrey Keyes. I presume he feels that he can say nothing complimentary and, therefore, perfers to remain silent.

Monday, July 3, 1944

Last Saturday I flew in my cub to see Clark at his Headquarters. He had asked me to visit him. I do not know why because we had nothing to discuss. After a few awkward moments, I said "Good-bye," and returned to the Division.

Wednesday, July 5, 1944

Received the following letter from Clark, dated July 4, 1944:
"Dear General Walker:

"My heartiest congratulations for your new appointment. I am delighted that The Infantry School will have such a skilled and experienced commandant.

"I know how much the 36th Division will miss you after all you have done for it. Few Divisions have had the good fortune to be guided continuously through as many different and important campaign phases by the same able hand. The long period of thorough training in French Morocco and Algeria, the initial landing at Salerno, and the bitter fighting which ensued; then the long, grueling winter campaign on the main Italian front, particularly hard on the Division commander because of unavoidable, slow progress in comparison to the splendid effort put forth; finally, leading your Division into the fight at the crucial moment of the beachhead break-out and the brilliant operations which resulted in the capture of Rome, all have associated you indissolubly with the 36th Division and the Fifth Army.

"The Fifth Army regrets the loss of one of its veteran commanders, but realizes the great role you are to play in the training of infantry for future battles.

"At this time, I wish to express my very best wishes for every success as Commandant of The Infantry School, as well as to extend my congratulations for the superior job which you performed as Commander of the 36th Division. With my sincere thanks for your constant and loyal cooperation, I am,
Sincerely yours,
/s/ Mark W. Clark
Lieutenant General, USA, Commanding

I am pleased, of course, to receive this letter. Wayne has gone out of his way to say some pleasing things. In fact, his letter reads like a citation for a distinguished service medal. The Rapido is very carefully avoided. Yet it was there that the Division fought with a courage and determination far greater than in any of the other mentioned operations.

In my opinion, this letter was written for the record.

Friday, July 7, 1944

I drove to Paestum to receive a farewell review in my honor voluntarily arranged by the officers and men of the 36th Division on the very same ground where they stormed ashore on the morning of September 9, 1943. This place was appropriate.

Truscott and Brigadier General Wolfe were present. After receiving the honors, I made a short farewell address in which I praised their past achievements, closing with the following:

"After the battle of the Rapido, I received a letter from the widow of one of our captains who was killed there. She praised her husband, saying that he had gone into the service because he wanted to help remove Hitlerism from this earth. She said that in each and every letter she had received from him he had praised the courage and devotion of his men; that he had spoken in the most complimentary terms of the unit commanders within his company and within his regiment. She said that she knew he had died the way he wanted to die, fighting for his country and the principles he believed in. She spoke with enmity and malice of the Germans and concluded her letter with these words, 'General, give it to them.'

"I know of no more appropriate last words to you than to repeat those of that brave and noble woman. The next time you meet the Germans, 'give it to them.'"

I found it hard to suppress my emotions during my talk.

After we observed a moment of silence in honor of those who gave their lives for the success of the Division, the troops passed in review in battalion masses. They marched well, looked well, but it was evident that they did not want me to go.

Afterward, my staff and many others came to say good-bye. I was so nearly overcome at times that I could not speak. Every one who spoke to me is deeply disappointed because I am leaving, and was most sincere in their praise of my leadership. This, I feel, is a great reward which few commanders receive from their troops upon departure from command.

I ate my last lunch at Division Headquarters today. With sadness in my heart, I returned to Rome since I do not desire to remain at Division Headquarters after the farewell parade and after saying good-bye to my staff and commanders.

Sorrento, Italy
Thursday, July 13, 1944

Last week, General "Sandy" Patch, Commander of the Seventh Army, asked me what I thought of Truscott as a Corps Commander. I told him frankly I felt that Truscott is a most competent commander. Patch replied that he did not want Truscott and that he preferred Keyes. I told him Truscott was professionally more capable than Keyes. Today, I talked to Patch's Chief of Staff, who stated confidentially that Patch has tried to replace Truscott, but that the Theater Commander would not approve it. I guess that was Devers. So, Sandy will have to go with Truscott in command of the VI Corps, which will be good for Devers, Patch, Truscott, and the USA.

Over the Atlantic
Saturday, July 15, 1944

At midnight we took off for the Azores. During the night, over the ocean, surrounded by clouds, the ride was monotonous so all of us settled back in our seats to get as much sleep as possible. We were flying at 8000 feet and it grew chilly during the night, but comforters were available for each passenger. I watched for the first light of day through the many clouds, but since we were flying west at 180 miles per hour, the rate of change from night to day, was quite slow. However, just when it was light enough to see the surface of the water, I was surprised to suddenly see land, and then, almost immediately, the airfield. We landed soon after in rain and fog.

After an hour and a half layover for breakfast and refueling, we took off for Bermuda. I was not particularly impressed with the part of Bermuda I saw. Just a spot of land in the ocean.

Washington, D. C.
Sunday, July 16, 1944

I arrived at the Washington airport at 11:30 AM and went immediately to Headquarters, Army Ground Forces, with all members of my party. There I arranged for a 21-day leave for them, and then saw them off at Union Station.

Monday, July 17, 1944

I reported to Ben Lear this morning as Commandant of The Infantry School.

The End

APPENDIX A

Sometime after the battle of Salerno, in a letter to General Walker, Brigadier General Miles A. Cowles, Commanding General of the 36th Division Artillery, described an incident in the defeat of the German tank attacks on September 9th in which he took an active part.

"You will remember that you and I went ashore on the same landing craft. We passed along the north side of the ancient Greek city of Paestum, with its famous Temple of Ceres, and were crossing a field of small Italian tomatoes on our way to a small section house on the railroad, when we received a bombardment from Germans who held the railroad station to the south. After the shooting stopped we worked our way north along the railroad tracks to a tobacco barn where we set up our command post.

"Since the first echelon of my artillery staff was following in another landing craft, I was the only artillery officer with you at the time. All this time there were two things foremost in my mind: (1) Where is the artillery battalion that is scheduled to be in position in this area? (2) When is that German counterattack coming which we prophesied would hit us early in the morning?

"I went looking for our artillery and at the same time keeping my eyes peeled toward the mountains and the Sele River. I saw 13 German tanks moving slowly northward along the base of the mountain. They were within easy range and I wanted to get our guns firing on them. At almost the same moment two of our DUKWs arrived about 400 yards southwest of the tobacco barn, each loaded with a 105mm howitzer and crew, commanded by a sergeant. These howitzers were from the 151st Field Artillery Battalion of the 34th Division, attached to my command, which had accompanied us from Bizerte. Of course, these men didn't know me for I had only met their battalion commander at Mostaganem a short time before we sailed. I ordered them to get their howitzers off the DUKWs immediately, and go into antitank positions, posting one man up in a bell tower nearby to give us warning. We knocked down some stone fences for a field of fire and I ordered them to cut fuses at 'delay' for tank penetration.

"Just as we had finished these preliminaries and were all ready to shoot, an alarm sounded. I saw four Mark IV German tanks to the north, coming over a low crest straight at us, about 200 or 300 yards away. All four were buttoned up and firing machine guns. Quick action was necessary.

"Our first round missed but kicked up a cloud of dust. Our second round penetrated its tank which went up in flames. The remaining tanks turned around and fled but we got one more. There were two more tank attacks in the vicinity of our CP, within 45 minutes. During this period other guns came up, including infantry cannon, and one of my lieutenants arrived to take over command of the two howitzers I had been supervising. All counterattacks were repulsed. A number of destroyed tanks were to be seen smoking here and there, and the men who had been in them were either dead or prisoners of war, some terribly burned.

"The first attack is more vivid in my memory and there is an amusing story that goes with it. Months later when I was back in the States in the hospital, I received a news release from the War Department describing that incident but with my name left blank, entitled 'Sergeant Bawls Out Brigadier General,' and requesting permission to use my name, which I granted.

"The release was written about a sergeant from Iowa, one of the gun crew commanders of the 151st Field Artillery Battalion. It reported how, after the first attack ceased, the sergeant yelled at his gun crew, 'Who was that damned jerk on number 5?' (Number 5 is the man who shifts the trails when the gun is being laid to fire.) I had moved away from the gun but was within hearing distance and when his attention was directed to me, I turned and met his enquiry with amusement. He was quite embarrassed to find that a general officer had been acting as a cannoneer in his gun section. I had been helping to shift the trails and lay the gun for, at that moment, speed was very, very important. During the excitement and rush of getting into position and repelling the tanks he had not noticed my insignia of rank."

APPENDIX B 411

Lt. Colonel Van W. Pyland's personal report regarding some of the activities of his 636th Tank Destroyer Battalion:

"On the afternoon of September 13th, Captain Austin, my S-3 and I, on reconnaissance in a jeep, were driving north across the flat ground beyond our position when we came onto a knoll. From it we could look across the Calore River in the direction of Eboli and could see German tanks milling around about 3000 yards away. I radioed back for two tank destroyers to come up. They began firing on the German tanks as soon as they arrived and kept it up until sundown. I am not sure how many tanks we destroyed. Just as the TDs were getting ready to move back to their concealed positions a German hedge-hopping plane zoomed out of the dark dropping bombs and firing machine guns at us. It was gone after a few seconds. Fortunately, only one man was wounded.

"Next day, the 14th, General Mike O'Daniel sent for me, telling me that he wanted a TD company brought up onto Chirico Hill just in rear of his position. I had one company and one platoon of the Reconnaissance Company, in reserve, away over on the south flank. I was already responsible for antitank defense of more than a mile of the low ground on the north flank and in addition was covering all terrain over which German tanks could attack and I didn't want to move any TDs up the slope and onto the top of that hill mass. So I lit out, to talk to General O'Daniel. As I came up to the brow of the hill I had no trouble locating the General. Everyone else was in some kind of a hole for protection against intermittent shell fire but he was walking along casually, now and then kicking at rocks in his path paying no attention to the shell bursts. I reported to him and he asked, 'Where are my TDs?' I told him they were in position covering the flat ground to the northwest where any logical tank attack would be made, and that I could not get any TDs on these hills. He calmly said, 'Well, if I had some TDs here now we would have some duck shooting. Look down there.' He was pointing. I clapped my field glasses to my eyes and there were 5 real German M-4s with marking clear and distinct, about 1000 yards away. They were refueling. I took another look, or two, and whirled on the run yelling to the General that I'd get TDs up there some way. I ran to my jeep and drove to my four nearest destroyers, hurried them along and guided them up a ravine on the back side of Chirico Hill. The going was rough. The third TD, in column, pulled off a track and blocked the fourth. My half-track vehicle also pulled a track. I yelled to them to radio for a wrecker, and, on foot, led the two leading TDs up a draw to the top of the hill. The crew of the leading TD lost no time getting into action. They destroyed the five M-4s and the refueling truck in just seven shots. For this feat each of the crew received the Silver Star from General Clark.

"After the duck shoot, German artillery laid onto that hillside with a vengeance, and General O'Daniel told me to get those damned TDs off the hill at once and not bring them back until he should send for them.

"We headed back down the hill the way we had come feeling that perhaps we had done a good job even if we did attract artillery fire onto the whole place.

"I found that the wrecker had about finished bolting the track back on the disabled TD and I sent the four destroyers back to their positions on the low ground to the north. The wrecking crew had trouble getting the track back onto my vehicle and it was some time before it was ready to go.

"I finally got back to my forward CP and found General Wilbur there. He said I had just missed the excitement of a big tank battle. This attack was made by 25 or more German tanks west of Altavilla toward the flat ground along La Cosa Creek just south of the Calore River. A few of them got between La Cosa Creek and our positions. The attack was smashed in a few minutes. Some 19 German tanks were destroyed. They were in the open, in full view, and my gunners had a picnic. My crews claim they knocked out most of them. We lost none. Later, I examined some of the destroyed tanks and noted that practically all penetrations were made by our 3-inch armor-piercing shells. Their brilliant tracer elements set fire to the gas fumes inside the enemy tanks and the members of the crew, if not disabled, came boiling out of the turrets. We had almost no casualties. The Germans made no more tank attacks after that.

"Later, on the late afternoon of the 18th, I received orders for my Reconnaissance Company to investigate the Altavilla area. The paratroops had been trying to drive the Germans off the high ground around Altavilla on the 17th and 18th, and had reported that the Germans had pulled out.

"With one platoon of the Recon Company and with Captain Kennison, the company commander, in my half-track we led out with the little column following us up the hill into Altavilla. The switchbacks and curves on that mountain road were more frightening than the thought of German antitank guns. The Germans had pulled out and we radioed back to that effect. We were told to remain there until relieved by the 141st Infantry next morning.

"After dark I left Captain Kennison in charge and drove a jeep back to my CP. Next morning at sunup I was back in Altavilla. I had orders from Division Headquarters to check the bridge across Calore just north of Altavilla and come back between the Sele and Calore to Persano to see if any Germans were there.

"I led the platoon down the hill and around to the northeast toward the bridge which was blown. There I picked up a German engineer soldier skulking on our side of the river. I also picked up an American paratrooper lieutenant who said he had jumped during the night and hadn't located his outfit. With the German prisoner and this paratrooper officer sitting on the hood of my jeep we turned back the way we had come to a small unimproved road leading down to the river. Sure enough it led to a ford across the Calore.

"The paratrooper left us here after wading the river to see if the water was shallow enough for my jeep. We saw a number of American dead on the wide gravel bar. They had 45th Division patches and had been dead for some time. On across we followed a good dirt road leading toward Persano. Heading that way we ran into a 45th Division patrol heading toward the river we had just crossed. Most of them appeared to be American Indians. Some of them spat at my prisoner; and as the aim wasn't too good I raised a little hell.

"A mile or so down the road (maybe more) we came to an area where it appeared that a terrible fight had taken place. I thought it might have been the area where the Somerville unit of the Jones Battalion (2nd Battalion, 143rd Infantry) had scratched their shallow foxholes to lie or die in. I found another ford near the outskirts of Persano and brought the platoon back to our lines. No enemy forces sighted other than one prisoner. So reported to Division."

APPENDIX C

FO 42   18 January 1944

Maps: Italy 1/50000 Sheets 106 I. II. III. IV., 161 III.
1.   a.   See current intelligence reports
      b.   Supporting troops.
         (1) Available Corps artillery reinforces preparatory fires of Division artillery between 1930 and 2030 hours on 20 January, 1944, neutralizing German strong points near the west bank of the Rapido River.
         (2) The 71st AAA Brig. provides AA protection for crossing points.
2.   a.   36th Infantry Division; (less the 142nd Infantry in Corps reserve) attached:
         1st and 2nd Bns., 19th Engineer (C) Regt., each Bn. less one company
         636th TD Bn.
         760th Tank Bn.
         443 AAA Bn. (less A Btry).
         Cos. A, B, and C, 2nd Cml. Wyns. Bn.
         Cos. A and B 16th Armd. Engr. Bn;
      crosses the Rapido River north and south of San Angelo on 202000 A January, 1944; captures San Angelo by dark 21 January, attacking from the north, south and west; establishes a bridgehead for crossing of CCB, 1st Armored Division in the vicinity of San Angelo on the night of D plus 1; protects the left flank of the II Corps.
      b.   (1) H-hour 2000 hours
         (2) D-day 20 Jan. 1944
      c.   For line of departure, boundaries and objectives see operation overlay, Annex No. 1.
3.   a.   141 Inf. Regt. (attached: 2nd Bn. (-1 Co.), 19th Engrs. (C) Regt.; Co. A, 2nd Cml. Bn.)
         (1) Crosses the Rapido River at 202000 A January 1944 and captures initial objective between Rio Pioppetto and Rapido River.
         (2) Makes a demonstration further south as shown on overlay to indicate a battalion crossing in that vicinity.
         (3) Continues the attack to the south and west and captures objectives within first phase line prior to daylight January 21st, 1944.
         (4) Attacks and captures San Angelo from the north and west either separately or in conjunction with the 143rd Infantry Regiment.

    (5) Protects right flank of bridgehead.

    (6) Continues the attack to the west on Division order.

b. 143rd Inf. Regt. (attached 1st Bn. (-1 Co.) 19th Engr. (C) Regt.; Cos. B and C, 2nd Cml. Bn.)

    (1) Crosses the Rapido River with two battalions abreast at 202000 A January, 1944, at areas indicated.

    (2) Captures, occupies and defends objectives within first phase line prior to daylight 21 January 1944.

    (3) Assists 141st Inf. Regt. to capture San Angelo, by fire and movement from the south and west.

    (4) Continues the attack to the west on Division order.

c. 36th Rcn. Tr.:

    (1) Crosses the Rapido River behind the 143rd Inf. Regt. on Division order.

    (2) Outposts the line of the Liri River west of its junction with the Rapido River.

    (3) Contacts 46th Div. (Br.) at junction of Liri and Rapido River, initially.

    (4) Maintains contact with the 143rd Inf. Regt. on its right.

    (5) Protects left flank of bridgehead.

d. 36th Div. Arty.:

    (1) 131st FA Bn.—direct support, 141st Inf. Regt.

    (2) 132nd FA Bn.—general support, priority to 143rd Inf. Regt.

    (3) 133rd FA Bn.—direct support, 143rd Inf. Regt.

    (4) 155th FA Bn.—general support priority to 141st Inf. Regt.

    (5) Div Arty. will fire an intense preparation on located German strong points near the west bank of the river from 1930 to 2030 hours, 20 January 1944.

    (6) After 202000 A January, 1944, the Div. Arty. will fire successive concentrations on enemy strong points preceeding the attacking units, time schedule for these fires to be arranged by regimental commanders with artillery units concerned.

    (7) Be prepared to engage promptly any hostile troop movements, particularly tanks, approaching the bridgehead from the west after daylight 21 Jan. 1944.

e. 636 TD Bn.:

Occupies firing positions near the east bank of the Rapido River, north of Cesa Martino after 202000 A January, 1944, prepared by daylight 21 January,

1944, to support the attack by direct fire on definitely located German positions or on tanks attempting to attack the bridgehead, and prepared to execute long range fires in support of the bridgehead after initial objectives are captured.

f. 760 Tank Bn.:

Occupies firing positions near the east bank of the Rapido River and south of Cesa Martino after 202000 A January, 1944, prepared by daylight 21 January, 1944 to support the attack by direct fire on definitely located German positions, or tanks on the west bank of the river.

g. 111th Engr. Bn.: (attached: Cos. A and B, 16th Armd. Engr. Bn.)

(1) Clears mines on east bank of Rapido River at selected crossing points, bridge sites and approaches prior to 20 January 1944.

(2) Constructs and maintains bridge approaches and exits.

(3) Maintains roads and clears mines within bridgehead when established.

(4) Constructs two class 40 Bailey, or armored treadway, bridges at indicated localities after initial crossing.

h. 1st Bn. (-1 Co.) 19th Engr. (C) Regt.:

(1) Reverts to Division control when assault elements of the 143rd Inf. Regt. complete crossing.

(2) Constructs 6-ton Infantry support bridges in area of 143rd Inf. Regt. on night 20-21 January.

(3) Constructs one Class 40 Bailey bridge on Main Supply Route in vicinity of San Angelo when San Angelo has been captured.

(4) Spots assault boats and foot bridge equipment on night of 19-20 January for crossing the 143rd Inf. Regt.

i. 2nd Bn. (-1 Co.) 19th Engr. (C) Regt.:

(1) Reverts to Division control when assault elements of the 141st Inf. Regt. complete crossing.

(2) Constructs 6-ton Infantry support bridge in area of 141st Inf. Regt. on night 20-21 January.

(3) Contructs a class 40 Bailey bridge on Main Supply Route in vicinity of San Angelo when San Angelo has been captured.

(4) Spots assault boats and foot bridge equipment on the night 19-20 January for the crossing of the 141st Inf. Regt.

j. 443rd AA Bn.:

(1) AA protection of artillery battery positions and forward assembly areas.

      x.   All units will carry yellow smoke grenades for identification of front lines to friendly planes and observers.

4.   a.   Traffic Control:

         (1) The Division Provost Marshall will establish an officer traffic control post at bridges 861156, 866172, 870135 and control posts at RJ 885159 and 903155.

         (2) Other control posts to be established as the situation requires.

         (3) Non-tactical vehicles (except ammunition carriers) heavier than 3/4 ton, restricted west of grade crossing 923150.

         (4) The Signal Officer will arrange communication with all traffic control posts and the Division Provost Marshall.

         (5) Traffic will be held to a minimum; night movements under strict blackout.

      b.   Miscellaneous:

         (1) The supply officers of the 141st and 143rd Inf. Regts. will establish QM Class I and Ord. Class V reserve dumps west of the Rapido River on positions accessible to their respective troops.

            (a) These reserve dumps to be established on the nights of D plus 1 and D plus 2 in sufficient quantity to serve the troops for two days, should the regular supply channels be interrupted.

            (b) Types of rations and ammunition to be determined by regimental commanders.

5.   a.   Communciation:

         (1) Index1A—49 to SCl.

         (2) Wire communication will be established and maintained across the river between regimental headquarters and headquarters of assault battalions.

         (3) Yellow smoke will be used to indicate our front lines to friendly aircraft.

      b.   CPs: No change.

      c.   Wire and radio communications will be established with traffic control points at all bridges across the Rapido River.

                             WALKER
                             Maj. Gen.

Official:
WALKER, G-3
       Annex 1—Operations Overlay
       Annex 2—Artillery Plan

Annex 3—Engineer Plan

The paragraphs of F.O. 42 pertaining to the employment of the Engineers were modified by Annex No. 3, which accompanied the field order, as follows:

1. Troops:
    a. 111th Engr. Bn.
        (1) Will clear mines from approach routes to river.
        (2) Will construct and maintain approach routes to river.
        (3) Will be prepared to perform normal engineer functions on the far shore after river has been crossed.
        (4) Will assist movement of 36th Div. Arty.
    b. 1st and 2nd Bns., 19th Engr. (C) Regt., each Bn. less 1 Co., attached to 36th Division.
        (1) 2nd Bn. atchd. to 141st Inf. Regt. will:
            (a) provide a minimum of 30 pneumatic reconnaissance boats; 42 M-2 assault boats and 4 improvised foot bridges for crossing infantry assault units.
            (b) Construct one 6-ton pneumatic treadway bridge at site shown on overlay as ordered by regimental commander.
            (c) Revert to division control upon completion of bridging operations.
        (2) 1st Bn. atchd. to 143rd Inf. Regt. will:
            (a) provide a minimum of 30 pneumatic reconnaissance boats, 20 M-2 assault boats and 4 improvised foot bridges for crossing infantry assault units.
            (b) construct one 6-ton pneumatic treadway bridge at site shown on overlay as ordered by regimental commander.
            (c) revert to division control upon completion of bridging operations.
        (3) 19th Engr. (C) Regt. will construct two class 40 Bailey bridges on proposed Main Supply Route in vicinity of San Angelo as soon as site is free of observed artillery fire or during the nite of D plus 1 or D plus 2 as ordered by Division Commander.
    c. Cos. A and B, 16th Armd. Engr. Bn.:
        (1) Co. A attached to 1st Bn. 19th Engr. (C) Regt.
        (2) Co. B attached to 2nd Bn. 19th Engr. (C) Regt.
        (3) Each company will construct one class 40 Bailey bridge for tank crossing at sites shown on overlay, beginning construction at H plus 4 or as ordered by the Division Commander.
2. II Corps Engineers will support 36th Division operations.

(a) By repairing and maintaining Hwy. No. 6 to 900183.
(b) By repairing and maintaining, for automobile traffic RR ROW, to 890158.
(c) Assist artillery, tank destroyer and tank units supporting the 36th Infantry Division.

WALKER
Maj. Gen.

Official:
WALKER
G-3

APPENDIX D

A CLASSIC STRATAGEM
ON MONTE ARTEMISIO

Ernest F. Fisher

Reprinted by permission of the author and of the **Military Review**, U.S. Army Command and General Staff College, Fort Leavenworth, Kansas.

Passage of a lightly held or unguarded sector of the enemy's lines by stealth and at night is an ancient stratagem—as old as the history of warfare.

In the Bible the Hebrew chronicler describes (in Samuel I, chapter 13 and 14) how, when King Saul and his son Jonathan besieged the Philistines encamped in Michmash, that Jonathan, accompanied by his armor bearer, slipped through the pass at Michmash, between Bozez and Seneh, to a place high up, about "half an acre of land, which a yoke of oxen might plow." There they surprised the sleeping Philistines who, when they awoke, thought that they had been surrounded by the armies of Saul and fled. Saul then attacked with his whole army. It was a great victory for him; his first against the Philistines, and "so the Lord saved Israel that day, and the battle passed over into Beth Aven."

In another Palestinian campaign, this one during World War I, a British brigade found itself before the same Michmash, with orders to attack toward Jericho and drive the Turks across the Jordan. Pondering the Scriptures the night before what promised to be a costly frontal attack, the brigade major and his commanding officer came across the account of Jonathan's stratagem at Michmasch. Determining that the terrain had changed little since that time, the brigadier decided to lead his troops over the path taken by the ancient Hebrew King. Moving up the mountainside under the cover of darkness, the British passed through the lightly held pass of Michmash to rout the Turkish garrison as the dawn's first light broke over the ancient town.

Familiar, too, is General Wolfe's clever tactic before the French stronghold of Quebec when he led his men up the slope of a woody precipice to overpower a small detachment at the Anse du Foulon, and to appear the next morning with his entire army drawn up on the Plains of Abraham before the eyes of the surprised French garrison.

The Allied campaign in Italy in World War II also produced a notable example of this stratagem, worthy of joining the three just cited in the annals of military history. This was the successful passage of the German lines at Monte Artemisio in May 1944 by the 36th Infantry Division, then commanded by Major General Fred L. Walker.

Hard Luck Division

The 36th Division, a battered veteran of the American 5th

Army's winter campaigns at San Pietro and along the Rapido, had acquired among American troops the reputation of being a "hard luck" division. Ever since September 1943, when it had come ashore on the Italian mainland at the ancient Roman settlement of Paestum near Salerno, the 36th Division had known difficult and costly missions. After being relieved from the Rapido front in February 1944, the division had been resting and training at Maddaloni and near Avellino where it had engaged in extensive mountain training in preparation for the 5th Army's May offensive across the Garigliano between the Liri Valley and the Tyrrhenian Sea, which was designed to link up with the Anzio forces and to capture Rome.

Anxious that General Lucian Truscott, his 6th Corps commander on the Anzio beachhead, have adequate strength for his breakout offensive, General Mark W. Clark, the 5th Army commander, changed his plans and sent the 36th Division instead to join the 6th Corps.

At dawn on 23 May 1944, General Truscott hurled the seasoned 3d Infantry Division and the 1st Armored Division against the center of the German 14th Army's defenses at Cisterna. After 24 hours of some of the costliest and bitterest fighting in a campaign which had long been characterized by such fighting, the two divisions broke through the German defenses on either side of Cisterna and swept up a three-mile-wide corridor, flanked by the Alban Hills on the left and the Lepini Mountains on the right. The object of the 6th Corps' drive was the town of Valmontone, an important road junction on the Via Casilina (Highway 6), the main line of communications between the German 10th Army, opposing the bulk of the 5th Army, and the city of Rome.

The Alban Hills

General Clark had long been concerned that his 5th Army reach Rome before the Allied armies landed in northern France. A possible solution to Clark's problem lay in the volcanic mass of the Alban Hills towering above the beachhead. This high ground provided the Germans with excellent observation which enabled their artillery to harass the 6th Corps stretched through the valley below. And through these hills ran the Appian Way (Highway 7), the most direct road from the beachhead to Rome.

It was to this area, then, that General Clark directed his attention and hopes for a speedy capture of Rome. Accordingly, on 26 May—one day after the linkup with 6th Corps had been accomplished—Clark ordered Truscott to turn the bulk of his corps to the left and to attack the German defenses along the southern slopes of the Alban Hills between Lanuvio and Velletri.

At 1100 on 27 May with the United States 45th Infantry Division on the left astride the Via Anziate, the 34th Division in the center south of Lanuvio, and the 1st Armored Division on the right, most of the 6th Corps wheeled left and attacked the Germans positions in the Alban Hills. Only the 3d Infantry Division and the 1st Special Service Force, a brigade-strength commando force assisted by an armored combat team from the 1st Armored Division, continued the offensive in its original direction toward Valmontone and Highway 6.

For the next few days the one armored and two infantry divisions launched a series of attacks against stubborn German defenders along the Velletri-Lanuvio-Campoleone line. Instead of breaking through quickly to "the most direct road to Rome," the 6th Corps struggled fruitlessly for four precious days along the southern slopes of the Alban Hills, and at the end found itself no closer to Rome.

Moreover, the relatively weak force which had continued northeastward toward Highway 6 in the original direction of the beachhead offensive had also been checked when elements of the Hermann Göring Division counterattacked between Valmontone and Artena. As night fell on 30 May, the 6th Corps offensive had definitely stalled on both sectors.

Meanwhile, the British 8th Army had captured Frosinone, the last major road junction on Highway 6 south of Valmontone, and the Allied invasion force in England had moved into its final assembly areas preparatory to the long-awaited invasion of northern France.

General Clark was understandably concerned about the unexpected delay in the offensive and realized that unless the German defenses in the Alban Hills were cracked within the next few days, he might have to wait for the 8th Army to pull abreast and join his own army in a coordinated attack on Rome.

On 26 May General Walker's 36th Division had relieved the 1st Armored Division in the sector immediately south of Velletri. It was General Truscott's intention then to use the 36th Division as a holding force and to shift the 1st Armored behind either the 34th or 45th Divisions to exploit any softening of the German defenses in the Alban Hills.

General Walker moved his command post from the Nettuno area into the shattered buildings of a dairy farm near Torrechia Nuova, about two and one-half miles northeast of Cisterna and five miles southeast of Velletri, while his 141st and 143d Regiments began the relief of the 1st Armored Division.

On 28 May Walker learned that Truscott now planned to use his division to relieve the 34th Division which had bogged down in a costly stalemate before Lanuvio. Recalling vividly an earlier bloody frontal assault against a well-entrenched enemy along the Rapido River, the 36th Division commander did not relish a repetition of this experience. He began, therefore, to search for a possible alternative to simply taking over from the 34th Di-

423

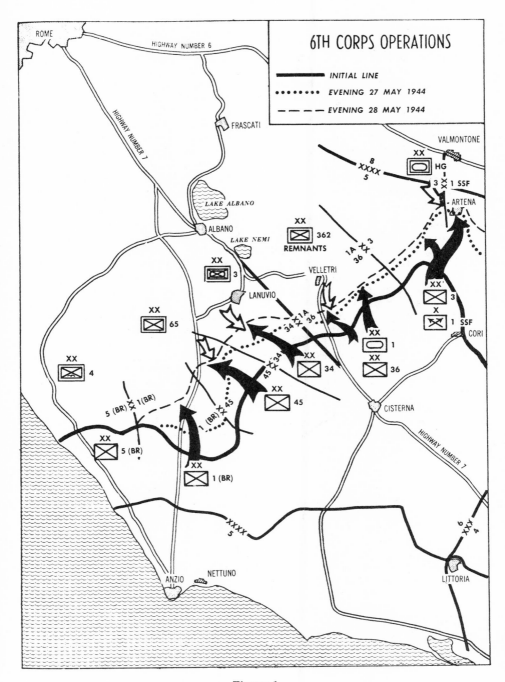

Figure 1.

vision an apparently hopeless task.

General Walker had studied the forbidding bulk of Monte Artemisio both from the cabin of an artillery observer's aircraft and from the forward observation posts of the 141st Infantry, then holding a line along the road at the base of the mountain. The division staff had also made very detailed studies of aerial photographs of the terrain before them and had found no evidence of enemy activity. When reconnaissance patrols reported on the 27th that they had found no enemy positions on the slopes of Monte Artemisio, General Walker called the division engineer, Colonel Oran C. Stovall, to the command post to discuss the possibility of locating a suitable trail leading over the mountain and through the German lines.

Conference

Meeting Colonel Stovall on the road just outside the dairy farm command post, General Walker held an alfresco staff conference, using the dusty road as a situation map. He explained to Stovall the problem facing the division and a possible solution. As he traced on the ground a rough map of the division's sector, the general confided to Colonel Stovall his concern that the corps commander might send the division into the 34th Division's sector, not to exploit a breakthrough, but to relieve a battered division whose repeated frontal assaults had gained only a few yards after two days of costly fighting.

The division commander now turned to consideration of the enemy's dispositions. The unexpectedly strong defense encountered by 6th Corps between Campoleone Station and Lanuvio and the appearance of the Hermann Göring Division in the vicinity of Valmontone led him to conclude that in order to build up these two sectors General Albert Kesselring must have thinned out a sector which he believed secure. Monte Artemisio, the heavily forested mountain wall to the front, seemed to the 36th Division commander the most logical sector for Kesselring to have left lightly guarded.

If the 36th Division could climb Monte Artemisio and slip in behind the German defenses, Walker explained to Stovall, Kesselring's grip on the Alban Hills would be broken. Walker doubted that the Germans would be able to establish another defense line south of the Tiber.

If two of the infantry regiments climbed the mountain and passed through the enemy's lines, Walker believed that he would also have to move armor and artillery in to support them if this action was to develop into a genuine breakthrough. Infantry alone would be unable to close the escape routes leading northward from Velletri; and he did not wish to expose the right flanks of the attacking regiments to possible enemy thrusts from the northeast. The force cutting the German withdrawal routes north of Velletri must be strong enough to check such counterattacks, as well as any attempt by the garrison to escape from the town. Moreover, until Velletri was taken, the infantry would be dependent upon a line of communication extending eight miles over a 3,000-foot mountain which possessed no roads and only few foot trails.

Success of the plan, as Walker saw it, turned upon the construction of a road adequate for tanks and tank destroyers as well as the necessary supply trains. Walker wanted to know if the engineers could build this road.

Unable to give an immediate answer, Colonel Stovall put his staff to work at once to study the terrain. From the air, from forward observation posts, and on aerial photographs the wooded slopes of Monte Artemisio were carefully searched for the most promising trail. The next day—the 28th—Stovall reported that the engineers had located a suitable route up the mountain and could do the job.

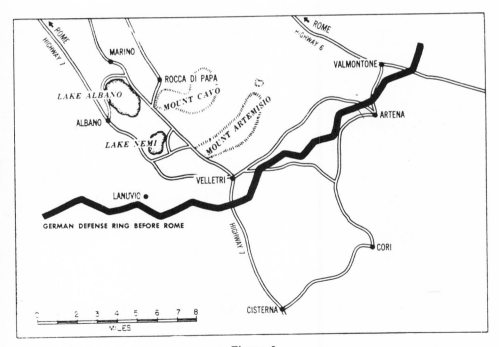

Figure 2.

A Gap

What General Walker and his staff had discovered was a gap, approximately two miles wide, between the left flank of the German 1st Parachute Corps and the right flank of the 76th Panzer Corps. Since the night of 27-28 May General Wilhelm Schmalz, commander of the Hermann Göring Division, had been agonizingly aware of this gap. Patrols, sent out by his right flank battalion, had gone as far as a fork in the road just northeast of Velletri before encountering troops of the 362d Division on the 1st Parachute Corps' left flank.

Although Schmalz had observed American patrols scouting this area during the 28th, there was little he could do to close the gap; his own division's front had been stretched to the breaking point. Realizing, however, the peril which this gap posed to the entire Caesar Line, Schmalz committed his right-wing regiment's last reserve, an engineer platoon, at Castel d'Ariano on Monte Artemisio, a small force hardly sufficient to close the two-mile gap.

The Hermann Göring Division's commander also sent an officer-led patrol to occupy a small group of houses at Menta on the corps boundary, and from the 28th through the 30th repeatedly requested 14th Army headquarters to direct the 1st Parachute Corps to establish contact with his right flank by means of a similar patrol. His pleas were unheeded.

Even as Schmalz was reporting the gap to his superiors on 28 May, Walker notified General Truscott of the apparent German weakness in the Monte Artemisio sector, and mentioned to the 6th Corps commander that he had directed patrols to take and hold any unoccupied ground. Although General Walker had not yet fully developed a plan to exploit this weakness, he informed the 6th Corps chief of staff, Colonel Don E. Carleton on the afternoon of the next day that he would keep on trying to work his way to the northeast, above the town, and approach the position from the rear. Colonel Carleton agreed that if the 36th Division could do this "the Boche in there (Velletri) would find themselves in a tough situation, and the town might just cave in."

Another Plan

Although prospects now appeared brighter for the development of Walker's plan, the corps commander had a plan of his own. Summoning his division commanders to his command post late in the evening of 29 May, Truscott confirmed General Walker's fears with an order for the 36th Division to move the next day into an assembly area in the rear of the 34th Division preparatory to taking over that division's sector on the night of 31 May-1 June. Returning to his own headquarters later in the evening, Walker issued warning orders for the move to his staff and, at a conference the following morning, a final oral order to his subordinate commanders.

While the division prepared for the move to the Lenuvio sector, General Walker and his staff continued to develop a stratagem to exploit the gap discovered on Monte Artemisio. The more they considered this plan and compared it with the situation they expected to encounter before the enemy stronghold at Lanuvio, the more convinced they became that their plan offered a better chance to penetrate the enemy's defenses at far less cost.

Since time was running short, General Walker resolved to lay the plan before the corps commander at the earliest opportunity. Walker's opportunity came when Truscott visited division headquarters shortly before noon on 30 May to inspect preparations for the move. The 36th Division commander outlined the division plan, pointed out its advantages, and requested that it be substituted for the mission which Truscott had already assigned.

The plan was simple. The 142d and 143d Regiments, with the former in the lead, were to pass through the lines of the 141st Infantry during the night of 30-31 May to seize the Maschio d'Ariano and Hill 931, two prominences at the northeastern end of Monte Artemisio. After reaching the crest, the 142d Infantry would advance southwest along the crest of the mountain to positions about two miles north and west of Velletri, where roadblocks could be established across the two remaining routes of withdrawal left to the enemy garrison in Velletri.

The 143d Infantry, meanwhile, would move northwestward to seize Monte Cavo and the Rocca di Papa, the highest points within the Alban Hills. After the two regiments had reached the summit of Monte Artemisio, the 141st Infantry would shift its attack to the west and capture Velletri by an encircling maneuver in coordination with the 142d Infantry. With the enemy garrison virtually surrounded, the 36th Division could then quickly destroy the remaining defenders of this part of the Caesar Line, and the "shortest" road to Rome would be open.

General Walker concluded with the statement that his reconnaissance had located a suitable cart trail crossing the enemy lines about three miles northeast of Velletri, and that his engineers were confident that this trail could be enlarged to enable tanks and trucks to follow the infantry closely.

Approval

General Truscott carefully questioned Colonel Stovall about his proposals to construct a road up the mountain, and, having satisfied himself that it could be done, agreed to discuss the plan at once with his staff at corps headquarters. Despite strong objections from the corps engineer concerning the plan's feasibility, General Truscott phoned Walker at 1300 not only to approve the plan, but to place the 36th Engineer Regiment to support Walker's division.

There was no time to be lost. Walker promptly issued a new warning order to his staff and called a meeting of his unit commanders at 1500 at division headquarters to give them final instructions for the operation which was to take place that night. The 142d Infantry was to move after dark by truck from its reserve position to the division's right flank where it was to pass through the 141st's lines and scale Monte Artemisio over the trail which the engineers would mark. The 143d Infantry in line before Velletri was to be relieved by the attached 36th Engineer Regiment. The 143d Infantry was then to move by truck via Cori to the right flank where it was to follow the 142d up the mountainside.

Colonel Stovall now moved his own engineer battalion into position to support the attack, and selected Captain Orval W. Crisman's Company B to construct the road up the mountainside. A minelaying platoon from Company B was attached to the lead infantry battalion to assist the infantrymen in establishing roadblocks behind Velletri.

As his division prepared to move against Monte Artemisio, General Walker noted that "our operations for tonight and tomorrow have promise of being spectacular. We are taking chances, but we should succeed in a big way."

Infiltration

At 2255 on 30 May, the 142d Infantry, commanded by Colonel George E. Lynch, crossed the line of departure in a column of battalions. Aided by a new moon, whose light was just sufficient to enable the men to pick out the trail, the leading company reached the road at the base of Monte Artemisio by 0130. From there the troops followed the trail up the lower slopes of the mountain through lush vineyards which provided welcome concealment. On the left the men heard the distant chatter of machinegun fire. This was the 141st Infantry Regiment probing the German defenses on the outskirts of Velletri.

As the silent columns passed darkened and presumably deserted houses, the bark of a nervous dog set off a cacophony of howls, punctuated by the braying of a jackass. Occasionally, a shot rang out, followed by moments of breathless anticipation as to what would follow. About 0300 the menacing rumble of aircraft engines shattered the night. Friendly antiaircraft fired a sparkling display at the invisible enemy aircraft which, in turn, dropped hundreds of flares illuminating the surrounding countryside for miles around.

Everyone hugged the ground and waited in silence. Bombs fell and strafing was heard in the direction of Velletri. Fortunately, the regiment had not been discovered; the aerial attack seemed to be aimed at the troops south of Velletri. The flares lasted about half an hour; as the planes roared away, the men scrambled to their feet and resumed the march.

It had been a close call, and the delay had cost the regiment valuable time. Dawn would soon be breaking, and the bulk of the mountain still lay before the marching columns. About 0415, as the first gray light began to obscure the stars, the lead battalion began to cross an open field, fortunately shrouded in an early morning haze. Tension increased as the troops started to climb the steeper slopes just below the summit. As the men saw their goal looming before them they quickened their pace, and by 0635 the advance guard, accompanied by artillery observers, scrambled onto the summits of Maschio d'Ariano and Hill 931. On the first peak they surprised and captured three German artillery observers—one was taking his morning bath. Not a shot was fired.

Even as the lead battalion of the 142d Infantry had begun its ascent of Monte Artemisio, Captain Crisman's company of engineers, under cover of darkness, moved forward to begin work. on the trail. The phenomenally rapid improvement of the trail into a rudimentary one-way road—but, nevertheless, a road—was largely the work of three bulldozers manned by skilled and determined operators.

Counterattack

Ironically, as the two regiments moved up the mountainside toward the Maschio d'Ariano, the German engineer platoon commander from the Hermann Göring Division, unaware of the size of the American force, reported to his battalion commander only that he had been engaged by some American infantry—nothing more. Consequently, General Schmalz was not immediately informed of the breakthrough, the danger of which he had so long foreseen. Not until the Americans were well established atop Monte Artemisio during the afternoon of 31 May did Schmalz receive from 14th Army an order to counterattack an enemy force which had penetrated the line between his division and the 362d Infantry Division.

But now the unfortunate general had only four or five operationally fit tanks left in his division, and they were engaged near Valmontone. The best General Schmalz could do was to throw a battalion of his **panzergrenadier** regiment into the breach late in the day. Already weakened by heavy losses, this battalion was no match for the 142d and 143d Regiments. The counterattack failed, and the Americans continued to widen and strengthen their penetration.

While the engineers worked on the trail throughout the morning, the 1st and 2d Battalions of the 142d Infantry moved southwest along the crest of Monte Artemisio toward the Maschio dell'Artemisio, overlooking Velletri from the northwest. Despite the German counterattack in the afternoon, the 142d Infantry continued steadily toward its objective, which it occupied by 1930.

430

Enemy tanks and 20-millimeter flak guns in the vicinity of Lake Nemi northwest of Velletri now opened fire on the regiment which held its ground throughout the night. But well supported by tanks and self-propelled artillery, the US infantry set up roadblocks north and west of Velletri and by dawn on 1 June had virtually surrounded the enemy garrison. Over 3,000 US infantrymen were firmly entrenched on the heights above Velletri in the enemy's rear.

The move had come as a complete tactical surprise to the Germans. American casualties had been relatively light. The 142d Infantry Regiment had lost eight men killed, 52 wounded, and one man missing. In the 143d three men had been killed, 94 wounded, and 11 missing—a relatively modest price for the ground gained.

Withdrawal

The 143d Infantry, which had followed the 142d up Monte Artemisio, had meanwhile marched straight across what had once been the ancient crater to capture Monte Cavo and Rocco di Papa, the two highest points in the Alban Hills. Deprived of their most important observation points overlooking the 6th Corps front, the Germans had no alternative but to fall back on Rome and beyond the Tiber.

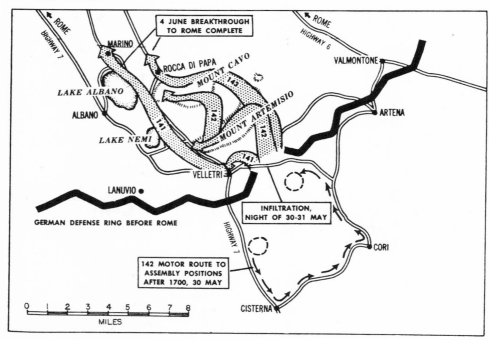

Figure 3.

American artillery observers accompanying the infantry quickly established themselves on these two heights to take full advantage of the excellent view they had of the German-held area. It was an artilleryman's dream and throughout the day they kept their guns busy pouring destruction and confusion onto the crowded network of roads behind the German lines.

Meanwhile, General Walker's communications people intercepted an order from the 4th Parachute Division to the 12th Parachute Regiment to withdraw from the town and fall back to the far bank of a stream about half a mile west of Velletri. Forewarned of the enemy's intentions, the 142d Infantry supported by tanks moved swiftly to cut off their escape.

It was now the 141st Infantry's turn to attack. Two of its three battalions closed in on Velletri over terrain made treacherous by numerous vineyards and orchards which restricted observation and made control of smaller units extremely difficult. Fighting back a last enemy counterattack early in the afternoon, leading elements of Colonel John W. Harmony's regiment entered Velletri at 1630, and one hour later had penetrated to the center of town.

The place was in ruins. Enemy dead and material littered the streets, and in the remaining buildings numerous dead and wounded were discovered. Hundreds of prisoners were routed from the extensive fortifications, tunnels, and reinforced gun positions —mute evidence of the important role Velletri was to play in the German defense plans. Despite the stubborn resistance of the survivors of the enemy garrison, the 141st Infantry incurred few casualties—one man killed and 38 wounded.

General Walker's stratagem had worked. An entire American infantry division now moved into the Alban Hills. Field Marshal Kesselring's last defense line south of Rome had been shattered, and General Truscott's 6th Corps, led by the 36th Infantry Division and the 1st Armored Division, now pursued the Germans across the fabled Roman Campagna toward the historic city.

"This was," General Truscott later remarked, "the turning point in our 'drive to the northwest.' "

Dr. Ernest F. Fisher has been assigned to the Office, Chief of Military History, Department of the Army, since 1959. He served with the 101st Airborne Division during World War II, holds a Ph.D. from the University of Wisconsin, and was for five years with the Historical Division, United States Army, Europe. This article has been drawn largely from material which will appear in a volume in the Mediterranean series of the official history of the US Army in World War II.

APPENDIX E

8183 ROTTACH-EGERN, 17-10-68
Sudl. Hpt. Str. 23 - Tel. (98022) 5305

HEINZ GREINER
Generalleautnant a.D.

Major General Frederick Walker
714 Fontaine Street
Alexandria, Virginia

Sehr verehrter Herr General Walker!

als Verfasser des jungst beim Verlag Kurt Vowinckel, Neckargemund erschienenen Buches:

"Kampf um Rom—Inferno am Po"

ist es mir Bedurfnis, Ihnen als meinem ehemaligen Gegner zu schreiben. Durch die gutige Vermittlung von Herrn Colonel Walton, der in seinem Buche "Rom fell today" Ihren tapferen Entschluss durch die damalige deutsche Armeelucke ostwarts Velletri (Mai 1944) ins Artemisio-Gebirge durchzustossen, in verdienter Weise gewurdigt hat, erfuhr ich Ihre Anschrift.

Auch ich habe in meinem Buch Ihre bewunnernswerte Tat eingehend hervorgehoben und darf Ihnen dazu jetzt—23 Jahre nach dem Kriegsende—personlich meine hohe Anerkennung fur diese Tat zum Ausdruck bringen.

Sie haben meine Division damals in eine sehr schwierige Lage versetzt, wie Sie aus meiner wahrheitsgetreuem Schilderung in meinem genannten Buche lesen konnen. Ihre Tat war wirklich uberragend tapfer und beinahe tollkuhn; denn hatte ich damals uber irgendeine Reserve verfugt, die man als nennenswert bezeichnen konnte, zum Beispiel ein Infanterie Regiment in Kriegsstarke mit 3 (statt 2) Bataillonen a 800 Mann, wie man zu Beginn des Krieges Reserven hinter Armee-Nahten hielt, so hatte ich einen Gegenangriff in ostwartiger Richtung gefuhrt. Dann ware vielleicht Ihre Division verloren gewesen.

Ich denke, sehr geehrter Herr General Walker, dass Ihnen diese Darstellung interessant sein wird. So konnen wirklich stolz sein auf Ihren Mut und vermutlich auf Ihre richtige Beurteilung der Lage, dass es unseren dezimierten Divisionen an starkeren Naht-Reserven fehlte.

Darf ich Ihnen als Ihr ehemaliger Gegner meine hohe Anerkennung aussprechen und Ihnen beste Grusse senden.

Ihr Ihnen sehr ergebener

17-10-68

Major General Frederick Walker
714 Fontaine St.
Alexandria, Virginia

Dear General Walker,
    As author of the recently published "Battle for Rome—Inferno on the Po" I want to write to you as my former opponent. Through the gracious assistance of Col. Walton, who in his book "Rome Fell Today" deservedly rated so highly your bold decision to strike through the inter-army gap east of Velletri, I obtained your address.
    Also in my book I have called special attention to your admirable deed, and may I—23 years after the war's end—personally express to you my high regard for this deed.
    At that time you had placed my division in a very difficult situation, as you can read from the accurate account given in my book. Your deed was really amazingly bold and almost rash; for had I then available any reserves worthy of the name, for example an infantry regiment at wartime strength with three (instead of two) 800 man battalions which at the beginning of the war were customarily held along an inter-army boundary, I would have counterattacked in an easterly direction. Then perhaps **your** division would have been lost.
    I believe, General Walker, that this recital (of the past) would interest you. Thus you can really be proud of your courage and presumably of your correct estimation of the situation, that our decimated divisions lacked strong reserves (along the inter-army boundary).
    May I, as your former opponent, express to you my high regards and send you my best greetings.
                                     Yours—

Contrary to what some people believe, Generals and Admirals do not start wars. Wars are started by politicians. They are conducted by military professionals under the control of politicians and they are concluded on terms imposed by politicians. The battles, however, are fought by men and materiel. The materiel —weapons, equipment, supplies—change from war to war. But the characteristics of men, and the principles of combat do not change. Only the application of combat principles change as dictated by changes of materiel. Soldiers of the future will use whatever materiel and techniques are provided for them at the time.

There are, however, a number of "musts" which are applicable to all times and to all wars. They were in use before Caesar invaded Gaul. They will be in use when man invades outer space.

The more important follow:

Administration

A Division does not spring into being from a collection of men and material. If it is to function properly—and that means each man knowing what his job is, for what he is responsible, and doing that job—there must be proper administration, a great deal of which is just plain housekeeping. There is an enormous amount of detail in the administration of a Division, and nothing should be overlooked. Paper work, the receipt and issue of supplies, and sanitation must be given emphasis equal to that given to tactical and mechanical training. Troop messes must be good. Living quarters, wherever possible, must be neat and comfortable. Administrative personnel must be required to conform to the rules for good order and discipline, and to maintain high standards of performance at all times.

The 36th Division was set up in accordance with these principles. As a result, our administrative personnel made a very important contribution to the high morale of the Division and had a feeling of belonging to and sharing in the successes of the fighting troops in whom they took a special pride.

When the Division passed through the Port of Embarkation with the remarkable record of only two paper errors, it received the praises of the Port Commander and his Staff. Train crews were surprised when all trains transporting Division personnel and equipment were ready to move out on schedule.

Training

Training is a broad term that includes both teaching and learning. Its principal purpose is to develop logical thinking, accuracy, skill, speed and discipline. These objectives were sought by Baron Von Steuben during those dark days at Valley Forge, just as we strive for them today. Training is not a one-time lesson—it is a continuous process.

Generally speaking, soldiers are instructed by the noncommissioned officers and officers of company rank. But they are supervised by higher commanders and staffs.

This supervision must never be neglected. It is not enough to pass by and note that units or classes are at their assigned places. Supervisors should listen to the instructor, observe his methods, check his instruction aids, note the use made of the facilities provided, and give special attention to the responsiveness and attentiveness of the trainees.

Corrections should be made on the spot and in an inoffensive manner. The interest of the trainee is renewed and he is reassured whenever the supervisor, especially a senior officer, takes over and conducts a part of the instruction himself, or cites some incident to emphasize the instructor's points.

Much of the pre-battle instruction of the soldier is theoretical and repetitious, but a resourceful instructor will never allow it to become boring. A good story, an unscheduled intermission, an introduction of personal competition are a few means by which the instructor relieves tedium and restores interest.

The excellent training of the 36th Division at all levels was a very important factor in its successes at Salerno, on the Bernhardt Line, and at Velletri.

Discipline

Discipline is the heart and soul of a military unit. It is a habit of willing obedience, but not blind obedience. It is as old as war itself and is developed, like any other habit, by repetition. A punctilious performance must be required in exercises such as precision drills and manipulation of instruments in order to inculcate the habit of willful obedience and establish proper standards of performance.

A greater freedom of action may be allowed in less exact exercises such as motor vehicle maintenance, care of and cleaning of equipment, cross country marches, tactical exercises, marksmanship, and sanitary duties. But satisfactory results must be required, which will develop and maintain the habit of obedience. Subordinate commanders must not permit slovenliness or carelessness at any time during formal instruction or performance of duty.

During periods of recreation, and when off duty, the habit of obedience will be maintained by conforming to the rules of military courtesy, customs of the service, uniform regulations and fair play.

There are good reasons for willfully obeying all general regulations in general use. They are like traffic rules, designed for a smoother, swifter and more harmonious performance.

It was discipline, the habit of willful obedience, that made the 36th Division a strong fighting unit.

Morale and Esprit de Corps

A high morale is absolutely essential to the success of any military unit. It is based on efficiency and built on mutual confidence. Disciplined soldiers know what is expected of them and what to expect from their comrades in arms. They have a sense of security. When they have confidence in their commander they can accomplish wonders because they will do their best as a member of their team.

High morale and what is called espirit de corps are developed in many ways. A soldier needs to think of his commander as one of the best. He needs to have confidence in him—but a soldier cannot be deceived for long. He needs to feel that his commander understands his problems and takes a personal interest in his welfare. He needs to feel that his missions will be planned intelligently and that he will have every possible advantage over his enemy. He is resigned to his fate and is prepared to go beyond the call of duty, but he does not want to be sacrificed by stupidity.

The soldier needs to feel that he is treated fairly and justly, caught up for slack work and praised for good. He wants to see his Division commander occasionally and to know that the top brass is aware of what he does. And he wants to see an efficient handling of supplies. He expects good administration. When these desires are fulfilled, the soldier's confidence and enthusiasm will follow.

The morale of the 36th Division was never higher than after the reorganization and preparation following the Battle of Salerno. It was this high morale that sustained the Division during its successes and reverses and hard fighting which resulted in breaking the Bernhardt Line in the bitter December of 1943.

Reconnaissance

Reconnaissance is an important element in every preparation for tactical action. This applies equally to an infantry patrol or to a grand attack. It is the means by which obstacles are discovered and by which advantages are revealed and verified.

Reconnaissance may prevent being surprised, or it may reveal an opportunity to surprise the enemy. It is made in many ways; on foot, by study of maps and aerial photographs, by radio surveillance, by reconnaissance planes, and by use of observation posts. When in contact with the enemy, reconnaissance must be continuous.

A reconnaissance that paid big dividends was the one made by foot patrols, followed up by Colonel Stovall, myself and others. It led to the Velletri breakthrough which opened the road to Rome.

Intelligence

Intelligence includes all available information concerning the enemy; his location, strength, disposition, equipment. The procurement, evaluation and dissemination of intelligence is an important and continuous process. Its sources, from a Division point of view, are observation posts, prisoners of war, deserters, the friendly native population, maps, aerial photographs, reconnaissance planes, ground patrols, captured papers and intercepted messages.

A good commander must have a thorough knowledge of enemy tactics and techniques in order that he may make full use of all intelligence available to him. Then he can foretell with reasonable accuracy the intentions and reactions of his opponent.

A great amount of intelligence was available concerning the fortifications of the German Gustav Line. This, plus a basic knowledge of infantry tactics, made it possible for the Staff of the 36th to foretell the German reaction to an attack across the Rapido.

Security

Tactical security is vital to success. It includes all steps taken to warn a military force of enemy offensive action, and to delay and break up enemy attack formations before they can advance to the main defenses.

The security of the 36th Division at Salerno was successful. The Germans made skillful dispositions of their forces to insure security of their defenses on the Bernhardt Line and at the Rapido. They failed to provide tactical security for themselves at Velletri.

Estimate of the Situation

An estimate of the tactical situation, a logical procedure of thinking as taught in our military schools, should precede every military action. When this estimate or study is omitted, or is carelessly performed, military planning becomes guesswork. Wishful thinking may dominate logic and lead to erroneous conclusions, impatience may ignore the factors of time and space, and success is frustrated. The failure of the 36th Division to cross the Rapido was the result of wishful thinking.

Military Education

The courses of instruction in the schools of our military system have been excellent. The Army, Navy and Air Force Academies, the schools of the various arms—infantry, artillery, engineer, etc.—The Command and General Staff College, The Army War College, and The National War College, to mention only a few, have had a great and beneficial influence on the qualifications of officers of our military forces. Except in the sciences, and in the operation of mechanical equipment none of these schools teaches the student a set way for tactical action. Rather they teach him to think and to reason.

The principles of war and combat are taught by applying them to theoretical military situations. No two military situations are alike however, and the student is taught to be logical in making his decisions, and practical in applying the principles involved. The tactical courses cannot cover every possible contingency, but the graduate is expected to be intelligent enough to make his own adjustments.

The successes of the 36th Division in Italy were the result of the application of the teachings of our military school system. The Division failed only when it was required to violate those teachings.

Qualifications of Commanders

Too often, military delays and reverses are due to unsound de-

cisions made by unqualified officers. There is no greater handicap
for a fighting force than inefficiency in command.

Commanders of combat units, large and small, are expected to
arrive at sensible decisions based on detailed knowledge, logic and
experience. Being human, however, they do not always do so.
Politics, personal ambition, wishful thinking, failure to recognize
facts, rashness, and despair sometimes lead commanders to assign
missions beyond the capabilities of their troops.

Therefore, the selection and assignment of an officer to command any combat unit, especially a division, corps, or army, is
serious business, and demands a thorough investigation of the
candidate's combat experience, personal characteristics and general
military reputation. Reference to his record of military service
is not enough. Seniority in rank is not enough. His military
capabilities will not be improved by changing an eagle to a star
on his shoulder. Stability, knowledge and experience are all needed
to make a good commander who must be fair, just and right.
No officer should be catapulted into command unless he has
had qualifying experience.

Censorship

Censorship is necessary because the enemy's eyes and ears are
always open for a chance word that could, unknowingly, betray
an important plan of action.

From another view, censorship seems burdensome to the soldier
and his family which quite naturally wants to follow his Division
in the newspapers. These accounts, plus letters, give them a
personal interest in, and a sense of loyalty to, his unit, and in
addition give them a feeling of continuing to be a part of his life.

Unfortunately, there are some censors who are overzealous or
overstimulated by power. When they resort to petty interpreta-
tions of regulations and to senseless cuts in the name of security,
they hurt rather than help morale. And when they overemphasize
the importance of the top command, to the exclusion of subordinate units, they are missing an opportunity to build both
morale and loyalty of the civilian population to support the war.

After Italy

As for the 36th Division, it gained in battlefield efficiency
with each operation, and after being transferred to the Seventh
Army under Major General "Sandy" Patch, it again proved how
well it had learned its lessons, and performed gloriously under its
Division Commander, Major General John E. Dahlquist.

INDEX

442

D

E

F

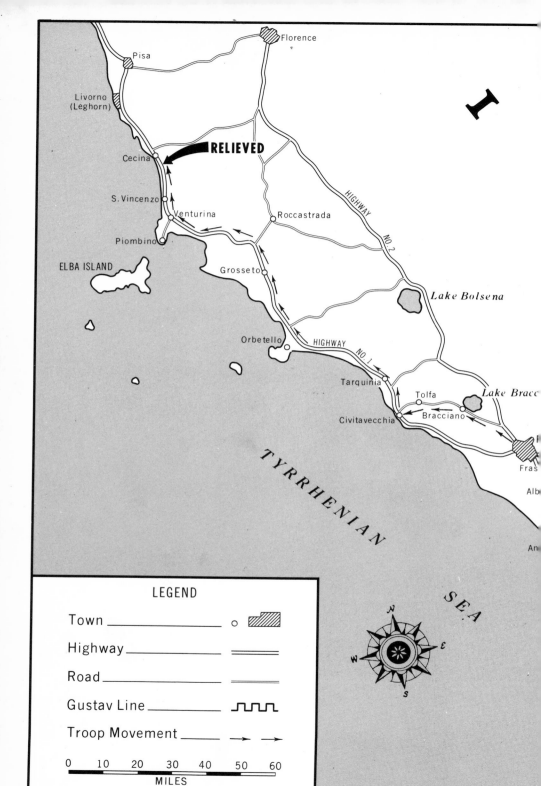

LEGEND

Town	○	▨
Highway		═══
Road		──
Gustav Line		⊓⊔⊓
Troop Movement		→ →

0   10   20   30   40   50   60
MILES